The Strenuous Life of Harry Anderson

The Strenuous Life of Harry Anderson

⚓

BY ROGER VAUGHAN

The author would like to thank the following for their support and insights:

Margaret Burroughs, Devereux Barker, Robert MacKay, Henry Fuller, Skip Barker, Gloria Pierce, Vanessa Cameron, Diana Russell, Nicholas Bell, Tom Baker

Mystic Seaport
75 Greenmanville Ave., PO Box 6000
Mystic, CT 06355-0990
www.mysticseaport.org

Edited by Andrew W. German
Mystic, Connecticut

Designed by Trish Sinsigalli LaPointe
tslapointedesign.com

Printed by GHP, West Haven, CT
www.ghpmedia.com

ISBN 978-0-939511-37-2

Vaughan, Roger.
The strenuous life of Harry Anderson / by Roger Vaughan.—1st ed.— Mystic, CT :
Mystic Seaport, © 2013.
   p. : ill. ; cm.
Includes appendices and index.

1. Sailors—United States—Biography. 2. Yacht racing. I. Anderson, Harry. II. Title.
GV812.5.A5 .B3 2013

For Kippy –RV

To William "Coach" Maclay and James "Jamie" Hilton, who were lifetime shipmates on many expeditions and escapades, and to the hordes of other shipmates I have sailed with. –HHA

The publication of this book was made possible by the generosity of the following friends and admirers of Henry H. Anderson Jr.:

Acorn Foundation Fund for History
  in Memory of Alexander Orr Vietor
Leith McLean Adams
Henry H. Anderson Jr.
David Anderson
Norman F. Angus
Hugh D. Auchincloss III
John R. Bockstoce
Warren A. Brown
RADM David C. Brown
Nicholas Brown
Mr. and Mrs. Howard S. Browne
W. Murray Buttner
Nancybell Coe
Mr. and Mrs. William T. Dalessi
Mr. and Mrs. Lawrence R. Glenn
Mr. and Mrs. Thomas J. Gochberg
Janet Gay Hawkins
Mr. and Mrs. James A. Hilton
Mr. and Mrs. Joseph C. Hoopes Jr.
Mr. and Mrs. Robert L. James
S. Edward Jeter
James Loran Kerr
William Koch
Charles S. Langston
Alfred Lee Loomis III
C. S. Lovelace
Donald G. Magee
Juliette C. McLennan
George S. Meyer
Willets S. Meyer
Mr. and Mrs. Clarence F. Michalis
Mimi Neff

David R. Pedrick
Richard W. Pendleton Jr.
Caleb M. Pifer
David Warren Ray
Elizabeth E. Roosevelt
Rounsevelle W. Schaum
James M. Schoonmaker II
Irving C. Sheldon
Jeffrey M. Siegal
Mr. and Mrs. C.R. Sonne
Luise Strauss
Richard Thursby
Charles H. Townsend
Stephen Van R. Ulman
Uncle Larry's Fund
Stephen G.W. Walk
V.ADM and Mrs. Thomas R. Weschler USN (Ret)
Mr. and Mrs. Richard M. Wilch
Mr. and Mrs. William G. Winterer

There is a sly bachelor from Mory's
From whom no answer will come,
'Tis Harry, the man of the drolleries,
And the quaintly impervious aplomb

CDRE. W. MAHLON DICKERSON

Contents

SANDRINGHAM HOUSE

    I am sure that in addition to the members of the Imperial Poona Yacht Club, there will be many conventional yachtsmen who will welcome this biography. The list of his connections, appointments and achievements in the conventional yachting world make an exhausting read, but to members of the Imperial Poona Yacht Club his position as the first Commode of the Revolting Colonist Outpost for 50 years is the only one that really matters.

    I think it is worth noting that no sooner had Harry Anderson stepped down as Commodore of the New York Yacht Club, than the 'America's' Cup was lost. Fortunately no such disaster occurred when he gave up the appointment as Commode of the Revolting Colonist Outpost and took up his present title of Pons Asinorum and enthusiastic supporter of the EIEIO Cup for Backwards Racing.

ONE | Accomplished Antecedents

Newport, Rhode Island, summer 1937:

In the movie version, the camera would take the viewer for a leisurely stroll along Thames Street, Newport's main drag bordering the east side of the large, deep harbor. On the inland side of the street there is a string of retail stores, bars, and restaurants, all busy with shoppers and diners on a warm summer day. The bright, white uniforms of sailors stand out in the crowd. Newport has long been a navy town. A facility for the research, development, and manufacture of torpedoes was built on Goat Island at the north end of the harbor in 1870. In 1937, 3,000 men are stationed there. A navy ferry runs regularly between the Island and a midtown pier, where off-duty sailors disembark and often make a beeline for the south end of Thames Street, with its dingy bars and brothels.

In 1884, the US Naval War College was established in Newport. In 1937, with a war between Japan and China ongoing, and Germany's young Chancellor Adolf Hitler busy concocting a mad Nazi philosophy, the War College is a busy place. The US Navy is preparing for the worst.

Across Thames Street on the harbor side, the docks are rafted two-deep with fishing boats and commercial vessels of many shapes and sizes. The camera pauses here and there to take in the loading and unloading, the handcarts and trucks coming and going, the salty faces of the fishermen and crews bent to their tasks.

Traffic on Thames Street is heavy. Notable for its size and luster, a passing, chauffer-driven Brewster—the American version of a Rolls-Royce—grabs the camera's attention. In the car is a family: mother

Orion, detail from page 5.

and father and several boys in their middle teens. The chauffeur is in black, with black tie and cap. The father is dapper in double-breasted yachting blazer and cap. The mother is in a sensible but stylish summer cotton frock of cream and white. The boys are in blazers and neckties. The family rides in silence along Thames Street, past the docks, past the brick, three-story Seamen's Church Institute—established in 1919 "to serve those connected with the sea"—past the shipyard where yachts are built and repaired. A few blocks further south, the limousine turns into Station 6 of the New York Yacht Club.

Station 6 is one of a dozen no-frills buildings that had been purchased or erected by the NYYC on waterfronts along the northeast coast of the United States in the late 1800s and early 1900s. With so few yacht clubs in existence at the time, the stations provided a place for members who might be cruising to tie up while purchasing supplies or changing crews. Station 6 is a simple, two-story wood-frame cube finished with cedar shingles. A small widow's walk topped by a cupola crowns a mansard roof. There are two covered porches on the south side. The first floor consists of one large room with a small bar at one end. Toilets and showers are at the other end. A ramp on the north side leads to a floating dock with deep water.

Station 6 is overseen by a club member and normally has a steward on duty who doubles as dockmaster. A cleaning crew comes in once a week to remove the cobwebs. But this is a special time. It is the summer of the sixteenth America's Cup, a "friendly competition [under sail] between nations" in the language of the Deed of Gift, the legal document that regulates the Cup matches.

The America's Cup began in 1851 when a fast schooner of radical design from the United States by the name of *America* crossed the Atlantic and went on to beat a fleet of British yachts in a race around the Isle of Wight. It was a significant victory. Britain ruled the waves at the time, both militarily and for sport. That event initiated an ongoing series of challenges in the largest, fastest, most impressive sailing yachts ever designed, challenges presented (and defended) by some of the wealthiest men on the planet. The races took place as little as one and as many as 20 years apart, and had always been won by the United States, the initial holder of the Cup. The USA's string of victories would last 132 years, but that's another story. The New York Yacht Club had conspired to send *America* off to beat the Brits, and had always been the official defender of the Cup.

For the summer of 1937, Station 6 had been generally upgraded for the occasion in an effort to compliment the glitter of the gaudy, 27-inch-high, eight-and-a-half-pound sterling-silver ewer the NYYC's yacht of choice was defending. The "cup" itself was bolted to a table in the Trophy Room at the NYYC's headquarters on Forty-Fourth Street in New York. Station 6 boasted freshly painted white trim without, and new varnish within. The photos on the walls had been dusted and straightened. The façade of the building had been dressed with a club burgee, American flag, and signal flags. All hung slack, so light was the breeze. The steward, also suitably dressed for the occasion in a navy blue serge uniform with an enlisted man's cut, opened the door of the Brewster with just the right amount of flourish as it stopped in front of Station 6. The steward greeted club members Mr. and Mrs. Henry H. Anderson formally, and by name.

There was little conversation between parents and teenagers as they walked down the ramp to the dock. The plan laid out by Henry Anderson was now being executed. The parents would be going to a friend's yacht to observe the first race of the America's Cup. The five boys—three Anderson brothers, Harry, Jim, and David, and their second cousins, Henry Stillman Taylor's boys—would be ferried to another yacht. On the dock, the group parted company without ceremony and boarded different tenders that had been standing off with engines idling. In their smart, white uniforms, the tenders' crews affected a military bearing.

The trip across Newport Harbor for the boys was rather a long one because their yacht for the day was the largest private vessel then in existence (measured in tons). It required deep water and plenty of space to maneuver. The harbor that hazy summer day was flat, with light wind brushing the surface. Even if the sea had been up it would have been a smooth ride. The tender was large and powerful, 40 feet of seagoing beauty in Bristol condition. The varnish and the brass fittings sparkled. The enclosed seating area discouraged spray from ruffling passengers' finery. Once its job was done, the tender would be craned aboard its mother ship *Orion* and would disappear in its rack on the main deck of the 1,422-ton yacht that measured 333 feet two inches from stem to stern. A Mrs. Cadwalader from Philadelphia owned a yacht a touch longer than *Orion*, but her vessel didn't equal *Orion*'s tonnage.

Orion was a steel ship built in 1929 in Kiel, Germany, by Krupp Germania Werft for one Julius Forstmann, former owner and CEO of the woolen company that bore his name. Forstmann had emigrated to the United States in 1903, having accurately appraised the burgeoning textile market the young country offered. Forstmann became the primary woolen company in America, branching out successfully into foundation garments for ladies and gentlemen. Even more astute than his business acumen was Julius Forstmann's early sense that the US was headed for a depression, which caused him to sell everything for top dollar in 1927 and commission *Orion*, on which he would take his family on a world cruise while the economy crashed, burned, and, one hoped, recovered. His timing could not have been better. The crash occurred a year later. *Orion*'s world cruise had been a great success, and now here Forstmann was in Newport on his enormous steel yacht to wine and dine 50 or 100 of his closest friends while watching the America's Cup.

In 1937, the America's Cup was a sporting contest unmatched for its elegance. It began with the lovely, slim lines of the 130-foot J-Class yachts that competed on the water. Few sailing yachts before or since would equal their stunning combination of grace, beauty, and power. Their masts towered 160 feet off the deck; their spinnakers measured 10,000 square feet. Crews of 30 professionals in white sailor suits did the hauling and pulling, while an afterguard of half a dozen yachtsmen handled steering, navigation, and tactics. Four of the J-Class yachts had arrived on the scene in 1929, having been completed just before Wall Street crashed.

The yachts' owners were men of sufficient means and prominence to have been household names in their respective countries, if not globally. America's predominant yachtsman of the 1930s was Harold S. "Mike" Vanderbilt, great-grandson of shipping and railroad tycoon Cornelius. When he wasn't running the family railroads, inventing a convention for Contract Bridge, or taking the lead in writing the Racing Rules of Sailing, Mike Vanderbilt owned and skippered a series of J boats to successful Cup defenses in 1930, 1934, and 1937. His challenger from Great Britain in 1930 was Sir Thomas Lipton, the tea baron. In 1934, British aviation pioneer and industrialist, Sir Thomas Sopwith, whose company had built 18,000 warplanes for the defense of England during World War I, had come within a hair of winning the Cup; close enough to warrant another try in 1937.

Add to all that pedigree the mouth-watering collection of gorgeous motor yachts making up the spectator fleet, and the ultimate richness of the impressive mansions on Bellevue Avenue and Ocean Avenue where the lavish, après sail formal dinner parties and dances were held, and the America's Cups of the 1930s looked like full-scale Hollywood productions.

To the Anderson and Taylor boys, all of whom were sailors, conditions for the first race of

The yacht *Orion*, 1937.

the 1937 Cup were disappointing. Harry Anderson had already experienced blue-water racing. The previous summer, when he was 15, he had participated in his first offshore race, Newport to Bermuda aboard George Roosevelt's 60-foot schooner *Mistress*. Leaning against the rail on *Orion*'s upper deck, Harry and the boys squinted into the haze and shook their heads. It was past midday, and the usually reliable sou'westerly breeze was a no-show. The sea was so calm that the only reason boats in the spectator fleet were rocking was from one another's wakes. Even if there had been wind enough to provide a good race, the boys realized they weren't going to see it from *Orion*. The ship's sheer bulk required she maintain a distance of more than a mile from the racecourse so her high sides would not block the wind. And now the bad news: there were very few people their age on board.

Harry, Jim, and David Anderson were particularly disappointed. All of them had a speaking acquaintance with Mike Vanderbilt, and they were eager to watch him perform on the racecourse. The boys' great-grandfather, Henry B. Anderson, who had started the first family law firm, had been counselor for the City of New York in the mid 1800s. As such, he had handled Cornelius Vanderbilt's license applications for the trolley lines running up Park Avenue that would play a key role in furthering Vanderbilt's railroad interests.

H. B. Anderson eventually became counselor for Cornelius Vanderbilt, then a friend. The family friendship had sustained through the generations to the point that Mike Vanderbilt had become a frequent visitor to the Anderson home in Oyster Bay, New York. Because Vanderbilt was an enthusiastic tennis player, and because one of his favorite partners was Mrs. Anderson (Helen), one of the Anderson boys was often dispatched to town to buy new balls when it was known he was planning a visit. The boys were often pressed into running the older balls through the Smiley Knapper, a device of the day that fluffed the balls, extending their playing time.

Teenage boys have a way of making the best of a situation. While they found the indoor pool on *Orion*'s upper deck tempting, they hadn't come prepared for swimming. It probably wouldn't have been appropriate. But they soon found the ping-pong tables, and close by on a shelf was a radio. Things were looking up. While the other guests were dawdling over a champagne lunch, the boys were soon playing a ping-pong tournament while listening to the tennis at Forest Hills on the radio.

The boys were too involved in their game to realize that one of the guests had paused to watch them, and was taking a few more sips from her glass of champagne as she pondered her next move. She was a tall woman, trim, shapely, with a shock of dark hair cascading to her shoulders. She was in her mid-thirties. Anyone who paid attention to the society pages would have recognized her face. She was one of New York's darlings of the day, a socialite people loved to love. She approached the table and set her glass down near the net, effectively stopping play and garnering the boys' full attention. They didn't read the society pages, but they knew that pretty face. It was Ava Astor, who was nine when her father, John Jacob Astor IV, had gone down with the *Titanic* after putting his pregnant wife in a lifeboat. Her great-great-grandfather was John Jacob Astor, who had purchased a very large chunk of Manhattan with money he'd made in the international fur business, and who had died with a fortune in excess of $100 billion (calculated in 2006 dollars) in 1848—more money than was in the United States Treasury at the time. That Ava Astor.

She asked the boys who was winning.

"Harry," the boys mumbled, more or less in unison. "He always wins," one of the Taylor boys said. "At everything," Harry's youngest brother David, age 12, chimed in. Harry said nothing. Even at 17 his long, serious face was hard to read. His expression was pleasant, his mouth showed a trace of amusement. His blue eyes were steady, missing nothing. Yes, he won most of the time, at everything as David had

said, from academic grades to tennis; from sailing to navigation and seamanship. Harry was glad of that; he enjoyed it actually, but he won with such grace, with such ease, and with so little affect that it was expected, commonplace, and inoffensive. None of his friends held it against him. That was just how it was if you hung out with Harry.

Flashing her famous pout at the boys, Ava Astor said that she didn't want to play with Harry. Then she looked him over, and allowed as how he seemed like an upstanding young man. Perhaps he would be willing to hold a few things for her while she played some ping-pong. With that, Ava Astor began removing the ranks of gold, diamond-encrusted bracelets that adorned her wrists. She scooped up the tangle of jewelry in one hand and handed it to Harry, who placed it in the side pockets of his blazer. Ava Astor picked up a paddle and brandished it.

⚓

THE BREWSTER, with Robert, the chauffeur, behind the wheel, was waiting at Station 6 when the tender returned the boys to the dock. Shortly thereafter, Mr. and Mrs. Anderson arrived. A World War I cavalry officer, Mr. Anderson put a high priority on promptness, even when the vagaries of boats and the water were involved. No one spoke about the day on the water as Robert drove up the hill from the waterfront and turned right on Bellevue Avenue. There was nothing to talk about. The light-air race had been completed, but it was a yawner. Vanderbilt and his "super-J" *Ranger* had prevailed with ease.

Bellevue paralleled Thames Street. In midtown the street presented a higher-quality selection of shops and restaurants in addition to the Newport Reading Room, an exclusive men's club founded in 1854, and the grass tennis courts of the Newport Casino (1880). Further south, in the mile before Bellevue made a 90-degree right-hand turn and became Ocean Avenue, the street was famous for the lineup of mansions that had been built there in the years between 1865 and 1914, the so-called Gilded Age.

That was a period when vast industrial fortunes were amassed, and what better way to display those fabulous successes than with the architecture of ultimate excess, marble and granite replacing brick and limestone. As the late journalist Brendan Gill, who for 50 years covered New York's social and literary life, wrote in his introduction to *Long Island Country Houses*, "the simple act of building is the surest means of announcing that one has made good. A man who puts up a

bigger house than his neighbor. . . . is a better man than his neighbor: the set of values that most of us live by is, I fear, as simple and undiscriminating as that." If in the Venice of the fifteenth and sixteenth centuries, "fanciful palaces leaped up in gaudy rivalry out of the shimmering waters of the lagoon," as Gill so eloquently put it, the barons of nineteenth-century Newport did their best to follow suit. In truth, while their efforts were worthy imitations built at enormous cost by teams of artisans brought over from the old countries, they were far less ostentatious than the fanciful palaces of Venice, or the 300-room extravaganzas of France's Loire Valley. But in Newport, the lesser mansions had the ever-changing, rock-bound, always dramatic, surf-struck coast of the Atlantic Ocean as their front yards. That was indeed both unique and hard to beat.

As Robert steered the big town car down Bellevue at a dignified pace, the Anderson and Taylor boys had time to glance at their neighborhood once again, commonplace as it was to them. Many of the houses were the size of government buildings in Washington, DC. On the right was the Elms, an enormous stone cube of a mansion designed after a famed French chateau of the mid-1700s, with seemingly more ranks of granite steps than the Philadelphia Museum of Art. The Elms was originally the summer residence of a coal industrialist from Pennsylvania. On the left was Chateau-sur-Mer, a high-Victorian Italianate stone villa built for a China trade merchant. Beyond Chateau-sur-Mer the massive façade of the Breakers could be seen through the trees. The Breakers is a 70-room Italian Renaissance palace built for Cornelius Vanderbilt II, grandson of Cornelius. Next was Rosecliff, modeled after a garden retreat for French kings at Versailles, owned by a silver heiress. Marble House followed, a "cottage" built for Mr. and Mrs. William K. Vanderbilt—Mike Vanderbilt's parents, his father being another grandson of Cornelius— an undertaking that required 500,000 cubic feet of marble. Finally they passed Rough Point, a more modest English-style stone home built by another Vanderbilt but now owned by a tobacco heiress, before turning in to Rockhurst, at the time the summer cottage of the Anderson boys' grandmother, Helen Jennings James.

Rockhurst was a wood-shingled, French-style country house, a long, three-story dwelling with a wraparound terrace on three sides, facing an expansive lawn that sloped down to Rhode Island Sound. There were two stories of bedrooms. Harry Anderson recalls a master bedroom on the second floor with the unique feature of a ladder in the closet leading to another closet on the third floor, where it was reputed the previous owner often visited

a mistress after his wife fell asleep. With its many sharply peaked dormers, Rockhurst's design was influenced by the chateaux of the aforementioned Loire Valley. Its 40 rooms included a solarium, and an enclosed arboretum on the main floor led to a ballroom. On the grounds was a stone gate cottage, a greenhouse, and stable-garage.

Helen Goodsell Jennings James was the daughter of Oliver Burr Jennings. In 1849, at age 23, Oliver was working at Browning & Hull, a dry goods store in New York City, when it was announced that gold had been discovered at Sutter's Mill in California. Jennings had a friend at B&H named Benjamin Brewster. It took little time for the two adventurous men to join the thousands heading for California.

The trip was rigorous no matter how one chose to get there. Jennings had a brother who had commanded half a dozen ships by the time he was 35. That was good luck, because getting space on a San Francisco-bound ship was difficult during the gold rush. But it was Brewster who went by one of Jennings' ships around storm-whipped Cape Horn, a ship loaded with goods advanced to them by B&H that he and Jennings planned to sell in California. Oliver Jennings traveled by a different ship to the Isthmus of Panama, made a 50-mile trek by canoe and mule through the fever-infested jungle, and caught a ship of chance on the Pacific side. Jennings arrived first (Brewster's voyage took six months), and he tried his hand at mining while awaiting his friend's arrival. He returned from the goldfields east of San Francisco having learned that sort of arduous labor was not for him. But he had made $1,200 for his efforts, enough to buy half the B&H goods being shipped. The two friends set up separate retail stores. After Brewster's store was destroyed in a fire, the two joined forces and became partners.

Business was excellent. Jennings & Brewster bought goods from B&H and other East Coast outlets for dollars, and sold them for gold. Credit was not accepted. Back east in 1854, Jennings married his old girlfriend, Esther Goodsell, and took her back to California, pregnant, this time via the new Panama Railroad through the Isthmus of Panama jungle and on to San Francisco. They would produce five children, including Helen, the Anderson boys' grandmother. Another of San Francisco's frequent fires burned Jennings & Brewster, but in 1862 they sold their interest for a large profit. Hence, Oliver Burr Jennings returned to New York a rich man, giving credence to his family's motto, "The Good Time Will Come."

Back east, Esther Goodsell's sister, Almira,

married William Rockefeller in 1864. That Jennings/Rockefeller connection would provide a most profitable venture for Oliver Burr Jennings and his descendants. It is said he returned from California with a net worth of around $360,000—$8 million in 2010 dollars. This fact was not lost on William Rockefeller, one of the entrepreneurs putting together Standard Oil. When innovative refining genius Samuel Anderson, William Rockefeller, his brother John D., grain merchant Henry Flagler, and whiskey baron and banker Stephen V. Harkness found themselves short of the capitalization they needed to complete the Standard Oil deal, they invited Oliver Burr Jennings to be the sixth initial stockholder. Jennings paid $100,000 ($2.4 million in 2010 dollars) for one thousand shares of what would become the country's richest corporation.

Helen Jennings James' husband, Dr. Walter B. James (1858-1926), had been a well-known New York City physician. A graduate of the College of Physicians and Surgeons in New York, Dr. James always maintained a staff position there. At the time of his death he was professor of clinical medicine at the College, as well as visiting or consulting physician at several New York hospitals. The list of medical associations he led or championed, and his various trusteeships—academic and otherwise—would fill several pages. One listing must have a star beside it. James was president of Georgia's Jekyll Island Club during eight of its golden years, 1919-1927.

Founded in 1886 by members of New York's Union Club, Jekyll Island was unrivaled when it came to social status and prestige. America's most powerful families wintered there. The plan for the Federal Reserve System was outlined at Jekyll Island over brandy and cigars. Many members would leave their private railroad cars on a siding near Brunswick, Georgia, and take the club ferry across the Jekyll River—a section of what would become the Intracoastal Waterway—to the Island. (Another relative, Anderson's Great-Uncle Walter Jennings, also had a "cottage" on Jekyll.)

Dr. James had succeeded his friend, Dr. Edward Trudeau, as president of the Adirondack Cottage Sanatorium for tubercular patients at Saranac Lake, New York. As a result, Dr. James would build a "camp" in the Adirondacks that his family enjoyed for many years.

Dr. James was the cousin of Arthur Curtiss James—the two men shared a great-grandfather. Arthur Curtiss James was the sole heir to his father's estate, worth $25 million (in 1920 dollars), an inheritance that included the Phelps Dodge mining interests. One of the country's wealthiest men, Arthur

Curtiss James was also an enthusiastic yachtsman who owned, in succession, the 131-foot schooner-yacht *Coronet,* fabled for its transatlantic race win in 1887, and a 218-foot, 659-ton bark named *Aloha* that was built for him in 1910. James was commodore of the New York Yacht Club during 1909-1910. His 125-acre Newport estate included a manor house that resembled the Plaza Hotel in New York, three other villas, a Swiss model farm, formal gardens, and a boathouse. It was the largest estate in Newport.

The Anderson boys shared another lineage

John Vanderlyn painted this portrait of Aaron Burr in 1802, during his vice presidency.

that is worthy of note. By marriage, they were related to the famous New York political figure, Aaron Burr. A Revolutionary War hero and an attorney, Burr was, in turn, New York State attorney general, United States senator, and vice president under President Thomas Jefferson (1801-1805). During his term as vice president he committed the act that would make him infamous, that being the killing of Alexander Hamilton in a duel in 1804. The marriage of Aaron Burr's second cousin Peter Burr (Aaron's second cousin) to Esther Jennings (the Anderson boys' great-great-great grandmother) in the 1700s made Aaron Burr a second cousin five times removed. His relationship to the controversial Burr would captivate Harry Anderson, causing him to become a certified expert on Burr, and a staunch defender of Burr's reputation.

One might say that Harry Anderson and his brothers had an embarrassment of accomplished antecedents.

VISITING THEIR grandmother's was always a pleasure for the Anderson boys. The house and grounds were a wonderful playground. Their bedrooms on the second floor had fabulous views of the ocean, and Helen James' kitchen most often

produced delicious seafood, fresh from the clear waters of Narragansett Bay.

"We never visited grandmother as a family inasmuch as Father and my uncles abhorred the frenetic and elitist social life in the Newport colony," Anderson recalls.

Mother did, however, take myself and my brothers for a week or two several summers. The house had many grandfather clocks, including one highly animated clock that chimed every quarter of an hour and that at night could be heard through much of the house. I remember being awakened at 6:00 a.m. every day by the sound of the groundskeepers raking smooth the gravel on the drive.

Among the rituals faced by a youngster such as myself were morning swims at Bailey's Beach, where ladies and children were not permitted on the beach until noon, and then only in full-length swimsuits. Another memory is being sent by Grandmother, accompanied by our French governess and driven by Robert the chauffeur in one of the town cars—most likely the Rolls-Royce or the Brewster—to pay a mid-morning call on a pre-teenage girl. Chatter was not even idle, since both of us were virtual strangers to one another. I suppose tea was served. It was quite awkward for both of us. But that's how things were done in those days in the Colony.

As Harry got older and started sailing in various grand prix events out of Newport, or when he was cruising on the family's New York 32, Rockhurst not only provided him with wonderful quarters, hot showers, and sumptuous meals, but a welcome freedom of movement and activity he did not enjoy at home.

The evening after the day aboard *Orion*, dinner was served in one of the smaller dining rooms at Rockhurst. As usual, everyone dressed for the occasion. Arthur, the butler who had been with Mrs. James for many years, was serving.

As he brought the soup course, Arthur bent down so he could speak quietly to Harry. He said there was a woman on the telephone asking if there was a young man in the house who might have a pocket full of her jewelry.

Arthur said the woman sounded a bit anxious, that she had been calling all the estates in town trying to find the young man in question. Arthur said her description seemed to fit him.

Harry looked startled for a brief second before he smiled just a little and told Arthur he could report that yes, he did have two pockets full of jewelry.

Many years later, Harry Anderson would comment on that moment. "That," he said with the dry chuckle that had become his trademark, "was only the first of many fortunes that slipped away."

TWO | Silent Giant

Harry Anderson turned 90 on June 2, 2011.

T wo weeks later, 400 people gathered at the New York Yacht Club's Harbour Court Station in Newport, Rhode Island, to pay homage to the man who had been in the vanguard of yachting's leadership for more than 60 years. It was a gorgeous late spring day, comfortably warm and sunny with great clumps of fluffy cumulous clouds passing in slow procession on a moderate southwesterly wind. On such a fine day, from its elevation on a steep hillside of mown grass, Harbour Court offers a panoramic view to the north across the harbor jammed with sailing and power craft of all shapes and sizes. To the right, the old town of Newport (1639), still salty and low-lying thanks to an indomitable preservation society, crowds the busy waterfront. Further to the left is Goat Island, now home to a marina, a hotel, and condominiums. Crowning the view is the two-mile arc of the Claiborne Pell suspension bridge connecting Newport with Jamestown on Conanicut Island to the west. The bridge spans the wide channel leading to Narragansett Bay, deep enough even for US Navy battleships. Beyond the bridge to the north is more broad water. One encounters Coasters Harbor Island, home to the US Naval War College, before moving into Mt. Hope Bay.

In the foreground, the large American flag and the New York Yacht Club burgee flying from the pole anchored 30 feet below the palatial, "French chateauesque" clubhouse, flung their colors against the sky. Harbour Court is the former home of the late John Nicholas Brown, real estate and textiles magnate from one of Rhode Island's First Families. The Browns helped start Brown University. Altogether this prime spot offers a magnificent vista, a glorious stretch of navigable water and prime real estate rich in history from Narragansett Indian days, to Giovanni Verrazano's

arrival in 1524, to the America's Cup—
a sailor's dream come true.

It was the perfect setting for honoring Harry
Anderson on his ninetieth year, since he has
been a sailor since childhood, and because
much of his life's work has been connected
with boats and the water. In addition to
friends and family at Harbour Court that day
in June, there were representatives from
many organizations that have benefited from
Anderson's membership, support, financial
contributions, administrative leadership, or

most likely all of the above: Mystic Seaport;
Herreshoff Marine Museum & America's
Cup Hall of Fame; US Sailing; American Sail
Training Association; Yale Sailing Center; The
Maritime Alliance; University of Rhode Island
Sailing Program; Ransom Everglades School;
International Sailing Federation; World Ship
Trust; International Yacht Restoration School;
National Maritime Historical Society; US Naval
War College; Seamen's Church Institute; Sail
Newport; Finn Class Association; Raven
Class Association; International 12 Metre
Class Association (of which Anderson was

Anderson was piped into his ninetieth birthday
celebration by his nephew Cameron Anderson.
With him was his brother David, and David's
grandson, Coleman.

the first chairman, serving with his friend, the Aga Kahn); the Aaron Burr Association; and the Robert Crown Sailing Center at the US Naval Academy.

Representatives and well-wishers from yacht clubs have to be in a class by themselves, since Anderson has accumulated 139 years total as a flag officer of the following yacht clubs: St. Regis Junior; Seawanhaka Corinthian (Junior and Senior); Pine Knot; Yale Corinthian; the Revolting Colonies Outpost of the Imperial Poona; Yale Sailing Associates; and the New York Yacht Club. Members were also in attendance from Anderson's dry land clubs, including Dauntless (of Essex, Connecticut, where he was the club's archivist in 2013); Union Club of New York; and the Newport Reading Room.

Anderson was born in Manhattan, grew up in Roslyn, New York; moved at a young age to Oyster Bay, New York; went to school near Saranac, New York, and Coconut Grove, Florida; attended university in New Haven, Connecticut; went to law school in Manhattan; and worked in Manhattan for a few years before moving to Newport, where he maintained a residence for most of his life. As mentioned, he has known Newport and sailed its waters since he was a boy, thanks to his grandmother's summer home there in the waning days of the town's Gilded Age. Because of Anderson's

varied interests and work, he has traveled extensively all his life, but if he would call anyplace home it is Newport.

For most people, being confronted with 400 of their relatives, friends, and associates on the occasion of the celebration of their ninetieth year would likely be daunting, emotionally draining—confusing at the least. For the event, Anderson was nattily attired in white trousers and his treasured crimson Congressional Cup blazer over a white shirt and the yellow necktie with the red dots of the Imperial Poona Yacht Club. He wore a straw boater bearing a band of New York Yacht Club colors. The blazer was an honor bestowed upon Anderson for "contributing exceptionally to the advancement of yacht racing and the success of the Congressional

17

Sculptress Leith Adams with her bust of Harry Anderson, done for the occasion of his ninetieth birthday.

Cup," the predominant match racing series in the United States since 1965. He served on its race committee for 35 years. The thirty-third Congressional Cup (1998) had been raced in his honor. The straw boater was left over from his days on the New York Yacht Club's America's Cup Selection Committee.

A spare man, with a slight forward bend from the waist and a left eye that acts up on occasion being the only visible nods to old age, Anderson took the party in stride, the way, it seems, he has always taken everything. Perhaps it was because he had taken the lead in giving purpose to the event. Former chairman of the board of the American Sail Training Association (doing business as Tall Ships America, or TSA), Anderson is a member of their Commodore's Council and Advisory Board. In March 2010, he attended a Tall Ships board retreat and brought up his forthcoming ninetieth birthday.

"He had a private conversation with a couple board members," says Bert Rogers, executive director of Tall Ships America. "The gist of it was, 'I'm going to be 90 next year, there's going to be a big party, so let's put it to work for Tall Ships.' And that's what happened." Rogers says the party, along with the endowment campaign that pre-dated it, raised around $320,000. "That's how he does things," Rogers says of Harry Anderson. "He's a fount of good ideas."

Caleb Pifer, age 27, skipper of the tall ship *Niagara* (a reproduction of Commodore Oliver Hazard Perry's flagship during the Battle of Lake Erie in 1813), is one of Anderson's younger friends. Pifer is the youngest person ever to be elected to the board of Tall Ships America (in 2012, he had become vice chairman of the board). He got to know Anderson when he was first hired by TSA in 2007. When Pifer discovered his compensation didn't include lodging, a deal breaker for him, Anderson offered him a room in his house on Corne Street in Newport. "I didn't have a clue who Anderson was, nor did he have a clue about me," Pifer says. "He was very gracious. He gave me a tour of his house with the big portraits of his ancestors on the walls, and he handed me the key. He said `just don't burn my place down,' and left the next day for a month. I about fell over, wondering who on earth was this trusting person."

Pifer says the way Anderson orchestrated his birthday party is typical of how he works. "Other TSA board members might think he is an elder who just enjoys coming to the meetings," Pifer says, "but that's not so. He's a silent giant. He takes meticulous notes, follows up meetings by having drinks afterwards with key people, and talks about what makes him unhappy. He's been a broken record ever since I have been on the board about creating a stronger endowment for TSA.

Others might have been more forceful about it, but Harry took a different approach. When you are of Harry's stature, you have to be careful what you ask of your friends, and I had never seen Harry bug his friends very much. But when he saw an opportunity—his ninetieth birthday—to attach his name to an endowment fund, and really reach out to everybody in his network, he put his entire weight behind it."

Anderson was his usual low-key self at the party. His working profile has always been that of the fellow in the wings quietly making things happen, not the gregarious spokesman reveling in the spotlight. He hung out with close friends and relatives, and graciously greeted all who passed by to wish him well, most of them by name. Given the list of schools, organizations, and clubs Anderson has been affiliated with for such a long time, one can scarcely imagine the thousands of connections and interconnections the man has made during his long and busy life. That makes his ability to put names with faces that much more extraordinary.

Anderson's remarkable memory is supported by his compulsion to keep records. He is a committed scribe—a reporter, an enthusiastic "blogger" long before the Internet was born and that term was coined—and a dedicated researcher of the first rank. When he was well into his ninety-first year someone asked

Anderson what he would have done differently if he had his life to live over. He gave even that tired cliché of a question a moment's thoughtful consideration, then said this: "I probably would have done more research and written more when I was in college."

Harry's brother David, who is five years younger, jokes that when he wants to keep his elder brother off his back, he'll give him a bit of information knowing he'll soon be off researching it. No subject is too arcane to satisfy Anderson's unbridled curiosity, his need to dig into the details. The idiom "God is in the details" is credited to architect Mies van der Rohe. "The Devil is in the details" followed. For Harry Anderson, the truth is in the details, and that's what drives him.

Chances are, if you have interacted in even a small way with Harry Anderson, he will have your contact information on file with a pertinent note or two scribbled alongside. There's nothing opportunistic about it. For Harry Anderson, there is a significant piece of the jigsaw puzzle we call life in everyone he has met, if only he can discover it. He carefully logs in names and numbers like he would file any other resource, toward that day when still another piece might fall into place.

Anderson moved to Mystic, Connecticut, in 2005. His ground-floor apartment at

StoneRidge, a sprawling assisted-living community, is more library than residence. Anderson doesn't need "assistance," but he has always displayed an enviable knack for keeping ahead of inevitable eventualities, like aging. The basics are there: two bedrooms, two bathrooms, dining/living room, and a kitchenette. But the comforts one associates with living arrangements for senior citizens—comfy recliners and wide screen entertainment systems—are absent. His TV is an old Sony Trinitron. Anderson has always preferred living with essential rather than luxury furnishings. When he owned the house at 209 Spring Street in Newport in the 1970s, some young sailing friends chided him about his penchant for wooden, straight-back, period chairs. The friends said he needed something comfortable, like a nice couch. He took their council to heart. Two weeks later a two-seater wooden bench with a straight back arrived. It did have a seat cushion, albeit a thin one.

Not only does that choice reflect Anderson's preference, his modus vivendi, but large, comfortable pieces of furniture would steal space from the innumerable bookcases and files that populate his rooms. His priorities are clear. The antique pine dining table in his StoneRidge living room is divided the long way by a rank of books and is always lightly cluttered with the current work at hand. ("Dining" is something Anderson does out.

He's not a cook. When he does eat in, he sits at a small corner table in his kitchen.) But Anderson's research files are in near Dewey Decimal order, labeled and numbered with his own system.

Twenty-five minutes after our first meeting, Anderson gave me the key to his apartment, saying he would be away the following week, and why didn't I stay there and spend a few days perusing his files. It was a replay of the Pifer story, complete with the portraits of the ancestors on the walls that had been moved from Newport. (The Anderson ancestors first emigrated from Londonerry, Ireland, to Londonderry, New Hampshire, in 1728.) When friends of Harry heard this, they laughed and said Harry would do anything for a sailor. Said one, "It's lucky you weren't a polo player." When I returned, his one "comfortable" settee—a three-person Victorian love seat in front of the bow window—and the wing chairs on either side, were covered with notebooks, folders, maps, books opened to key pages, all aflutter with sticky notes bearing helpful comments and directions for finding more on the subjects.

The subjects Anderson has researched over the years are encyclopedic, but those of prime significance include several relatives. "After my mother died," Anderson says, "I discovered a locker full of books and family papers.

She had never mentioned the material was there. It was new stuff on both sides of the family, Anderson and Jennings. That got me going, I guess."

A scholar who chooses to concentrate on his own family could be dismissed as parochial, but the family in Anderson's case is so illustrious, and so significant during various seminal developmental stages of the United States, that to ignore it would have been verging on the irresponsible. Anderson's response to his mother's locker full of family papers was that of a student who had been dropped, wide-eyed, into a private, special collections archive of many rooms—with a pocket full of keys.

Chief among Anderson's ongoing research projects is his cousin, Arthur Curtiss James. Writing in *Fortune* magazine in February 1930, Alan Schumacher labeled James one of the world's richest men. The worth of his railroad holdings alone—one-seventh of the existing track mileage in the United States at the time—was valued in excess of $30 million ($387 million in 2010 dollars). And that was the tip of the iceberg. Schumacher writes that James did not fit any models of famous patrician dynasties of the day like the Harrimans, the Rockefellers, or the Astors: James "is something more nearly comparable to a landed proprietor of nineteenth-century

English life, a man who has inherited a great property, who feels the responsibility of his inheritance, who intelligently increases it, but who does not make his holdings his career. Arthur Curtiss James is one of the first examples, and perhaps the best example, of the great, funded proprietors Industrial Civilization must produce."

That James was an esteemed yachtsman and an enthusiastic tennis player would have been enough to attract Harry Anderson's attention to his cousin, but there is more. Schumacher reports that James was the least known of any other man of comparable importance and wealth in the United States. He sought to avoid publicity, and in fact he had done nothing "dramatic" to deserve it. That James apparently sought to avoid the dramatic makes him something of a kindred spirit for Harry Anderson, if not a paradigm. Behind the scenes, James was a vehement agitator against Prohibition. His enormous charitable gifts were unpublicized, and it was said he never "abused" his wealth or power. Those times James did appear in print, what he said was both pithy and worthy of note—another Anderson trait. In 1931, the *Sacramento Bee* quoted him as follows on the subject of the Great Depression: "We should not allow drunken speculation to prevail again as we did in 1928." If James' humor had had a dark side, he would have chuckled at the financial manipulations and subsequent recession of 2010: more hangovers from "drunken speculation."

Anderson's 50-page working paper on James includes a map he has drawn showing the railroad routes west from the Mississippi River that James controlled with the Chicago, Burlington & Quincy; the Northern Pacific; the Spokane, Portland & Seattle; the Denver & Rio Grande Western; and the Western Pacific lines, all of which he owned.

Anderson recalls meeting James a few times when he was a youngster. "He owned a house in Coconut Grove, Florida, quite near the Adirondacks-Florida School (now Ransom Everglades) where I studied," Anderson says. "He sometimes included me for Sunday lunches on his power yacht. He was so much older that I didn't get to know him well. But I remember he always brought his big yacht, *Aloha,* to Seawanhaka each spring for the opening of the club. *Aloha* was built in 1910, painted black. He went to cruise the Mediterranean one summer and had it hauled and painted white so it wouldn't be so hot. At the end of the summer, he had it painted black again. He was Commodore of Seawanhaka, and very popular. They wanted him to run again but he had other plans."

James died in 1941, when Anderson was 21.

Annie Burr Jennings (1855-1939) is another favorite relative Anderson has researched over the years. She was Anderson's great aunt, the daughter of Oliver Burr Jennings, Anderson's great grandfather, the forty-niner who became one of the initial investors in Standard Oil. Ms. Jennings was a powerful and formidable matriarch, an outspoken and influential spinster. Her 75-acre property in Fairfield, Connecticut, was known for the county's showpiece, Sunni-Holme, its sumptuous dwelling of 19 bedrooms and 14 bathrooms, and nationally acclaimed for its acres of formal gardens that required a full-time staff of 30 gardeners.

Known equally for her philanthropy and her liberal-mindedness, Ms. Jennings was the town's and the county's First Lady. Few decisions of any magnitude were made around Fairfield without first consulting Annie Burr Jennings. On her death bed she told friends she knew her large property would be broken up. "Just don't let them make it into an airport," she cautioned. It wasn't.

Annie Burr Jennings was another Anderson relative who shunned both display and publicity, although the aggressive stands she took on public welfare issues kept her name in the newspapers. "Causes that appealed to her intelligence," *The Hartford Courant*'s obituary read in part, "seldom failed to enlist her generous support." At the Parks Commission, she cast the deciding vote against requiring men to wear bathing tops at the local beach. She was against women's suffrage initially. Many women of her stature were, fearing it would dilute the unique influence they enjoyed. But Annie B. quickly embraced the crusade when it gathered momentum during World War I. She campaigned actively for the repeal of Prohibition, saying that liquor should be available to all, not just to those (like her) who could afford Prohibition prices. When debt-plagued Fairfield was about to combine high school and grammar school students under one roof, Annie B. Jennings bought a house and gave it to the town for use as a high school. She disliked Franklin Delano Roosevelt so intensely she became a Republican, saying she would rather go without sewers than encourage New Deal involvement in the town. When the front door was stolen off a house in Fairfield she was restoring, Annie B. wrote the following letter to her contractor: "I am so disgusted and disappointed over the fact of the stolen door that I have lost all interest in the house and will do nothing more at present. . . . dismiss everybody connected with it and I will pay the bills for what has been done up to date." Her monogram bore this Latin inscription: "Otium sine literis mors est." Translation: "Leisure without literature is death."

Anderson attended several of the legendary, annual Christmas parties Annie Burr Jennings hosted at her town house at 9 East Seventieth Street in Manhattan. They were masquerades, with stated themes such as "wild west," or "Spanish," and substantial effort was expected of her guests by Annie B. in that department. The guest list numbered in the fifties and was limited to relatives. Younger children were excluded.

"The parties were on Christmas night," Anderson recalls.

> The men were down on them. Everyone had eaten Christmas lunch in their homes on Long Island, then they had to get dressed in costumes and drive into the city. But Annie B. was a strong-willed woman so everyone showed up. No one dared cross her. The servants wore red jackets and wigs. Two of them would carry in the boar's head, and two others would carry in the wassail bowl while singing God Rest Ye Merry Gentlemen. The wassail bowl was passed from person to person for a sip much like the Green Cup at Mory's Temple Bar in New Haven. Aunt Annie would remark that this was a form of passing on the family germs.
>
> There was always an entertainment. One year she had Edgar Bergen and Charlie McCarthy before that puppet act had gotten famous in Hollywood. And there were always presents.

A rare photograph of one of Anderson's Great-Aunt Annie Burr Jennings' costume parties that were held annually on Christmas night during the 1940s at her Manhattan town house. Miss Jennings is seated in the middle row, center, to the left of the gentleman in white tie.

She liked Fleur-de-Lis perfume, so one year everyone got a bottle. She was high on William Lyon Phelps, an English professor at Yale who wrote What I Like in Poetry, *so we all got autographed copies. But people were used to that kind of party in those days. In the '20s and '30s New York people went out to a fancy dress party a couple times a week. With no television or movies to speak of, people entertained themselves.*

Annie B. was crazy about Yale. Two of her brothers had gone to Yale, which may have accounted for her strong support of the university. When he was an undergraduate there, Anderson attended lunches at Sunni-Holme before Yale/Harvard crew races, beginning with an overnight at the mansion. "I recall one moonlight night," Anderson says, "walking with Mother through Aunt Annie's gardens. I was especially struck by the pool surrounded with white roses on the wall that enclosed the garden. A pair of swans floated majestically on the pool.

"There was always a huge Yale banner hanging in the port cochere, the bulbs in the lights along the drive were switched to blue, pieces of Yale goalposts [it was the practice pre-World War II to tear down the goalposts after major games] adorned the left-hand wall of the loggia, blueberry ice cream was served that had been molded in the shape of the

university's bull dog mascot, and Annie's pet parakeet would shrill `Boola Boola!' when the cover was removed from its cage."

After lunch, guests were transported from Fairfield aboard Annie B.'s hired railroad car coupled to the train to New London. "Great Aunt Bell James," Anderson says, "who had been secretary to the wives of two presidents—Republicans for whom Aunt Annie became an elector for the State of Connecticut toward the end of her life— was so obese that she could not enter the railway car, so she sat on a wicker chair on the back platform."

Bleachers had been erected on flat cars on either side of the crew course on Connecticut's Thames River. The cars would keep pace with the shells for optimum viewing. Anderson says a casual sailboat race between the two schools prior to the crew races one year marked the beginning of intercollegiate sailing, the second oldest college sport—crew being the oldest.

"Annie B. had bad eyes and couldn't keep track of what was going on," Anderson says, "but a relative using field glasses would report to her how the race was going. She was quite blind toward the end. When she held her tea cup to be filled, she would move it around causing the butler to follow it with the pot." She had seats for Yale's home football games just one row behind the president's seats. When Annie B. died, Yale President Charles Seymour remarked that she was "The best Yale man of the last 60 years."

Anderson remembers when Annie B. acquired a pistol. The Lindbergh kidnapping in 1932 had engendered a wave of paranoia. People began erecting cyclone fences around their property. Friends had urged Annie B. to arm her chauffeur. When the man expressed his distaste for guns and refused to take firearm training, let alone carry a weapon, Annie B. bought a pistol herself and kept it beside her in the back seat. "People were horrified," Anderson says, "wondering what Annie B. might do if someone wanted to get in the car, who she might shoot who wasn't deserving of getting shot."

Anderson says he heard from his mother that Annie B. had once proposed to an Irishman who was running for mayor of New York, saying if he won the election she would marry him. "I never heard any more about that until I was in Louisiana in 1943 on maneuvers with the US Army," Anderson says. "We were at Camp Polk, outside Leesville that was once featured on the cover of *LIFE* magazine as the town with the highest VD rating in the country. A bunch of us went to a nightclub there. There was a small band playing, led by a black chap. I got into conversation with him and it turned

out he was not only from back east, he knew Annie B. She had apparently spoken to him about playing at her wedding. The wedding never occurred, but that verified the story."

Annie B. Jennings' estate was valued at $10 million ($157 million in 2010 dollars). Among the long list of her charitable bequests was half a million to her long-time maid and traveling companion, and a tidy sum to the gun-shy chauffeur. The treasure for Harry Anderson was her accumulation of original family documentation. "I've spent years tracing Aaron Burr's life and death," Anderson says. "Annie B. gave me so much work to do posthumously that I named my lobster boat after her."

Both Annie B. and Harry Anderson are collateral descendants of Aaron Burr, who is certainly the most controversial of the founding fathers, and one of the most controversial figures in all of American political history. He was an attorney, an enthusiastic military man who actively sought out field commands. As such, he was known as a stickler for honesty and protocol. He is called the father of modern political campaigning. His innovative enabling of suffrage for male citizens without property is what obtained the working class vote for Thomas Jefferson in 1801. He was an abolitionist, and pro women's suffrage. He believed in the equality of the sexes, prescribing education and training in the classics, language, horsemanship, and music for his daughter at a time when that sort of program for a woman was against the norm. Despite his successes in battle during the Revolutionary War, Burr was not a favorite of General George Washington. President Thomas Jefferson never trusted Burr, using the bully pulpit to label him a traitor (he was acquitted). Literally hundreds of books (fiction and nonfiction) and plays have been written about Aaron Burr's long and complex life.

Anderson has been in the thick of the Burr controversy for years. He is an active member of the Aaron Burr Association, founded in 1946 "To keep alive the memory of Colonel Aaron Burr as a student, a soldier, a lawyer, a politician, a patron of the arts, an educator, a banker, and as a husband and father, and to secure for him the honor and respect which are due him as one of the leading figures of his age." Anderson never fails to release a broadside review of the latest books on Burr. Of Gore Vidal's novel, *Burr* (1973), Anderson wrote: "Don't bother. It's populist fiction." Of David Stewart's *American Emperor: Aaron Burr's Challenge to Jefferson's America*: "Don't read it. It's opinionated. While . . . bringing very little novel to the table, (the author) has an almost insidious way of arriving at conclusions that are skewed against Burr." He says the best and most well researched book on Burr is *Fallen*

Founder, by Nancy Isenberg. He should know. Anderson's Burr Collection, consisting of more than 100 items—books, newspaper clippings, original letters (one from Dolly Madison), manuscripts, paintings and plates, and memoirs—was given to Rutgers University in 2000.

Anderson's extensive research has surfaced in several books and articles on Burr, including two endpapers in Oliver Perry Sturm's *The Conspiracy Against Aaron Burr* (revised edition 2005) having to do with the verification of Burr's second family in Philadelphia. And he has written exhaustively about the authenticity of the Aaron Burr desk, a clever piece of furniture that converts from an elegant elliptical table to a utilitarian writing desk with a built-in seat. Anderson inherited the desk from Annie B. Jennings, an avid collector of "Burrabilia." Here is an excerpt of his article on the desk: "The nails holding the bottom of the drawer to the side pieces are flat-sided and tapered with the head formed by bending the end at 90 degrees, i.e., machine-cut sprigs perfected after 1810. . . . Likewise the machine-milled ripple three-tiered decorative trim outlining the side panels mitigate against the desk having been made before 1840."

William Rockefeller has been another subject of sustained interest for Anderson. While William was not a blood relative, the marriage of Anderson's great-grandfather, Oliver B. Jennings (the forty-niner), to the sister of William Rockefeller's wife was the fortuitous event that (in perpetuity) connected the Anderson family to the Standard Oil fortune. And while the name "John D." Rockefeller has sustained to this day as a signifier of wealth and power, the younger brother William Rockefeller is, by comparison, relatively unknown.

Anderson's interest in William Rockefeller was furthered by Rockefeller's 50,000-acre estate on Lower St. Regis Lake, a half-day's paddle and portage from the Adirondack-Florida School where Anderson studied. The large estate was even closer to his grandfather's Adirondacks camp, where he spent many summers as a boy. "The St. Regis River flows through the Rockefeller estate to the St. Lawrence," Anderson says. "There was terrific trout fishing on his property, and a couple of us from the school wanted to try our luck. Mother would tell us to call over there and ask if we could fish. So we did. We got William Rockefeller's son on the phone, and he gave us permission. We caught some sizable trout."

William Rockefeller started out in the grain business and was recruited into oil by his older brother. The two had different roles at Standard Oil. When the company began to expand from Cleveland and buy refineries in New Jersey, William was sent to New York where he opened Rockefeller & Co., a sub-corporation to develop foreign markets for Standard Oil. "He had a connection located in Amsterdam," Anderson says. "That fellow would cable the prices of oil daily so William knew when to buy and sell."

"The story is that John D. would tell William he was going to sell some of his Standard Oil stock and William would tell him he was crazy, and he'd buy it. He had a huge mansion up the Hudson River [in Tarrytown]. Every day he'd walk a mile to the New York Central station on the river, then walk from Grand Central Station in Manhattan to Wall Street, quite a distance."

There has never been a biography of William Rockefeller published, but Anderson does have a manuscript by George Levy, complete with footnotes and photographs. Working with Levy to get it published, finding a home for it on the shelf of posterity, is one of Harry Anderson's ongoing projects.

Then there is missionary Rufus Anderson Jr., Harry's great-great-great grandfather. Rufus Anderson Senior was born in Londonderry, New Hampshire, in 1765. At the age of two, his mother elicited a promise from her husband on her deathbed that her son be educated in the ministry. It was a promise he kept.

Rufus entered Dr. Wheelock's Dartmouth College in 1787, driving two cows from Londonderry to Hanover to pay the tuition. After graduation, he joined the Presbyterian Church and became a lifelong preacher. Among the papers he published was *Fast sermons designed to resist the ingress of French infidelity and licentiousness.*

Rufus Jr. continued in his father's footsteps, finishing a work his father had begun called *Modern Missions to the Heathen*. In the 1820s he set off to Hawaii to put theory into practice. He would become secretary of the Foreign Commission of the American Board of Commissions of the American Missionary Society during a period when the United States and Great Britain were vying for control of the Islands. Harry Anderson has accumulated 64 of the sermons that he gave during that time. Anderson says Rufus Jr. so angered the Right Reverend Bishop of Hawaii with alleged misstatements, that the ranking cleric devoted an entire sermon to lambasting him and his work. Rufus Jr. subsequently went to missionary outposts in Turkey and Greece. "The only difference today," Anderson says, "is we are trying to turn societies into democracies instead of converting them into Christians."

A large portrait of the Reverend Rufus Anderson Jr. hangs over the worktable in the

living room of Harry Anderson's Mystic apartment. Despite the lifelong evangelistic work of the four- and five-times great-grandfathers, Harry Anderson says his father did not inherit their religious passion. "Father said he was a Christian, but that he didn't need to go to church. Mother took us to services." Once beyond prep school, Harry Anderson gave up church-going as well. Anderson says he has the portrait by default. But it is hung, dutifully, in its proper place. For Harry Anderson, an ancestor is an ancestor. But he has made an effort to move Rufus to a less immediate, while no less respectful, location. "Each generation," he says, "these family portraits get divided and subdivided, so I wound up with Rufus. I've been trying to give the portrait to Bowdoin College, where Rufus was on the board, but they don't seem to respond on the subject."

The Reverend Rufus Anderson Jr. (1796-1880).

———————— ⚓ ————————

THE SECOND BEDROOM in Anderson's Mystic apartment has been turned into an office, with wall-to-wall shelves and many rolling files. Behind the sizable desk are Anderson's computer, printer, and his most-prized and most-essential piece of equipment, a copy machine. It is a copy machine of good quality, late-model, four-color, fast, capable of servicing a workforce of a dozen people. The copy machine has been indispensable to Harry Anderson for the constant barrage of mailings (broadsides, memos, letters) to various groups he has arranged by commonality of interest. Extra cartridges, reams of paper, sticky notes, and other office supplies are plentiful, and arranged on the counter of the adjoining bathroom.

Behind the large, utilitarian desk, his computer screen and keyboard are on a table, having been raised by a construction of cardboard boxes and books to a height enabling him to work standing up. He believes sitting at a computer is not good for you—recent research confirms this. Anderson got his first computer in 1980, when he was 60 years old. Trish McKenna, then-girlfriend (now wife) of Jamie Hilton, then captain aboard Anderson's sloop, the New York 40 *Taniwha*, was working for a software company at the time. Anderson asked her to help him get set up with a PC.

"Back then, large corporations were just beginning to adopt PCs in large numbers," Trish says, "but they were still exotic items for home users. Harry and I had lots of discussions about what brand to buy, what software to get. He dove in a lot faster than many people who were much younger."

That makes Anderson a computer veteran, an enthusiastic e-mailer who has great fun with online fusillades, usually signing off with the amusing Franglais word of his own invention, "Cordialement," followed by one of several, ever-changing, always arresting quotes:

> ——"*Fatal handicaps are few, but the most fatal of all is the faculty of seeing the other person's point of view.*"

> ——"*A leader is someone who can adapt his principles to circumstances.*"

> ——"*Never tell people how to do things. Tell them what to do and they will surprise you with their ingenuity.*" Gen. George Patton

> ——*May our mission be to* "*Free fact from fiction,*" *and our credo:* "*A young man who is not a liberal has no heart; an old man who is not a conservative has no head.*" HHA Jr. and Samuel Johnson

—*"I shall not waste my days in trying to prolong them."* Jack London

—*"The art of celestial navigation is finding out where you are by looking at where you aren't."*—*cf: "A penguin walks backwards because he would rather see where he's been than where he is going."*

—*"Modesty is a virtue that can never thrive in public."*

—*"Don't be fixed like a plant in a particular spot to draw nutrition, propagate, and rot."* Cdr. David Porter, USN

—*"How well the politicians of today have heeded John Adams! A measure of drop in standard of living: no longer antimacassars on AMTRAK seats."*

Those on his lists can still expect packets delivered by USPS because old habits die hard, and perhaps because Anderson takes fiendish pleasure in his ability to stuff record numbers of sheets into a letter-sized envelope. For recipients, the bulging packets are a treat to open, and they don't often disappoint.

When the spotlight does swing his way, it doesn't faze him. At his ninetieth birthday, after all the toasts and kudos; the ten minute highlights video of Anderson's life (compiled by master of ceremonies for the event, and head of US Sailing, Gary Jobson); and the presentation of the enormous, half-faux theme cake assembled and decorated by Tall Ships staff; after all of this, when it was Anderson's turn to say his piece, he did so with eloquence, displaying another of his talents.

After a deafening round of applause for Anderson subsided, the honored guest said, "I guess I should run for office." More applause. As he had used his ninetieth birthday as the trigger for a fund-raiser, he used his time on the podium to promote the various organizations he supports. He thanked those who had traveled long distances to be there. He recognized his old friend Bill Maclay, longtime Naval Academy coach, saying the two of them were anachronisms since they were the only two people left who had competed in Bermuda Races in schooners. And he thanked the young sailors from the University of Rhode Island who had raced with him in the 1980s: "They kept my perspective on life from prematurely maturing."

THREE | Man's World

Roslyn, New York, where Harry Anderson grew up, is a small village on Long Island's north shore, east of Port Washington and Manhasset. It's located at the foot of Hempstead Harbor, a finger of water extending to the south off Long Island Sound. Northern Boulevard (Route 25A), one of the first roads to run the length of Long Island, runs right through Roslyn. The Anderson family home (actually in Roslyn Heights), was a three-story wood frame structure with wings on either side and third-floor dormer windows in the central roof. Built in 1920, the house was the center of a 40-acre complex that included a garage over which there were living quarters for Burberry, the family chauffeur, and his wife and three children; a horse barn with four stalls and living quarters above for the groom; and a tennis court and swimming pool. One wing of the house included accommodations for a cook and three maids. It was, as Harry's youngest brother David recalls, a big operation.

"We were all fortunate," says David, who is five years his brother's junior.

> Our great grandfather Oliver Burr Jennings married the daughter of a cabinet maker from Fairfield, Connecticut. His son, Oliver, first worked in a shirt company, then as a clerk in a New York department store. He took off for San Francisco in 1849 with his friend Brewster, and the rest is history. The moment that changed the trajectory of Harry's life and mine was in Cleveland in 1872 when John D. Rockefeller came up short of the million dollars he needed to create Standard Oil, and his brother William suggested our great-grandfather as an investor. And so Harry and I have enjoyed a very privileged life. The Standard Oil money is still there. When Teddy Roosevelt broke up the company, it made everyone richer because there were seven companies instead of one. Harry has put his fortune to good use in yachting and education.

33

Anderson family portrait, ca. 1924. From left, Harry, Henry Hill, Helen with son David, and son Walter (Jim) seated. The dog, Monte, was one of two Pyrenean Shepherds in the family. The other, Carlo, was absent for the photograph.

When we were young boys, Harry and my middle brother Jim, who died in his sixties of a heart condition, had a governess. I had my own governess. Theirs was French. Mine was Scottish. It was a very Victorian upbringing. Emotions were a sign of weakness. There was lots of discipline, the playing fields of Eton, that sort of thing. Children were to be seen and not heard. After supper it was goodnight, goodbye.

Father never dandled me on his knee. He was afraid of emotions because he basically had no mother. She died when he was four, giving birth to his brother. So he was brought up by a man, my grandfather. I often think the fact there was no woman in his life had a lot to do with how my father behaved. The man who really brought him up was Carl Cutler, who co-founded Mystic Seaport. He was hired as a tutor to teach my father Latin and Greek. In 1904, my grandfather sent father and his brother Larocque, my uncle, off to the Adirondack-Florida School, an all-boys private school that had been started on a boat in Florida in 1893. The fall and spring semesters were in the Adirondacks. The winter semester was in Florida. It cost a bundle.

Father was not warm and fuzzy. He was very accomplished, highly disciplined, a very bright guy, a great horseback rider. And he took up skating and was good at it. But he was stern. He would take out the razor strop and order us to drop our trousers and kneel if there was a problem. It was hard on Mother.

Henry Hill Anderson, the father, was the third generation of his family to practice law. The boys' great-grandfather, also Henry Hill Anderson, founded the first Anderson law firm. It was dissolved after his death in 1896. Harry's grandfather, Henry Burrell Anderson, and his great-uncle Chandler Parsons Anderson formed Anderson & Anderson in 1898.

A Yale graduate (1916), Henry Hill Anderson was active in the Yale Battery of the Student Army Training Corps until 1917, when he enlisted in the US Cavalry and went to Ft. Leavenworth for training. He was on several expeditions into Mexico's "Rim Rock Country," pursuing marauding bands of Mexicans who were crossing into the United States and murdering civilians. Anderson was honorably discharged in the fall of 1919 with the rank of major.

Henry Hill Anderson graduated from Columbia Law School in 1922 and was admitted to the bar in the same year. After a few years at Carter, Ledyard & Milburn, in 1925 he became a partner in the family law firm that was then known as Anderson, Gasser, Ferris & Anderson (that being Henry Hill). He had married Helen James in 1920, while still at Columbia. The couple moved to the Roslyn house, built for them by Harry's grandfather, in 1925, with their three young boys.

Harry Anderson says his upbringing was both rigorous and strict.

My mother's side, the Jennings family, was close knit, definitely not spendthrifts. And Father, a World War I Cavalry officer, had us riding Cavalry style. We learned how to jump without a saddle by using our knees to hold on. When we were 10 or 11 we were shooting rifles on the small range we had on the place. A target area was built from timbers and filled with sand twelve inches deep. Our chauffeur, Burberry, belonged to the American Legion in the village. He said they had a great shooting system there, and offered to take me and my brothers to shoot. But my family was elitist. The upper crust didn't want their children mixing with average people. They were afraid we might pick up some bad language or associate with ruffians. It was snobbish. It wasn't until we got to the Adirondack-Florida school and met black workers and guides that we got to deal with the non-elite.

It would have been a good idea if we had gone shooting in the village with Burberry.

If we chose to rebel we'd get a licking. The usual instrument Father used was a stropping leather for his straight razor to administer

whacks on the rear end. As the oldest child, I was always under control. The oldest is always under more family restraint. He's the parents' first experience so they keep tight control. David, being the youngest, could get away with all kinds of things. He was the most rebellious. He knew how to dodge the discipline, and could get away with murder.

From David Anderson's perspective, the Roslyn scene had an isolating effect on him and his brothers. "We had the horses and grooms and plenty to do, but we didn't have much of a social life," he says. "Burberry had a boy my age, and we became really good friends. My parents didn't appreciate that, and gave me a hard time about it. But how could they forbid me hanging out with him when we

Harry Anderson on *Tommy*, his Arabian polo pony, at Roslyn, New York, in the 1930s.

lived right next to one another on the same property? That friendship gave me a different perspective because we went to Greenvale, a highfalutin private school run by the same people who started Buckley. One of my classmates was Gloria Vanderbilt."

What further exacerbated the boys' isolation was the Lindbergh kidnapping in the spring of 1932. That event had an impact on society equivalent to a terrorist attack in the twenty-first century. "One of our sports at Greenvale," Harry Anderson says, "was to cross Route 25 and play cops and robbers in the woods. After the Lindbergh kidnapping that came to an end. A cyclone fence was erected around the school. Children of the very wealthy families such as Deenie Hutton (daughter of Marjorie Merriweather Post and E. F. Hutton) and Gloria Vanderbilt came to school driven or accompanied by a detective."

Harry's and his middle brother Jim's perspective went global in 1928, when they sailed with their family aboard the Cunard liner *Mauritania* to spend three months skiing in Switzerland (David, only two years old at the time, remained at home). The Andersons were close friends of Paul and Frances Pennoyer. Frances was a daughter of J. P. Morgan, America's leading financier in the early 1900s. Paul Pennoyer was a young American attorney who had worked in his firm's London office. On weekends he joined co-workers there who went skiing in Switzerland and Germany, thus becoming one of America's skiing pioneers who helped acquaint his countrymen with the joy of the sport.

"Winter weekends," Harry Anderson says, "my family would meet the Pennoyers on the New York Central sleeper to Tupper Lake, then drive to Uncasa, J. P. Morgan's 1,100-acre summer camp in the Adirondacks, on Raquette Lake. Walking through Grand Central Station with pairs of skis on their shoulders caused a sensation, inasmuch as most of the other travelers had no idea what they were."

In November of 1928, the Anderson family, along with the Pennoyers and a few other friends, boarded the *Mauritania* bound for Cherbourg, France. Harry Anderson was only seven years old at the time. He recorded his recollections of the trip some years later.

Because of pea soup fog, Mauritania *couldn't depart until the next day. At breakfast in the sparsely filled dining room, Father asked the waiter why there were so few passengers. The reply was that many passengers, hearing the foghorns in New York Harbor during the night, had become seasick. The ship had hardly passed Sandy Hook when my brother and I got into a pillow fight resulting in goose feathers* festooning the stateroom and Father having to pay the purser to replace them. It was "on your knees and lower your trousers" for a half dozen lashes with a razor strop.

After debarking at Cherbourg we took the train to Gstaad, Switzerland. Gstaad in those days was a small village. For tourists there was only the Grand Hotel above the village outskirts. Not far from the village is the winter campus of Le Rosey, an international boarding school that was a popular depository to which Americans and families from other nations committed their sons while they took the grand tour (today it is co-ed).

Absent the modern-day ski lifts, Gstaad was attractive for ready access to the Alpine rail system, which our parents and friends took to their highest elevation, then walked on skis to the top of a mountain. Seal skin covers over the ski enabled one to walk in herring bone fashion up the slopes; the hair follicles on seal skin run in one direction so that one could slide, or walk, one ski uphill while the skin on the other ski kept it from sliding back down. It was arduous work, and as late as college days in the early 1940s it was not unusual at resorts such as Stowe to get off the top of the lift and climb farther up the mountain in this manner up an abandoned logging road. As skiers swooped down a mountain through moderating temperatures, the dry fluffy snow became more

damp and sticky requiring changing the wax on the skis. This was done with a metal holder with perforations into which a stick of wax was placed and heated with a miniature blowtorch as it was dragged down the ski. There were no "huts at the top" serving food and wine, so luncheon was carried in rucksacks on one's back. Guides were essential since there were none of the packed trails found in our heavily traveled slopes of today.

For the youngsters, there were moderate slopes near the Grand Hotel where we took daily ski lessons. From time to time we would ride on a luge into the village, pack it with supplies and tow it back uphill to the Hotel. Unlike the flexible flyer sleds in the States, which are used mostly for fun, the luge for the Swiss was a work-horse, higher off the ground with metal runners the full length of the luge and steered by dragging the left or right foot. We brought a luge home with us. As for schooling, there was no let-up as our French governess was part of the expedition. Between her and Mother, classes were conducted daily. At age 7 I could ski and speak French better than at any other time in my life.

With the advent of spring, the trip came to a close, but an outbreak of typhoid fever made travel in a public conveyance too risky. Hence the return trip to Cherbourg was by hired limousines.

The Seawanhaka Corinthian Yacht Club
clubhouse at Oyster Bay, ca. 1896.

Harry Anderson doesn't remember family hardships caused by the Great Depression, other than failure to turn off a light when vacating a room resulted in further application of the razor strop. He recalls his father having to give IOUs to local merchants during those times when the banks had been closed by presidential edict. Some of the family's staff suffered when their savings accounts disappeared along with the banks that held them. "That atmosphere kept everyone on edge," Anderson says. "We could sense the tension." But he was too young to remember many details of those dark days. School and the routine of life went on without particular interruption. He does have in his files a pristine copy of a dinner dance invitation issued by his parents and four other couples calling themselves "The Long Island Committee for the Suppression of Depression." It is for Saturday evening, September 12, 1931, and states: "In order to definitely crack the present crisis we earnestly request that each guest bring one quart of non-inflammable champagne to be delivered at the door and drunk on the premises." The hand-printed invitation is decorated with drawings by a *New Yorker* magazine cartoonist of the day who drew high society characters. The invitation specifies fancy dress.

"People played hard and drank hard in those days," Anderson writes in a brief recollection titled *Life During Prohibition*, "with some going blind by reason of bootlegged liquor spiked with wood alcohol."

At the family home in Roslyn there was a walk-in vault located behind the coal-fired furnace which served to screen it from possible revenuers. Recall being woken by noise circa 2 AM which was the arrival of the bootlegger's truck, and Father in pajamas and wrapper going downstairs to let them in the cellar door. . . . At Cove Neck across from the Seawanhaka Corinthian Yacht Club on Centre Island, adjacent to T. R. Roosevelt's Sagamore Hill home was a water tower. When the bootleggers bringing booze from Connecticut approached Cold Spring Harbor and Oyster Bay, a red light was displayed on the tower to report "coast all clear." Kenney, a young employee of SCYC, once described how he was sent with a shotgun to close off the causeway while the bootleggers unloaded.

Dinner parties were the norm weekdays as well as weekends. Bill Willetts brought a spare tuxedo to dinner into which to change after he (regularly) rode his bike off the high diving board (to be au courant the upper crust installed new swimming pools with diving towers as well as the new, red brick dust composition en-tous-cas tennis courts which originated in France).

Life at Roslyn for the Anderson boys was focused on achieving responsibility. They walked the dogs before breakfast, and they often went riding as well before the morning meal. Each had a horse and was expected to take care of the animal. "You could ride almost anywhere on Long Island in those days," Anderson says. "There were horse gates everywhere you could open from the saddle with a pull string. It didn't matter who owned the property. Father taught us to ride, and we also went to a riding stable run by Cossacks for lessons. They were tough, those fellows, but good. They trained us to jump. I had an ex-polo pony. He was part Arab. He liked to prance when he heard a band."

David Anderson's memories of childhood riding with his father are not fond. "My father got a horse for my middle brother, Jim," David says. "It threw him. Father made him get back on. It threw him again and he broke his arm." David recalls that his father gave him a horse with a mean disposition. "If you went near his head he'd snarl," David says. "Our groom commented it wasn't a very good horse for a nine-year-old boy. The horse had a habit of suddenly whirling while cantering through the woods, and I would go off into the branches. I wasn't old enough to train it. I went to Mother and asked her to intercede with Father, tell him I wasn't riding anymore. And I didn't, not until my kids were grown."

David kept several of his nine children in horses during their teenage years, and unlike his older brother, he resumed riding for pleasure in his forties.

Life and the acquisition of Responsibility, wasn't all serious. As befitted young people of their social position, there were commensurate pleasures. Anderson recalls robust games of bicycle polo played on the bicycle-diving Willetts' wooden tennis court. Cut-down polo mallets were used, and tennis balls substituted for the willow polo balls. "Collisions were frequent," Anderson says, "and the mallets wreaked havoc on the spokes of the front wheels."

For sailing, the primary activity of the Anderson men, they traveled 10 miles northeast on Route 25A to Oyster Bay, home of the Seawanhaka Corinthian Yacht Club (SCYC). Of the boating clubs in the United States that have run continuously since being founded, only the New York Yacht Club (1844) and the Southern Yacht Club in New Orleans (1849) are older. The Seawanhaka was established in 1871, the same year as the Eastern Yacht Club in Marblehead, Massachusetts.

The formation of Seawanhaka was a logical development in the rapid growth of Long Island as a summer colony for notable New York families. The Island had been a seasonal retreat since the seventeenth century, but it was construction of the Long Island Railroad (begun in 1834) that made the Island readily accessible. By World War II, nearly 1,000 estates belonging to captains of finance and industry, with their mile-long driveways and immense acreage, would turn Long Island into one of the most socially desirable residential areas in the United States. The excellent harbor at Oyster Bay had made the surrounding area a most coveted—and disputed—ground since the 1650s, when the Dutch and English arm wrestled over how the land might be apportioned.

It was upon this harbor, in September 1871, aboard a 41-foot yacht named *Glance* owned by a gentleman named William L. Swan— said to be from one of the area's foremost families—that 12 men gathered to found the Seawanhaka Corinthian Yacht Club. Their stated purpose: to become proficient in navigation; to personally manage, control, and handle their yachts; and (to commit themselves to) all matters pertaining to seamanship. William Swan was elected the first commodore.

That pledge to "personally manage, control, and handle their yachts" was a departure from yachting's status quo at the time, a response by young amateur sailors to the professionally sailed big boats at the New York Yacht Club.

The Seawanhaka Yacht Club would migrate to New York Harbor—the center of yachting at the time—in 1875, leasing a basin on Staten Island (1881) and a clubhouse in Manhattan (1887) "Corinthian" was added to the name in 1881. But the SCYC would return to permanent headquarters in Oyster Bay in 1892. As Robert B. MacKay writes in his introduction to *Long Island Country Homes,* co-authored with Carol A. Traynor and Brendan Gill, "Estate development on Long Island was spurred on by 'Corinthian,' or amateur yachting, which was coming into vogue in England. . . . Ideal conditions were present [here] for the nurturing of the new sport, many of whose adherents were collegians and young men who considered it a matter of personal pride to scrape, paint, rig, and sail their own boats. This activity stood in marked contrast to the professional stakes races . . . of the time in which owners considered it below their dignity to assume command of their own vessels."

In "A Short History" of Seawanhaka (1994), past-Commodore P. James Roosevelt writes:

> *Yachting depends upon discretionary income. Few Americans enjoyed such a luxury until post Civil War prosperity. . . . [Even then] the sport was unrecognizable by today's gauge. It was more like horse racing with gentlemen hiring professional skippers and crew to man their*

vessels which raced each other as a betting proposition.

The tactics of the game had their births among the "sandbaggers." These were 15 to 30 feet, shoal draft, wide beam, planing, over-canvassed vessels with enormous bow-and stern-sprits. Their nickname derives from the dozen or so 50-pound bags filled with sand that the crew moved across the wide, open cockpit with every tack. . . .Various taverns, teams, and villages backed 'their own.' With the prizewinner often determined by a post race barroom brawl.

The concept of Corinthian sailing caught on, and the Club grew like a fire. In his final speech as Commodore, Swan charged:"Prosecute vigorously the popularization of Corinthian races with which Seawanhaka is so closely identified, as I feel assured it will not only be to it a tower of strength, but also that it is the only true and enjoyable kind of yachting."

Among the first yacht racing rules passed by Seawanhaka was one outlawing movable ballast, a direct swipe at sandbagger racing.

"Seawanhaka's approach to the sport marked the death knell for sandbagger racing," Roosevelt concluded. "Seawanhaka members, with their emphasis on Corinthianism, had transformed the entire motivation, methods, and objectives of the sport."

In an article titled "Blue-Collar Boating," written for *The Log of Mystic Seaport* in 1996 when he was curator, Benjamin A. G. Fuller blames the industrialization of municipal waterfronts coupled with the rise of "Corinthianism" for the gentrification of sailboat racing. Industrialization cut off access to the water that hundreds of little boat clubs had enjoyed. Fuller says in their pursuit of the Corinthian ideal, the members of the Seawanhaka club were in the forefront of shifting sailing from "wide-open, developmental participation to an elite, regulated sport." The rules Seawanhaka imposed on its first fleet, which happened to be Sandbaggers, not only prohibited movable ballast, but they required the boats had to be exclusively crewed by amateurs. Entrants had to supply crew lists complete with occupations and addresses. "This hit Sandbagger racing hard," Fuller writes, "because Corinthian (amateur) yachtsmen, professional watermen, and hired captains and crews had [heretofore] always mixed it up merrily on the race course."

If all that sounds hauntingly familiar, 125 years later the debate over amateurs and professionals would still be going on. Sailboat racing's administrators would be bent over their computers in an effort to define "professional," putting sailors in a variety of categories based on their chosen careers, experience, the brand of beer they preferred, the color of their foul weather gear, and establishing conditions under which they could or could not crew on various boats (or take the helms of those boats) in various races, to the extent that one had to carry a copy of the resulting guidelines in one's seabag for reference. It is also significant that Harry Anderson, having been raised within the privileged, gentrification of the sport and steeped in the Corinthian spirit of the Seawanhaka Corinthian Yacht Club, worked to popularize sailing when he had a chance to help direct the sport's future. Harry Anderson did not want sailing to be associated with what Robert MacKay has called "the American experiment in aristocracy."

The SCYC's decision to build a clubhouse on Centre Island in Oyster Bay in 1892 had induced nine of its members to build mansions there by 1912. MacKay writes that in the general vicinity of Oyster Bay, over 30 members had built houses by 1932, following their election to the club.

One of those elected to the club was Henry Hill Anderson. The Corinthian concept was tailor-made for his outlook and merged perfectly with the way he was raising his boys. And he was a lifelong sailor. He had grown up on his father's yachts, using Long Island Sound as his childhood playground. His father lived at Sands Point, Port Washington. When they

wanted to visit friends 10 miles away in Oyster Bay, Henry Anderson and his pals would row a dinghy into the Sound and hook a ride on the undertow of a barge. He had polished his sailing skills at the Biscayne Bay campus of the Adirondack-Florida School, sailing in small boats, skippering a Malay proa, and cruising on the tops'l schooner *Hickory* that had been given to the school by his father.

In 1912, the year before he entered Yale, he had sailed from New York to Honolulu around Cape Horn as an unpaid crewman on board the three-masted, 203-foot steel bark *Foohng Suey*. His father had provided a drawing account of $1,000 for him with the ship's owners. Anderson kept a log of the voyage that indicates it was not what one would call champagne sailing. Ten days out he writes: "There is a heavy cross sea on, and the old bark rolls first one rail under and then the other, pouring water all over the main deck. Snow, sleet, and rain all day. I lost my breakfast but managed to keep down the rest of my meals by staying on deck as long as possible and turning in as soon as I went below." Fifteen days out: "We were laid to in a southerly gale. A wave struck aft and came over the poop so hard it was all I could do to hang onto the belaying pin and keep from getting washed to leeward."

If Harry Anderson's grandfather had intended

this to be a coming-of-age trial-by-sea for his son, he wasn't disappointed. In a letter written to his father upon arriving in Honolulu five months after leaving New York, Harry Anderson's father writes: "We've had a rather exciting trip. Our Chinese cook shot one of the sailors, who died that night. . . . The mate is a bad egg . . . He can't handle his watch. . . . He can't see a squall coming ten feet off. . . He's got no use for me at all, and sends me up to overhaul buntlines every chance he gets. We had a fairly hard blow off the Horn, but not so bad. I saw her roll 40 degrees one way off

the Horn by the gage . . . I've been sewing on sails till I can handle a needle fairly well. . . . I've gotten so I can do pretty well on a yard handling sail. I've been up [aloft] in the heaviest weather we've had."

In 1926, Harry Hill Anderson had skippered his father's Alden schooner, *Trade Wind*, in the Bermuda Race. He joined the Seawanhaka club prior to 1930. His boat at the time was the S-Class sloop *Clotho*, named for one of the oldest and most powerful goddesses in Greek mythology. (Daughter of Zeus and Themis,

ABOVE: the crew of *Trade Wind* for the 1926 Bermuda Race. RIGHT: the Alden schooner *Trade Wind*, owned by Harry Anderson's grandfather, Henry B. Anderson, 1926.

Clotho spun the thread of human life.) Harry Anderson's first sail was on *Clotho*. He says it was his job to sit behind his father and light his cigarettes. He recalls one dramatic encounter on the S-boat during a race at Seawanhaka during a fresh sou'wester:

"On that occasion, Mother was on board, although she did not race regularly. Father and Philip J. Roosevelt, who also had an S-boat, had an ongoing difference of opinion over the interpretation of one of the racing rules. By happenstance, with one S-boat on port, the other on starboard, the disputed situation arose. Both skippers decided to assert their version of the rule. I well recall the bow of Roosevelt's S-boat coming aboard over the leeward coaming, which crumpled under the impact, and cracked the main boom. I don't recall the rule in question or which yacht the protest committee upheld—today both yachts would be disqualified for failing to avoid collision. I do recall that Mother was not the least bit amused at what she considered a sophomoric prank."

The Andersons would move from Roslyn to Oyster Bay around 1937 to be closer to the sailing. Harry Anderson says his father was frustrated by the weekend traffic on Route 25A that passed by the end of their driveway. It often required a wait of 15 to 20 minutes before he was able to pull out onto the road.

That had to have been exceedingly annoying to a man who used William K. Vanderbilt's privately built highway across Nassau County, the Long Island Motor Parkway. Vanderbilt lived in Northport, in Suffolk County, on a lavish estate complete with moat and drawbridge. An auto-racing enthusiast, in the early 1900s Vanderbilt offered a trophy for races on local roads. After two spectators were killed, Vanderbilt underwrote a company to build a graded, banked highway suitable for racing. A toll road, it was the first limited access roadway in the world.

Handy Hill, the house in Oyster Bay purchased by the Andersons, was on Cove Neck Road, across from Old Orchard, the property of President Theodore Roosevelt's son Ted. The president's home at Sagamore Hill was just up the road. The Andersons had intended to build, but the 1937 second dip in the Great Depression made it less expensive to buy an existing house and property. Handy Hill was on 18 acres and included a garage with a chauffeur's apartment above it, a horse barn, a tennis court, an icehouse, a boathouse, and a greenhouse with a small cottage for the groom and his family. "The ivy on the house had been smuggled from England in the overcoat pockets of family members," Anderson says. "When the head gardener appeared to meet Father in coat and tie, this was too elaborate for Father, so he was retired and the gardener's cottage was rented."

The property ran to the beach at the entrance to Oyster Bay Harbor, directly across from the SCYC on Centre Island. On the beach was a two-bedroom house with a dock and a float. Harry Anderson says that rowing across to SCYC was quicker, especially on weekends, and more fun than driving. A further excerpt from his *Life During Depression* depicts life among the privileged:

> *The dinghy I rowed to the Club was a heavy version of the International 14 dinghy. Our next-door neighbors, the Philip J. Roosevelts, and the Van Merle-Smiths had similar ones. The Van Merle-Smiths also had* NancyPat, *built as a rumrunner with three Liberty engines. It was never put into service because of the termination of Prohibition. At 55 knots, it was faster than taking the Oyster Bay branch of the Long Island Railroad to Lower Manhattan. Van Merle-Smith's cousin, Wilton Lloyd-Smith (their respective parents had decided that plain "Smith" lacked prestige, so added the prefixes) flew a seaplane to South Street. Childs Frick (son of the Pittsburgh coal and steel magnate Henry Clay Frick, creator of the home on Fifth Avenue that became the Frick Collection) in Roslyn went even further. He had one of the first snowmaking machines. He would ski to a footpath overpass to cross the Shore Road, board his commuting yacht, and*

en route to Manhattan would shower, shave, and have breakfast. After World War II families such as Baker and Gubelmann regularly flew to work in their seaplanes, landing near the Twenty-Third Street Marina on the East River.

One of the highlights of Harry Anderson's boyhood was the advent of the New York 32 [32 feet on the waterline, and 45 feet four inches overall], a legendary sloop designed in 1935 by Sparkman & Stephens as a club class for the New York Yacht Club. Twenty of them were ordered by members. Several were sailed by college kids whose fathers had bought the boats for them. Number 9, also named *Clotho*, went to Harry Anderson's father. Anderson remembers Saturday drives from Roslyn to City Island to watch the progress of the boats being built at the Henry Nevins Yard.

"It was a sight to see what was probably the first mass production line of a large boat," Anderson says, "with framing being laid up over an upside-down mold and the planking then attached. The hull was turned right-side up to install the interior and plank the deck. I remember the adze man hollowing out the mast sections. Two long planks were glued together in pairs, after which the adze man would straddle a pair and hollow out the insides. When the second pair was finished they were glued edge to edge with Resorcinol heated in a pot. Then the outsides were rounded with the adze."

In the spring Anderson's father took delivery of the boat and sailed it to Oyster Bay with his son Harry. With the bulk of the fleet situated at the Seawanhaka, Larchmont, American, and Cold Spring Harbor Yacht Clubs, there was lots of weekend racing in addition to Larchmont Race Week. Special trophies for the 32s were put up by various clubs. "Most of the 32s had crews made up largely of family," Anderson says.

> *During prep school and college years the boats constituted a sort of extracurricular education. For example, I would sometimes skipper at Larchmont Race Week if Father could not get time off.*

> *My sophomore year at Yale, my father and another 32 owner decided on the spur of the moment to keep going to Maine after the New York Yacht Club Cruise. When Father had to get back to New York City to work, he turned the boat over to me and we spent another couple weeks scouring the coast. I wasn't entirely without supervision, as Capt. Low, who had worked on my grandfather's schooner* Trade Wind, *was the pro on board.*

> Clotho *was also the platform for learning celestial navigation. In 1939 as war broke out,*

> *Commodore George Roosevelt ran an evening course in celestial navigation which Father took as a refresher when applying to become an officer in the navy. The Commodore assigned me the task of rounding up books, forms, and instruments for the course. I found plastic sextants for $45 each that were acceptably accurate, and were being produced in the inventor's home in an area zoned residential only. The other purchase was parallel rulers with three pairs of roller bearings along one edge that made them usable in the roughest weather without slipping. I still have one.*

BEFORE THE move to Oyster Bay, the Anderson boys' boating skills had been advanced in the Adirondacks, a sportsman's paradise in the northern section of New York State, located between Lake Erie (to the west) and the north-south mid-point of Vermont, an area dominated by the Adirondack Mountains.

This area began attracting wealthy families from Manhattan in the mid-1800s, when a man named Apollos (Paul) Smith started a primitive hotel at the north end of the St. Regis Lakes that he hoped would appeal to canoeists, campers, hunters, and fishermen. There was no running water in the hotel, and

Clotho, the Anderson family's Herreshoff S-Class sloop racing off Seawanhaka in the 1930s.

a trip to the spring under the bank of the
lake with a pail supplied drinking water.
"Roughing it" at Paul Smith's became a fad
among the wealthy that escalated into the
building of "camps," small villages of wood
frame buildings each with a separate function.
The buildings evolved from tents erected
on platforms. The camps are often called
"rustic," which is a bit of a stretch. While in
most cases the architecture and materials were
kept simple, aimed at blending the buildings
into their woodsy surroundings, they were
well built and most accommodating. The
camps were considered "old-shoe" retreats for
families with nationally recognizable names
that spent summers sharing the beautiful,
isolated Adirondacks boondocks with
Bichnell's thrush, black-backed woodpeckers,
the spruce grouse, land-locked salmon,
northern pike and muskies, brook trout, deer,

beavers, and other indigenous residents. Most
of the camps were only accessible by water.

Under the headline, "Pleasures At Paul Smith's,"
the *New York Times* reported in the spring of
1903: "Of camp life in the Adirondacks this
season it may be said that it is the most
fashionable of years, for the Vanderbilts, the
Rockefellers, the Reids, the Morgans, the
Blaines, the McCormicks, the Stokeses, the
Mortons, and many others are in their camps,
some of which were enlarged in anticipation
of entertaining many friends. . . . the St. Regis
Chain of Lakes will be the rendezvous of many
persons distinguished in the financial and
business worlds as well as the social world."

Some of the camps were downright elegant,
showcasing wealth and displaying whim. The
Vanderbilt camp's two-story main house was
redesigned to look like a pagoda after the family
had visited Mt. Fuji. Their boathouse took on
the traditional Irimoya roof form of Japanese
temples. The Rockefeller camp consisted of
50,000 acres. One of the more elaborate
camps included 68 different buildings.

In her book about the region, *Camp Chronicles*
(1952), Mildred Phelps Stokes Hooker wrote,
"I tell you if there is a spot on the face of the
earth where millionaires go to play at
housekeeping in log cabins and tents as they
do here I have yet to hear about it." Mrs.

One of the individual sleeping cabins at
Camp Junco in the Adirondacks.

Hooker was the second-youngest child of the New York banker Anson Phelps Stokes, She was two years old when she first went to her father's camp in the Adirondacks in 1883.

Playing at housekeeping involved a wholesale move of servants and supplies from Manhattan to the north woods. Mrs. Hooker quotes her mother's description of packing for the trip in 1883: "Patrick left in the afternoon with horses, Muggins and Sport (the dogs), and a truck load of freight. Papa chartered what they call a special parlor horse car direct from 42nd Street to Ausable [across from Burlington, Vermont, on Lake Champlain] for $100, and we take in it our horses, carriage, all camping outfits, extra trunks, stores, etc. They go to Plattsburg and arrive tomorrow evening. Then to Ausable where the freight will be taken off by wagons to Paul Smiths."

She then reviews the master list of people, pets, and supplies: "Anson Phelps Stokes, wife, seven children, one niece, about ten servants, Miss Rondell [a tutor for the children, one supposes], one coachman, three horses, two dogs, one carriage, five large boxes of tents, three cases of wine, two packages of stovepipe, two stoves, one bale china, one iron pot, four wash stands, one barrel of hardware, four bundles of poles, seventeen cots and seventeen mattresses, four canvas packages, one buckboard, five barrels, one-half barrel, two tubs of butter, one bag coffee, one chest tea, one crate china, twelve rugs, four milk cans, two drawing boards, twenty-five trunks, thirteen small boxes, one boat, one hamper."

Henry Hill Anderson Sr. had become familiar with the St. Regis Lakes area by virtue of his attending the Adirondack-Florida School from 1906 to 1911. The Adirondack campus was near the small village of Onchiota on Rainbow Lake, a brisk, three-hour paddle and portage by canoe northeast of Paul Smith's Hotel. When Anderson began dating New York debutante Helen James, the couple spent time at Camp Junco (named after the bird), the Adirondack camp that her father—Dr. Walter Belknap James—had built on Upper St. Regis Lake (southwest of Paul Smith's) around 1900.

Dr. James built Camp Junco because of his close personal and professional association with Dr. Edward Livingston Trudeau, the first person to promote isolation, rest, and moderate exercise in cool mountain air to combat tuberculosis. During the nineteenth and twentieth centuries, TB was the leading cause of death in the United States, and greatly feared throughout the world. Dr. Trudeau (great-grandfather of cartoonist Gary Trudeau) had contracted the disease from his older brother, whom he had cared for until his death. Once diagnosed, Trudeau left his

Adirondacks woodsmen. The Anderson boys, from left, Jim, David, and Harry, with Henry Kingman, guide in charge at Camp Junco.

practice in New York and moved to his favorite resort in the Adirondacks—Paul Smith's—presumably to die in pleasant surroundings. Instead, he recovered. Convinced that healthy diet, rest, and outdoor exercise had restored him, in 1885 he opened a clinic in the woods near Saranac, New York, to make available the curative process he had discovered. Part of the cure was sitting on an open porch in winter weather. Novelist and poet Robert Louis Stevenson was just one of the clinic's famous patients. Trudeau encouraged his friend, Dr. James, to take over the clinic when he was no longer able. Dr. James agreed, and he built Camp Junco to be closer to the clinic. James was president of the clinic for 25 years. Antibiotics effectively began to cure TB beginning in 1943, but the Trudeau Institute today continues work on TB and other infectious diseases that attack the immune system.

Henry Anderson Sr. and Helen James were married at tiny St. John's Church in the wilderness that had been built near Paul Smith's in 1919. Dr. Walter Belknap James died in 1926, leaving Camp Junco to his daughter because his wife preferred to summer in Newport. The camp had upwards of 15 buildings counting the boathouses, icehouses, servant's quarters, and many individual sleeping cabins to accommodate the family and guests. Old film footage of the camp shows a large dining room building with a spacious screened outdoor dining area and a walk-in granite fireplace; several two-story guest cabins with dormer windows and porches that could amply house a family of four; a living room building with another large screened patio; and a row of four, two-story sleeping cabins each with a large walk-in shower off the living room on the first floor, and a dressing room on the second floor with an outdoor screened sleeping porch. All were wood frame buildings finished in cedar shakes.

Harry Anderson was nine years old when he first went to Camp Junco. Downstairs, the living room in the boy's sleeping cabins had been converted to a playroom and nurse's room. On the waterfront were four canoes, two Adirondack guideboats, three launches, and a sailboat. The place was a young boy's dream, as Anderson's written recollection indicates:

Life was never dull at Camp Junco. Each day commenced with a pre-breakfast dip in the lake off the dock. As September approached, this became a macho challenge.

After breakfast it was roll the all-weather, red clay tennis court, and get in a couple hours practice. Mother was an excellent tennis player and would coach us. My friend George Willets and his mother, who lived a short bicycle ride away from our house in Roslyn, regularly spent a month or so at Camp Junco. George was quick and nimble and usually bested me.

Before lunch it was overboard with a heavy brush to wipe the slime off the hefty centerboard sloop known as a Swampscott O Boat, designed by John Alden. After lunch we rubbed yellow laundry soap on the bottom of the O Boat, then sailed it to the start of the afternoon race. The laundry soap was a trick taught to us by a guest, Russell Dench, a ranking Star class sailor from Edgartown. No doubt most of the primitive form of polymer rubbed off by the time we reached the starting line. He also provided us with a novel wrinkle to reduce the weather helm of the O Boat. He nailed a vertical row of shingles jutting out ahead of the stem to add to the windage of the fore triangle.

If weather compelled canceling the race, a cannon was fired from either Upper St. Regis or Spitfire Lake. Cannon signals, more reliable than the party phone line, were also used for fire and other emergencies. By reason of the irregular conformation of the Lake and its islands, the racecourse could be up to 13 legs.

Post-race fun was usually swimming.

The narrow passage or short slough connecting Upper St. Regis Lake and Spitfire was too shoal for most boats on the starboard side going north so a small light was mounted mid-channel connected by a low power line to the shore. We found, at some peril, that if one demounted the boat's signal flag staffs, lay in the bottom and kept the outboard at planing speed, one could just clear under the wire. Predictably, this became a prime challenge for us youngsters. The closest I would ever come to a similar rite of passage was when training as an artillery observer in Piper Cubs. When there was a hiatus in the traffic on a two-lane road we would fly the Cub under the telephone wires. It was not like flying under the George Washington Bridge. The clearance was so tight that one could see the grain in the field behind the airplane flattened by the prop wash.

Another sport involving Lake Spitfire—it was played there so that our parents could not witness what we were doing in their Hackers, Chris-Crafts, Fay & Bowens and other launches—was water polo with a basketball and a guideboat oar or canoe paddle instead of a polo mallet. The boats were our ponies, with the potential for horrific collisions. A somewhat similar form of sport—more like jousting— took place annually in the O Boats. The objective was to sail through the slough into Spitfire Lake and thence through another slough that meandered almost two miles through marshland into Lower St. Regis Lake, land next to Paul Smith's Hotel, pick up a marked postcard and finish back in Upper St.

Regis Lake. While in the slough all racing rules were suspended. One object was using spinnaker poles to joust crew members on another boat into the water. It did not matter how many crew one lost this way as long as they all were rescued on the way home.

John Trevor, whose father, it was bruited about sotto voce as though it were top secret, was a founder and head of the Secret Service, was in charge of the racing marks for the regattas. The marks were a simple crossing of two pieces of wood on which a flagstaff with burgee was mounted. They also made challenging turning marks for us youngsters in our outboards, challenging because if you passed too close to them, the marks were dismasted. John, frustrated by having to replace them, smartly assigned the St. Regis Junior Yacht Club the job of maintaining them, thereby reducing the breakage. The Ralph Earles from Philadelphia (his brother George, who had a camp on adjoining Spitfire Lake, was governor of Pennsylvania) made available a tented deck sleeping porch as a sort of clubhouse for the Junior Club. Their daughter was commodore, or commodorable as some wags called her. I was vice commodore. She may have been one of the first female yacht club commodores in North America. Many years later when I was asked for my resume before becoming a flag officer of the Seawanhaka Corinthian Yacht Club, I did not list this Jr. St. Regis post, fearing that the

taboo versus woman might contaminate my chance of selection.

After dinner we would practice carrying canoes in order to develop muscles and beef up for future portages, which were required to go from one body of water to another on canoe trips. Each canoe had a yoke carved to match the shape of one's shoulders. This was attached across the middle of the canoe. One knelt beside the upright canoe, swung the boat over one's head, settling the yoke on the shoulders, then rose up. On a canoe trip, the sleeping bag was packed at the forward end, with cooking utensils, food, clothes, etc., carried in a woven pack basket on your back. A two-man canoe weighed 50 pounds less the gear and backpack. If you wanted to go many miles, you'd carry to the railroad track. The freight train would stop, you'd put the canoe on a flat car, and get dropped off.

At night, when George was visiting he would be in the two-story cabin adjacent to mine. After curfew we would communicate by Morse Code, using home-made telegraph tappers.

The family had a pure-bred bulldog, no doubt by reason of Father having attended Yale. Bulldogs are almost brainless, or ultra-stubborn. This one had a habit of chasing after boats leaving the dock. The heavy bone structure of the beast meant it couldn't float.

My job was to dive in and retrieve the dog that I would find walking along the bottom with bubbles streaming from its mouth. It never learned not to chase the boats.

Life at the camps was very communal, partly because young people from various camps intermarried. There would be a hymn sing every Sunday night, and every month Mrs. Marjorie Merriweather Post Hutton would invite all to view the latest Hollywood movie before it had been released. Also on Sunday most drove their launches from Spitfire, down the winding slough in the marshes separating Spitfire and Lower St. Regis to the docks at Paul Smith's. From there it was a half-mile hike to St. Johns in the Wilderness for Sunday Episcopal service conducted by a visiting clergyman. The exceptions were those whose camps were accessible by road. The Huttons went to church on Sunday in one of the five cars they shipped to the Lakes in one of their private railroad cars. A car with two armed detectives would follow them (recall this was the post-Lindbergh kidnapping era).

An aside: Later on, Mrs. Hutton's daughter Deenie was being wooed by Frank Trudeau, grandson of Dr. Edward Trudeau who started the tuberculosis clinic. At Yale, Frank roomed with Stan Rumbough. One football weekend, Frank invited Deenie for the game, after which Frank and Stan gave a party that jammed their dorm room wall to wall. Stan left to get

ice, and as he was walking back and passing below his dorm room, Deenie fell out the window. Stan dropped the ice, and caught her. After graduation, it was Stan who married Deenie, with Frank acting as best man.

One Sunday, Bishop Kinsolving (father of Mrs. John Nicholas Brown) was the minister. After the first hymn he pronounced it a poor performance, and said, "We will try that again." Few of the fur-clad ladies had ever been so scolded in church. Obediently, they chimed in with more enthusiasm.

The small electric organ had an emergency hand crank in case the electricity quit, which it often did in thunderstorms. Frank Trudeau and I were the standby crankers. One Sunday we had to go to work pumping fast enough to keep a white power indicator card in full view on the glass. A woman named Mrs. Chase sang during the passing of the collection plate, and enjoyed it so much she often did an encore even though it wasn't requested. This time we let the white card recede enough to slow down the organ. This was too much for her, so she halted, never realizing the trickery.

The highlight of sailing on the St. Regis Lakes was provided by the Idem class (Latin for "one is like another one"), a lovely, gaff-rigged skimming dish of a race boat designed for the Lakes' light winds. Members of the St. Regis

Yacht Club had commissioned Clinton Crane (a member of Seawanhaka) to draw a boat for them in 1897, the same year the club was founded. The Idem was the result. Crane was 27 years old at the time. He would go on to design J-Class and 12-Metre yachts. The Idems were delivered in 1899.

The Idems are 32 feet overall, with only a 19-foot waterline length. They carry an enormous 600 square feet of sail designed to capture the Lakes' lightest zephyrs. Bright against the dark, pine-green backdrop of the Lakes' shorelines, the fleet of fragile Idems— now antiques—are a lovely sight to behold. Harry Anderson recalls racing once or twice on the boats. "With their huge mains, the boats were a bit much for us young sailors," he says. "The main trimmer sat in his own cockpit behind the helmsman. With no winches, trimming that sail was a workout for a strong man."

Life quickly got very busy for Harry Anderson. Strenuous. He apparently liked it that way because the rapid pace he set would sustain into his 90s. As if Camp Junco didn't provide enough activity, for two years Anderson attended the more regulated summer camp run by the nearby Adirondack-Florida School. Summers weren't spent entirely in the Adirondacks. There was also sailing at Seawanhaka. Before long, there would be a change of schools that would provide even more time on the water.

FOUR | Obedience to the Unenforceable

W hen he was 12, Harry Anderson went for an interview at the Adirondack-Florida School at Onchiota, New York . . . by canoe. His mother and father were in one canoe. Harry and a guide were in a second boat. It was a four-hour trip altogether, with two portages that were long for a boy of his age. The party set off from Camp Junco on Upper St. Regis Lake, paddled into Spitfire Lake, navigated the slough into Lower St. Regis Lake, carried about a mile to Paul Smith's on Church Pond, paddled across Osgood Pond up a narrow stream leading to Jones Pond, after which there is another carry of about a mile into the south end of Rainbow Lake. The school is a two-and-a-half mile paddle from there.

It wasn't Harry's first trip to the school. When he was 10 he'd been to the summer camp run by Adirondack-Florida—Camp Meenagha, named after the nearby mountain—but not by canoe. Meenagha, according to Anderson, is Native American for "blueberry." For the trip to camp, the family would take one of its launches to the dock at the Landing on Upper St. Regis Lake where the cars were kept, and drive an hour and a half. When Anderson was 11 he'd attended the funeral of Alice Ruth Carter Ransom, who had run the school after her husband's death in 1907. That had been his first trip to the school by canoe.

The interview was more or less a formality. Harry's father and Uncle Larocque had entered the school in 1906, after the northern campus had opened. The school authorities had gotten to know Harry as an upstanding young camper who was as enthusiastic and capable in the woods as he was on the water. There was no question he fit the demanding profile of the Adirondack-Florida student

Sunday evening sing at Adirondack-Florida School in 1938. Harry Anderson is at center with pocket handkerchief in place.

Alumni.
magazine
Fall 1997

as outlined in the extraordinary letter written in 1903 by the founder, Paul Ransom.

Son of a prosperous Buffalo, New York, family, Paul Ransom was a popular Williams College professor with a Harvard degree whose promising legal career was cut short when he was diagnosed with Bright's disease, a kidney disorder without a cure at the time. Urged to seek a warmer climate, in 1893 Ransom traveled to Titusville, Florida, the end of the railroad line. He crossed Lake Worth by small boat, then hired a sloop with a captain to take him to Coconut Grove on Biscayne Bay. He

was looking for Kirk Monroe, a well-known writer of boys' adventure books. He had a letter of introduction to Monroe. The two men met and got along so well that Monroe sold Ransom seven acres of his land in Coconut Grove in 1896.

With a school in mind, Ransom spent several years getting organized, erecting some rudimentary buildings, pumping drinking water by hand, and taking on a handful of students who had their lessons in the boathouse. In 1898, Ransom built the first tennis court in southern Florida.

Along the way, Ransom married Alice Ruth Carter, daughter of the president of Williams College. The improved health and vitality he had experienced from spending the winters in a warm climate had spawned the idea of starting a migratory school. His wife shared his enthusiasm for the project. Toward that end the Ransoms bought an old lumber camp, Meenagha Lodge, near Saranac. Adirondack-Florida school was opened in 1903 with seven boys and three teachers in addition to Ransom. The seven boys, as this excerpt from his Letter to Prospective Students makes clear, were of the "Third Class":

Your parents have asked me to accept you as a pupil at my school, and I have consented to do so provided I find you are in accord with me as

LEFT: **Harry Anderson as a student at Adirondack-Florida School in 1938.**

Map shows the canoe route from Camp Junco (lower
left), on Upper Saint Regis Lake, to the Adirondack-
Florida school on Rainbow Lake (upper right).

to the purposes for which you would come here and are willing to agree to certain things which I consider necessary if those purposes are to be attained.

The people in this world may be divided roughly into three great classes, according to the attitude they hold to life. The people in the first class believe, or seem to believe, that they were put into the world to see how much they can get out of it. Provided they are comfortable themselves, it does not distress them that others are in misery. Their object in life being to get all they can, and keep all they get, it sometimes seems a matter of little consequence to them if they get some things that rightly belong to other people. The people of this class are often rich, sometimes they are talented; but if the world is better off for their living in it, it is not because of any conscious effort of theirs. They never find the contentment and happiness they seek so eagerly.

The second class is those who do not give life any thought at all—who do not like to think very deeply of anything. They are content to drift along and take what comes, but they are too lazy to take the trouble of deciding difficult problems. They are often well-meaning, amiable people; but if all the people in the world belonged to this class no progress would be possible and things would soon come to a standstill.

The people of the third class believe they are in the world not so much for what they can get out of it as for what they can put into it. They are unwilling to give up their lives for the selfish pursuit of pleasure. They believe in work, and are willing and anxious to do their share of it. They do not shirk the great problems of life, but meet and solve them. It is to these that the world is indebted for all the progress that has been made in the past, and to them it must look for all hope of progress in the future. The people who belong to this class are very busy—too busy to think very much of themselves—but they are really the happiest people in the world.

Now if you want to belong to one of the first two classes, this is not the school for you. We have no time to waste in training boys to be selfish or lazy. You would not be in the spirit of the school if you came here, and you probably would not remain in it long. If all you care to think of is the fun you are going to have—the hunting, fishing, and cruising—and if you have no thought to give to the serious matters of life, to your work, to honor, and truth, and purity, and helpfulness—you would only be a hindrance to us here, and you would yourself be disappointed, for while we believe in fun, and in all the pleasures of the outdoor life we try to give our boys, we believe more in the higher things, and we intend to give them the first place. But if you find that it is your wish to belong to the third class—to live not for yourself alone, but to serve your God, your country, and your fellow man, with all your heart and mind and strength—why then, my boy, this will be a good place for you and we will welcome you here with all our hearts. And if this is the life you wish to train yourself for, you will not find it difficult to commit yourself to the promises that I ask you to make to yourself and to me, for they are part of the training. If you wish to become an efficient, helpful, trustworthy man you must begin by being an efficient, helpful, trustworthy boy, and to do this you must accustom yourself to obey, to work, and to resist self-indulgence.

As this decision is of such extreme importance, I shall ask you to think over this letter at least one day before deciding. If you decide that you want to come to us, you will date and sign one of the enclosed letters and return it to me. . . .

Of the other two copies, one is for you to keep . . . in your Bible so that you may refer to it . . . and thus refresh your memory of what you have promised.

Harry Anderson doesn't recall Paul Ransom's letter from when he was 12 years old. Today, the philosophy expressed in the letter remains the school's creed. The school is now called Ransom Everglades,

and is co-ed with two campuses in Coconut Grove. Ellen Moceri, head of school in 2013, reads Ransom's letter to the assembled students at the start of each semester. Anderson appreciates how accurately the letter reflects the day-to-day philosophy of the school, and how profoundly the school influenced him.

The depth of that influence on Harry Anderson can be measured by his long association with the school. He calls his relationship with Ransom Everglades "a lifetime pursuit." The school is his number-one philanthropy. He began serving on its board after World War II when he was a student at Columbia Law School, and he played a significant role in ending the school's migratory design. It was an early example of the pragmatism Anderson would become known for bringing to the organizations he has been associated with. In 1949, with financial collapse the alternative, Anderson and the board regretfully closed the northern campus and consolidated the school's resources on Biscayne Bay.

"The greatest wrench," Anderson wrote as a contribution to the book, *Ransom-Everglades, Reflections of a School, 1893-1978,* "was parting with the Adirondack campus, especially for one who always took the Adirondack side of the never-ending argument over which site was the favorite. . . . The association taught

THE STRENUOUS LIFE OF HARRY ANDERSON

63

us that in the field of education one takes economic risks in which a prudent businessman would not engage, and we recognized the verity of the values laid down by the Ransoms three-quarters of a century ago. Not until one spends the pre-breakfast hours in the headmaster's office does he begin to comprehend what education and its administration is all about."

Anderson served continuously on the board, becoming a Life Trustee in 1985. He was the first recipient of the Founder's Alumni Award. The gymnasium and the sailing center at Ransom Everglades both bear his name.

In 1933, when Anderson entered Adirondack-Florida School, he was one of 35 boys from mostly affluent families gathered on the northern "campus," an old, basically unaltered logging camp. There were seven masters. Maids tidied the rooms, made the beds, prepared and served meals. Other than those services, the school was a do-it-yourself experience. Old film footage shows students—in jackets and ties other than when hunting, fishing, or working in the woods—having classes in small rustic rooms, tramping through woods covered with early fall snow on the way to meals, chopping and lugging wood to stoke potbellied stoves, and celebrating various occasions or relaxing in simple common rooms.

The building of small, crude log cabins started spontaneously in 1903 when three students disappeared most afternoons into the woods to work on a secret project. When the cabin they had built was revealed, the idea caught on, with upwards of a dozen student cabins being built over the years. Harry Anderson and two other students who were handy with tools built one. "It was just one room," he recalls, "with a couple bunks, a table, a fireplace. It was an escape for cookouts on weekends. Nothing fancy."

Both the north and south campuses of the school stressed proficiency in activities that could sustain through life, in addition to the usual sports, of which soccer was predominant. "The school Paul Ransom started," says Ellen Moceri, a petite, resolute woman in her sixties who became head of school in 2001, "stood for young men who were strong of mind, body, and spirit. Ransom was a follower of philosopher and educational reformer John Dewey, and naturalist John Burroughs. He believed in experiential learning. He liked the idea of man against nature better than competitive sports, especially sailing. That is still the first sport at Ransom Everglades. We're probably the only prep school in the country where learning to sail is a prerequisite for graduation. Paul Ransom's idea was, 'Let's have an adventure, we'll sail to Key West!'"

In one of the school's oldest buildings, a large, hand-carved wooden plaque is prominently displayed. It reads, "Obedience to the Unenforceable." It's a school motto. "It means that character is what you do when no one is looking," Ellen Moceri says. "Character doesn't come from having rules and regulations or student handbooks. It's who you really are. Ethical values are universal, not situational."

If the Adirondacks provided one of the best possible places for practicing the wide range of woodsman's skills, the school's Biscayne Bay campus is ideally suited to the mariner. The 35-by-8-mile Bay starts in the south at Key Biscayne (to the east), fronts Miami to the west, and defines the inside shoreline of Miami Beach. The South Bay is one of the East Coast's prime sailing venues—Olympic trials are often held there—and the school is ideally located at its midpoint on the mainland side. Biscayne Bay is shallow, with an average depth of ten feet, but for most small sailboats that's more than adequate.

When Harry Anderson was there in the 1930s, the campus was called "Pine Knot Camp," Paul Ransom's original name for his land. It was just as untamed as the north woods. Scorpions were commonplace in the buildings, poisonous coral snakes slithered by on occasion. On spring nights one could hear the scuffling of crabs crawling out of the Bay and heading for the Everglades. There was no hot water, and fireplaces were the only way to temper the chill of cold nor'westers. As Anderson quips, "Adirondack-Florida offered a variety of challenges unmatched by the customary prep school."

The Florida campus boasted a fleet of 16 small sailboats: six gaff-rigged sneakboxes, six Herreshoff 14-footers designed for the Bay, a few Moths, one Suicide-Class boat, a Malay proa, and a few nondescript craft. There were two larger sailboats for weekend cruising. One was a 65-foot tops'l centerboard schooner, the other a smaller sloop. Coveted trips on the cruising boats were available to students based on their accomplishments in academics and seamanship. Anderson was always near the top in both categories. He was also vice commodore of the school's Pine Knot Yacht Club, another of the many flag-officer positions he would hold in eight different yacht clubs.

Anderson's accomplishments made him a hard act for his brothers, David and Jim, to follow. "One of my parents' big mistakes was to send all three of us to the Adirondack-Florida School," David Anderson says today. "With so few students, there was no escape for Jim and me from Harry's predominance. Harry was kingpin. He was a good student, a good sailor, a good tennis player, a good horseman. My father was hard on Harry as the first child,

and he responded to all that pressure. I was fortunate, too much of a shrimp rat to bother with. And Jim was a happy slob with not much intellect, and not a mean bone in his body. No ambition either. He ended up a sergeant in the Army, married a woman with money and raised cows. But it was impossible for us, coming into the school with Harry being such a star. If there had been 100 students there would have been a place to hide, or do your own thing."

David Anderson says what saved him was discovering Dostoyevsky's *The Brothers Karamazov.* "I read that book and had a transformation," he says. "It was mind changing. I'd grown up in a Dickensian atmosphere where things were black and white, good or bad. Harry has that old-fashioned view. But that book changed my life, showed me that my family was living in an unreal world where everything was so rational. In *Brothers* there is a bunch of people crazy as coots, but to me that was the real world. I became very interested in Russia. *Brothers* broke me free."

David says his early rebellion involved an interest in jazz stimulated by trumpeter Louis Armstrong and others. His interest was a radical departure from the classical music that prevailed in the Anderson household. He was 14 at the time; the year was 1938. "It drove

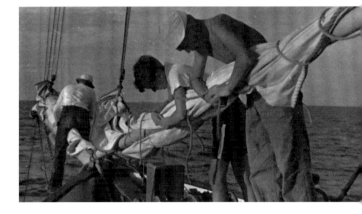

my mother crazy," David says. "I'd sit in my room and listen to old Bluebird records. The breakthrough was when I persuaded mother to take me to the famous Benny Goodman Carnegie Hall Concert. She didn't exactly get in the aisle and dance, but she liked it."

Harry Anderson excelled in the classroom not only because he was smart; he was enthusiastic. He seems to have been born with an unbounded, insatiable curiosity. His love of learning began early and has lasted a lifetime. Perhaps his father's lengthy and detailed log of his passage on *Foohng Suey* set an example for the son. In any case, it appears Harry was keeping records and notes of various events and encounters from the time he learned to write. Behind the proficient sailor and woodsman was an introspective young man, an inconsolable romantic for whom words were important, as this sonnet

67

LEFT: *Winslow*, the schooner belonging to the Adirondack-Florida School, at Coconut Grove when Anderson was a student there in the 1930s. RIGHT: Harry Anderson (middle) furling the jib with classmate John Richardson aboard *Winslow* during a student cruise in 1937.

he wrote as a student at Adirondack-Florida School attests:

Corregio Pro Melancholia

Among the fickle paths of life, so far
From fixed as is the eagle to his nest,
There waver the uncertain moods
    that bar
Us from adhering to what suits us best;
And therefore where there comes to
    mend your wrong
The inspiration to your life's desire,
Tender it as 'twere a spark in grip so
    strong
That it might ever be a mounting fire;
Not like Mars, who blinks from red
    to blue
And quickly back to red by way of white,
But like the steady, staring lynx pursue
That which inspires you by its guiding
    light;
Because an opportunity once lost
Detracts from life far more than just
    its cost.

The insight is keen. The message bespeaks advanced maturity and uncommon sensitivity. Anderson's early struggles with philosophical questions relating to his own identity go beyond standard-issue schoolboy confusion. That and the oppression of his childhood are evident in other early writings preserved in his files, and in the school's literary periodical, *The Hickory*

Log. One *Log* piece in particular stands out. "From Delight to Dreariness" is a rumination on a "cold brick wall partly bordering a gray gravel drive" that existed at Anderson's boyhood home in Roslyn, New York.

Barren and dreary this scene has always represented my life, the very spirit of my soul. Not only is it a symbol of failures, longings, and melancholies, but also of happy days, pleasant memories, and former delights; for past joy is a present sorrow. . . .

Many times in the early morning the sunrise would cast on the wall, just as in the evening, the same weak light, the same dim shadows across the ivy. Thus would begin a gloomy day for me, during which I would succumb to morbid despair. Every time the instructor chastised me or someone else reprimanded me, I would cringe deeper into desolate gloom. Finally toward evening the oaks would console me in grief— grief which, mingled with my abject terror of the dark, would hound me all through the night, until the light of dawn passed across the red brick wall.

Later in life, when I became passionately fond of persons, places, and pursuits, the dying sun and deepening shadows on the red brick wall would set my mind to poignantly craving familiar sights. With distressing regret I would wrench myself from the sound of the wind

which sent clouds scurrying beneath a Florida moon and which went whispering through the dry palm branches above blanched coral sand. Out at sea a yacht lifting ahead in each puff and sliding through the sighing swell would render me helplessly desolate. Likewise the heaving shoulders, sweating side, and groaning leather on a winded horse would reduce me to a grievous longing for those scenes that can never be repeated. In the same way the quiet of an Adirondack balsam thicket, occasionally still yet more by a snowflake swirling gently downwards, would surround my existence in an enshrouding mantle of sadness. Always the beauty of life has for me been my past recollected in tranquility.

Still the long brick wall, dark ivy clumps, long

Officers of the Pine Knot Yacht Club at the Adirondack-Florida School in 1938. From left, Fleet Captain Spotswood Bowers, Rear Commodore Devens Osborn, Commodore George Nichols Jr., and Vice Commodore Harry Anderson.

black shadows, and pale yellow glow stimulate my morbid nostalgia. There can be read into this symbol of my life an intricate and complicated meaning, such as that the dying light of past joys are waning into long shadows of my future which come slowly forward to grip me in their dark clutches. Yet I prefer to perceive the picture in its entirety. To me it represents the vanishing of my present happiness as it is being slowly entombed by my longing to relive past pleasures.

Sailing seems to have provided the shield Anderson needed to keep the shadows' clutches at bay, offered the refuge he needed to free himself from dark ivy clumps, and promised the discovery of new pleasures. There was sailboat racing every afternoon at the Biscayne Bay campus. There was also the *Winslow*, a tops'l schooner that had been built in Nassau, for weekend cruising. "The engine cost more than the boat," Anderson recalls. "There were pipe berths below. We'd harpoon whip rays and chop them up for shark bait and hang hooks in the water. Hammerheads won't eat anything dead, so we'd bail the blood out of the dinghy and the sharks would come in during the night. We had trip lines tied to pots and pans so we'd wake up when the sharks struck. We went aloft to set the tops'l, and we were taught the basics of celestial navigation."

An event that would greatly enhance Anderson's status in the school's sailing community was his participation in the 1936 Bermuda Race on SCYC Commodore George Emlen Roosevelt's 60-foot schooner *Mistress*. Anderson was 15 at the time. The opportunity to go on the race came about because of his growing reputation as a superb young sailor at SCYC Jr., coupled with his family's friendship with the Roosevelts. "Someone asked my father why he let me go on the race at such a young age," Anderson says. "He said because there were three helmsmen he would trust in an emergency at sea. Sherman Hoyt and George Roosevelt were two of them." Hoyt, a talented helmsman who had rescued the United States from the brink of defeat in the 1934 America's Cup—one of the craftiest and best known sailors of his day—had designed *Mistress*, which was launched in 1930.

"Sherman told me you should be able to close your eyes and sail a boat to windward," Anderson says. "Because if you are at sea in the driving rain and the compass is obscured and you have nothing to go by, you should be able to feel the wind on your neck and your cheek and tell exactly what angle you're sailing at. Sherman was a colorful character, no question about that. More colorful than they write about him. He never had an automobile, or a license either as far as I know."

Anderson also had great respect for George Roosevelt, whom he considers the embodiment of the Corinthian ideal. George Roosevelt (1887-1963) became one of his mentors. In a letter Anderson sent to Julian Roosevelt Jr. in 1999, he writes: "Of your three Roosevelt ancestors, George was a genius, especially in mathematics; he was with Admiral Weems on the advisory board to the US Navy for navigation; on night watches he would deliver long accounts of the days of the Egyptian Ptolemy dynasty and the discovery of celestial navigation; and, I believe, at one time he was President of the International Chess Association. I recall him describing how in 1939 at a breakfast in London with an international group they drew the basis for the atomic bomb on the table cloth—missing were the quantities of each ingredient needed to coalesce it into a functioning weapon. Subsequently he went to Moscow with Russian Foreign Minister Molotov in his private railroad car and was the last westerner ever to see Molotov."

The 1950 Bermuda Race crew lines up on *Mistress*. From right, Commodore George Roosevelt (owner) at the helm, Pat Merle-Smith, Frank V. Snyder, Sven Rasmussen (cook), Julian K. Roosevelt, George Nichols Jr., P. James Roosevelt, Harry Anderson, and Captain Titcomb with Ollie (mate) behind him.

To this day Anderson considers Roosevelt one of the best seamen he ever sailed with. When Anderson boarded *Mistress* for the 1936 race, it was not long after the black schooner had finished third in the 1935 Transatlantic Race to Norway, a race marred by the deaths of three participants. Roosevelt admitted after the finish that he had been so scared during the race—so consumed by his navigation, and by keeping a vigilant watch for ice—he had averaged only three hours sleep a day. In his book, *After the Storm*, John Rousmaniere reports that Roosevelt told reporters after the race, if all experienced sailors didn't feel fear before heading offshore they should take up farming. What was unusual about that sentiment, as Rousmaniere noted, was Roosevelt's willingness to go public with it.

Anderson kept notes about his first Bermuda Race with George Roosevelt:

> The Commodore was a firm believer in introducing young blood to the sport and a firm believer in every member of the crew learning the ropes including taking their stint at the helm. It was not long after the start that mal de mer set in, but fortunately not for long. . . . In the 30s and 40s safety-at-sea had not been standardized, but the Commodore, who was ahead of the times, taught us a quick recovery method for a man overboard. (On a later race on Stormy Weather

> we carried two dozen polo balls painted orange, the theory being that if we threw them over at 15 second intervals they would lead us back to the man overboard). There were no specifications for lifelines, a flare consisted of a canister filled with chemicals that when immersed in water emitted a plume of pinkish smoke, and three chronometers were carried to determine Greenwich time. Courses were given the helmsman in cardinal points—for instance North by East one quarter East—so one had to know how to box the compass. . . . Identifying the Gulf Stream was done by putting a thermometer in a freshly dipped bucket of seawater.

Based on that blue-water racing experience, and his high seamanship standing at school, the following year Adirondack-Florida Headmaster Kenneth Wilson invited Anderson to join him on the crew of *Actaea*, a Frank Paine-designed, 38-foot cutter owned by an alumnus and his wife, for the Miami-Nassau Race. It turned out to be a darkish comedy of errors. The steward had disappeared with the money he was given to buy provisions for the boat. The captain had lost his false teeth, making him difficult to understand. When it became necessary to reef, several of the ties holding the luff slides of the main to the track broke. Ken Wilson was confined to his bunk after irritating an old back injury. The log line was severed when the helmsman ran over it (making sternway) when he got stuck in irons while shaking out a reef. The navigator was seasick for the first 24 hours. With only three left to sail the boat, Anderson did one five-hour trick at the wheel.

"My first purchase when we reached Nassau was a shorter belt," Anderson wrote recently about the trip, "so much weight had been lost. We were one of five out of fifteen starters to complete the race. The largest yacht, the schooner *Augusta Verdi*, for which the race was supposed to be the first leg of a trip around the world, sank during the night with all but the ship's cat being rescued by the US Coast Guard. Having experienced a minor hurricane in the 1936 Bermuda Race, and the pounding in the Miami-Nassau Race, I was under the impression that every ocean race involved a calamity of some kind. In retrospect, after a dozen or more Bermuda Races, the tragic Fastnet Race of '79, and several really tough Sydney-Hobart Races—not to mention the lives lost in races off California in 2012—the impression is not far from reality."

⚓

THAT SAME YEAR, 1936, Harry Anderson was appointed commodore of SCYC's newly formed Junior Club. For Seawanhaka, creating a junior club was a way to formalize a junior sailing program, and it also got the juniors out from under the adults on the main clubhouse porch. "The concept," Anderson says, "was to create a mini-yacht club and make the juniors responsible for its operation, race scheduling, discipline, and maintenance—subject, of course to the supervision of a junior instructor. It was a form of experiential training, a term not in vogue in those days. The junior club boasted its own launchcommittee boat that picked up juniors from the family docks around Centre Island, Cove Neck, and Oyster Bay."

One of his first duties as junior commodore was to go with Rod Stephens, one of the legendary sailors of the day, to the Penn Yan Boat Company north of Ithaca, New York, to test the first hull of the Sea Bird, a 24-foot keel boat that had been designed for the Junior SCYC by Rod's brother, Olin Stephens. "Above all," Anderson says, "the boat was to be safe, unsinkable, and indestructible. We went after Christmas, wearing coonskin coats. We tested that first boat in a blizzard. It was blowing a gale. Rod was in ecstasy. He was wearing one of the first pairs of Topsiders. There was ice on the mast, and Rod started climbing to see if the shoes would hold. The weather influenced the decision to reduce the size of the rig, which was unfortunate because the boat could have used more sail on Long Island Sound."

As a junior, Anderson was one of several boys from Seawanhaka who tried out for the Sears Cup, the oldest youth championship of sailing in the United States. It was held at the Pequot Yacht Club in Southport, Connecticut, that year. The team from Seawanhaka didn't make it, but they did have an adventure. "We were staying with Briggs and Lucy Cunningham," Anderson recalls. Briggs S. Cunningham (1907-2003) came from a wealthy Cincinnati, Ohio, family. He would become famous as a race-car driver, and would make the cover of *Time* magazine (1954) as the builder of a line of racing cars bearing his name. In 1958 he would win the America's Cup as skipper of *Columbia*. He was a committed supporter of junior sailing on Long Island Sound. He donated his Sparkman & Stephens-designed schooner *Brilliant* to Mystic Seaport in 1953 as a sail-training vessel for teenagers, and he funded its maintenance until his death.

"One day after racing," Anderson says, "Briggs took a few of us for a run in his super-charged Ford that had garish stainless piping on the outside of the hood. We went up the Merritt Parkway at 55 miles an hour in third gear. On the way back we were hitting 100. One of the boys asked Briggs why there was no traffic on the highway. There wasn't another car in sight. Briggs explained he was a director of the Merritt, and had asked that the section we were on be closed for half an hour."

Those who remember young Commodore Anderson say he led quietly, and with good humor. Marjory Gerdes Fates, one of the founding members of the Seawanhaka Junior Club, recalls Harry was "Cool, not outgoing and backslapping at all, but he was a leader. He wasn't domineering, but he wasn't warm either. He was a good sailor, he won in all aspects, but he was a cool customer. He did all the right things. We respected him, but we didn't love him."

In the 1930s young people tended to socialize in groups. Heavy dating and "going steady" was not the fashion. Marjory Fates says plutonic relationships were the way of it, but more likely a bunch of young people would simply go out together to a movie or a party. Harry Anderson says the Seawanhaka juniors had what they called a "Riot Squad," a collection of half a dozen boys and girls who would occasionally go into New York City to night clubs that stayed open until 4:00 a.m., or to private parties. Or they would go to Playland, an amusement park on the Sound in Rye, New York. "Alcohol was definitely involved," Anderson says.

"We had a mascot," Anderson recalls, "a pet hen that lived at one of the girls' houses. When the Riot Squad went on parties, or into the city, we would take the hen with us and bring it in under cover. One nightclub in New

York featured ice hockey on the stage. The hen got loose in there one night and we had to chase it around behind the stage."

Marjory Fates says they would sometimes visit Rothman's, a landmark restaurant-bar on the corner of Route 25A and the turn off to Oyster Bay. "We were too young," she recalls, "but it was our secret place."

Anderson would never marry, a situation friends and acquaintances have often puzzled over. He usually offers a new, humorous rejoinder for every inquiry, but one loss he feels he suffered as a teenager made its mark. The girl's name was Marion Johnson, a co-founder of the Seawanhaka Junior Club. She was regarded as an uncommon beauty, "the belle of the ball," Anderson says. "She wore those Grecian gowns to the dances. But I lost out to a fellow sailor, Hutchinson "Hutchie" DuBosque. It was very competitive in those days. He beat out a lot of people who were interested in her. It was love lost, some sadness."

Hutchie DuBosque died in 2008. Marion Johnson DuBosque, now in her 90s, lives in an assisted living complex in Essex, Connecticut. She was totally surprised to learn that Harry Anderson had had a strong interest in her. "That's not something I ever knew about," she says.

Seawanhaka was a very social club in the 1930s, renowned for the black-tie dances held there on Saturday evenings. There were several "commuters" in the harbor, streamlined power yachts in the 60-to-150-foot range built for speed and comfort. High-ranking corporate officers used them to travel from Long Island (or the Hudson River) to Wall Street. Often on a Friday evening, one of the commuters would motor from dock to dock, picking up nattily attired partygoers and dropping them at SCYC. When it was time to call it a night, the commuter would be on hand to deliver the revelers back home.

But at both Seawanhaka clubs, sailing was the main attraction. The instruction and the fleet racing for juniors in the Sea Birds and other one designs was superb. They raced every day during the week. On weekends, they raced with their families on bigger boats. Once a year the senior members took the juniors on a three-day, point-to-point racing cruise on their larger yachts. "We had a many as three 12-Metres on those cruises," Anderson recalls. "One got to be at the helm of a 12 as a teenager, even starting it. Pretty good fun."

When he turned 16, Harry received a Ford Phaeton from his grandmother James. She gave similar gifts to his brothers Jim and David when they reached 16. "Father was fit to be tied," Anderson says, "grandmother giving us

sports cars at our age. During the party season that winter I managed to wreck the Phaeton. I went to a luncheon deb party out on Long Island. I had a dinner party to go to that evening in the City at the Waldorf. Deb party season was hectic, all those mothers thinking about marriage. Driving toward the city on a narrow road, I skidded on a patch of ice, hit the curb, and went into a telephone pole. The engine was demolished. The tow truck took me to a garage in Manhasset. I could catch a train to New York from there, but by the time I got dressed I was a little late. I was supposed to sit on the right hand of the girl coming out, and she wasn't very happy. But they saved my seat." Anderson chuckles at the memory. "I wasn't hurt. Not a scratch. But the car was totaled. When Burberry drove father to Manhasset in the morning to get the train, he stopped to look at the car. He wasn't very happy."

Also when he was 16, Anderson was grinding winches on 6-Metre sloops at Seawanhaka, the cradle of international yacht racing in those days. The 1930s were the hey-days of the lovely 6-Metre Class. It was also the apogee of yachting's period of gentrification. It was no accident that most of the leading skippers of the day also happened to be from some of the wealthiest families of the day. It took big money to play in that league.

There were many legendary yachtsmen in that 6-Metre fleet. Briggs Cunningham was one. Cornelius Shields (1895-1981) was another. Dubbed "the gray fox of Long Island Sound" for his habitual, winning ways, Shields' brother Paul had started the investment firm of Shields & Co. in the 1920s. Cornelius worked as a salesman. His father had been president of the Lake Superior Corporation (steel, pulp, and paper) in the early 1900s. Shields was father of the International One Design Class, and would commission and co-design (with Olin Stephens) the Shields class. Twice he won the coveted Seawanhaka Cup, an annual international contest. Harry Morgan, later commodore of the New York Yacht Club, was a grandson of J. P. Morgan. Ace helmsman Bob Meyer was an uncle of Cord Meyer, a CIA higher-up who would become embroiled in the Kennedy assassination investigation. Meyer's grandfather had made a fortune in Cuban sugar, and in property. He had given

On board the 12 Metre *Seven Seas* moored off Seawanhaka in the 1930s. From left, Harry Anderson, Pat Merle-Smith, Pat's father and SCYC Commodore Van Merle-Smith seated at helm, and Robert B. Meyer.

each of his grandsons a farm on Long Island. "One of them got Queens County," Anderson says, only half joking. Herman Frasch "Swede" Whiton, heir to a sulphur fortune, was the first American sailor to win back-to-back gold medals in the Olympics (London, 1948; Helsinki, 1952—in 6-Metres). The irascible and brilliant Sherman Hoyt, who was a generation older, made up in talent what his family lacked in super wealth. There was Bill Luders, the designer of fast, lovely hulls, and to top it off with a royal touch, King Olaf of Norway was a dedicated 6-Metre sailor.

The younger sailors on Long Island Sound in those days were no less impressive. Anderson was racing against the likes of Bob Bavier (1918-2001), who would win the America's Cup (1964) and become publisher of *Yachting* magazine; future two-time America's Cup winner (1964 and 1967) Bus Mosbacher; Frank Snyder, a future commodore of the New York Yacht Club; George Nichols; and Henry "Bimmy" Duys, an ace helmsman.

Harry Anderson says he got a berth on a 6-Metre because his father was a member of a syndicate. In an English paper he wrote about American teams from various yacht clubs on the Sound (Larchmont, American, Manhasset Bay) competing at Seawanhaka for the honor of representing the US in the Gold Cup in 1937, he describes crews gathering half-awake at SCYC in the pre-dawn darkness, standing among piles of sail bags, foul weather gear, and lunch boxes while contemplating the "somber moan" of the wind blowing 30 knots.

"For what reason," he wrote, "did fifty or more hard-working businessmen get up at 6 AM every day for seven days and spend those seven days on the water, regardless of weather, racing as persistently as they possibly could? Their goal, that was resting on a marble base, was a solid gold oyster shell with frilled edges and artistically decorated on both sides by two large pearls. The winner of this lavish trophy will have attained the highest achievement in the yachting world because the Gold Cup is challenged not by two nations, like the America's Cup, but by the best yachtsman from every foreign country." [At the time, the Gold Cup was in the possession of SCYC].

Anderson's paper describes the windward leg:

"For the next two miles. . . . *Jill* smashed into the seas, sending a veritable deluge of water inboard as she ate her way into the wind. Incessantly coming about, we were continuously hauling on ropes, winching sheets, passing the genoa around the mast and tightening backstays. Finally we rounded the mark as fifth boat. Immediately we hoisted our largest spinnaker while the paid hands crawled on deck to pass out the pole. The sail broke free [of the stops] and with a rush the half-gale sent the tremendous spread of canvas kiting ahead. Riding the wave crests and then sliding down into the troughs she rolled so violently that we had to lash the main boom and lie on the floorboards to keep from being pitched against the sides of the boat."

After the finish, the weather worsened, raising seas large enough to prevent the tenders from towing the yachts back to the SCYC. After a long day of racing in rugged conditions, the crews had to pound back to the harbor upwind, under main alone. "Soon the torrents beat down the sea, killed the wind, and chilled our stinging backs," Anderson's paper concludes. "In this dripping condition we reached our mooring and returned home to gain a good night's rest as part of our training for the next day's grind." (The paper received a C- grade, with "mechanics" cited as something he needed to work on.)

There might have been a less arduous way for Anderson to purge his demons, but comfort can't be a consideration when seeking an alliance with power. When that is the goal, it's difficult to beat what the sea has to offer. And such robust activity was wholeheartedly endorsed at the time by what Anderson often calls "the upper crust" of society. It began with a speech that Theodore Roosevelt delivered in 1899, 22 years before Anderson was born.

The speech was titled "The Strenuous Life." Roosevelt argued that strenuous effort and confronting hardship were ideals Americans should embrace for the betterment of the nation and the world as the twentieth century dawned. "I wish to preach," Roosevelt said, "that the highest form of success comes to the man who does not shrink from danger, from hardship, or from bitter toil, and who out of these wins the splendid, ultimate triumph. . . . it is only through strife, through hard and dangerous endeavor that we shall ultimately win the goal of true national greatness."

Roosevelt's macho challenge was well timed, falling on the receptive ears of eager young men facing the increasing industrialization and urbanization of America. It wasn't just talk emanating from on high. As a schoolboy Roosevelt had taken up boxing at his father's insistence. After graduating from Harvard, when told he had a heart condition that required benign activities, he rejected his doctors' advice and played tennis and polo, hiked, rowed, and practiced jujitsu. When his young wife died, he became a rancher in rugged North Dakota for two years, and when he delivered his address he had only a year earlier led his Rough Riders up San Juan Hill during the Spanish-American War.

In retrospect, the Strenuous Life speech was the perfect motivational message for many men like Harry Anderson's father, whose lot was to fight in two world wars. The notion had served them so well they felt it was their duty to pass it on to their children. Thus Harry and his brothers had endured the tough discipline at home, lashes with the razor strop, being sent off to remote prep schools and camps based on the same self-reliant, athletic philosophy, all in the company of men. For Harry Anderson, it was the sea that provided the biggest attraction.

The literature Anderson and his classmates were reading is rife with seagoing challenge, if not recommendation. In *The Tempest,* Shakespeare offered a seminal riddle that's been analyzed by scholars ever since: "Nothing of him that doth fade, but doth suffer a sea-change into something rich and strange." Rich and strange is certainly intriguing, and "sea change" has become part of the literary vernacular. Joseph Conrad, who saw the sea as a refuge for those unsuited to life on land, offered this romantic vision: "The ship, a fragment detached from the earth, went on lonely and swift like a small planet." In his poem about the famous misfit, J. Alfred Prufrock, T. S. Eliot's besotted character considers this grim alternative: "I should have been a pair of ragged claws scooting across the floors of silent seas." And there is Frederick Marryat's wonderful disclaimer, "I haven't the gift of gab, my sons—because

I'm bred to the sea." Bred to the sea. It has a nice ring to it. For Harry Anderson, it might have been the case—although his gift for gab has never been lacking.

In a recollection addressed to Ransom Everglade School's students in 1991, Anderson wrote: "With the Everglades still only a few miles to the west, Key Biscayne not yet connected by a causeway so that we could sail over and walk across the Key and go skinny dipping in the ocean, and Biscayne Bay to the lower keys constituting a vast extension of the campus for sailing and cruising; and in the Adirondacks the chain of lakes and streams and unlimited woodlands available for expeditions by canoe or trekking, and for fishing and hunting, one was continuously exposed to the challenge of nature. This challenge not only made one intensely aware of the need for conservancy of our environment. . . . but the unpredictable vagaries of the elements taught us resourcefulness and teamwork."

FIVE | Rites

A fter Harry Anderson had been at Adirondack-Florida School for five years, his father assessed the situation and told his son he had a choice: he could take his last year at a junior college, or he could attend Phillips Academy in Andover, Massachusetts, an exclusive, very expensive preparatory school founded in 1778. At Adirondack-Florida, Harry Anderson was ahead of his class, needing only one or two more credits for college. His father thought it was time for a strong finish. Harry picked Andover. "Andover, Exeter, and Lawrenceville had just cooperated on offering advanced courses for seniors that were elevated enough to be accepted for credit from Ivy League colleges," Anderson says. "American History courses at Andover were superior to those offered freshman year at Yale. Latin too. So I wouldn't have to take those courses at Yale, a good thing."

The only student Anderson knew at Andover was Jim Mooney, a neighbor from Oyster Bay. Mooney showed him around the campus, and Anderson joined him on the debating team. Their friendship as sailors at Seawanhaka was enduring. If Anderson's year at Andover was uneventful, the vacations often made up for it. Anderson recorded these notes about one memorable night in Manhattan:

During Christmas and Easter vacations my brothers and first cousins and I would frequently stay at the 'James Hotel,' my grandparents Dr. Walter and Helen James' seven-story townhouse at 7 East Seventieth Street, two doors east of the Childs Frick home (now a Fifth Avenue museum).

The seventh floor was grandfather's medical office and laboratory lined with bookshelves topped with casts of primates shot by him in Africa in his search for the missing link to man. The third and fifth floors were bedrooms, one for servants, and others with twin rooms on the street side and twin or single on the rear

The 12-Metre *Seven Seas* on a spinnaker run, 1939.

courtyard side. The second and third floors contained a huge library on the street side, and a ballroom with a balcony for an orchestra. Ground floor was reception-sitting room street side, and spacious dining room to the rear with full-length portraits of members of the family.

Although by then buildings in this part of the city were heated by the New York steam system, the cellar held several tons of coal for a boiler and pipe-and-valve system purchased by grandfather from an ocean liner that was being scrapped. Apparently he considered the city steam unreliable, subject to strikes, etc., and wanted an in-house source of energy. This was destined to face myself and cousin Walter James with a daunting challenge on a New Year's day when staying at 7 East to attend a white-tie dinner dance.

In sub-freezing weather New Year's Day near dawn we left the dance and could not find a taxi. By happenstance we hitched a ride on a milk wagon up Park Avenue to Seventieth Street. On opening the massive, 20-foot iron-glass doors at the bottom of the stairs at 7 East, and a second set of doors at the top, we heard the sound of running water. On opening the elevator we found solid water running

down the sides of the shaft. Fortunately the service elevator was dry and took us to the seventh floor to assay the situation. The seventh floor was an inch deep in water, so in our evening clothes and pumps we accessed the roof and found water pouring out of the red cedar storage tank [most homes in those days had water tanks on the roof to provide pressure]. The overflow pipe had frozen, resulting in gallons of water pouring out the top of the tank and onto the building.

No plumbers were responding at that hour on New Year's Day, so Walt and I set out to cut off the water intake to the building. With a flashlight in one hand and a piping plan in the other we went into the cellar and combed through the maze of building plumbing, turning off what appeared to be key valves. Each time a trip to the roof was required to see if the flow was stemmed. After half a dozen tries, success was ours. The aftereffects of the flooding took days to rectify. The floors were several inches of concrete with a layer of cinders for soundproofing, and thereby waterproof, so they had to be pumped dry and the carpeting dried out. Neither Walt nor I received a bonus for the foray, but inasmuch as grandmother always supplied some lucre when we went off to parties in order to advance our prospects with the girls, we could not complain. It was her way of vicariously enjoying what we were doing.

Harry Anderson, age 18, sporting chin whiskers on board *George B. Cluett*, bound for Labrador in 1939.

The James townhouse was next door to Annie Burr Jennings' townhouse at 9 East Seventieth Street, where her famous Christmas parties were held. "The two grand dames led such busy lives," Anderson recalls, "they would communicate by turning the switch that signaled the local Western Union office to send a boy on a bicycle to pick up a telegram from Number 7 to Number 9—or vice-versa—take it back to the Western Union office and then bicycle it back to the house of the addressee."

As a one-year student at Andover, Anderson was a latecomer to student organizations. "All the good jobs were gone," he says, "like getting on the newspaper." Andover did not have a sailing team, so he played soccer and focused on getting the credits he needed for Yale. He also joined KOA, one of Andover's powerful secret societies. George H. W. Bush, who was two years behind him, was a member of a different secret society. Anderson says he only knew the future president Bush casually. Anderson was a KOA legacy via his great-uncle Oliver Gould Jennings, who had been student, trustee, and benefactor of the school. Jennings had persuaded his sister, Annie B., to donate her collection of banjo clocks and some fine ship models to the school's Addison Gallery.

KOA was located in a handsome pillared brick house built for the society by its alumni. The interior was as elegant as any big city men's club, complete with a billiard room. Old photographs indicate that the KOA house was dark paneled (partly in Hawaiian koa wood), hung with large paintings of landscapes and sailing ships, and furnished with quilted brown leather chairs and sofas. Reports of those days indicate that initiation for the secret societies often included arduous hazing. Pledges were often required to spend several nights at local cemeteries. There are stories of boys being punched and paddled, baptized in water tanks, and placed in coffins for interrogation. Two years before Anderson arrived at Andover, a pledge had died during a night of hazing. In 1943 there was another scandal related to hazing. Finally, after a pitched battle among alumni factions, in1950 Andover's secret societies were abolished.

Anderson says his KOA initiation was more benign. "One had to wear a prep cap and do chores for a senior, which ended if we won the game against Exeter," he recalls. "Fortunately, Jim Mooney was my mentor, so the chores were light and we beat our rival Exeter that year. The physical aspect was some paddling plus delivering newspapers to KOA officers, shining shoes, and memorizing doggerel. Being a senior I probably got off lighter than normal."

Given his family's longevity at Yale, attending that school was his destiny. When Anderson's nephew applied to Yale in 2005, Harry and his brother David compiled a list of 75 relatives who had gone to Yale.

Before his son set out for New Haven, Henry Anderson had a rite of passage in mind. The purpose was twofold. He thought his son had attended a sufficient number of debutante parties and fancy dances—Harry Anderson says if boys his age weren't attending at least three parties a night they were considered pikers—and there was tradition to consider: Henry Anderson's father had arranged his passage on the *Foohng Suey*, and that had been instructive. Arranging such rites for their sons was something many fathers of Henry Anderson's social standing did at that time. The value of the Strenuous Life was still prized.

Anderson first tried to book his son as crew on a German square-rigger in the Flying P Line that hauled grain between Australia and Europe. When that effort failed, he was looking for an alternative when he encountered Dr. Alexander Forbes from Harvard at a Cruising Club of America dinner. When Forbes mentioned he needed manpower for an expedition to Labrador he was mounting that summer, Henry Anderson told Forbes he had a couple hands for him.

A member of a prominent Boston Brahmin family, Alexander Forbes (1882-1965) was a physiologist, a geologist, and a cartographer who had sailed his 90-foot schooner to Cape Chidley, in the far north of Labrador, in 1931 on a mapping expedition. Three years later, he combined aerial photography with sailing. The American Geographical Society published his book, *Northernmost Labrador, Mapped from the Air*. What began as a mapping mission for Forbes at the suggestion of his friend Sir Wilfred Grenfell, who ran the well-known Grenfell Mission in Labrador, turned out to be accelerated by England's dire need for fighter planes. The object was to find a base in the far north where short-range fighters could take on fuel before they flew the shorter great-circle route across the Atlantic. Forbes documented that effort in his book, *Quest for a Northern Air Route*, which was published by Harvard University Press in 1953.

Professor Vinto Tanner of the University of Helsingfors in Finland was co-commander of the expedition. Dr. Tanner was a professor of geography, a leading authority on Norse sagas and runics, and an expert on the Lapp and Inuit cultures. He had devoted considerable study toward establishing a geological time correlation between Labrador and the Scandinavian Peninsula in the 12,000 years since the last ice age. This led to his study of currents and winds as they might have affected the early Viking and Norse explorations. The purpose of the 1939 trip was to undertake geological and botanical studies, with attention to geographical conditions, and to verify Norse landings on Labrador. The coastal islands would provide logical places to interview elders about tales handed down through generations, and to do some excavating. The expedition was a follow-up to an initial Labrador voyage Tanner had made in 1937. In the detailed, 800-page book he would write about the two trips, *Outlines of the Geography, Life and Customs of Newfoundland-Labrador*, Tanner would spend nearly 400 pages on the races of men, their ethnology, and human geography.

While the Norse had sailed along the Labrador coast in 986-87, John Cabot is credited with discovering Labrador in the late 1400s. For 500 years, explorers from Scandinavia, Portugal, England, and France had made many subsequent visits to the jagged coastline of that large, northern Canadian province, which would measure more than 10,000 miles if straightened out. By the mid-1930s, Labrador had been mapped with some accuracy. But geographically, oceanographically, and anthropologically, the surface had barely been scratched.

Anderson left for Labrador in June 1939, three days after graduating from Andover.

His second cousin, John Nash, had also been booked on the trip by *his* father. With them were two other boys joining Tanner's expedition, George Peabody and Peter Gilman. The four sailed north aboard a Grand Banks fishing schooner that had been retired because it leaked so badly. It was hauling cargo up the coast for the Grenfell Mission, which had been started in 1892 to improve the plight of the coastal inhabitants and fishermen of Labrador and Newfoundland. "Most people think Grenfell was taking care of the Eskimos," Anderson says. "In truth he was taking care of the white residents, mostly Scots. The Indians were only on the coast in the summer when they came to sell skins." By the 1930s, Grenfell had established hospitals, schools, and even an orphanage. His mission initiated work projects and conducted social work.

The old schooner was the 140-foot, Lunenburg-built *George B. Cluett II*. It departed the Boston Army Base on June 24, bound for Lunenburg, Nova Scotia, the first leg in the passage to St. Anthony, Newfoundland, where it would rendezvous with the expedition's vessel, *Strathcona II*. Since *Cluett* was not insured or inspected, it could not carry passengers for hire. The boys were signed on as crew, and paid fifty cents a day. Anderson, as always, compiled a log of the trip:

Cluett *was in bad need of overhauling (scheduled for a year or two from now to mend some bad planks, rotten bulwarks); carried loose-footed jib, staysail, foresail and triangular main cut to clear deck cargo and black from diesel exhaust. Cargo below of fertilizer, hay, etc. On deck oil drums, crates of hens (live), hogsheads of water (one undrinkable), 2 huskies. Nothing to make one feel more at sea than the smell and cackle of fowls and the barking of dogs.*

Captain Iverson's father had made his pile cod fishing off the banks in the heydays before the depression; Capt. Iverson himself had made his running rum and evading the Revenue cutters, the Cluett *still bearing bullet holes in the cabin house from those days.*

Charlie, the cook, was a hunchback by reason of having been standing on a pier as a young man when a cargo sling let go overhead. Fortunately the planks of the pier were rotten so that cargo and Charlie went through and he suffered only a broken back. . . . One night he came close to another severe accident when the coal-burning stove fell through the cabin sole—fortunately on an even keel. His sense of hygiene was unique. Before cooking he would dab a drop of essence of perfume (extremely expensive stuff on which he had spent, years before, some of his rum-running earnings) in each armpit.

The mate was a burly chap. He delighted in plucking a freshly laid egg from one of our crated hens, biting off the end, and sucking it down in one swallow. Of scientific bent, he frequently experimented with the hens, determined to find out whether they could swim, by dropping one overboard. The fog made his experiments difficult to assess.

The fare was less than fair in either sense of the word. Salt cod three times a day with Charlie's toast (he'd made it at home and brought it on board in an onion sack) and java with a dollop of condensed milk—the skipper sent forward daily from the stores one can for the entire fo'c's'l' for the day.

The head was a "gunch house" the name for a sea-going "Chic Sale." Lashed to the port rail

The crew of the Tanner Labrador Expedition aboard *S/S Strathcona* in 1939. Alexander Forbes is at left front, next to V. Tanner (hatless). John Nash is far right, second row. Harry Anderson is just behind Nash, under the furled sail.

forward, it had under the seat a scoop leading overboard. In heavy weather when on the port tack the scoop pointed skyward rendering it useless, whereas on starboard tack it periodically would scoop up sea resulting in salt water douche. The case of the huskies was even more constricting as they had been house broken not to foul their cages. On being let out after 36 hours they hastened to relieve themselves—guess where—on the halyards coiled at the foot of the main and foremasts.

[The third day] we had 35 knots NE and turned and sailed before the wind (100 stokes of the pump per hour and bald-headed with cutaway main and the chicken coops awash could not make progress against the NEaster.)

[The fourth day] Passed into the long channel entrance into Lunenburg in pea soup fog and flat calm at night—for two hours was at the helm as Skipper yelled course changes—swung to north and let her shoot as engine was killed—glided toward distant twinkling lights into a dock—still and cool and fresh in fog and night darkness—catted anchor caught on a piling and almost decapitated two huskies.

For two days stayed at Ich Dein Hotel (no bunks available on board now that no watches being stood). George discovered egress and ingress quicker using the rope ladder fire escape. Hired car and toured countryside.

A few days later, *Cluett* set sail for St. Anthony near the northern tip of Newfoundland and met Tanner's 150-foot *Strathcona*, which was powered by a triple-expansion steam engine. It also had steadying sails. There were a few other scientists among the party, including palynologist Carl-Gosta Wenner who studied pollen as a way to identify time periods and the existence of various flora. The objective of Wenner's mission was to learn more about events in the area since the culmination of the ice age, since which the ocean levels had risen.

"The levels rose in a series of steps," Anderson says. "The scientists' instruments would be using measured vertical angles. You find sea level by studying the barnacles. They have to be wet 50 percent of the time. You go out in a dory and find the highest barnacle you can find, and that's half tide. You can calculate sea level from that."

Alexander Forbes would only stay a few days on the trip. Before he was to join *Strathcona II* in St. Anthony, Forbes and a pilot had departed in a float plane for Hamilton Inlet, Labrador, 300 miles north of Newfoundland. On the way out they blew a cylinder and had to make a forced landing. "We waited two days for them," Anderson says, "and Tanner said if they didn't show up soon we'd have to head north. The season was so short that every day was precious."

They turned up. A fishing boat had found them. But without the plane, which was his adjunct to the expedition, Forbes went home."

Anderson and his five young shipmates were called WOPs (work without pay), and provided the grunt labor on the trip. Grunt they did, lugging scientific gear ashore and setting it up, hauling water for the boiler in dories, chopping wood, and joining scientists on reconnaissance trips ashore. They wore sealskin boots with sewn canvas tops, gloves with canvas cuffs, and belts around their midriffs to prevent flies and mosquitoes from getting in. They wore hats draped with mosquito netting. *Strathcona II* had an Inuit pilot on board because many of the bays they entered had not been mapped. "His name was Simon Lusick," Anderson recalls. "He'd been at the Chicago World's Fair in 1893. He was asked how he liked it. He said, 'You got a good country. Me, I got syphilis.' "

Anderson's log documents the arduous days on board *Strathcona II*, where the accommodations were considerably more confined than on *Cluett*.

[June 1939] Went ashore and climbed hill into next valley with [W]enner. Lake mis-charted, forced to walk a long ways through swamp and thick trees. Mosquitoes and black flies unbearable. Green head net useless as flies bite

and crawl through. [W]enner said George would throw himself into the swamp and roll over and over and scream under circumstances like this. Your scribe badly chewed by black flies. . . . Late in evening reached town of Nain, where the huskies howl, the church bell rings and the mosquitos bite. . . . George made inquiries as to getting home and finally received permission to go on the coastal steamer Winifred Lee, *which had just come in. . . . He did not seem sorry to depart. . . .*

Made a stop at which both [W]enner and Tanner surveyed, each at a different spot. [W]enner was deliberate, much to his satisfaction and Tanner's annoyance. Hard work to get the dory off the beach. . . .

In afternoon all hands made sorties to the other side of Sculpin Island with supper, spades and countless tripods. At great length and detail measured and staked out in archeological fashion the foundations of houses. . . . The lead to the diggings was via a tale passed down from generation to generation of Inuit (Eskimo) about a tribe of large persons who inhabited the coastal islands and occasionally raided the Inuit settlements. It was thought this might be related to a Norse settlement which would be identifiable by the presence of charcoal which they brought with them for cooking with metal utensils as distinguished from the Inuit who used blubber and seal or whalebone utensils. No sign of charcoal, however. . . .

Surf rolling in on rocks made for ticklish rowing. Tanner thought the specimens we had collected were wrong, so we took him ashore. He picked a poor spot. We landed on rocks, and receding surf nearly tipped us over. His samples were the same as ours. . . .

House Island. Huge iceberg grounded outside the sand bluff protecting the harbor. . . .

Evening found us looking for an anchorage in Mudford Tickle (tickles are narrow, usually winding; rattles are even tighter, with more current and navigational hazards and choke points). Sheer 1,000 foot cliffs, rough and jagged, rising from both sides of the passage. . . . Gulls wheeling, sea pigeons floating below the cliffs like drops of water from a falls, and a sunset for which words are wanting. Northern lights galore—backdrop, footlights, and limelights all in the stage set. . . .

July. John Nash and I scuttled ashore and scaled the shale slopes to the 3,750 foot peak which towered over the ship. . . . Later, driven underway by mosquitoes, we roused two hawks. The descent, made by hurling our gear down before us, was at great risk—down for a long stretch by bracing back, arms, and knees against the side of the rock chimney while the hawks

did plunging dives toward us. Arrived on board in the evening. Loaded one doryful of fresh water collected from falls to complete the filling of the boilers which had been blown out with alkali. Rowing a dory full of fresh water out through salt water is paradoxical. We would row the dories to the beach with the 25-gallon wooden barrels that held our fresh water for drinking, cooking, washing, and fill them under the falls. Next we would pour the water into the dory until the freeboard was down to a few inches. One would sit in the water and row the dory to the vessel where the water would be bucketed out and poured into the boilers—an arduous and awkward process. . . .

[W]enner missing. John and I haul water while others took motorboat and searched for him. [Wenner found.] He simply miscalculated his time and had gotten caught in the dark. The night had been cold and he soon developed a brief cold. Actually Tanner had allotted 48 hours to find him to avoid being trapped in developing ice. . . .

While [W]enner slept and Tanner surveyed, we chopped wood at breakneck pace. Sweat poured off us. In desperation I took a swim and changed winter underwear for the first time since leaving Boston. Diving overside amidship I came to the surface and did not (could not) take a breath until I climbed up the boarding ladder, a tortuous process. . . .

Hopedale. Loaded coal by derrick and motorboat from 1600 until midnight. Long, dirty, black job. Heavy work. 145 and 200 lb bags. Sometimes Hudson Bay Co. would dump 250 pound sacks of coal on some rock at the entrance to a harbor. We'd put that in the dory, row it out, hoist it on deck. Loaded water. [W]enner late for start. An hour out had to return to pick up [W]enner's drill bag. Tanner and [W]enner furious at each other. . . .

Expedition was underfinanced with respect to being able to purchase coal, hence all the wood chopping. The same goes for food. Once or twice a week we heaved to and all hands jigged for cod fish. The cook varied the menu, fried cod for breakfast; boiled cod for luncheon; cod with brains, tongues and livers for dinner. One Sunday everyone set to shooting seagulls. A couple were bagged and served up for lunch under the guise of ocean turkey—the only attempt to try and make this oderiferous bird reeking of dead fish, edible.

In August, on the way back to St. Anthony, Tanner got word that war was about to break out in Europe. Not only was Tanner well known for his academic and scientific prowess, he had formerly served in the foreign offices of Finland and the USSR. At Cartwright, a whaling center, he encountered a Scandinavian skipper with a shortwave radio, and heard from well-informed associates in Europe that war would commence within a few days of Labor Day. Tanner considered the information reliable enough to alter course directly for St. Anthony. From there he and Wenner would take *Strahcona II* to St. John's and hope to get home with the samples and specimens they had collected before hostilities commenced. "As we were later to find when we returned home," Anderson wrote, "in Labrador we had received information to which neither the State Department nor Whitehall were privy."

There was time for a brief two-boat party when they encountered *George B. Cluett* moored next to the passenger vessel *New Northland* at a stop on the way to St. Anthony, but the war news had floated a cloud of anxiety over *Strathcona II*. It was one more thing for Tanner and Wenner to debate while juggling plans. "We are afraid," Anderson wrote, "war will break out in a few hours. Quickly we secured passage for ourselves on *Northland*, packed all Tanner's gear and research equipment, loaded both Tanner and Wenner aboard another boat, the *Kyle*, loaded our stuff in a rush, said good-bye and barely made the *Northland*. It was August 29."

The bad news was that while passage on *Northland* cost half the price of *Kyle* for the trip to Boston ($21), the boys got what they paid for. "Our quarters," Anderson wrote, "were one-quarter the size of

Strathcona's and one-tenth the size of *Cluett*'s, without ventilation and with only one dim light. They consisted of three triple-decker pipe berths with steel slats for mattresses and so placed as to give room for only one person to move in and about the quarters at a time. All our 37 pieces of luggage stayed in the passageway. Our ticket did not include meals, which cost an additional 53 cents each. We were short of funds, so discovering that the night galley cook enjoyed having someone to talk with, we took turns on successive nights engaging him in conversation in haltering French and coaxing him to cook up a huge pot of tea and enough sandwiches to take us all through breakfast and lunch until we could blow ourselves to supper."

The good news was that Sir Wilfred Grenfell was on board, and eager to meet a group of Tanner's WOPs. It was against regulations for steerage passengers to mix with cabin class, so Grenfell went below and ate with the boys in steerage. "It was interesting," Anderson wrote, "listening to him tell about the early days on Labrador and how, in the first *Strathcona,* they hit an iceberg the first day out, holed her and she sank. Later, a costume party was being planned for the passengers, so several ladies came below to find out if we had some clothing they could borrow. This led to a couple of widows inviting us up to the bar late at night to slake our thirst."

Anderson sent his cousin John Nash a copy of his Labrador log a few years ago. In a letter of thanks, Nash quipped, "I don't remember you keeping such a detailed account of our trip. Were you doing it while I was doing your work?" Nash clearly remembered the cook aboard *Cluett*. "I remember how that dirty old cook, Charlie, made his bread. He would mold the dough in a battered old pan, take the pan with him to his upper bunk, place it between his legs, and pull a dirty old blanket over it. That is how he raised the dough. . . . I also remember you trading your long johns which you had worn all summer to an Eskimo for a seal skin which he had slept on for God only knows how long. . . . An event you did not mention was your thought about buying a small sailboat in Lunenburg and the two of us sailing back to Boston. . . . I don't believe," Nash concludes, "I have ever worked so hard before or since, and under such adverse conditions."

By the time they reached Quebec the boys had had their fill of steerage life. They jumped ship, spent a night in Quebec, took a train to Montreal the next day, and finally the sleeper to New York. Anderson says they must have had the train fare wired to them. But they arrived home "without a sou."

COLLEGE HAD TO BE on the dull side, or perhaps a relief, after such a rugged summer. But there was sailing. The Yale Corinthian Yacht Club (YCYC) had been established in 1881, just ten years after the Seawanhaka Corinthian and Eastern Yacht Clubs were founded. In 1894, Yale sailors raced against Harvard (who else?) on the Thames River in New London following the Yale-Harvard crew race (crew being the oldest intercollegiate sport), thereby staking claim to holding the first-ever intercollegiate regatta. The boats were 40-footers on loan from the families of students. "My grandfather was commodore of the Yale Corinthian Yacht Club in the 1890s," Anderson says. "There was something like 15 yachts in the 50-foot range that undergraduates had when they were at college—very different from the dinghy sailing of today. I suppose World War I pretty much finished that off."

Two years later Yale had one of the earliest one-design fleets, New Haven 21-foot dinghies. Other types of dinghies came and went, until World War I focused attention elsewhere. But sailing had taken hold in the Ivy League. Harvard sailors included Franklin Delano Roosevelt, Samuel Eliot Morison, and Harold S. Vanderbilt.

The Intercollegiate Yacht Racing Association (ICYRA) was born in 1928, thanks to Yale freshman Briggs Cunningham. As a Yale student and sailor, Cunningham promoted the idea of a regatta involving Harvard, Yale, and Princeton after the school year ended. There was no end of sailing talent among the Ivy League schools, so Cunningham's idea was well received. Invitations were sent out, a trophy was donated, the regatta turned out to be the first of a series, and the nucleus of the Intercollegiate Yacht Racing Association was formed.

Eleven years later, in his freshman year at Yale, Anderson recalls that the Yale Corinthian Yacht Club had a few Class X dinghies that were kept under the New Haven Yacht Club on the eastern shore of New Haven Harbor. When he returned sophomore year, the boats had disappeared. It turned out they were owned by seniors who took them home when they graduated. Yale sailed at Milford, Connecticut, in those days, a half-hour drive west along the coast. The combination of the drive, plus the uncertainty of available boats in addition to their upkeep, and all the other rigmarole of sailboat racing (the need for a chase boat for setting course marks and aiding the race boats, a race committee, and some sort of starting sequence) required high degrees of enthusiasm and creativity from participants.

"We had no club boats, no boathouse, no lunching site," Anderson says. "But our teams were hand-picked; we had plenty of talent from which to choose. All racing took place weekends at other colleges and service academies." Some of the regattas were quite elegant. Anderson was on the team that went to the first regatta held in 44-foot yawls at the US Naval Academy. And in his sophomore year he was crewing in the ICYRA national championships that were held at Marblehead in the International One Design (IOD) Class, lovely 33-footers on loan from local owners. Yale lost to Dartmouth by one point. Dartmouth's skipper was Emil "Bus" Mosbacher, who would go on to win eight IOD season championships, the 1959 Southern Ocean Racing Circuit, two America's Cups, and be selected for the initial class of the National Sailing Hall of Fame. Seventy years later, Anderson grimaces and his moustache twitches rapidly when he talks about losing to Mosbacher and Dartmouth.

The summer after his sophomore year, Anderson crewed aboard the 12-Metre *Seven Seas*, under charter to the father of George Nichols Jr. Among the crew was a Seawanhaka sailing contemporary, Eric Olsen, with whom Anderson would enter into a business partnership in the 1960s. Also on board was another Seawanhaka sailor his age, Hutchinson "Hutchie" DuBosque, who

would win the hand of Marion Johnson.

Beating into Camden Harbor, Maine, in 20 knots of wind, *Seven Seas* picked up a lobster pot buoy that wrapped itself around the propeller. After executing a difficult dock landing under sail in a lot of wind, they lay alongside a large ferry pier while cutting it free. Anderson recalls asking a man standing on the pier when the next ferry was due in. The man said he didn't know. Anderson asked when the last ferry came in. "'Bout a year ago."

Later, at anchor, with a celebration going on ashore, Anderson made these notes:

> *In the swathe of the lowering sun with the fitful gusts of wind there sighs the swell of voices singing a national song or communal hymn. In a land of rocks and forest—storms and seas—where people garner a slim livelihood in their struggle against the elements, life means loneliness and isolation. Wind and sun measure time, for man's own creation is too artificial to withstand the demands of natural forces. A storm means delay of days, a run of mackerel means days of fishing—one's actions must be attuned to the varying moods of nature rather than to the automaton of a time-tick.*
>
> *Distance and isolation make man dependent on his neighbor and thankful for his own*

preservation. The community means fellowship and security in the face of the warring elements. In distress it bands together; in success it joins in giving thanks.

This evening, the sincerity and measure of human values of the lonely dweller, of the man who knows both sunrise and sunset, is reflected in the rough but hearty hymns in celebration of the 150th anniversary of the founding of Camden.

So endeth this day on which we navigated across Penobscot Bay by celestial, crossing moon and sun lines—a rare opportunity for finding out where you are by looking at where you aren't.

(signed) HA—a Yale sophomore

One morning a few days later, Anderson recalls that his cousin, Walt James, came running out of the head during breakfast shouting "fire!" "We had all been brought up not to stuff toilet paper in the bowl," Anderson says, "since heads in those days were more prone to jam, but to toss it in and light it with a match to reduce the wastage. But the toilet seat was made of flammable plastic, which in Walt's case caught fire. It was easily put out, but we spent the rest of the cruise on a charred seat."

Anderson regularly sailed on the 12-Metre

Seven Seas during his summer vacations from Yale. *Seven Seas* was Commodore Van S. Merle-Smith's flagship. Anderson and other young crew members would drive to the New York Yacht Club station at Glen Cove, Long Island, where members' yachts would be moored for the week, and take *Seven Seas* across the Sound to Larchmont with the paid hands. "Father, Bob Meyer, Sr., with Commodore Merle-Smith came from town on his commuter, *Nancy Pat*, changed into yachting clothes and had a quick sandwich before going out to the starting line. Commodore Harry Morgan would do likewise except he arrived by seaplane. After the race we would all steam back to Seawanhaka on *Nancy Pat* with Commodore Merle-Smith. The trip was so fast there was only time for one drink. There would be a stop at the Club for more drinks, then we were delivered to our respective docks."

With more than 10 privately owned 12 Metres sailing in those years, the class had its own start at the big race weeks like the one hosted by the Larchmont Yacht Club. *Northern Light* (US-14), designed by Sparkman & Stephens in 1938, was Merle-Smith's second 12. Briggs Cunningham owned *Nyala* (US-12), also designed by Sparkman & Stephens in 1938. Anderson raced on *Vim* (US-15), which Harold "Mike" Vanderbilt had built in 1939. Vanderbilt had been a frequent visitor to

Anderson's family home in Oyster Bay since Harry Anderson was a boy. And Rod Stephens, Vanderbilt's regular deck boss on *Vim*, was so often a visitor at Handy Hill that his toothbrush was a permanent fixture in the guest bathroom.

Mike Vanderbilt and Rod Stephens. It would be difficult for any current racing sailor to come up with more enticing objects of time travel than those two legends. Harry Anderson was there. Mike Vanderbilt's three America's Cup wins at a time when grand-prix yachting was worthy of a *Time* magazine cover story, piled more accolades upon one of the country's most prominent family names. Railroad magnate and champion bridge player, Vanderbilt also invented a popular contract bridge "convention." He also took the lead in rewriting——with Harry Anderson's father and Commodore Merle-Smith——the Racing Rules of Sailing, a task that took more than thirty years from start to world-wide acceptance.

When Anderson began racing on *Vim*, he learned to appreciate firsthand why Rod Stephens was so revered as a sailor. "If you never sailed with Rod," Anderson said at a dinner in honor of the Stephens brothers at the New York Yacht Club in 1977, "you have missed what can best be described as a form of continuing education in how to do it inculcated through convincing suggestion resulting in willing compliance. Rod's

implementation of hull and rig speed from Olin's drawings has stood the club in good stead over the years in defense of the America's Cup, and has provided a graduate school education in the marine field for countless helmsmen and crews.

"The two of them together were a study in being meticulous," Anderson said in an oral history interview at Mystic Seaport in 1990.

They would do things like practice jibing the spinnaker downwind, jibe after jibe after jibe. Rod would time the movements of each of the crew. Just like plotting the movements of a factor, or working up a play, he would retrace and cut down the steps each man would take. Sometimes he would reduce the time by 30 seconds. Before long, the whole maneuver had been speeded up.

I learned a lot about the trim of spinnakers from Rod. He was quiet, intense, serious. He had it timed by stopwatch how long it took him to get from his office at Sparkman & Stephens to Grand Central Station for his train. Rod had a black book. Every time we set the mains'l he'd write down the temperature and the humidity, how far we pulled out the foot and stretched the luff. Before the start he'd send me below to make sure the toilet seats were down to lower the center of gravity. When in a tacking duel, he noticed the paid hands on the other boat

*threw their cigarettes overboard when a tack
was called, so we'd watch for that and be ready.*

*One afternoon when Rod was sailing on the J-
Class* Ranger *in 1937. The mast top catch-pin
for engaging the headboard failed to work. Rod
went aloft in a bosun's chair and shinnied the
last part of the climb to the top—150-feet off
the water—with a replacement pin between his
teeth. He was seasick, but never dropped the pin.*

When I was in college, I raced on Vim *in the
American Yacht Club series followed by the New
York Yacht Club series. That year we ended up
in Marblehead for a week of match racing
between* Vim *(Marblehead's Eastern Yacht
Club), and* Northern Light *(Seawanhaka).*

Junior and senior year Anderson served as
rear commodore of the Yale Corinthian Yacht
Club. "Most of our time," Anderson says,
"was spent walking the waterfront from New
Haven to New London eastwards, and from
Milford westwards searching for a location
for sailing at Yale." He would finally find a
location, but it would take many years.

Academics were almost as important as sailing
to Anderson at Yale. "Sailors" are traditionally
thought of as an unruly lot for their pursuit of
good times and debauchery after doing battle
with unruly vessels on unrelenting seas. From
Shakespeare on, the sailor in literature has
been associated with strong drink, gaudy
tattoos, and general unaccountability. While
he is not tattooed, Anderson has never been
adverse to strong drink. Mory's Temple Bar in
New Haven was only the first of many friendly
bars he got to know so well. But by all accounts
he was one of those involved students who
fully embraced the subjects he studied, when
they engaged him. A scholar long before he
arrived at Yale, he approached academia the
same way he tackled any challenge, from
canoeing and woodsmanship to tennis, sailing,
and seamanship: with curiosity, determination,
satisfaction—and success.

Anderson was a professor's dream, a
student who always wanted to go beyond
the classroom, find out more. During his
senior year at Yale, he and a group of five
other students hired a Russian Orthodox
priest to teach them Russian language and
history (Yale had no Russian course available
at the time). The boys met with the priest, a
former Cossack, for two hours twice a week.

Since Anderson had taken Latin all four years
at Yale, culminating that study with a course in
Roman Law seemed logical. That course met
Saturday mornings at 8:00 a.m., a schedule
that had other Yale seniors rolling their eyes in
disbelief. Saturday classes? Most seniors didn't
schedule any classes on Fridays so they'd have
longer weekends.

The 12-Metre *Vim*, 1939.

Harold S. "Mike" Vanderbilt at the wheel
of the J-Class sloop, *Ranger*, 1939.

Roman Law was not offered in the catalog, but a Professor Bellinger in the Classics Department offered to teach it if at least six students signed up for it. It had not been offered since Bellinger had taken the course from Yale President Arthur Twining Hadley when Bellinger was an undergraduate. In a note of advice and counsel to his nephew Ross Anderson when that young man entered Yale in 2005, Anderson wrote:

The [Roman Law] course was further distinguished by the Justinian Code—the main body of law developed during the period of the Roman Republic and codified under Emperor Justinian during the time of Imperial Rome, and which formed the basis of the Napoleonic Code that applies in Western Europe, the State of Louisiana, and Puerto Rico, settled under French and Iberian influence. It was never translated into English. Hence, there were no "trots," which meant genuine application of one's mind further exacerbated by the lack of texts available. There were two in the reference room of the Sterling Library, and one in the Law School Library, so sometimes it meant waiting in line to access one or studying late at night. I found that I could accomplish twice as much studying in an hour between five AM and breakfast as I could in an hour between 10 PM and midnight; the mind is fresher and translating and mathematical problems are resolved with

greater alacrity. I doubt you view this schedule with enthusiasm, but try it.

No doubt that gave young Ross Anderson something to contemplate as he perused the Yale course catalog.

His uncle went on: "Do not underestimate the high level of Roman Culture and system of government; one professor used to maintain that the leading poets in the history of the world were chronologically Lesbia, Horace, Catullus, Goethe, Shakespeare, Shelley, Keats, and Wordsworth. `Nota Bene,' I am working on a paper re-affirming—in the face of many theoretical revisionists claiming that Shakespeare's plays and sonnets were written by a consortium as he did not have the education or background to have been able to do so solo—that Shakespeare was indeed the only author of works so signed."

He also offered his nephew a bit of history, and a dollop of political philosophy.

In my day, with war on the horizon, a piece of legislation that was to be critical to the role of the USA in WWII was up for renewal in Washington—the universal conscription bill. It was in jeopardy of not being renewed [it was renewed, in 1941, by one vote] inasmuch as the prevailing sentiment in the 1930s was isolationist, favoring high tariffs and pacifism.

The latter was partly fueled by Communist (Russian) money in support of the distribution of pacifist periodicals in the high schools, and of socialist cells in the colleges under the guise of the Student Unions, and a general disillusionment over the capitalist system as a result of the depression. Several seniors, including Kingman Brewster, who became President of Yale in the 1960s and was a close friend . . . George Bundy and others who later rose to high government posts were circulating a petition in favor of renewal which provided the opportunity for us lowly freshmen to meet some of the BMOC (big men on campus) seniors.

Anderson still has his final Roman Law exam from 1942 filed away with care. Here is Question V: "A and B have land on opposite banks of a river. An Island forms equidistant from the banks. A plants three apple trees, one in the exact center of the island, one on the bank on each side. B gives X the usufruct on his land. What action has A if X – (a) picks up the apples that have fallen; (b) picks the apples from the trees; (c) ties boats to the trees on the banks; (d) cuts the trees down."

At Yale, Anderson lived at Pierson College, a hotbed for international relations students at the time thanks to its master, Arnold Wolfers. "He was a proponent of the theory that history is influenced by great men who appear on the scene," Anderson recalls, "or who are elevated by crisis, often by happenstance. Another prestigious presence was Professor Nicholas Spykeman of Holland, an early advocate of the 'power political' concept, under which politics, economics, natural resources, and geographical positions keep nations in constant competition, and the ultimate struggle erupts from time to time in warfare."

Anderson says one seminar he attended met in the professor's living room with the man's Afghan hound curled up in front of the fireplace. An English major, he gravitated to Yale's Elizabethan Club, founded in 1911 "to provide a forum for undergraduate discussions on literature and art, and to offer a congenial environment for social and intellectual interaction between junior and senior members of the University," according to Stephen Parks, for many years the club's librarian. The Elizabethan Club was the idea of Yale alumnus Alexander Smith Cochran, a Yonkers, New York, carpet manufacturer who owned the famous schooner *Westward*. Cochran founded the club with the donation of a house, a $100,000 endowment, and his "important" collection of early English literature because he said what he missed most as a Yale undergraduate was good conversation. Fifteen undergraduates are elected to the club from each class each year. Tea is served every day with a different kind of sandwich on a rotating, seven-day schedule.

Anderson frequented the Elizabethan Club on a regular basis as a student, and, as with so many of his early associations, his connection to the place has been lifelong. A note he wrote to Stephen Parks in 2005 reveals scholarly aspects of the club that he enjoyed: "I recall the presence of Professor Eugene M. Waith who was my advisor for my major in English. In my files is a letter from him in 1989 in response to my aim to view all of the contemporary portraits extant of Elizabeth I, an aim not yet achieved." Anderson happily recalls the club's simple pleasures: "the clay-stemmed pipes of the members in the overhead rack, the special tobacco shipped from Canada complementing the special teas that are still served today, the floor that creaked causing the teacups to rattle."

As always, family entered the picture. "Joining the Lizzie," Anderson wrote to Parks, "put me in touch with my cousin by marriage one generation removed, Wilmarth (Lefty) Lewis, who married a niece of my great aunt Annie Burr Jennings. Aunt Annie was a close friend of Yale Professor William Lyon Phelps, who wrote *What I Like in Poetry* she once gave as Christmas presents. . . . Coincidently, I knew in connection with sailing the late Drayton Cochran, son of the founder of the Lizzie, but never ascertained whether he was ever a member."

He only took one graduate course in his time at Yale, the subject of which was the tying of fishing flies. It was taught by the head of off-campus sports, and it met one evening a week. "The final test was a matter of art," Anderson says. "In those days one could purchase the scruff of a Chinese hen or rooster. Why Chinese? Because scratching for worms was tougher in China, making the hairs tougher and stiffer."

In addition to sailing, Anderson was on Yale's pistol team as both shooter and manager. He says it was most fun competing against the service academies, where the pistol matches were held shoulder to shoulder, with members of each team positioned alternatively on the firing line so that one had an "enemy" on each side. "This heightened the tension considerably, as well as the decibel level."

Anderson was also in the Reserve Officers' Training Corps (ROTC). He says his father's advice for Yale was to join ROTC, given that war was imminent; to learn boxing; and to make sure he took a course in either The Age of Johnson, or nineteenth-century Romantic poets, both taught by Professor Chauncey Brewster Tinker, under whom his father had studied in 1919. Tinker was the person who had found the Boswell papers in a croquet bench on the grounds of Malahide Castle in the outskirts of Dublin. (James Boswell was the author of the classic biography, *The Life of Samuel Johnson*.) "A rather stern and taciturn man," Anderson says. "Tinker was unable to integrate himself (socially) so he was rebuffed by the matron of the Castle when he attempted to obtain or purchase the papers." A more gregarious member of the Yale English Department successfully handled that task.

"Advice from father amounted to a command," Anderson says. "Two-thirds of the advice worked out well. The boxing was short-lived. Despite the directives couched as friendly advice, the strict Victorian family regimen, and the quasi-military upbringing with its razor strop whippings, father was proud of his sons even though he never explicitly said so. I learned that from mother. He was even prouder when all three of us joined the armed services."

In college—in fact in all his life—Anderson always made time for adventure. In the summer of 1941, before his junior year, he and a couple of friends drove out to Sequoia National Park in California for a camping trip. They packed to economize, with tents, sleeping bags, and cooking equipment lashed to gates on the running board of Anderson's 1938 Chevrolet. Somewhere in Ohio they stopped for the night, set up camp in a field, and fired up the grill. Not long after their hamburgers began cooking, they were attacked by a bunch of hogs from a nearby

farm that had sniffed the aromas and broken out. "We scrambled," Anderson says. "One fellow climbed on the roof of the car. We didn't do much camping after that."

They had planned to stay overnight in Santa Fe, New Mexico. After a bad thunderstorm, they drove to a plateau for a look at the city. Spying a rabbit, Anderson pulled out his pistol and took a shot at it. Suddenly the lights of a car hidden in the darkness came on revealing other cars and a group of men involved in monkey business of some sort. "We had to assume something illicit was going on," Anderson says. "Maybe they thought we were revenuers. We were turning to leave when they fired a shot at us. We fired a shot back. We had no idea what we were getting into. They chased us on the highway back to town. There's a big square in the middle of Santa Fe. We ducked off the road around the square into a side lane, came out on the other side, and kept going."

For Harry Anderson, getting shot at was a portent of things to come.

In Sequoia, Anderson recalls fishing for golden trout, so named for the color the fish take on from the bottom coloring of the Kern River. Many years later, when he would have the duty of hosting President Eisenhower during an America's Cup race, fishing for golden trout would put him a leg up on the president, who in all his fishing experience had never had that privilege.

Driving back, the boys took the northern route so they could visit the Bonneville Salt Flats west of Salt Lake City, Utah. Anderson wanted to try out his Chevy on the famous speed course. The speedway runs northwest/southeast, so they took a shortcut off the highway and broke through the salt crust that gets thinner toward the edge, like ice on a lake. Working in 110-degree heat on the flats, the boys unloaded the car, then jacked it up and stacked salt chunks under the wheels. By repeating the process several times, they were able to push the car out of the soft area and get to the speed course.

Back in New Haven, Anderson attended a talk by First Lady Eleanor Roosevelt. She had stayed overnight in the visitor's suite at Pierson College, and spoke the next morning in the Chi Psi fraternity's large meeting room. Anderson doesn't recall the subject of her talk. "She ran a daily column on home and other topics," he says, "and was known as 'fuzzy brained Eleanor.'" Halfway into her talk, an aid approached Mrs. Roosevelt and handed her a piece of paper. She paused briefly, looked at it, and continued speaking. Twenty minutes later, she concluded her remarks. After acknowledging the applause, Mrs. Roosevelt indicated the slip of paper she had been given and told her stunned audience she had been informed that Pearl Harbor had been attacked by the Japanese. It was December 7, 1941.

SIX | War

T
hanks to his association with Professor Tanner during the Labrador expedition, Harry had early warning about the imminence of World War II. Tanner's information turned out to be accurate. Anderson returned from Labrador in mid-August 1939. Germany invaded Poland two weeks later on September first, just before he began his freshman year at Yale. He joined ROTC, as his father had advised. As a commissioned officer in training, he followed the mounting conflict in Europe with keen interest. A year later, with the passing of the Selective Training and Service Act, the first peacetime draft in US history, millions more men between 18 and 45 were suddenly very interested in what was transpiring in Europe.

The war's escalation was anything but subtle. In the spring of 1941, America's neutrality was tested with the sinking of a US warship by a German submarine, causing President Franklin Roosevelt to declare an "unlimited national emergency." An oil embargo on the Axis countries followed that summer. A portent of the inevitability of war was the signing, by Roosevelt and Winston Churchill, of the Atlantic Charter in August 1941, which specified postwar Allied goals. After a second US warship was attacked by a German U-boat, Roosevelt issued a shoot-on-sight order for Axis ships sighted in US waters. Another torpedoing in October that year resulted in the first American deaths associated with the war (11 were killed). In November the US Navy took command of the Coast Guard. The day after Pearl Harbor, the United States officially declared war.

The response of Yale and other universities was to compress their schedules. Anderson's class would be the first to lose its summer vacation to the classroom, and graduate in December 1942, instead of the following June. Final exams were taken, but senior theses were waived. There was no time.

Second Lieutenant Harry H. Anderson Jr.

At Yale, dorm space had been allotted to the V7 Naval Reserve Officer training program. Anderson and his fellow ROTC mates went home for Christmas. On January first they took a train to Oklahoma City and a local to Ft. Sill. All were given the rank of corporal because they hadn't satisfied their senior year summer camp requirement. At Ft. Sill, they would go through three months of Officer Candidate School consisting of fieldwork and class training. "There were no uniforms for us," Anderson recalls. "The first couple weeks we were in tweeds. In the middle of winter we were on this high hill conducting artillery fire in our tweeds. It was cold as blazes."

Different schools with ROTC units had different specialties. At Yale it had always been artillery. Anderson's father had been in the Yale Battery. In Harry Anderson's day, ROTC students became familiar with the 75 mm howitzer, a popular infantry support weapon that could fire high-explosive shells a distance of seven miles. "The ones we had at Yale were left over from World War I," Anderson says. "They had wooden wheels and were horse-drawn. If you went out for polo at Yale you didn't have to have a horse. You used the Army's horses. By sophomore year, our howitzers got rubber tires. We didn't have live rounds. They used to take us out to the harbor entrance and simulate firing on German submarines, which never ventured that far."

Figuring they would be running up to Oklahoma City from Ft. Sill on weekends, Anderson and his classmates brought liquor with them and stashed it at the hotel before they left for Ft. Sill (Oklahoma City was dry). They needn't have bothered. In three months not one weekend pass was issued. But after three months they were pronounced second lieutenants in the US Army. Anderson was one of the few not assigned to a military unit. Because of his high grades in both classroom and in the field, he was asked to stay at Ft. Sill as an instructor in gunnery and survey operations. Survey is the essence of artillery, with transit and traverse being used to locate targets (observation posts, gun positions, etc.) in connection with the control of firing

Inductees in the Yale class of 1942 for Cannon & Castle, the honorary military society. Anderson is second from right, back row.

batteries. At Ft. Sill, gunnery training included a brand new weapon, the bazooka, a handheld, anti-tank rocket launcher fired from a man's shoulder, which went into production in 1942.

Yale was the first ROTC unit to go to Ft. Sill for training. Princeton was next. "I had some good friends in that class," Anderson says. "The Princeton people turned up with golf bags and tennis rackets. We weren't sure what they planned to do with them out there. As an officer you could play polo. As a corporal you weren't going anywhere."

After his teaching stint at Ft. Sill, Anderson was assigned to the 95th Division in San Antonio, Texas. Given leave, he went home to Oyster Bay for a few days before heading for Texas. His father, who had accepted a commission as a lieutenant in the US Navy, was also home on leave. The senior Anderson was one of many men his age who would serve in two world wars. Within seven months he had been promoted to lieutenant commander and given command of a 225-foot former Coast Guard patrol vessel with a crew of 120 men. The ship was assigned to amphibious forces in the North Atlantic.

"Father told me that Admiral Marquand, who was in charge of the Naval District at 30 Church Street in Manhattan, wanted to see me," Anderson recalls. "Father said the Navy had heard about the bazookas at Ft. Sill." The next day, Lieutenant Commander Henry Anderson took Second Lieutenant Harry Anderson to 90 Church Street. The admiral spoke about the Corsair Fleet, private sailing yachts that had been requisitioned by the US Navy to cruise the East Coast of the United States and listen for submarines. While their mission was to hear a submarine and report it, the sailing vessels carried some hedgehogs, an anti-submarine weapon developed by the Royal Navy that exploded on contact. Admiral Marquand thought the bazooka might also work on the yachts if a submarine surfaced. "He opened his safe and pulled out three bazooka rounds that had been stolen from the Army," Anderson recalls. "Imagine, the Navy having to steal from the Army. You'd think the services would cooperate."

Anderson explained that the 20-foot back-blast of the bazooka would burn up whatever was behind it, and that it wasn't suited for use on a sailboat.

The 95th Division was sent to Louisiana for maneuvers, then to the California desert for war games. In a letter written in 1952 to a fellow officer with whom he had fought later in Europe, Anderson wrote about the desert:

I would spend hours, such as they are in Army life, or in Kipling's Barrack-Room

Ballads, *looking 30 miles across the desert from our tent encampment under the outcropping of a row of jagged hills, hours looking at the dip of the desert and then its subsequent rise to the next divide of hills purple in the distance. The only vegetation was a few scattered smoke trees and the coarse desert bush growing in the arroyos cut by the rare rains in the lava flows which usually extend from the foothills. Always the incessant, almost mystical wind across the valley of sand and the persistent sun suddenly replaced at night by a coolness and a darkness so penetrating that only by looking centuries away towards the stars could one tell there was anything but black.*

The same sort of setting must in part account for the vivid descriptions in the Bible. *One feels when at sea on an ocean race in a small sailing craft the same tremendous forces of nature, the same power pervading against which men and mankind seem but helpless dwarfs.*

"In California it was division against division," Anderson says.

We almost had a civil war. We were all supposed to be using dummy rounds. But one all-black division had been issued live ammo by mistake. We came close to shooting each other up. That would have caused a furor. We lost a couple of fighter planes that were supporting us, strafing the mock enemy. Flying over the desert is like flying over water when there is no wind to define the surface. Depth perception isn't good. The planes got too low and crashed. I had a friend in Long Island who did the same thing with a seaplane.

Sundays we had time off. We practiced artillery fire with dummy rounds. A checkerboard was laid out, and they would set off a little pod of smoke where your round was calculated to have landed. We had Piper Cubs for observation, and for conduct of fire. One of my best friends was a pilot, so we'd go up and chase coyotes, shoot at them with a .45. You had to be careful the wing strut wasn't in your line of fire.

The frail, tail-wheel Piper Cub airplane entered the artillery picture in 1942. The Cub's slow speed (a 65-hp engine drove the plane at a maximum of 85 knots) and low-level operation (under 1,500 feet, usually lower) made them ideal for close communication with ground batteries, and for adjusting artillery fire with considerable precision. The Cub's equipment consisted of compass, throttle, and fuel gauge. Their only armament was a .45 pistol carried on the pilot's hip. The artillery observer conducting fire faced to the rear for optimum observation. Their low-level operation preempted the need for parachutes. Most pilots carried a bullet-hole repair kit consisting of canvas and glue. For airborne observers like Anderson, and his pilot friend, the excitement of training gambits like shooting critters, bombing cows with bags of water, and flying under telephone wires would seem tame once they arrived in the war zone. German soldiers were often able to down the Cubs with small-arms fire. The Cub's defense against enemy fighters was to roll over and dive at Allied antiaircraft batteries that would open fire on the pursuing enemy aircraft. Talk about dodging bullets. Their defense against ground fire was their radio, with which they could direct artillery fire on the enemy battery. The Cubs suffered an attrition rate of 100 a month during 1944 and 1945.

In 1946, Anderson would receive a certificate of commendation from Major General Harry L. Twaddle "for outstanding meritorious service during the period 20 October 1943 to 21 February 1944." The certificate authorized Anderson to wear the Army Commendation Ribbon. Anderson was commended for the training of his battalion survey team during the desert training period that resulted in the highest grade yet scored in the firing tests at Iron Mountain, California. The certificate reads in part, "By his exceptional professional ability, aggressiveness, loyalty and constant devotion to duty, Lieutenant Anderson made an outstanding contribution to the accomplishment of this coveted record and consequent superior preparation for combat."

Anderson was assigned to S-2 (intelligence, survey), and S-3 (fire direction center).

His unit, the 920th Field Artillery Battalion—part of the 95th Division   came east in the spring of 1944 to a staging area at Indian Gap, Pennsylvania, then to Camp Edwards on Cape Cod prior to debarkation for England. They moved to France to join the First Army, run by General Courtney Hodges. But the 95th Division's commander, General Twaddle, didn't think much of Hodges. Twaddle intervened with SHEAF and got his group assigned to the Third Army under General George S. Patton. The First Army was in the north, and would fight the Battle of the Bulge. The Third Army was in the south. "That was lucky," Anderson says. "We had Patton, and we had a much more interesting life."

The 920th Field Artillery Battalion landed on Normandy Beach without resistance 30 days after D-Day. "I was ashore directing our units where to go," Anderson recalls, "and these three officers stepped off the boat. One of them had been my French teacher at Adirondack-Florida School. I welcomed him back to France."

Perhaps what Anderson refers to as "a more interesting life" had to do with the Battle of Metz, a so-called "fortress city" in the northeast of France at the confluence of the Seille and Moselle Rivers. Metz is about

30 miles west of the German border. In November 1944, Metz was held by the German Army. Ten divisions of the American Third Army were stalled en route to the Siegfried Line—a defense system of forts, bunkers, tunnels, civilian personnel, and tank traps stretching 400 miles from the Netherlands to Switzerland—in the vicinity of Metz. In his detailed, unfailingly objective report of the battle that he wrote much later from notes scribbled on the backs of confiscated German letterheads (and from unit histories and several books on General Patton), Anderson writes that while Metz had not been taken by storm since 451 AD, "Patton intended to change history in this respect."

After attacking Metz, the XX Corps to the north and the XII Corps to the south were ordered to drive past the city and on to the east, each leaving a division to mop up the forts as the main thrust continued toward Germany. Anderson writes: "The XX Corps ordered the 95th Division to attack south along the Moselle to Metz. The 920th Field Artillery Battalion . . . would support this drive. The straightforward mission of moving upstream along the west bank of the river was complicated by the added requirement to execute a feint across the Moselle. This feint, it was hoped, would distract the enemy from the main effort of the XX Corps to be made by the 90th Division further north.

The 1st Battalion, 377th Infantry, selected for this dubious honor, would be supported by the 920th."

To help sell the deception, the 377th sewed on new shoulder patches. Radio call signs and vehicle markings were changed, vehicles moved up into crossing positions, and each of the 920th's guns was allocated a separate radio channel. Having thoroughly alerted the Germans to the probability of an American crossing of the Moselle, higher authority changed the orders. No longer was the effort to be a feint. Instead, the 377th—with the 920th's support—was ordered to carry out the crossing and establish bridgeheads at several specified locations. "Not only could a violent enemy reaction be expected," Anderson writes, "but in addition the heavy rains of the preceding week had brought the Moselle to flood stage."

After dark on November 8, the 920th began the proceedings with a 15-minute shelling of landing areas and known enemy positions. Then infantry teams paddled across the river in pontoon boats. "The men attempted to lay cable, but the highest water in 29 years snapped the line," Anderson wrote. "German mortar and 88 mm gunfire caused casualties and wrecked boats. The combination of enemy shells and flood water prevented the engineers from constructing a Treadway footbridge."

Meanwhile, two companies of foot soldiers crossed the river and worked their way 300 yards inland. The two units were isolated. But a bridgehead had been established. "A continuous series of fire missions were radioed by a 920th observer to prevent the enemy from exploiting the vulnerable situation of the two companies. In the first twenty-four hours the 920th fired 1,411 rounds."

The mission of the 377th and the 920th was in a perilous state for several days. Attempts to ferry supplies across the river failed. Troops in the bridgehead were running out of ammunition, food, radio batteries, and all other necessities. "Appeals to the 920th brought immediate aid. Artillery observation planes [Piper Cubs] . . . dropped essential items as well as sleeping bags and socks to the beleaguered men. These Army aviators made a total of fifty-one supply trips over the bridgehead."

The battle at Metz was significant (and brutal) enough that General Patton himself visited the 95th command post a week after the attack had begun. Patton reported that 80 men had been killed and 482 wounded, and he announced that a new task force had been assigned to help mop up the city.

In his report, Anderson mentions little about his role at Metz. He says the winter weather

took its toll. None of the men had winter boots, and frostbite was rampant. Living in tents was wretched. When Anderson does feel his presence should be noted for the record, he refers to himself briefly by surname. When he reports that the new task force had pushed south and reached the remnants of the 377th at Imeldange and Bertrange north of Metz, Anderson duly notes that "Lieutenant Colonel Thomas R. Brown, commanding the 920th, with Lieutenants Lee and Anderson of his staff, crossed the bridge at Thionville, drove south, and reported to Colonel Bacon at Imeldange." He goes on to say that Lieutenant Lee relieved the forward observer. But alas, he does not—will not—elaborate on the role of Lieutenant Anderson.

He did not put this in the official report of the battle, but later he was more specific about his duty:

> As Assistant S-2—an intelligence rating—
> I led survey teams to plot positions of the
> guns, observation posts, and key points in
> enemy territory; conducted the fire direction
> center coordinating the fire from three batteries
> of artillery; did some forward observer firing;
> and quite a bit of air observer firing from a
> Piper Cub.
>
> One day I was across the Moselle in my jeep
> with Paul Ward, driver and machine gunner for

*the 55 mm antiaircraft weapon mounted in the
vehicle, with our commanding officer, Colonel
Brown. The task force, of which we were a part,
provided the only friendly troops on the east
bank of the river. There was no way of knowing
what enemy were on our left flank as we
proceeded south up the river bank. At one point
we were attacked by tanks and infantry point
blank; an attack we repulsed by calling in
artillery fire.*

*Perhaps the hairiest aspect of the operation was
when Col. Brown sent us back to bring up the
artillery batteries. It was night, and no sign of
friends or foe as I sat with grease gun at the
ready (guns with short barrels used by tankers
where space was constricted, or in a jeep where
the barrel of a carbine was too long to be
swung rapidly at a target) and a couple
grenades in hand (if there was sniper fire, to
return fire would create a flash that revealed
one's position, whereas a hurled grenade did
not). It was miles and hours of tenseness.*

Later on, as the task force "entered country
with steeper hills and rougher terrain, and
patches of woods provided concealment for
enemy guns," as written in Anderson's report,
it encountered three German 88 mm guns.
Fire support was called for. "Major White
and Lieutenant Anderson," the report reads,
"who were accompanying 'A' Battery, turned
themselves into an informal fire direction
center. The battery dropped trail, and in three
minutes had rounds on the way. Two of the
88s were hit. The enemy destroyed the third
(blew the tube). The rest of the enemy force
withdrew.

"At dusk, all three batteries (of the 920th)
moved forward to night firing positions. . . .
As three wars had been fought in the area
during the previous 70-odd years, the maps
were accurate. This helped White, Anderson
and the other 920th officers register their
night firing without mishap." Anderson adds:
"Survey for the battalion was done by
inspection, batteries laid by compass. Next
day these initial data were checked against
metro corrected data applied on a checkpoint
registration. The variation was but one mil
[mm] in elevation, and the same in deflection."
Harry Anderson has always put his trust in
the details.

Anderson says the interrogation of prisoners
yielded good information. The infantry had
a Native American assisting the interrogator.
"Behind the scenes he would put on war
paint and a head dress of feathers and grab
a hatchet as though it were a tomahawk.
When faced with a stubborn prisoner of war,
the interrogator would ask the man if he knew
about the American Indians and their custom
of taking scalps. At that point the Native
American would charge in and plant the

hatchet in the wall next to the prisoner's ear. The psychological approach usually worked. The practice might have been pushing the Geneva Code, but not as much as my one-time observation of the German shelling of ambulances."

It was Anderson's good luck not to be in Lieutenant Lee's forward observer team when they reached Fort Belacroix, at the northeast entrance to Metz. Enemy troops had abandoned the fort, and mined it. When the 377th reached the wall of the fort, the Germans blew it up by radio, causing 125 injuries and a slew of deaths. But Metz had been taken, and within the ten-day time limit set by General Patton. Command was turned over to General Didot and his French units.

"In the campaign," Anderson wrote, "the 95th division learned that heeding Gen. Patton's advice resulted in fewer casualties and more prisoners; i.e. keep moving, keep shooting, and don't give a damn about your flanks. . . . Finest praise of all to the ears of the 920th FA Bn were the laudatory expostulations of the infantry for the artillery support furnished them. . . . Artillery support was close, continuous, and concentrated. . . . Total number of rounds fired was in excess of 8,000—a number close to the number of prisoners taken by the Division in the operation."

SON OF A PROUD, World War I cavalry officer who had ridden under General "Black Jack" Pershing, Harry Anderson had grown up with that dramatic history as his legacy. From a young age the concept of war fascinated Anderson both politically and tactically. As a budding historian, war was a natural focal point for him. His experience in the field—his front-line participation in a patriotic war—only expanded his interest in affairs martial. Add to that his keen powers of observation, his obsession with note-taking and reporting on his experiences, his dedication to research, and it made sense he would be the one to write the account of the 920th's battle at Metz. Many soldiers are permanently traumatized by the blood and gore of the battlefield. For Anderson, it was another learning experience, the lessons of which he would retain, in surprising detail, for the rest of his life.

When he has the chance, Anderson encourages young men he knows to take military training. An example is Andrew Hilton, the son of Jamie Hilton, one of Anderson's former boat captains and a godson by proxy. Andrew is one of Anderson's many godchildren, one who needed little coaxing about the military. He says he wanted to join the Army when he was eight years old. "But Harry fueled it," Hilton says, "helped me make the right decisions when I was joining. He wrote me tons of letters and emails, and not just random Harry letters. They were full of knowledge. As a kid I had a fascination with military history, and General Patton. Harry and I shared all that. I didn't really read his letters when I was 12, all I cared about then was presents, but when I got home after my first tour in Iraq I re-read a lot of them. I realized Harry had been talking to me like an adult. It was going over my head then, but it registers now."

Anderson's advocacy of military training is part of a strong belief in a national service requirement for all eighteen-year-olds, be it civilian or military. "We've become very soft, mentally and physically," he says. "Youngsters aren't tough enough. I'm very much in favor of a national service requirement in which everyone spends time with his fellow countrymen on the same level. Andrew Hilton matured more in a few months than most kids his age do in a few years. We need jobs. Look what FDR did with the Civilian Construction Corps (CCC) in the 1930s and '40s. Imagine the outcry if the present administration told people they had to do such hard, physical work. But it would create jobs."

On leave seven months after the Battle of Metz, Anderson found himself at an old haunt, the Stork Club in New York. Anderson says the socially prominent club was considered "safe" for undergraduates by their families. There he ran into a classmate from Yale who mentioned he was attending a course in military government. The Army had encountered a shortage of personnel in North Africa and Europe, which had delayed getting basic utilities and transportation back in service, to the detriment of ongoing military operations. So for the upcoming landing in Japan, military government units were going to land with the third wave. Anderson's classmate bemoaned the lack of people with field experience in his class, or of any manuals on the subject. He said they needed someone who had been in the field to speak to his students about the reality of military occupation.

As it happened, Anderson's battalion had spent more than a month serving as the military government for a section of Germany in the spring of 1945. The Allied front had moved so fast that the manual for the occupation of Germany had not been completed. Combat units were ordered to fill the gap until the three-way division of the country among Great Britain, France, and the US could be made official. Anderson's unit was responsible for organizing trucks to bring in food, and for getting banks and utility companies back in business.

"The way it was quickly divided up meant that

we might have a branch bank, but the main bank was in some other unit's territory," Anderson says.

On top of that we had several thousand prisoners of war the Germans had taken— mostly Russians and Italians—who were housed in this huge stud farm where they bred work horses. We had to get the Russians out so they could train for the Eastern Front. I was judge advocate for my Battalion. The end of each day I had to go to the courthouse because people had been stopped on the street and held because they didn't have proper papers. I always kept a pistol in hand during that walk, and scanned the windows of the houses for a possible sniper. I had to decide what to do with those who had been stopped. We were busy in all aspects of civil jurisdiction. For example, an American soldier had stolen coffee from a house. He could only speak Spanish. The witnesses could only speak German.

One case Anderson had to handle with care was when his jeep driver, Paul Ward, whom he had fought alongside at Metz, and who had become a close friend, left his sentry post one evening in search of a cup of coffee. It was a punishable offense comparable to desertion. The captain, who didn't like Ward, recommended he be court-martialed. "The legal issue treaded a fine line," Anderson recalls, "inasmuch as hostilities were over.

But we were in occupied territory. Plus Paul was an independent person not readily malleable to military discipline. A jail sentence would have broken the spirit of a fine soldier. Recognizing the captain was prejudiced against Paul, but probably did not have the confidence to press charges without our recommendation, we remained non-committal thereby leaving the captain in limbo."

That evening at the Stork Club, Anderson told his classmate that he'd be glad to speak with the students. The official invitation was quickly tendered by the colonel in charge, and Anderson rushed off to the Elizabethan Club in New Haven to scribble notes for his talk. He still has a copy of the 15 pages of handwritten notes he polished at Mory's the evening before his talk. They reflect the chaos encountered by a military unit trying to make sense of a war-ravaged, defeated country. Some excerpts:

From Army group on down unit boundaries failed to coincide with the political subdivisions of the occupied country. . . .

The Burgomaster of an area must send a truckload of food per day to a certain town, but we cannot grant him a pass because it is beyond our authority to do so. . . .

The veterinarian must have a pass to care for

the horses in this town, but that is out of our jurisdiction. . . .

Russians from the British sector ran riot pillaging and raping in our section, but we had no power to try them. Russians in our sector did the same thing in the British territory with the same result. . . .

Must have public officials who are not the do or die war party types, and who can be trusted. . . .

The aim of a military government is to set policy and direct, not administer.

Summary: set working hours—not working with Army personnel but with civil affairs and civilians; must talk, send for people, tradesmen; make people govern themselves; use common sense.

The talk was a reality check for the students, prompting this note from the colonel to the commanding officer, 920th Field Artillery Battalion, 95th Infantry Division: "Lt. Anderson delivered a most interesting and instructive lecture which was of great value to his listeners, who are preparing for similar activities in the Far East." Anderson received a forwarded message from General Harry Twaddle to the commanding officer, 95th Division. "He said it was a good thing to have

a soldier using his leave for something productive," Anderson said, "but there was no promotion."

Fifty years later, Anderson would write to a colleague at the Naval War College about establishing bridgeheads, referring to events in Metz like it was yesterday: "Our crossing of the Moselle River demonstrated how ill-prepared we were in terms of equipment. It was with extreme frustration that we scoured the farms and villages for boats of any kind, and especially for rope with which to suspend communications wire so it would not be snapped by the rushing river current. At great cost of manpower, primarily infantrymen, the bridgehead was secured thanks to the enemy not realizing how fragile was the force holding same and to having their armor beaten back initially by artillery and bazooka fire."

Anderson was an admirer of General George Patton long before he found himself under his command. Watching Patton operate at close range—with his own life at stake—confirmed his high opinion of the general. "I greatly admired him," Anderson says.

He was a bold leader, innovative, a man who tolerated a minimum of red tape. He had an incredible knowledge of military history. He knew every major battle back to the days of the Romans and Greeks. He drew from tactical situations of the past when they mimicked what he faced. He suffered from dyslexia all his life. He had to repeat courses to graduate from West Point. Maybe that's why he had that tough demeanor.

Patton spoke to the 95th Division when we joined him in Alsace Lorraine, where some of the population were sympathizers for France, and some for Germany. His order was, "I don't care who you sleep with—just don't fraternize." In addition, he ordered that whenever the troops were tempted to swear— an institutional predilection of his—that we exclaim "son-of-a-bitch-German." He paid a visit to one of our forward observation posts when we were at Metz. We were ahead of the troops, conducting fire on the Siegfried Line. He shouldn't have been there, he was very exposed.

Anderson has read every book about Patton. With his firsthand knowledge of what went on in the European Theater of World War II, and the additional research he has devoted to the subject, authors who dare tackle Patton have to deal with Harry Anderson. If they should fail to be aware of that, Anderson will find them. Patton's grandson, Benjamin, who wrote *Growing Up Patton*, sent one of the first copies of his book to Anderson in May of 2012. Anderson's response reads like a final World War II history exam:

During the preliminaries of the Battle of the Bulge you mention that our forces were driving eastward. Actually Third and First Armies were stalled smack against the Siegfried Line. My Division, the 95th, was at the Saar River inching its way along. Behind the town stretched tiers of Siegfried pillboxes for half a mile or more reinforced with up to 14 inches of concrete and manned by the Volkssturm (people's army). Earlier, when Third Army was stalled at Metz for lack of fuel, maps, etc. the Germans had abandoned the line, but the delay at Metz later gave them time to re-man it.

As an indication of the slow progress, it took our infantry three days to cross an area the size of a small hotel ballroom, and we had observers in the second floor of a house conducting 105 mm fire on the house across the street. . . . Myself and my driver/survey Corporal spent three days at the edge of the river where every morning as we crept forward to a 3rd floor observation post in a house there were signs of German occupancy during the night. The objective was to knock out pillboxes with artillery fire using one telephone to conduct the fire from a 240 mm Howitzer positioned 20 miles away to the read (the dispersion directionally is +/-10 yards and laterally 5 yards—the larger the caliber the greater the accuracy); a 155 mm rifle (the WWII Grand Puissant de Feur) mounted on a tank chassis and firing at almost point blank range, i.e.

2000 yards; a battalion of 155 mm Howitzers and 4.5 mm mortars provided by the infantry. The objective was to breach a pillbox with a concrete piercing fuse and drive out the occupants with white phosphorous.

Very few artillery officers have ever had the luxury of conducting so much fire power at one time. With only one phone line and several missions simultaneously it was hot work.

The disappointing part of the exercise was knocking down the church steeple that the Huns were using as an observation post to fire on our forward elements (in the course of moving eastward I climbed numerous church/cathedral steeples/towers both out of interest in their construction above the interior decorative false ceilings and to observe how many were, in violation of the Geneva Convention, being used by the Germans. Panoramic sketches and telephone wire were a giveaway).

Anderson also related this story to Benjamin Patton: "When General Eisenhower called a conference when the Battle of the Bulge broke out, he asked Gen. Montgomery of the Second Army, Gen. Hodges of the First Army, and Gen. Patton for their recommendations. The first two said they would hold, or move into defensive positions. Patton said, 'You fellows may hold, but I'm going to drive those

bastards up their hairy assholes.' His actions saved the beleaguered troops in Bastogne. Those words I was told by a reliable source; wonder if you have run across them?"

In a long, page-by-page critique Anderson wrote in 1995 to Carlo D'Este, author of *Patton, a Genius for War,* he includes this story that took place not long after his unit had arrived in Europe, and while General Twaddle was negotiating the reassignment of Anderson's 95th Division from the First to the Third Army—Patton's command.

Our fire control officer had taken his jeep and a low trailer to Epernay to load up with champagne. It turned out to be Pieper and Charles Heidsick 1934 and 1937, prime vintages. When he got into First Army territory, he of course could not find the 95th, which had been rerouted to Third Army. Having disobeyed orders and loaded with illegal booty, he was in deep trouble, but lucked out finding in the G-2 section a close friend who, also committing a courts martial offense, revealed the change of plans for the 95th that was traveling without shoulder patches. What followed was an even greater risk—an all-night blow out popping champagne. The hangovers the next morning were so bad that my immediate superior, Capt. Jones S-2, and I for recovery drove to the headquarters of a neighboring Division commanded by a general who had taught ROTC at Yale and whose daughter the two of us had squired on occasion when our Division was in the California-Arizona desert maneuver area. As we arrived, his headquarters was being shelled by enemy fire which snapped us back into shape instantly—a tough cure.

It was 44 years after the Battle of Metz that Harry Anderson wrote his report that was published in *Military Collector & Historian, Journal of the Company of Military Historians* (1978). The question arises how even a man with Anderson's formidable powers of recall could remember events in such detail. He explains.

After ten days, our units had reached the south edge of Metz, and units coming downstream from the north had reached the north limits, hence our infantry liaison officer called a cease fire for further artillery. Our battalion headquarters that evening were set up in a building housing a café. Some of the officers, including my direct superior, a Captain Jones from Texas, a West Pointer with imagination and verve who was S-2, were playing poker.

Several members of our Battalion had explored a breached fort and recovered Luger pistols as souvenirs, including the sergeant in charge of headquarters. He was seated behind Capt. Jones cleaning, or fondling, a Luger, which unfortunately, and to his ignorance, was

loaded. It went off, hitting Capt. Jones almost point-blank in the back and killing him instantly. Imagine the trauma amongst all of us, having lost comrades in action during the 10-day battle, and now this senseless tragedy. Further imagine being the commanding officer having to write Jones' family that he was killed by friendly fire!

Under the circumstances trying to sleep that night was impossible, so I wrote up the details of the battle, finishing as dawn broke. At hand were the maps and coordinates for each phase of the battle. I penciled in the coordinates (latitude and longitude survey numbers.)

J UST AFTER the Battle of Metz, Anderson's father was admitted to the naval hospital in San Diego with chronic nephritis, an incurable ailment at the time. While he was on leave, in June, Anderson visited him at home in Oyster Bay. Then he went off to Mississippi, where he had been reassigned. The forward elements of his regiment, which did not include artillery, were on the West Coast in preparation for being shipped to Japan when the atomic bomb was dropped on Hiroshima on August 9, 1945. A week later, at the age of 51, Anderson's father died from nephritis.

Anderson traveled to Oyster Bay for the service. "It was small, family mostly," Anderson says, "because it was wartime and everyone was all over the place." His youngest brother, David, was in the Coast Guard at the time. On August 16, he was at the helm of a transport passing the Rock of Gibraltar en route to Marseilles with a few thousand troops on board. David said his executive officer came on the bridge, walked over to him, and said he just wanted to tell him his father had died. "It was a military funeral. Navy chaps fired salutes. The American flag was folded up and handed to my mother."

Anderson's unit in Mississippi was "demobbed" (demobilized). He was transferred to the Fourth Army at Camp Butner, North Carolina, where he kept busy by writing the unit history for the 29th Field Artillery Battalion of the Fourth Division. His unit was scheduled for deployment to Ft. Dix early March in preparation for being released. "No one wanted to go to Ft. Dix that time of year," Anderson says, "and since I was the officer in our unit in charge of assigning where everyone went, I sent us to Ft. Bragg, North Carolina. We knew a fellow officer there with a house. The Airborne Division was at Ft. Bragg, and we wanted to make a jump, but without training they wouldn't let us."

Harry Anderson was discharged from the

US Army on April 1, 1946, with the rank of captain. He had been awarded a Bronze Star, and an EAME (European African Middle Eastern Campaigns) ribbon with three battle stars. The Bronze Star was for the battle of Metz. The citation concluded: "His outstanding service frequently rendered under heavy enemy fire during this momentous period of combat reflects great credit on Lieutenant Anderson."

Anderson joined the 77th Reserve Division based in Manhattan, which included monthly meetings (blackboard sessions) and a two-week field commitment every summer at Camp Drum in northern New York State. The 77th was one of the last divisions to be fully integrated, and aside from the officers, his field artillery battalion, the 453rd, consisted mostly of black personnel. Anderson had worked with a Third Army anti-tank battalion in Germany that was all black. "The unit originated in the Philippines during the Spanish-American War," Anderson says, "and had developed an esprit-de-corps the likes of which the Marines boast. They operated self-propelled anti-tank guns that did not have the protective armor of a tank, and therefore needed to fire from concealed or protected positions. As liaison with the anti-tankers, my job was to guide the weapon into position before dawn when the mist over the river obscured observation. They would pour direct fire into a pillbox or other fortified position. When the mist lifted they would get the hell out before the Krauts could pinpoint them. Word was that General Patton thought highly of them."

Anderson says his reserve duty often turned out to be riskier than combat. One summer because of a lack of military vehicles, the Army hired school buses to transport the men to summer camp. "The drivers had no experience with military conveys," he says, "which are divided into units of 20 vehicles maintaining 45 mph with a fixed distance between units. This prevents the accordion action that occurs when starting and stopping. It was mayhem as drivers tried to catch up and then suddenly had to halt. Drivers would swerve into the oncoming lane to avoid rear ending the bus in front."

Then there was the summer when a battery of nurses doing field training nearby cut up the 77th's carefully laid telephone wires to tie down their tents. They had been issued tent pegs, but no rope, and made do with what they could find. "The next day," Anderson says, "communications teams spliced the wires back together and in their haste the phone lines from one battery were attached to the wrong battalion fire direction center. As the observation party of our battalion called for fire on target X, rounds would suddenly explode behind us, or fly into a farmer's field."

Not all the bizarre risks were lethal. It seems Julius Ochs Adler, president of the *New York Times*, was commanding general of the 77th. The first morning of one summer camp, there were two stacks of newspapers at the officers' mess: the *Times,* and the *New York Herald Tribune*. "Only the first morning," Anderson says. "After that, Ochs had his aides buy up all the *Tribunes*. On Sunday, the *Times* headline was a double-column huzzar about the general's leadership of the division."

One summer Anderson and another officer were assigned to special duty with drivers and vehicles to entertain several French Reserve Officers by taking them to dinner at a hunting club on one of the Thousand Islands in the St. Lawrence River. "France, unlike the USA, required its reservists to serve at summer camp annually whether or not they were home or abroad. By doing so with the military of whatever nation they were visiting, the requirement was satisfied."

Anderson would move to Connecticut, where the commute for monthly meetings became prohibitive. He retired from the Army Reserve short of the requirement for a lifetime pension.

CHAPTER

SEVEN | Commerce Interruptus

H arry and his brother David were released from the military at the same time. They reconvened for a brief period at the family home in Oyster Bay. Their mother thought it would be good for their business careers if the boys got acquainted with golf, so she sent them off to the Piping Rock Club for lessons. They tried it for a week. Neither of them has addressed a golf ball since.

David went off to finish college. Harry entered Columbia Law School in the fall of 1946. His first interest had been the State Department. The postwar policy of the State Department was to waive certain course requirements for military officers, which Anderson found an attractive proposition. But despite his independence, Anderson felt he wasn't sufficiently endowed financially for the line of work he wanted. "I thought about fellows like Arthur Bliss Lane," he says, "a career diplomat, Ambassador to Japan when Pearl Harbor occurred, a classmate of father's at Yale. He had a pretty good family income. You didn't have to be wealthy to be in the State Department, but it helped if you were planning to go up the line."

Among people with money, the definition of what constitutes "wealth" is an ongoing discussion. The outcome of the discussion is based on comparison, the perception of one's limits, and in the end is in the eye of the particular beholder. Lists of comparative wealth like the Forbes 500 establish the top end. That helps the rest of the potential clients for services advertised as "wealth management" figure out where they stand, financially speaking. Degrees of wealth range from "comfortable," to whatever ultimate, descriptive phrase one prefers. In most instances, those degrees are understated by the beholders. In the past, it was mannerly—politically and socially correct—to downplay one's wealth. In the twenty-first century the flaunting and display of wealth is more acceptable. But in any

The Raven about to make a splash in its debut
at a breezy Larchmont Race Week in the 1950s.

case, the discussion rolls on. Based on the comparison of his family resources with those of Arthur Bliss Lane, Harry Anderson's perception was that the diplomatic corps was too rich for his blood.

Both his father and grandfather had gotten their law degrees from Columbia after graduating from Yale, so the path was well beaten for Anderson. "I'm sure father would have liked it if I had gone to law school," Anderson admits, but denies that the pressure of family tradition influenced his decision. His brother David disagrees. "Harry really identified with my father," David says, "followed in his footsteps in every way including going to law school."

Anderson hadn't been at Columbia very long before he got a call from a man named C. Townsend Ludington, who had been a student at Adirondack-Florida School from 1909 to 1913 (he transferred to the Haverford School at that point, graduating in 1915). With his brother Nicholas, Townsend Ludington had started a small airline in Philadelphia in 1930—Ludington Airlines—that grew rapidly. With flights to New York and Baltimore, Ludington Air had carried a record 100,000 passengers in just 21 months. Aircraft like the Stinson SM 6000 Tri-motor zipped travelers to New York in only two hours. In 1933, Ludington Air was acquired by what was to become Eastern Airlines.

Townsend Ludington was also chairman of the board of the Adirondack-Florida School. The school had been forced to close down during World War II, and in 1946 an effort was underway to get it restarted. That year, Ludington asked Harry Anderson to join the board as secretary. It might have seemed a bit of a stretch, asking a first-year law student of 26 to fill the secretarial position on any board, but Anderson had the right pedigree. His father had been in one of the earliest classes at Adirondack-Florida (1911), and had been a member of the school's first board of directors. Fellow directors, Ludington and the senior Anderson had known one another from student days.

Harry's legacy at the school included seven family members over four decades. In addition to his stellar performance at Adirondack-Florida, his devotion to the school was well known. Military service had matured him, and being financially independent is never a hindrance when it comes to board membership. Getting the campus ready for use after a time of abandonment was obviously going to require capital outlay. And ironically, if he accepted the invitation, Anderson would be filling the board seat of his father, who had died the previous year. Harry accepted the invitation with pleasure, and he tackled the complexities of restarting the school with enthusiasm while he continued his studies at Columbia Law.

And it was complex. The board had put the Coconut Grove campus up for sale during the war, but a collection of loose ends and a raft of legal issues—not to mention a hurricane that damaged the then-uninsured campus—had resulted in a pricey cancellation agreement. On top of that, Kenneth Wilson had resigned as head of school because of a war injury that curtailed his movements.

Ludington and a few devoted alumni provided the funds necessary to pay off the cancellation agreement and establish a fund covering campus rehabilitation. A new head of school was found. Meanwhile, Harry Anderson started tracking down some bonds that had been issued by the school in the 1930s. The search took him on a circuitous path that had all the qualities of film noire. The missing bonds were linked to a former trustee and secretary, a partner in a small law firm, an inveterate gambler who spent his afternoons playing bridge or backgammon for high stakes in various New York clubs. He had a habit of losing. He invested in marginal financial schemes that rarely paid off. Meanwhile, his mother and wife were putting on the pressure to fund the way of life to which they were accustomed. He ended up taking some securities from the family's trusts. The Attorney General of New York was going to prosecute him, so the trustee attempted suicide by jumping out the window of the Yale Club

Library. That too was unsuccessful. Friends came to the rescue, moved him to California, and set him up with a few gasoline stations. But he was still kiting money and having bad luck. When a wholesaler shut him off, he hired a truck to move gasoline from one station to another. During the transfer, the driver had run a stoplight and had been killed.

Anderson found himself in the thick of an intricate financial predicament. Had the trustee retired the bonds? Was the school liable? If the bonds were outstanding, the worth of the school property would be compromised. He calculated the bonds were still outstanding. "The school paid off the bonds held by the Ransom heirs," Anderson says. "By doing that, we saved the school a significant amount of money based on the premise that the other bonds had been retired by the wayward secretary-trustee. It was complex, but it worked." With his astute handling of his first challenge as a trustee, Harry Anderson had, as they say on *The Sopranos*, made his bones.

The Adirondack-Florida School reopened in the fall of 1947 with nine students and a faculty of six. One of those students was C. Townsend "Towny" Ludington, son of the former chairman of the board. After a brief stint teaching at the school, in 2013 Towny Ludington was the Boshamer Professor of

English and American Studies at the University of North Carolina, Chapel Hill (retired). One of his biographies is about novelist John dos Passos. "In spite of what my father would say if he were alive, or Harry," Ludington says, "the school wasn't strong academically when I was there. In those days, anybody they could find on the street they let in just to get the numbers." There were 17 students in 1948.

The hundred-year commemorative book, *Honor & Excellence*, published by the Ransom School in 2003, reflects the slim financial edge the school had been treading during the restart. Citing the dire need to increase the student body to a break-even number of 40, the head of school at that time spoke of competing for students with military schools and other independent organizations, and being underbid for students by other private schools. He referred to the process as "the business of boy procurement."

In 1949, faced with the specter of bankruptcy, board chairman C. T. Ludington broached the idea of closing the northern campus. It was an unpopular concept, but not without merit. The pragmatic Harry Anderson, who maintained that he always loved the northern campus best, helped Ludington sell the idea, painful as it was to him and all concerned. Ludington maintained that the school would

be successful drawing day students from the more densely populated Florida area (today, as Ransom Everglades, it flourishes as a day school). Finally, a consensus was reached. Before the northern campus was sold, Anderson took it upon himself to spend a few days in the Adirondacks packing up all the documents and photographs he could locate. That material is a significant part of the well-organized archives at Ransom Everglades.

The only puzzling thing about Harry Anderson's matriculation at Columbia Law School is that he didn't graduate. With the excellent record of scholarship he had compiled at Adirondack-Florida School, Andover, Yale, and the US Army, he was certainly equal to the academic challenge of law school. During his time at Columbia, Anderson formed a business partnership with a prominent International 14 dinghy sailor and engineer, Eric Olsen, to start a company called Gull Reinforced Plastics. The plan was that Gull would use the latest molded plastics (fiberglass) technology to manufacture parts for a variety of industrial uses. But Gull, for which Anderson was listed as vice president and treasurer, would not incorporate until 1951. Anderson was set to graduate from Columbia in 1948. One would have thought that having a treasurer with a law degree would have been an added benefit for Gull.

David Anderson says he always wondered why his oldest brother never got his law degree. The two brothers were never close. A five-year difference in age is a significant gap from birth through the teenage years. The brothers' diverse natures sent them off in different directions, and World War II served to further isolate them. So when David happened to run into Harry's Columbia Law roommate at a social gathering a few years ago, he was eager to find out why on earth Harry hadn't graduated after putting in two years and all the effort required. "Without any hesitation he told me because there was a big yacht race the day of the exam," David says.

When asked if a boat race got in the way of finishing Columbia, Harry Anderson says only, "there were a lot of boat races." And he chuckles, putting his moustache in motion. But he avows there was no boat race that took precedence over his law exams. It seems he just lost interest in pursuing a law degree. "My grades weren't that good," he says.

In fact I recently looked back at my Yale records, and I only had a C average. Yale was a problem because of the acceleration caused by the War. I had all this material accumulated for my thesis, and there wasn't even time to read it. And I got very involved with the Gull start up. We had to start working, raising funds. In addition to Eric Olsen, who was from MIT, we

had John Newman, a Harvard graduate, and Larry Ely, from Princeton, a great innovator who designed a lot of products for us. We all knew each other from intercollegiate sailing. John Newman and I were often judges at ICYRA regattas, driving from Philadelphia, after judging at University of Pennsylvania, to Annapolis to judge at the US Naval Academy during a weekend before the Delaware or Chesapeake Bay bridges had been built— or taking the Washington, Baltimore and Annapolis Railroad known as the Wiggle, Bounce and Agitate.

One has a better understanding of why law school might have been discontinued— and why Gull wasn't incorporated until 1951—after becoming aware of Anderson's activities in 1948 and 1949. Having proved conclusively that he could do well academically, his lackluster grade average at Columbia is a strong indication that Anderson wasn't particularly entranced by law school, despite his duties as judge advocate for his field artillery battalion during the war having provided an introduction to legal practice. In any case, Anderson chose an alternative vocation.

An indication of his lack of focus on his law studies was the build-it-yourself Thistle Class kit Anderson purchased in 1947. The Thistle, a 17-foot, cold-molded performance boat that was a larger version of the

International 14, had arrived on the scene in 1945. It required a crew of three. "Weekends while in law school," Anderson writes, "I would work on assembling the kit—no mean job since the family boathouse had no electricity and I had to hand drill through the oak rub rail. There was a grand party at the launching. Absent a ramp, the guests carried the boat afloat."

Having taken direction and toed the line for 25 years, having lived up to parental expectations in all of his endeavors, having won acclaim from classroom to battlefield, the European trip Anderson happily helped engineer in the spring of 1948 has "breakout" written all over it. His brother David's rebellion from his chilly, dickensian upbringing started early, was out front, and resulted in Russian scholarship, three different careers, a marriage, and the fathering of nine children.

Harry's was longer in coming, and while it was more subtle it was no less defiant. It was the precursor to his departure from the traditional path: his embarkation upon a self-styled life with no bosses, no mate, and no agenda other than his own, and that of organizations he chose to support in his own way, for the most part as a volunteer. The 1948 European trip revealed his need to be traveling at a strenuous clip and at his whim, while hungrily ingesting the curiosities of

the world. It was a method of operation he maintained the rest of his life.

Anderson says the original plan in 1948 was for a summer trip with James Lane Buckley, an older brother of William; law school classmate Richard Wheatland II, whose uncle was Fairfield Osborn, a renowned conservationist; and William Grayson, whose father was an admiral who had become head of the Red Cross. The stated goal of the trip was to trace Rudyard Kipling's haunts in the Far East from India to the Malay Peninsula. "T.S. Eliot had just published the best of Kipling [*A Choice of Kipling's Verse Made by T. S. Eliot*], thereby arousing widespread interest in his work," Anderson says. The trip has all the earmarks of a late night scheme conjured at Mory's over several rounds of strong drink.

"Financing the trip was going to be a lead cinch," Anderson writes in a recollection of the trip, "inasmuch as Dick's uncle would give us an introduction to each Indian Maharajah in in order to raise several million dollars to support agricultural development for their country—sort of a Marshall Plan for Asia. We would be taken on tiger hunts, and receive a commission based on the amounts raised. The plan crashed when Dick developed mononucleosis. His Uncle Fairfield had no idea who Buckley and myself were."

From the sound of Plan B, it was the result of another even more creative evening at Mory's: "Travel primarily in France to evaluate the effect of Kipling's writings on modern French culture—the principle venue of research to be cafes as a counterpart to British pubs." If only Chevy Chase and John Belushi had been privy to this idea in the 1970s we all could have enjoyed the movie. The Yale-blue blind spot played a key role in the preparations. "Because Jim Buckley and I had been listening for years on Monday nights to the Yale Whiffenpoofs singing the paraphrase to Kipling's "Gentlemen Rankers," *To the Tables down at Mory's*, and spent time at Ye Old Cheshire Cheese in London, off Fleet Street a few doors down from Dr. Samuel Johnson's house, we were well acquainted with the Kipling legacy in England and the States." While Kipling was living at his American home, Naulakha in Waite, Vermont, in 1895, some Yale sophomores established a Kipling Club and invited him to their 1896 annual dinner. He declined in a poem titled "Mulvaney's Regrets." Anderson has a copy of Kipling's poem in his files:

> Attind ye lasses av Swate Parnassas
> And wipe my burnin' tears away
> For I'm declinin' a chanst av dinin'
> Wid the bhoys at Yale on the fourteenth May.
>
> The leadin' fayture will be lter-ature
> (Av a moral nature as is just and right)

For their light and leadin' are engaged in readin'
Me immortal worruks from dawn till night.

They've made a club there and staked out
    grub there
Wid plates an' napkins in a joyous row,
An' they'd think it splendid if I attended
An' so would I – but I cannot go.

The honest fact is that daily practice
Av rowlin' inkpots, the same as me
Conshumes me hours in the Muses' bowers
An' leaves me divil a day to spree.

Whin you grow older and skin your shoulder
At the world's great wheel in your chosen
    line,
Ye'll find your chances as Time advances
For takin' a lark are as slim as mine.

But I'm digressin! Accept my blessin',
An' remember what ould King Solomon said,
That youth is ructious an' whiskey's fluxious
An' there's nothing certain but the mornin'
    "head."

And so they were off on a Bernstein Line passenger ship out of New York bound for Amsterdam, a banana boat replacement for ships seized by the Germans during the war. It had slatted doors opening on deck, great for the tropics but not well suited to transatlantic service. "One of the engines," Anderson writes,

The grand tour spawned at Mory's in 1948.
Somewhere in France, Harry Anderson shot this
picture of his cohorts. Top, from left, Tom
Nihol, Jim Buckley (the Citroen was his
family's), and Bill Grayson.

"had been replaced with one substantially lighter than its partner on the opposite side, so the ship had a five-degree list. Her speed was a little over ten knots, so it took 13 days to get to Antwerp. We were passed by the *Queen Mary* three times. One of the highlights of the trip occurred on Bastille Day when there were theme performances by French groups on history and nostalgic subjects. Jim and I translated the "Whiffenpoof Song" into French, which our group sang. When we came to 'les pauvre petites agneaux,' slowing the tempo, many of the ladies broke into tears."

From Amsterdam they took a train to Paris. Anderson sent a letter home letting everyone know his forwarding address was the Automobile Club de France. As with all his travels, he never missed a contextual tie-in of any historical significance.

> Bill Grayson joined us, having flown from Berlin in General Draper's plane right after one of the most dramatic moments in the Cold War. Recall that Draper was in command of our occupation forces conducting military government. Gen. Clay was the key chap in Washington. It was Draper's team that, from a London enclave, had produced the handbook on military government for the occupation of Germany. The Russians had already made a couple of moves to encroach on the Allied portion of Berlin, and had suddenly threatened to take over the entire city. Unable to contact President Truman, the two generals told the Russians, no further or we shoot. The ploy worked, but the Russians wound up blocking our supply routes, a situation that required the establishment of the "Corridor and Airlift."

In Paris the group inaugurated the trip's mission by dutifully spending evenings at insider cafés like Les Deux Maggots, a haunt of intellectuals like Ernest Hemingway and Gertrude Stein. Anderson recalls that Deux Maggots had become renowned when *LIFE* magazine featured the maitre d'—a teenage girl in a tight-fitting navy blue sweater—on its cover. After that, the trip's mission gave way to other ventures.

After driving around Switzerland for a few days, Anderson left the group for Munich. His assistant commanding officer from the 920th Field Artillery Battalion, Major Ed White, attaché to SHAEF, who had been assigned to inspect Polish installations in Munich, had arranged for military orders to be cut so Anderson could join him. "Munich had suffered severely from bomb damage," Anderson writes. "There were few smiles on the faces of the populace. Joining White and myself was a young Romanian countess who had escaped with the family jewels under her fur coat. A protégé of White's, she was studying at University of Munich that was without roofs.

She went to classes in her overcoat while she awaited transfer to University of Pennsylvania." Anderson's tour included a tour of Hitler's Eagle's Nest at Berchtesgaden, and a trip to Linderhoff Palace, which "mad" King Ludwig of Bavaria had built as a replica of Versailles.

Back in Switzerland the group sought a different perspective by taking turns riding an inflatable mattress in streams paralleling the road. In Florence, they frequented museums. "One day we noted an exhibit of Hitler's paintings. We had always heard of Hitler as a painter of houses, and had assumed he was in overalls on a ladder painting exteriors. Not at all. These were canvasses of houses, dreary and boring."

Fully into tourist mode, the group took in the bareback horse races and fifteenth-century pageantry (Il Palio) in Siena, Italy; the annual horse show in Dublin; and a side trip to Scotland before heading back to the States.

The trip was so successful that Anderson and his friends contemplated forming the Poor Man's Riviera Society, with the slogan "If it's travel you're after, go Gaelic for laughter." The purpose was twofold. First, to establish in a community on the south coast of Ireland, a Riviera in native habitat to which the poor man could go, with modest accommodations and no casinos. Second, the directors'

trips (holidays) to Ireland would be tax-deductible, and if the corporation were liquidated, "the assets having been spent in invisible corporate expenses by its officers in Ireland reconnoitering, and the stock bought by same is deductible as a short term loss." Alas, the Poor Man's Riviera Society was never incorporated.

Work for Gull Reinforced Plastics suffered another delay the following year, when Anderson took the better part of a month to race 6 Metres in the British-American Cup, an international team race in keelboats that was initiated at Seawanhaka in 1922. Racing was held off Cowes, Isle of Wight, United Kingdom, with four boats on each team. Of all the racing he has done, the 1949 British-American Cup is among the most memorable for Anderson. A photo of *Goose*, the boat Anderson sailed on as tactician and foredeck man, hangs in a place of honor (above the toilet) in his Mystic apartment. Designed by Sparkman & Stephens and launched in 1938, *Goose* was the most successful of the prewar 6 Metres.

It started with a London dock strike that resulted in immobilizing one of the US boats. Owner James Sheldon's exhaustive attempts to engineer an unloading scheme that would satisfy both labor and management ended in frustration. The British team graciously

The 6-Metre *Goose* racing in the British-American Cup on the Solent in 1949. Bow man Anderson hanks on the jib for the next upwind leg. In the cockpit, from left, are Rob Morgan, Ted Janeway, Nancy Nichols, and Dr. George Nichols at the helm.

chartered a boat to Sheldon for one pound sterling. It was a dog. The regatta was a long series requiring a comeback by the American team. It was sailed on the Solent, which separates the Isle of Wight from Southampton on the United Kingdom's south coast. Sherman Hoyt once said this about the Solent: "When yachting was revived after the Middle Ages they picked the worst location for strong currents, choppy seas, and shifty winds."

The Solent is indeed a mean-spirited body of water with an extreme wind range that can change from flat calm to white caps in a London minute. An extreme tidal rise and fall of four meters (14 feet) produces ferocious currents. On a practice day with little wind, one American boat was slammed into a cage (channel marker) by the four-knot current, while another took a bite out of a teammate's stern by misjudging the tidal effect. The

The crew of *Goose*. From left, Rob Meyer, Harry Anderson, Nancy Nichols, George Nichols, Ted Janeway.

American team consisted of Herman Whiton (*Firecracker*); Bus Mosbacher (*Llanoria*); Dr. George Nichols Jr. (*Goose*); and Mrs. James R. Sheldon (*NOA*, on charter). George Nichols, as it happened, was a classmate of Anderson's from Adirondack-Florida School, an Oyster Bay neighbor, and a fellow member of the SCYC.

The report on the regatta Anderson compiled is 14 pages single-spaced, complete with charts of the course and photographs. It is presented race by race, with the course, tidal situation, and wind conditions noted. The denouement of the first race will be recognized as a classic by anyone who has ever competed in the Solent. *Llanoria* and *Goose* had worked out an eight-minute lead with one leg to go to the finish. In a team race, a 1-2 finish by a team is an unbeatable combination. As Anderson wrote, "Only a miracle could prevent an American victory. The Solent, however, is an unceasing source of miracles, and one was in the making."

Llanoria and *Goose* both took the port jibe on the downwind leg, and soon found themselves becalmed without steerageway. The trailing boats took the starboard jibe, and they were first to pick up an incoming southeasterly breeze that blew them to the finish. *Llanoria* and *Goose* finished next to last, and last. The lesson was not lost on Anderson. "In the fluky winds and strong tides of the Solent," he wrote, "*Llanoria* and *Goose* should have kept further apart on the run in order that they would not fall victims of the same fate."

Race two turned out to be the most significant of the series because of the rules question that arose. *Llanoria*, skippered by Bus Mosbacher, rounded the last mark with a lead of several minutes. "Suddenly an astonishing maneuver took place," Anderson writes. "Instead of heading for the finish, Mosbacher, realizing the American team did not have a winning combination, turned *Llanoria* back along the leg of the course from which he had just come, tacked ahead and to leeward of two British boats, and by forcing them onto a higher course attempted to allow *Goose* to sail through them to leeward and secure a winning combination. It was a gallant challenge, but *Goose* was too far astern for it to work." For his efforts, Mosbacher was beaten across the line by one second, losing the always-valuable ¼ point for placing first. The *London Times* gushed that it was "a day of prolonged, and at times scarcely bearable, excitement."

That Mosbacher's gambit didn't work out wasn't the question. The lively post-race discussions at the bar centered around the propriety, under the racing rules, of a boat turning back to help a teammate by harassing a competitor. "It was the consensus of both

teams," Anderson wrote, "that the rules do not, and never have been adequately explicit to cover situations occurring in team racing events." This led a few years later to the formation of a large committee that included Mosbacher, Whiton, and Anderson to draft a supplementary set of rules for intercollegiate team racing in the United States. The final code was completed by a subcommittee consisting of George O'Day, William S. Cox, and Henry H. Anderson Jr., and later adopted with little variation by the North American Yacht Racing Union (NAYRU) . . . and later (with one variation consisting of a complete prohibition on the practice of going onto another leg of the course to engage an opponent) by the Royal Yachting Association.

Smoke from cannon indicates the start of a British-American Cup race in 1949 off the Royal Yacht Squadron's Cowes Castle.

After losing the first three races, the Americans won the next three, accumulating enough points in the process for the overall win. In looking for differences between the two teams, Anderson mentions that the Americans put more emphasis on practice and training than their opponents—"Although," he reports with ill-concealed pride, "while *Goose* had the fastest average spinnaker setting time of any boat in the fleet, the combined times of each team for all six races when averaged are almost identical." He adds: "The Americans for the first time brought lady crewmembers aboard: Whether this move comes under the heading of progress or not, is not within the scope of this report to determine."

The regatta aside, British hospitality was in full cry: racing Flying Fifteens with their designer Uffa Fox one evening at the Island Sailing Club, relaxing lay day cruises on larger yachts, and wonderful dinners at the several host yacht clubs. Anderson writes:

There were always speeches after dinner, one in particular by Uffa Fox, the great dinghy sailor and designer of the first planing hulls. I had met Uffa as a youngster at Seawanhaka around 1936 during team races in the International 14-foot dinghies. He was a character. Prince Philip had turned Prince Charles over to Uffa so he would teach him how to drive a race-car, sail, and swear. In a good Cockney twang, Uffa

spoke about the historic sights on the Isle of Wight, the Roman roads and castles and the many pubs, including the Half Way Inn better known as the Disappointed Lady. When it was my turn to speak, I told the male aspect of Uffa's punch line:

Jim Buckley and I were settling our nerves in London in 1948 at Ye Old Cheshire Cheese at Wine Court Street No. 1. Over the entrance there was a sign, "Recently renovated in 1777." We would ask the bartendress to screw us up several pegs, a reference to the screw mechanism on the keg taps, and the measured peg projections on the insides of the old pewter mugs. We met a British top-sergeant we had known during the war. He told us he was teaching cadets at Sandhurst how to make gun stocks out of hardwoods like "ash, 'ickory, and h'oak.' When an Oxford student present questioned his pronunciation, he said, "Those woods are so resilient, they are used as piles for piers, and for the benefit of that h'over educated bastard in the back row, when I says piles for piers, I don't mean to convey the meaning of hemorrhoids for aristocracy."

There was also Poona, the Imperial Poona Yacht Club to be more specific, that was founded in 1934 by a group of Oxford students led by Reginald Bennett, as a send-up of the ever-proper Royal Yacht Squadron and Royal Yacht Club. Poona was one of several sailing clubs founded by Bennett, who went on to be doctor, psychiatrist, aviator, member of Parliament, and helmsman of the J-Class *Shamrock V* in 1934-35. In Bennett's obituary (2001), the *Guardian*'s Andrew Roth wrote that Bennett was "a jovial yachtsman who sailed with Prince Philip, an eager free-tripper and a willing accepter of consultancies and directorships." In articles for the doctor's magazine, *Practitioner*, Bennett sought to prove that mothers-in-law will the failures of their children's marriages, and, Roth noted, "In a debate on homosexuality he welcomed the fact that their then fear of imprisonment helped their treatment." Bennett was also a skipper for the British team in the 1949 British-American Cup, which is how Anderson met him.

Imperial Poona's by-laws begin, "For 'white' read 'black,' and for 'coloured' read 'coloured'" throughout." An Indian/Hindustani influence predominates the club. The name comes from Poona, India, the town in the British Empire farthest (or at least a long way) from the sea. The IPYC's slogan is "Chhota hazri," meaning "good health" in Hindustani (Bennett's translation: "There is nothing worse than a Continental breakfast"). Notes II in the IPYC constitution read: "In order to conform to the relevant legislation, to wit the Abolition of the Sex Differentiation Act 1975, the Parthenogenesis Act 1976, the Androgyny

Act 1977, and the Universal Hermaphrodism Act 1978: Rule 6, last sentence, shall be deemed to read 'No memsahib, male or female, is eligible.'"

After a certain amount of strong drink has been consumed, Poona members compete in an annual sailing race in dinghies that must be sailed backwards. The race is most often against Oxford, and held on the River Thames alongside Port Meadow in Oxford. The starting line is between two gateposts on one side of the river, and a cow strategically placed on the other side. The slamming of the gate is the starting "gun." The rules are all backwards (port tack and windward boats have right of way) to match the backwards sailing.

Reasons for cessation of membership in Poona include death, failing to "Think Imperially," imprisonment, or deportation. Outposts of the club include the Inverted Colonists in New Zealand; the Repulsive but not Revolting Outpost in Canada; and the Reactionary Colonists Outpost in Bermuda.

In the course of events, Bennett invited HRH Prince Philip, an enthusiastic sailor, to join Poona. Prince Philip accepted, was immediately given the club's most elevated honorary office, and titled His Highness the Maharaja of Cooch Parwani. When he was moved to send personal notes bearing his royal crest, or telegrams to fellow IPYC members—as he did on the occasion of Bus Mosbacher winning the America's Cup with *Weatherly* in 1962—Prince Philip signed them with his Poona title.

The whole thing had great appeal for Anderson. Bennett and the Poona crowd instantly recognized him as a kindred spirit. Anderson was not only warmly welcomed to Poona's ranks, but also charged with setting up a "Revolting Colonists" outpost on Long Island when he returned home. Titled "Commode," Anderson was head of the Revolting Colonies outpost for more than 50 years. When he retired he was given the title, "Pons Asinorum" [Bridge of Asses, from Euclid].

Anderson's report on the regatta concludes, "No effort was spared to make the visitors feel at home and give them a jolly good time." All that, and they took home the trophy. No wonder the British-American Cup of 1949 lives on with such vibrancy in his memory.

⚓

ANDERSON ARRIVED home in time to sign on as tactician and navigator on board the 12 Metre *Anitra* (1928), which was under charter to W. Mahlon "Bud" Dickerson for the 1949 New York Yacht Club cruise. Dickerson was an admiralty lawyer known for his successful defense of the captain of a Moore-McCormick liner had who shot and killed a demented seaman who had attacked him. Dickerson would become commodore of the New York Yacht Club in 1967. When asked why he belonged to so many clubs in New York, Dickerson is said to have replied, "You wouldn't want me to have to defecate in public facilities, would you?" His father, John Stiles Dickerson, known as "Ironsides," had broken ponies for Wild Bill Cody, and had steered the schooner *Madeleine* to victory in the 1876 America's Cup. His grandfather Mahlon had been secretary of the navy in 1834.

On the 1949 cruise, *Anitra* would win the King's Cup, held on the final day. The day before, the boat had suffered damage on the run to Marion, Massachusetts. As Anderson wrote in his report on that cruise:

> The load of the synthetic genoas was too much for her original, puny winches designed to handle porous cotton sails. One had actually egg-shelled, gone out of round so that the ball bearings had fallen out of their casings and rolled overboard. If that were not deterrent enough for racing the next day, Bud and his brother Jack, who had put Larchmont Race Week on the yachting map, had received the news of their father's passing. The double crisis prompted a soul-searching debate between the brothers

over whether to scrub competing. Their consensus was that the old man would have wanted them to race. In the meanwhile I had been down below lying on a bunk with drift and hammer in ninety degree heat knocking the bolts out of the port side spinnaker winch to use as a substitute for the defunct starboard side genoa winch.

The next day, *Anitra's* crew went out and won one "for the gipper." Anderson's report continues:

We executed a tactic first taught me by Commodore George Nichols, owner of the J-Class Weetamoe. *Once able to lay the spindle on Cormorant Rocks off Mattapoisett, we tacked to port and proceeded inshore as far as possible to get the header off the beach that the sou'wester provided. The first yacht to enter this zone where the volatile breeze coming off the land hits the more stable air over the water and deflects, can tack to starboard and enjoy the lift that puts her ahead of the trailing yachts. By the time* Anitra *tacked back to starboard, sure enough she was to weather the competition and pointing higher when suddenly potential disaster loomed. The leech of the mainsail began to split a foot or so above the end of the boom. Jack Dickerson immediately crawled aft along the boom, depending on the yacht's heel to keep his balance, and rove a line through the first reef cringle and under the boom to keep the sail*

from splitting further. During this tense action it was necessary to reassure the helmsman that Jack was attending to a minor problem.

Also that summer, the historian and also junior instructor at Seawanhaka, Bill Swan, became aware of a new design called a Raven. A 24-foot, open-cockpit boat, the Raven was the first design by a Rhode Islander named Roger A. McAleer. McAleer's lofty goal was to design a boat of 21 feet or more that would outperform the Star and the Indian, a 21-footer raced in Boston and Narragansett Bay in the late 1940s. The boat he envisioned was a centerboarder with light displacement, a long waterline length, and a big mainsail. The first one was built of molded plywood in Rhode Island in 1948. Bill Swan showed the boat to Briggs Cunningham, who was impressed enough to race it in *Yachting* magazine's initial One-of-a-Kind Regatta the following year. It met expectations. Anderson recalls that in one of the first races, Cunningham, on the wind, went by the Star to leeward and sailed across its bow. He did the same thing to a 30-foot Atlantic. The long, light, shallow hull with only a 30-inch overhang, a hard turn at the bilges leaving a flat bottom, and without the drag of a deep keel, gave the Raven very exciting planing characteristics off the wind. After the regatta, Cunningham purchased the boat.

As fleet captain at Seawanhaka for Commodore

George Roosevelt, Harry Anderson quickly got interested in the new design, and as would become his habit when he encountered a project that excited him, he jumped in with both feet. He visited Roger McAleer in Rhode Island, promoted the boat, and helped secure orders. He also bought a Raven for himself. Anderson helped get a national class association started, and became its first president. The first fleet was at Seawanhaka.

He also campaigned the boat. Liz Roosevelt, a woman ten years his junior, was one of his regular crew. Her response to the gossip about her being the closest any woman got to marrying Harry Anderson: no comment. A dignified, unpretentious woman who favors jeans and friendly old sweaters, Liz Roosevelt still lives in Oyster Bay. She works as a bookseller and continues to race in Seawanhaka's Sonar fleet. A third cousin twice removed from Teddy Roosevelt, Liz says she was more closely related to Eleanor than Eleanor was to her husband. "Eleanor was a Roosevelt from my side of the family," Liz Roosevelt says. Liz was a high school history teacher for many years. "Teaching history seemed a logical thing to do," she says, "since my family made so much of it."

Liz Roosevelt resides on Cove Neck Road just a few feet from the water in the old boathouse for Teddy Roosevelt's Sagamore Hill estate that is several hundred yards up the hill. "During World War II there was a subsistence farm on this property," she says. "There were a couple cows. My younger sister and my mother and I made butter on Saturdays. One of us would take a pound up to Sagamore Hill. Mrs. Roosevelt was still alive. If she was feeling well she would invite us little kids in. I got to sit on the polar bear's head of the rug in the living room."

Liz has known Harry Anderson since she was a child. "If I asked to stay late at a dance," Ms. Roosevelt says, "my parents trusted me to get a ride home with either my uncle, or Harry Anderson."

Because the biggest Raven builder was in Sandusky, Ohio, a fleet developed in the Midwest. The national championships were held there in alternate years. One year Harry asked Liz and another crewmember to drive his boat to the regatta. He had work to do at Gull. He told them the trailer would need new tires at some point, which he had loaded into the boat. Their trip was eventful, including the difficulty of removing the rusted wheels from the trailer, and a few hills their vehicle barely made it over. "We arrived at 5:00 a.m.," Liz says. "I was sleeping in the car in the parking lot, and the other crew was sleeping in the boat. Harry showed up at 8, bright and cheery having flown out, ready to get on the ferry."

That was a regatta at Put-in-Bay, Ohio, an island east of Toledo on Lake Erie, during which Anderson and a friend decided to climb the 350-foot memorial to Oliver Hazard Perry late one evening. "It had bricks that stuck out and provided footholds," Anderson says. "But we didn't get very far." Alcohol, as Anderson likes to say, was involved.

Anderson's backing of a trailerable, affordable boat in a day when 6 Metres and larger, even more expensive yachts ruled the roost, was significant. Here was a classic product of a most privileged upbringing, a young man who had had the rare opportunity of steering 12 Metres as a teenager, and who was a well-regarded, dues-paying member of yachting's

Racing upwind in heavy air, the new Raven Class competes in its first national championships, held at the Seawanhaka Corinthian Yacht Club in 1950.

gentry, blithely putting his effort, enthusiasm, and money behind what could be considered a "people's boat." Having Briggs Cunningham in his corner certainly helped. In yachting, that was akin to having LeBron James putting his name on a shoe in 2012. There's no indication that at the time his backing of the Raven was a conscious crusade on Anderson's part. He simply saw the Raven as the way of the future, and as a young, athletic sailor, he liked the challenge offered by this "performance" boat. But promoting the Raven was a move toward the democratization of sailing. For Anderson, it would be the first of many such moves.

Anderson provided a clue to his actions many years later. In a letter titled "As It Was" that he wrote to a nephew who had entered Yale in 2005, he spoke of "the three most profound events during my lifetime in terms of coalescing society, improving national morality, and opening up opportunities: The Great Depression; World War II, which in the military service brought persons from all ranks of society into a common effort—made it possible to know one's fellow countrymen in a committed manner not available, so far, to your generation—and engendered the concept of service for one's country; and the GI Bill of Rights which dramatically changed the complex of higher education by making it available to hundreds of thousands of mature

persons who previously would never have had the experience. It diminished the elitism of the Ivy League, and affected teachers and their approach to teaching. To the degree that it resulted in diversity on ethnic, economic, and religious levels it provided some of the mixing that marked the first two events."

There was a flicker of snobbish backlash about the Raven from some of the Seawanhaka membership. Centerboarders on trailers? Anderson recalls the unrest: "What are we doing handling this kind of class?" some people wondered. "At the first Raven nationals at Seawanhaka, one skipper arrived in a chauffeur-driven car from the Lakes. Someone else came by helicopter. Another bought champagne for everyone. After that, not many talked the boat down."

A rarity these days, the Raven had a long, happy life, with fleets on America's East Coast, and in the Midwest. Around 350 of the boats were built. It was the first one-design class to be built in fiberglass, thanks to the United States Coast Guard Academy in New London, Connecticut, which wanted a fleet in the 1950s. Cape Cod Shipbuilding, in Mattapoisett, Massachusetts, now owns the molds, and has built 40 Ravens since 1961.

One of the basic principles of old-school yacht racing that would stay with Anderson as he

championed new boats, and helped expand and guide sailing's future, was the Corinthian spirit of the sport. In 1953, when Sheila Curtain Gross, who was vice commodore of the Seawanhaka Junior Club when Anderson was commodore, died an untimely death, a trophy was generated in her memory. It was to be awarded to that sailor who best exemplified the Corinthian spirit. The signature at the end of the text on the trophy is that of Harry Anderson. It reads:

A "Corinthian" is a person who plays a sport as an amateur; that is, for the love of it without thought of personal gain, and who brings to the sport the finest qualities associated with the terms 'sportsmanship,' and 'gentleman.' Historically the term Corinthian stems from the town of Corinth, a port located on the isthmus joining the two parts of Greece. The Corinthians were seafaring men of renown and were gentlemen sportsmen who handled their own ships and hunted with their own horses instead of paying others to do so. Undoubtedly, the yachting fraternity adopted the term Corinthian and incorporated it into the names of their clubs because of the world-wide reputation that the men of Corinth acquired for maintaining such high standards of conduct as amateurs in the pursuit of sports.

ANDERSON SAYS it was Eric Olsen who generated the concept for Gull Reinforced Plastics. A brilliant sailor, Olsen was the US representative in the two-man dinghy in the 1956 Olympics. A successful ocean racer, Olson also won major titles in International 14s, 505s, Tiger Cats, Tempests, and Shields. He was an inventor, an engineer, and a yachting journalist. During a previous employment, Olsen and a coworker had designed a sink basin/toilet combination similar to those made of metal on Pullman cars, or for use in house trailers. They thought this would make a nice proprietary product upon which to anchor Gull. Until the title could be cleared, Gull opened a one-room office in Essex, Connecticut. Anderson moved to New Haven, 30 miles south. "We held board meetings on Saturday mornings in the bar of the Griswold Inn in Essex," Anderson says. "The bartender liked to play the organ, leaving it up to the guests to mix their own drinks and sign for them."

Gull rented a former garage in Deep River, near Essex, and installed presses, molds, and mixers for resins, a major draw on funds. More old classmates from Yale and Columbia Law School were hired as attorneys. Anderson says his daily tasks were bookkeeping, the payroll, tax returns, and pricing products for

The Raven: loa 24' 3"; lwl 21' 7"; beam 7'; draft (board down) 5' 4".

customers in addition to working on one or more molds on the production floor. "There was time between laying up fiberglass and resin in a pair of molds, and the time the product took to cure, to dash into the office and tend to accounting details," he says. He had taken a crash course in accounting from the accountant of a local tobacco company. The Connecticut Valley was a major grower of tobacco wrappers in the 1940s and '50s. He devised the use of a 20-column analysis sheet to list all the costs of making a product. "I used the same techniques later when I was executive director of US Yacht Racing Union," Anderson says.

Gull was among the first companies to use the more heat-resistant, nonporous epoxy resins that were first commercially synthesized in the early 1930s. Resistance wiring was buried in the molds to speed up the curing process. Gull made film-developing trays for Eastman Kodak, housings for magnetometers (metal detectors hung from aircraft), and nose cones for Sparrow missiles. They made prototypes for lighter-weight submarine bunks, retractable hardtops for a projected Ford model, and worked on developing a surface for the exterior fabricated concrete panels of Manhattan's Pan Am (now MetLife) Building across Park Avenue. None of those went into production.

While they were unable to raise the capital

needed to produce the original proprietary basin/toilet bowl that had launched the company, Gull did have a proprietary salad bowl that started off as a lamp shade. "It was in the form of a wide bowl, upside down," Anderson says. "In clear resin the light sparkled off the fiberglass strands. We convinced our partners to make the product into salad bowls using different pigments for coloring. This was made from polyester resins that retain an odor after being cured. We solved the problem via a Yale classmate who had married the second-wealthiest producer of perfume essences in France. By introducing a few drops of essence of garlic into the resin mix, it killed the odor of styrene and definitely improved that of the salad."

The idea of making reinforced plastic caskets with veneer overlays to make them look like wood seemed to be another potential winner for Gull until they ran smack into the death business collective. "Caskets are way overpriced, we discovered," Anderson says. "The monopolies of the casket makers and undertakers is more solid than Crane plumbing had in its heyday. Gull overcame the problem of finding inks that would not dissolve in polyester. The sons of the President of International Chemical, who made the inks, were good friends of Anderson and his partners (Yale men, no doubt; sailors for certain). But as practical and potentially lucrative as the casket project was, Gull could not overcome the industry monopoly. Anderson illustrates:

Van Alan Clark, who was a major force in developing the first US Yacht Racing Union Olympic training center at Association Island, on Lake Ontario, was visiting his mother-in-law in Palm Beach when she died suddenly. The Clarks owned most of Avon Products, but when Van found out he would have to rent a new hearse each time he crossed a state border because of the monopoly, he purchased a cheap pine casket and rented a U-Haul to drive her body north to Marion, Massachusetts, where he lived. When overnighting in the Carolinas, he awoke to discover the trailer had been hi-jacked. The police were unable to track it down, so he had to call his wife and report he had lost her mother. The funeral service took place without a body. Months later the trailer was found in a nearby river, indicating the thieves had panicked when they discovered the contents. The insurance companies would not pay off for seven years because there was no corpse.

The failure of the casket project was another nail in the company's coffin. In 1953, Gull Reinforced Plastics was sold to a company in upstate Connecticut that made marine products.

In the early 1950s, Anderson got involved with another small boat, the Finn dinghy.

The Finn, still probably the most physically and mentally demanding single-hander afloat, was designed in 1949 for the 1952 Olympics at Helsinki. The Finn has been in the games ever since, setting a record for Olympic longevity. Anderson's good friend Glen Foster, a world-class helmsman and member of Seawanhaka, was enthusiastic about the boats. Both Foster and Anderson were dismayed that nothing was being done to bring Finns into the United States, so they got the ball rolling and officially started the national class association. Foster was president, Anderson was secretary. "Glen was sailing International 14s at the time," Anderson says. "He told me we needed a boat to sail in the mornings before the crews woke up."

Foster and Anderson, who was now a member of Seawanhaka's race committee (he would go on to become chairman), introduced the powerful, 15-foot dinghies to Seawanhaka, where the first fleet in the United States was started. Many Raven sailors, including Liz Roosevelt, gave them a try. Despite her six-foot frame, the Finn proved to be too much of a handful for her. Today's Finn sailors tend to be large, strong men who spend a lot of time in the gym, and even they are tested by the Finn. Being well over six feet tall and at least 220 pounds—and extremely fit—gives one a fighting chance to manage the overpowered dinghy in heavy wind. John Rousmaniere

Harry Anderson sails his Finn, *Ghorindinky*,
off Seawanhaka in the 1960s.

says Harry talked his father into buying him a Finn when he was 16. "The light air helped us weaklings," Rousmaniere says. Anderson, at around six feet and 170 pounds was no bruiser, but he loved the boat, and tried out for the 1952 Olympics, finishing out of the money. Foster was even shorter, but he did well in the Finn, winning several national championships. "Glen was a great helmsman," Anderson says of his friend, who died of cancer in 1999 at age 69. "He had a way of feathering a boat upwind." Foster would go on to win in 8 Metres, 6 Metres, Dragons, 5.5 Metres (three Scandinavian Cups and a Gold Cup), International 14s (the coveted Prince of Wales Cup), and Tempests (bronze medal at the 1972 Olympics). "He was fully employed as a specialist on the New York Stock Exchange at the time," Anderson says, "making him possibly the last bona-fide amateur to win an Olympic medal." Foster's son, Colin, is another of Anderson's godchildren.

As Anderson has said, there were a lot of boat races. He was sailing at Seawanhaka every summer, traveling to regattas, organizing and promoting the Raven and Finn classes, and generally enjoying himself. He had joined the New York Yacht Club in 1948, and that club's annual 14-day cruises were the focus of every summer. The cruises were held in various sections of the East Coast and consisted of racing from harbor to harbor. A highlight of those early cruises for Anderson was the presence of 13 to 15 New York 32s on the starting line. Anderson's family still owned *Clotho* that his father had bought in the 1930s. Essentially offshore one-design racers 45 feet overall, the 32s were designed by Sparkman & Stephens in 1936, and considered treasures by those who owned them. "I was always told," Anderson said in an oral history interview at Mystic Seaport in 1990, "that once the class had been built—and 20 of them were built at Nevins yard in City Island, New York, at the same time—S&S were told to burn the plans so no one could try to copy them or improve the boats. This was refuted by Olin Stephens."

During the New York Yacht Club cruises, elegant cocktail and dinner parties were scheduled at each port of call. Some were held ashore. Others were hosted on the larger vessels. One of those was the 200-foot, three-masted schooner *Guinevere*, the second of two schooners of that name owned by Edgar Palmer, president of New Jersey Zinc Corporation, and a trustee of Con Edison. Palmer gave the stadium in his name to his alma mater, Princeton University. *Guinevere* had been commissioned into the Corsair Fleet during World War II. One of its commanders had been Lieutenant Henry H. Anderson.

"Mrs. Palmer was a jolly lady," Anderson recalls.

She'd invite her friends out to the boat for cocktails, dinner, and after-dinner games. In one, a person was blindfolded and his shoes and socks were removed, the idea being to identify various objects that were presented with your feet. All kinds of things would happen. Somebody's boobs would be there, or they'd warm up half a melon, or bring down a ventilator cowling. That wasn't as wild as the pearl game. Several of the big yachting families—that of real-estate magnate Walter Gubelmann, the Moores of Moore-McCormack, Avard Fuller of Fuller Brush—would have a big mother ship along. On one cruise they gave everyone 12 pearls on the first day. After dinner, you paired off, boy and girl. You both bared your belly buttons, inserted pearls, and the object was to make the other person laugh before you did, causing the pearl to drop out of their naval. Whoever had the most pearls at the end of the cruise was the winner.

Anderson had loved his family's New York 32, savored the history, and respected the tradition embodied by the class, but after World War II he became fascinated by the future. Racing Finns was uppermost in his mind in the early 1950s, but he found time to get involved in a hydrofoil powerboat designed by Englishman Christopher Hook that Hook was promoting for commercial and military use. He ran into the hydrofoil at the New York Boat Show. Anderson and his Yale roommate Rob Meyer—son of the 6-Metre sailor—had gone to the show to help Roger McAleer promote the Raven. When they saw the hydrofoil, it stopped them in their tracks. "We had a long talk with this tall skinny Brit, Christopher Hook," Anderson says, "and wound up buying the boat. We made some deal that gave him the right to take it here and there for demonstrations, like for the Society of Naval Architects and Engineers at MIT. We did demos for them on the Charles River. We could do figure eights on the foils at 20 knots. The boat was 12 feet long, and would hit 25 knots. Later on, I became an investor in The Atlantic Hydrofoil Corporation, a company we formed to produce hydrofoils."

As might be expected, the history of the boat was of interest to Anderson. During his last years, Alexander Graham Bell's experimental interests turned to boats, namely hydrofoils. He called them "heavier than water" boats because while in motion they are sustained not by their displacement, but by the lift of foils just as wings support aircraft. Bell, and Casey Baldwin, who managed Bell's lab, worked together on a number of hydrofoil craft, including designs for submarine chasers they proposed to the US Navy. After first refusing their plea for the loan of powerful

Liberty engines, the navy relented, sending two of the coveted 400-hp power plants to Bell and Baldwin. The result: the HD-4, a 60-foot hull with an outrigger that attained a marine world speed record of 70.86 miles an hour riding on two sets of fixed, multi-tiered hydrofoils—in 1919.

"Once up and clear of the drag," wrote one who experienced a ride in the HD-4, "she drives ahead with an acceleration that makes you grip your seat to keep from being left behind. The wind on your face is like the pressure of a giant hand . . . an occasional dash of spray stings like bird shot." The novel aspect of the boat was its articulating foils. Forward feelers "read" the waves and changed the pitch of the foils, keeping the boat airborne in rough weather. The foils could also be banked, enabling tight turns. The prospect of this maneuverability, all-weather utility, and speed on the water was irresistible to Anderson and his friends. A hydrofin one-third the size of a displacement vessel and manned by fewer crew could carry the equivalent cargo using much less fuel.

Having taken delivery of his boat, that he named *Icarus,* after the failed, seminal aviator of mythology, Anderson wasted no time putting it to the test with a crossing of Long Island Sound from Old Saybrook, Connecticut, to the Seawanhaka Yacht Club.

"Joining *Icarus* for the trip," he wrote in a 50-page summary of the hydrofoil project in 2010, "was James L. Buckley, William B.'s next-older brother. When his law firm in New Haven learned of the 'perilous voyage,' they stipulated that he complete his will. My cohorts at SCYC had arranged for the firing of cannons and a small band to herald our arrival. Disappointment reigned when the strong northwest winds driving across the ebb and flood tide created the short, steep seas characteristic of Long Island Sound, plus the mechanical deficiency of the shock absorbers for the hydropeds that read the waves to automatically adjust the angle of attack of the foils, aborted the trip."

When Christopher Hook was informed about Anderson's trip, he was dumbfounded. In a letter, Hook cautioned his overly enthusiastic customer: "I managed to shoot down the coastal trip, but you had to have your cut at crossing the Sound! Please remember that your boat is not finished and far from being in a state to do these tricks." Hook's letter goes on to discuss several technical points, complete with mathematical formulas, and requests Anderson's input on same. Two days later Hook writes again. "I realized afterwards that the wave system (you encountered) was the one type which a hydrofin will not take, depending on the size of the boat. I have never experienced it myself, only in theory, and was therefore slow to realize the fact that it was actually (a limiting factor) when encountered head on. . . . If you get a chance to check over the various nuts and bolts, especially the pivot of the foil to see that nothing came loose, it wouldn't be a bad idea. If the weather isn't favorable, I would advise taking it easy on any long hauls until the pressure can be raised again in the hydraulic system and the air can be removed."

Anderson wrote back to Hook a week later, a four-page, single-spaced typed report that was detailed and comprehensive. It included (on page 3) an aside of a capsize that Anderson and his friend Ted Janeway had experienced while trying to foil in rough easterly conditions in Oyster Bay. "The foils forward had shock absorbers that weren't designed for salt water," Anderson recalls. "We hit a wave, the attack was positive on the starboard foil that lifted us up, but it froze, and successive positive hits flipped the boat. Ted was on the high side, and was thrown out. I was to leeward, and was pinned under the boat. Fortunately, we weren't wearing life jackets or I wouldn't have been able to sink down and swim out. It was a close call. A friendly powerboat pulled us in. The only ignominious part of the operation was that a 6 Metre under spinnaker passed us just as we capsized."

Anderson went on his fourth Bermuda Race

in 1954, while still involved with the Gull Products start-up. He went on *Stormy Weather* (1934), a beamier, two-foot longer version of Sparkman & Stephens' famous *Dorade,* the transatlantic race winner in 1931 that skyrocketed the Stephens brothers to prominence. *Stormy Weather* was owned by Jim O'Neill, a Seawanhaka member who lived in Centre Island, who would become Anderson's employer. They raced hard, and when they got to Bermuda, they played just as hard. Toward the conclusion of his long report on the race, Anderson writes:

> The skipper took the helm as we beat for the finish. . . . It only took three-quarters of an hour, but the tension was terrific. Every man had washed that morning, although none of us had shaved, and each man was so keen on his station one might have thought we had fooled around the whole rest of the trip. . . . A motorboat drew alongside and kept up with us. Aboard were Maggie O'Neill, the skipper's wife, and a few ladies interested in other boats. Seeing Maggie made Jim even more excited, and it was a real job keeping his mind on sailing the boat. . . .
>
> Jobs done and anchor on deck, the skipper ordered us below. Without the knowledge of most of us, except for Tom Morris who was by this time the ship's undisputed cellarer, the skipper had put six quarts of imported French

champagne on the ice that morning. These were opened one by one, each man taking a turn at trying to shoot the corks through the skylight. Each man made a toast, and before we knew it, there was only one bottle left for toasting the other boats in the harbor.

Mistress *had been seventh boat to finish, an accomplishment given the sleeker designs she had beaten. It was therefore within our scope of cordial duty to circle* Mistress *as she lay at anchor. Our crew lined the rail and with glasses in hand gave Commodore Roosevelt three cheers. The Commodore was obviously very pleased with this demonstration of good fellowship on our part, so we repeated the ovation.*

The arrivals of loved ones aboard were exciting. . . . Ed Scheu had sad news when Maggie O'Neill told him his wife was not coming because of sickness in her family, but the other ladies made sure he was consoled with encouraging words and strong cocktails.

The 1960 race to Bermuda was memorable for an unpredicted tropical storm that hit the fleet at night after three days of racing in light winds. The storm carried winds hitting 70 miles an hour that shifted often and suddenly. John Rousmaniere was a watch-mate of Anderson aboard *Stormy Weather* that year. As Rousmaniere quoted Anderson in his book,

A Berth to Bermuda, "We were a little shy about shaking out reefs and setting more sail until daylight. There was a big sea and the easiest sail to set was the mizzen staysail. We set it all right but after a while someone looked aft and noticed that the transom was lifting right off the boat. We finished the race with our transom lashed to the mizzen mast."

Bermuda was a frequent port of call for Anderson in the 1950s and '60s. Before he started sailing with Jim O'Neill, Anderson sailed three Bermuda Races on *Mistress*. The rivalry between *Mistress* and DeCoursey Fales' more lively schooner *Niña* was both friendly and intense. Anderson was on *Mistress*, and his close friend Bill Maclay—who had advanced his own racing skills as the director of offshore sailing at the US Naval Academy—was on *Niña*. Commodore Fales, a banker, attorney, and member of one of Rhode Island's founding (as in *Mayflower*) families, always rented a sizable crew house in Bermuda. He would often ask the butler to have a pitcher of daiquiris available at breakfast.

The parties held there were legendary. Late one evening, Anderson climbed on his motorbike, accelerated into the night, and after 200 feet his bike came to a screeching halt, hurling him over the handlebars. He dusted himself off and discovered an anchor line tied to the bike. The other end was secured to an immovable object. On another evening, Anderson and a few pals thought it would be a great joke to lash a friend of theirs who had passed out to a closet door they had removed from its hinges. The idea was to float the door with its passenger into Hamilton Harbor, where he would awaken with the dawn. Luckily, the joke proved too complicated to be executed given the weakened condition of the pranksters, and the lateness of the hour. "It was fortunate we didn't go through with it," Anderson says, who often manages to come up with a classical reference. "By dawn the seagulls would have plucked out his liver, like *Prometheus Unbound*."

As Anderson recalls, "The bar at the Royal Bermuda Yacht Club was comparable to the interchanges on the New Jersey Turnpike, since everyone had to pass by it, or through it, on the way to the dock. One usually paid toll, too, so that if one commuted frequently between Hamilton and the anchorage, one was not likely to last long during the day."

There were many trips to Bermuda for small boat racing in Finns and International 14s. Glen Foster and his wife spent their honeymoon in Bermuda. A sign of things to come was when sailmaker Sandy Van Zandt delivered a new mains'l to Foster when he went through the receiving line at the wedding. Foster

shipped both his Finn and his 14 to Bermuda, an indication that he would be engaged at least part of the time in activities other than those normally associated with honeymoons.

Ding Schoonmaker, for years a top-ranked Star sailor, did six Bermuda Race Weeks in Finns in the 1950s and '60s. Later on, he would work closely with Anderson on the boards and committees of various yachting associations. "Harry was not only instrumental in purchasing Finns for American sailors to use, and then having them shipped," Schoonmaker says, "but he negotiated with those in charge to get the Finn accepted into Race Week." Schoonmaker says there was never a dull moment during those regattas. "One time after racing was over," he says, "Harry and a guy named Bob Bellamy, who was new to the class, and I got on our motorbikes and went off to Tom Moore's Tavern to have lunch. Bellamy's bike was slower, so he had his head down trying to catch up. Harry came to a fork and stopped, undecided which way to go. I stopped beside him. Bellamy missed Harry and plowed into me. I slid across the street, blazer all torn up. Bellamy hit a stone wall, landed on his head. We were bleeding. The bikes looked like trombones. Harry said 'now I remember, we go left.' We got a taxi, held the bikes outside the door. We walked up to the bar and the bartender put a bottle of iodine in front of us.

Said it was the worst road rash he'd seen that day. Then he made us a round of Dark and Stormies."

Anderson says he had actually stopped at the fork to show his friends the old railroad embankment. "In the old days the railroad was the only way to get from Hamilton to St. George's. There were no automobiles. Just garbage and fire trucks."

"Harry used to wear his father's blazers," Schoonmaker says. "When they got even more worn out, he still wore them. Once when I was sailing with him he told us to go ashore without him, he had to get dressed up. When he showed up, he still had on the shorts he'd sailed in, and the tattiest old ragged white shirt I've ever seen. It should have been in the rag bag. But that was one of his quirks. Even in Bermuda, which was classy in those days, he was frayed and tattered. I don't think he ever threw a piece of clothing away."

Anderson was a partner in another reinforced plastics company in Bermuda with International 14 sailor Bruce Lee, a friend from Oyster Bay who would later coauthor *Pearl Harbor—Final Judgment*. In those days, in Bermuda, you could register a corporation in six hours. Anderson and Lee zipped across the harbor in a Boston Whaler to attend board meetings. Bermuda Plastics made lawn furniture, and also built the Finn designed by four-time consecutive Olympic gold medalist (three in Finns), Paul Elvstrom. Research involved a trip to Finland to watch how Elvstrom's plant was building the boats. "We happened to sight down the rail of one of the boats on the line," Anderson says, "and it wasn't straight. It rose and fell quite a bit. Finally we realized that in order to create a space for resin between the deck and the hull, the workers were using pebbles from the driveway, and of course all of them were slightly different." Anderson's involvement in Bermuda Plastics was short-lived.

In the 1950s Anderson also worked on a project called the Medical Practice Letter. The concept was to consolidate a person's medical records in one computer program so that it could be accessed by different physicians, hospitals, clinics, and insurance companies. It was an idea so far ahead of its time that in 2013, despite a federal push to expedite a consolidation of medical records—and despite the available technology—the project is still "in committee." In pre-surgical preparation for eyelid operations he required in 2012, Anderson was required to fill out separate hand-written questionnaires for the surgeon, the hospital, the MD, two eye doctors, and a heart specialist—an all too familiar situation. "In hindsight," Anderson says, "we should have hooked up with IBM for technical and financial assistance."

Sailing on *Stormy Weather* led to a job for Anderson with the Columbia Lincoln Corporation, started by *Stormy*'s skipper, Jim O'Neill, who also owned the Lincoln Warehouse Corporation. Anderson became assistant to the president for a project that involved the conversion of the first fireproof storage building in New York (Sixty-Ninth Street and Lexington Avenue) into offices for the FBI and the New York Telephone Company. The conversion would include a firing range for the FBI. Anderson was vetted and received a "secret" clearance.

"There was a special office with access by a private elevator for J. Edgar Hoover," Anderson says.

> *Whether or not he used it is a question, but he certainly spent time in the city as two of us discovered one night when we sat down at the first table in Toots Shor's night club. Toots came over and said the table was permanently reserved for his close friend Hoover who was prone to drop in unexpectedly.*
>
> *On completion of the project, Jim O'Neill gave a small reception for the VIPs involved. Guests were given a tour before dinner that included Hoover's office, and the bathroom with its monogrammed towels (JEH). At dinner the chief counsel, a former Yale Whiffinpoof, sang the "Whiffinpoof Song." The next morning we*

> *found that the ladies had taken everything monogrammed home as souvenirs, right out from under the noses of the nation's top security force.*
>
> *Business in the Big Apple was tough sledding, with the city paying contractors months late, thereby driving up the cost of doing business by reason of them having to borrow funds to tide over; the Mafia controlling the waste-paper collection; and the building maintenance and cleaning companies virtually owned by the unions. When Columbia Lincoln tried to negotiate a maintenance contract with another company, the leader of the union for the existing contract was paid $20,000 in cash under the table.*
>
> *When "Gentleman Jim" O'Neill was receiving bids to purchase his company, William Zeckendorf was a bidder even though he was on the edge of bankruptcy. Selected was Wellington Associates, second only in the amount of New York real estate owned to the General Services Administration. Wellington also owned the Chrysler Building with offices in the top aerie for its head, Sol Goldman, and chief exec, Alex DiLorenzo. They were thoroughly vetted by the FBI. Yet when Jim O'Neill, counsel, and myself showed up for closing, neither DiLorenzo or counsel appeared, a no-no in real estate transactions. They were using this as leverage to lower the price, but the deal finally went*

through. They offered me a job, but it was not up my alley.

Later in his life, Anderson would contemplate his brief but varied career in the business world and consider it a failure. In 1958, when his job at Columbia Lincoln Corporation came to an end, while he didn't have a specific plan, he removed himself from the job market. As he told head of school at Ransom Everglades in 1991, "commerce didn't suit me."

As it happened, in 1958 the America's Cup would be reestablished after a wartime hiatus that began after the 1937 match. That would definitely suit Harry Anderson.

EIGHT | Now or Never

F or the first race of the 1958 America's Cup match between *Sceptre* (K-17, challenger, UK) and *Columbia* (US-16, defender, USA), Harry Anderson found himself aboard the destroyer USS *Mitscher* as liaison between the New York Yacht Club and President Eisenhower and his party. This was not only the first race of America's Cup XVIII, but the first race of the first match since 1937, after which America's Cup racing was temporarily abandoned because of World War II and its aftermath.

In 1956, England's Royal Yacht Squadron suggested to the New York Yacht Club, then holder of the Cup, that the Cup should be revived. The RYS had an agenda. They were eager to challenge. Their suggestion started internal debate at the NYYC. Building more J-Class yachts was financially out of the question in 1956. Money was tight. The war had surely saved the country from a depression and gotten industry going, but war is expensive.

Commodore Henry Sears wanted the Cup to be revived. According to Dyer Jones, current head of the Herreshoff Marine Museum/America's Cup Hall of Fame in Bristol, Rhode Island, and former commodore of the NYYC, Henry Morgan was dead set against it. "His attitude was," Jones says, "let's not ever drag that thing out again." Morgan, youngest son of famed financier, J. P. Morgan, was a powerful force at the NYYC. He had well-earned global respect in the yachting community. At the time, American yachting organizations shunned foreign entanglements for fear of losing control of their own racing programs. Harry Morgan had begun reaching out on his own, and was representing the United States in Europe as an unofficial observer long before the North American Yacht Racing Union (NAYRU) joined the International Yacht Racing Union in 1952. The IYRU had celebrated Morgan's efforts by naming him an honorary vice president. "For a generation," Jones says, "no one

The 12-Metres *Sceptre* (foreground) and *Columbia* cross tacks during the 1958 America's Cup series.

had a leadership position at the NYYC without Harry Morgan's approval. He was running a benevolent aristocracy."

Morgan lost the Cup battle. The Cup was revived. The NYYC successfully petitioned the New York Supreme Court to modify the Deed of Gift to a minimum waterline length of 45 feet for competing yachts, allowing the more affordable 12 Metres to become the yachts of choice. "But Morgan won the war," Dyer Jones says. "He was Chairman of the America's Cup Committee—better known on the waterfront as the Selection Committee—for the rest of his life. If the event had to be revived, he was going to be in charge of it."

Harry Anderson is not quite sure how, as

a fledgling member of the race committee, he landed the classy, presidential liaison assignment. "My second cousin, Henry Taylor, might have had a hand in it," Anderson says. "He knew the press officer at the White House." That would be the father of the Henry Taylor with whom Anderson had watched the Cup races and who had played ping-pong with Ava Astor in 1937, aboard *Orion*. In 1958, Taylor was owner of the elegant Sparkman & Stephens 72-foot yawl, *Baruna* (1938).

Anderson met with *Mitscher*'s skipper, Commander Douglas Pate, the Friday before the race, which was scheduled for Sunday. Anderson was given a sound-powered telephone so he could communicate on a private, secure line from O Deck, where he would be with the presidential party, directly with Pate on the bridge. He was very familiar with the instrument. It was a field artillery phone that had been standard equipment in the US Army. Anderson had also been informed by Commander Pate—who would become commander of the Atlantic Fleet— that the ship might proceed directly to Norfolk after the race without stopping at Newport in order to speed the president to Washington. Eisenhower was weighing what to do with his advisor, Sherman Adams, who was under fire for his wife having accepted the gift of a vicuna coat from an arms supplier. "In today's climate of augmented graft," Anderson

As the New York Yacht Club liaison to the presidential party in 1958, Harry Anderson briefs President and Mrs. Eisenhower at the first America's Cup held in 12-Metre yachts.

says, "this would hardly rank as a peccadillo." At the time it was a cause celeb.

On Sunday, Anderson reported to *Mitscher* in yachting attire—double breasted yachting jacket, dark trousers, cap, with field glasses around his neck—where he was introduced to President Eisenhower and his wife Mamie, and several of the president's golfing partners. These included Eisenhower's personal physician, Major General Howard Snyder, and W. Alton Jones, then president of Cities Service. Anderson had prepared plastic cutouts of the yachts, buoys, wind direction arrow, and starting line with magnets glued to them so they would stick to the ship's steel bulkhead. Anderson says Eisenhower was friendly, easy to get along with. "I briefed the group on pre-start maneuvers," Anderson says, "a useless exercise inasmuch as there was so little wind the start was postponed. When it was resumed, neither yacht hazarded tacking on the other for fear of stalling out." To while away the time, Anderson and the president talked about their common love of trout fishing, with Anderson one-upping the president with his story of fishing for golden trout on the Kern River in Sequoia National Park. In a report on his day with President Eisenhower, Anderson writes:

By then lunch—sandwiches were being served by way of a Marine stationed behind each of us who would hold the sandwich plate or the field glasses, depending upon whether one was eating or viewing. Because of the postponement, the vast Sunday spectator fleet was no match for the casual patrol system (never again was an initial Cup race held on a Sunday). The starting area was a cacophony of yachts of all shapes and sizes. As Mitscher *blasted its horn several times while getting underway after the start, the President looked over the side and remarked, "This reminds me of a drunken cab driver in a Paris traffic jam."*

We watched part of the first leg of a dull race in little wind, with the challenger being no match for the defender, before we peeled off at flank speed for Newport. The President had made the decision to cashier Sherman Adams, and wanted one last round of golf before leaving for the capital on Monday. In those days, they docked destroyers without a tug assist. This required coming in with enough speed to have steering control, but not so much that you couldn't back down. They backed Mitscher *down just right and dropped the lines over the bollards. A month later a destroyer going too fast piled into a pier. Tugs were required after that.*

Between Alton Jones and the Newport community, the President was kept active ashore and afloat. He also played golf with Howard Cushing, then head of the Newport Reading

Room. A notable photo of the two hung in the Reading Room shows them on the course surrounded by several young men in business suits. On close inspection, one sees their golf bags are holding guns, not clubs. Cushing also invited Ike aboard a lobster boat to see how crustaceans are trapped. The day before, the skipper of the boat was sent out to put lobsters in the traps so the President would not be disappointed. The next day the man pulling the traps was aghast to see that the skipper had neglected to remove the rubber bands from the claws. As he was tossing the shorts over the side, the President asked why. He was told they were illegal. The President said to keep a dozen of the shorts, having been told they had the most delicate flavor. When he was advised he might be arrested for taking shorts ashore, the President said he thought he could take care of that situation.

After his job at Columbia Lincoln Corporation came to an end, Anderson got more involved with the NYYC. His credentials were excellent. Having started his flag officer career in the Adirondacks as vice commodore of the Upper St. Regis Lake Yacht Club at age 12, improved his skills as vice commodore of the Pine Knot Yacht Club at Adirondack-Florida School at age 14, and having been the first commodore of the Seawanhaka Corinthian Junior Yacht Club at age 16, he was both seasoned as a yacht club administrator, and totally conversant

with the Racing Rules of Sailing. He was so conversant with the rules that after the British-American Cup of 1949, during which Bus Mosbacher had doubled back to help his teammates by blocking a British boat, Anderson had helped re-write the rules for team racing. That ad hoc committee sounded like a who's who of yachting: Leonard Fowle (former secretary of the ICYRA), Bob Bavier, Bill Cox, Swede Whiton, Glen Foster, and Anderson. "We finalized the draft at 5:00 a.m. at Bill Cox's house in time for breakfast before commuting to work in Manhattan," Anderson recalls.

He had become chairman of the race committee at Seawanhaka in 1950, and he entered the flag officer line of ascension as rear commodore of Seawanhaka in 1961. Diplomacy, the other key attribute needed to successfully run a private sporting club where those who sail to compete and for pleasure have to coexist, while graciously making room for the bridge players and the diners, is something Anderson appears to have been born with. By joining the race committee at the NYYC, Anderson was identified as a potential flag officer of the yacht club.

An indication of Anderson's early involvement at the NYYC was his presence at a little-known meeting at the 21 Club, one of New York's timeless high-society restaurants located just a few blocks south of the yacht club's Manhattan station. The meeting was called by Jim O'Neill, Anderson's owner-skipper on *Stormy Weather,* and his boss at Lincoln. It was about money; namely, how to raise the money the syndicate needed to put its defender, *Columbia* (US-16), on the starting line for the 1958 match. "21" was the right choice for the meeting. One pays dearly for average food at "21," but the ambience is wonderfully camp. The vintage lawn jockey hitching post at the entrance and the scores of antique model airplanes and other toys that hang from the ceiling appeal to the restaurant's socially conscious clientele. And as *New York Times* food critic Pete Wells has written about the 84-year-old restaurant, "A meal at 21 sails along on a river of alcohol and high spirits."

"Commodore J. Burr Bartram headed the *Columbia* syndicate," Anderson says.

He and past Commodore Henry Sears had advanced the money for tank testing. They had picked the afterguard except for the skipper. They wanted Briggs Cunningham, but Briggs was reluctant to jump in. If Briggs didn't come in, and both add and attract some money to the pot, they'd be in a bind. Jim O'Neill had the idea of doing an IPO. At lunch that day were Bartram, Sears, O'Neill, and me. O'Neill's idea was discussed, and rejected. They ended up persuading Briggs to be the skipper, which helped fatten the financial pot.

One of the races in the defender trials in '58 illustrates the financial woes. The race committee had set the course, and Vim *(US-15) was out there sailing around, but there was no sign of* Columbia. *Pretty soon the race committee had to start the countdown, and it would be a sail-over for* Vim. *Suddenly* Columbia *appeared off Ft. Adams, being towed out at flank speed. The people who had cast the keel for the boat hadn't been paid. They had put a lock on her. Henry Sears had to write a check for a couple hundred thousand to get her released.*

Another indication that Anderson had stepped into the New York Yacht Club's inner circle at an early stage was his co-authorship, in 1958, of what was known as the "Assignment and Acceptance" document. This important document was, in essence, the first of what would be several America's Cup protocols. As Commodore Dyer Jones explains, Assignment and Acceptance covers the following conditions: "A Cup match having taken place, and the Cup having been won by X, New York now agrees to assign and X agrees to abide by the Deed of Gift, and X acknowledges that jurisdiction regarding the Deed of Gift will be the state of New York Supreme Court. At the time we didn't know how important that would become," Jones says. "That document had to be signed following the final race."

Anderson says the document he wrote with Commodore Don Kip and Robert Erskine specifies how the defender chooses the challenger of record. By signing the A&A, the challenger agrees to abide by the Deed of Gift and take proper care of the Cup. The idea behind A&A is the defender only has to deal with one club. "Along the way," Anderson says, "when the Royal Thames Yacht Club was challenger of record, their commodore—Elmer Ellerworth-Jones—called Harry Morgan and said they couldn't get the challengers to agree on conditions for the trials. Morgan called me and Bud Dickerson, who was commodore at the time, to have lunch with the RTYC commodore. Morgan said tell them when they meet in May if they can't agree then the NYYC will tell them how to run the trials. That's how to handle that kind of situation. It all got too egalitarian after that.

"Various 'protocols' have been written to adjust conditions or interpret the Deed. For example Hood began to sell his superior sail cloth around the world, blurring the concept of 'built in the country of the challenger.' Boats and equipment were supposed to be designed and built in the country of the challenger. But what about a winch that was made in Italy but used parts made in other countries? Or the Hood sailcloth? We finally had to add a protocol that if it were a 'shelf item' you could buy in a marine store, it didn't matter where it was made. That's how we slowly gave away our technology."

It was 1958 when Anderson began frequenting the Newport Reading Room, a gentlemen's club founded in 1854. Considered to be one of the centers of Newport social life for men, the Newport Reading Room is one of five clubs of the Victorian era that remain established in the east. The others are in York and Bar Harbor, Maine, Edgartown, Martha's Vineyard, Massachusetts, and Saratoga Springs, New York. The Newport club, which has quietly and steadfastly maintained its gentlemen-only membership policy through an age of women's liberation, extended privileges to the New York Yacht Club race committee during the match in 1958. The reading room's large, wood-frame clubhouse on Bellevue Avenue was built as a home in Greek Revival style in 1841. Handsomely

Harry Anderson with Cdre. Mahlon Dickerson and his wife, Betty, at the Savannah Club in New York's Greenwich Village after a ball in the 1950s.

The NYYC Race Committee, photographed aboard
Chauncey Stillman's yacht *Westerly* in the mid-1960s.
With Captain Sewall on station, the committee
included, from left, Willis Fanning, Briggs Dalzell,
Joe Bartram (under awning), U. S. Navy Commander
Richard J. Dermody (front), Jerry Bliss, Harry
Anderson, and Rob Wessman.

restored and enlarged, it is elegant and well kept on the outside, unpretentious and comfortable inside. The walls of the long, inviting bar of dark wood that has been polished for many generations by the elbows of navy blazers and tweed jackets, are hung with amusing caricatures of the members. There are two dining rooms serving good, basic fare, and several cozy libraries for reading and conversation.

"We told them we'd like to come up in non-Cup years," Anderson says, "so they initiated a nonresident membership." When Anderson eventually moved to Newport, the Reading Room made him a full member without

Anderson with Tim Dolman (left), David Brown, and Dr. Charles Langston, at the Newport Reading Room bar.

having to first be a subscriber; a compliment. The subscriber category is typical of Newport clubs. Subscribers are on probation, and have to be reelected every year until they prove their mettle. Anderson has proved his time and again, including one late night after a prolonged session at the Reading Room bar when he and another member of the Race Committee were seen energetically directing traffic at the corner of Bellevue and Memorial Drive, one of Newport's busier intersections, in an attempt to unravel a traffic snarl.

⚓

ANDERSON FOUND himself fully involved in the administration of yachting. It wasn't something he planned. He had let his consuming interest in boats and the water, in combination with his scholarly approach to life, lead the way. "I don't know if Harry ever made conscious decisions, or if he ever had a plan," says Dr. Charlie Langston, a Newport Reading Room cohort and personal friend. "If the whole world is your cousin, you don't need a plan."

Langston recalls some guidance Anderson gave him when he was going through a divorce. "I got talking to him one evening at the Reading Room," Langston says. "I was having a tough time of it and thought he might give me some

words of advice. Harry looked at me and said, 'You'll probably need a new boat.'"

As early as the late 1940s, Anderson was already well known as a first-rate judge with a have-rulebook-will-travel outlook. He made an annual trek to the US Naval Academy in Annapolis, Maryland, to be on the jury for the MacMillan Trophy, the oldest collegiate sailing event, sailed in the Academy's fleet of 40-foot yawls. Anderson was a popular judge by virtue of his willingness to spend time with the sailors discussing the rules. He also relished the social, apré-sail aspect of a regatta. After officiating at the annual collegiate Timme Angsten Regatta in Chicago in 1950, the principals sent him this morning-after "toast" penned on stationary of the Terrance Plaza Hotel in Cincinnati:

We met you in 218
Under the influence of grenadine
Now here's to Harry, he's back East
He's missed by all who rest in peace—
Cease those stories about geese from Greece
And conquests of the golden fleece;
Buy yourself a third-hand Raven
And tack back, Jack,
To old New Haven.

Seriously, Harry, your presence at our little snowbound party was the climax to a wonderful week.

Along the way Anderson had become president of the Yacht Racing Association of Long Island Sound (YRA LI), a volunteer position. He was also head of Seawanhaka Race Committee, and a member of the YRA LI Appeals Committee charged with unraveling tricky protests. He recalls one incident at Seawahaka in particular. "It was a starting situation in 20 knots or more. A phalanx of 70-footers descended on the committee boat with *Bolero* on the weather berth. All were early for the gun by reason of not having properly calculated the set of the tide. On *Bolero*, Corny Shields was tactician for (owner) John Nicholas Brown, and one could hear him admonishing John to bear off as he was going to be over early. To leeward were two other big yawls, and then, to the detriment of all three, Harry Morgan's *Djinn*. Harry, of course, was instrumental in getting Harold Vanderbilt's new rules accepted internationally, and knew them by heart, especially the new barging rule. Hence he lodged a protest, and the Appeals Committee of the Yacht Racing Association of Long Island Sound disqualified the three yachts to weather of *Djinn* for barging—the first appeal on the barging rule to come before a protest committee. The NAYRU Appeals Committee agreed about the disqualification of *Bolero*, but exonerated the intervening yachts as having been innocent victims, not perpetrators.

Once during his race committee chairmanship at Seawanhaka, Anderson conducted two regattas in two different locations on the same day. One was a Long Island Sound multi-club, multi-class regatta. The other was a feeder race from Oyster Bay to Newport for Bermuda Race entries. Having started the race to Newport in the morning, he set up the YRA multi-club race to finish late afternoon. In order to get to Newport in time to finish the feeder race, the race committee chartered a rear-engine Grumman Seabee floatplane. With Anderson was his friend Glen Foster, who wanted to scout the Newport waterfront for a Bermuda Race berth, and David Jewett, who carried the freshly calibrated race chronometer.

"By dark," Anderson says, "we were off Watch Hill at the eastern end of Long Island Sound and could see that a fresh sou'wester was kicking up whitecaps. We stayed offshore hoping to sight the progress of the yachts, but a sudden thunder squall blotted out all visibility. By the time the squall cleared we were over the stretch of beach and salt ponds that extend from Watch Hill to Pt. Judith. Fuel was low, and weather interference blocked radio transmission, so the pilot announced we would make an emergency landing on one of the salt ponds. He mentioned there was no way of knowing what rocks, stumps, or other impediments might be lurking below the dark surface."

The landing was successful, but the long walk across the ponds and marshes on decades of old oyster shells was tough on the feet. The party homed in on the water tanks of the Charlestown Naval Auxiliary Air Field. There they were met by the chief, who took one look at their bloody feet and arranged for tetanus shots at nearby Quonset Naval Air Station, and bunks at the bachelor officers' quarters. "But the first antidote he suggested was a few swigs from his bottle of bourbon to which no one objected," Anderson says.

As race committee chairman, Anderson hadn't forgotten about finishing the boats in Newport. "It turned out that David Jewett had served during World War II in England under the admiral currently in command of Quonset. He phoned his former CO. The next morning the duty officer was duly impressed when the admiral's limousine arrived with flags flying to pick me up.

"Being chairman of the SCYC Race Committee had put me in a position to lead YRA LI," Anderson says. "When you are president of the YRA in your region, that doesn't involve enough action to interfere with your business. You can do it on the side." But when the executive director of the YRA LI died suddenly, Anderson found himself pinch hitting in that more time-consuming job. The thought and

effort he put into it is evident in excerpts from two letters he wrote, the first of which is to commodores and race committee chairmen of the 60 member clubs then under YRA governance. It's fair to say the recipients were uplifted, energized, and also amused by their president's words:

Portia, in her argument to the court, apostrophized, "The quality of mercy is not strain'd, it droppeth as the gentle rain from heaven."

With the increase in Sound, area, and fleet racing, additional starts for new classes and more and more juniors graduating into the YRA, Portia could not very well address the situation on the Sound today in similar terms. The race committees are more strained than ever, and quality of performance, unfortunately, is not heaven sent. . . .We would be remiss in not emphasizing that the success of these programs rests with you gentleman of the race committees. Good racing is the result of good committee work, and in the long run it is the race committees who set the pace, who keep the courses short in light airs, and who goad the skippers to sea in heavy weather to try their mettle and their gear.

Quality in committee work is the result of the chairman's training, planning, and overseeing of his committeemen and is achieved, to quote

Commodore DeCoursey Fales' renowned counsel to his watch captains, by "'tention to details!"

Whether you operate on the wide open Sound or in the inner recesses of the Bay, the impact of your contribution to the sport is felt and recognized throughout the YRA.

May wind and weather droppeth favorably for you from the heavens.

Anderson's second letter was to all YRA members, and it tackled a subject that will always be a thorny issue for sailing, especially racing. His forthright approach was refreshing, his admonitions timeless. He began by recounting an incident in which a life was saved because two yachts "heeded the traditions of the sea" and abandoned their own race to help a yacht from another class that was in distress. Dated October 1966, the letter continues:

The increasing frequency of fatal accidents, to say nothing of the close calls which have occurred in sailing craft during the past few years demands a radical revision of our approach and attitude towards the sport of yacht racing in North America.

In each case, almost without exception, the cause of the accident has been the failure to observe one or more of the cardinal Rules of Safety, for example, the wearing of an adequate life jacket

when conditions warrant taking such a precaution, staying with the boat when capsized, etc.

While organized racing on Long Island Sound has been spared such a fatality for over two decades, tragedy struck home waters during the Labor Day weekend when two junior sailors, after being expressly instructed to wear life jackets, removed them on the race course. Moreover, they carried several pounds of weights in their pockets—an outright violation of the racing rules—so that when they attempted to right the boat after a second capsize, the crew member no longer had the energy to support himself in the water. In spite of the valiant attempts of the helmsman to keep him afloat, he went under, and the helmsman himself was only saved from drowning by the quick action of the crew of another sailboat. . . .

To try to outwit the elements or to beat the canons of the sport is to brook disaster. The tragic and needless drowning of a junior as a result of the blatant flaunting of the safety rules drives home in a traumatic way the dilemma facing the yachting fraternity today: either we must enforce conformance with the time-tested safety procedures, or reduce the scope of our exposure by racing only in enclosed waters on extremely stable boats under light to moderate weather conditions.

To move in the latter direction, in addition to being patently unpalatable, would serve only to intensify basic deficiencies which already exist in our adult and junior programs—lack of exposure to heavy weather and sea conditions and failure to develop competence in capsizable, high-performance boats. It is shocking to realize that existing standards of seamanship and gear in many classes raced locally render them incapable of competing in breezes of twenty knots or more.

The life jacket, which is readily worn by European sailors, must become recognized as a "badge of battle" rather than a "sign of shame" as it is all too frequently regarded in North America....

It must be the aim of your YRA LI executive committee to develop regulations for incorporation into sailing instructions providing for the mandatory wearing of life jackets by all crew members in centerboard and high-performance keel boats whenever whitecap conditions exist. The penalty for failing to do so would be disqualification....

Never have the words of Joseph Conrad rung so true: "Of all the living creatures upon land and sea, it is ships alone that cannot be taken in by barren pretenses— that will not put up with bad art from their masters."

Anderson was also vice commodore of Seawanhaka at the time. He missed a trustees meeting at which it was decided that Rear Commodore Julian K. "Dooley" Roosevelt would be removed from the line of ascension to commodore. As son of the venerable George Roosevelt, Julian K. had a tough act to follow. But he had some impressive accomplishments on his résumé, including his leadership of the 1964 Olympic team that had won medals in all classes in Japan. And he'd worked hard for the club as a flag officer. Roosevelt's nickname came from a fictional bartender created by Chicago humorist Finley Peter Dunne. "Mr. Dooley" appeared in Dunne's political sketches, often casting barbs at President Teddy Roosevelt (Julian K. was a first cousin once removed from the President—Teddy Roosevelt's father and Julian K's grandfather were brothers). The nickname was well applied. Excessive drinking was in vogue in those days, but it was bedeviling Roosevelt, often causing him to behave in an unseemly manner at club social events. Anderson didn't have a quarrel with the trustees' decision, but he thought it unfair that the trustees hadn't told Roosevelt of their resolve. Roosevelt was in Europe at the time, officiating at a regatta. As a friend of Roosevelt's, Anderson took it upon himself to let Dooley know of the decision. It's hard to imagine dealing with such a delicate subject in a more palatable way than Anderson managed.

After a cheery opening greeting, Anderson's letter reported on the trustee meeting. "In order to move ahead with the selection of a Nominating Committee, the Commodore sought the opinions of the trustees respecting future officers and their assessment of the extent to which resistance exists among segments of the membership against his being succeeded by yourself." (Note: that deft, comprehensive construction requires at least one more read through.)

Anderson continues: "Unfortunately, the consensus was that strong enough opposition exists so that such a slate would be voted down, and it was the observation, therefore, that the result would be serious friction and be most embarrassing for everyone, especially yourself.

"For this reason, the advice of the board members to the Commodore was to apprise the nominating committee, when selected, of this situation and to suggest withholding your name for office of Commodore until sometime after the 1968 Olympic Games. . . . Gossip being what it is, I felt you should know the picture as it now stands first hand before you hear a re-hash via the grapevine."

Testament to the virtue of Anderson's letter was a response he received from George Roosevelt Jr. after the letter had been shared

with him. "Your perceptive letter regarding Dooley was gratefully received," Roosevelt writes, and goes on to discuss his brother's dire need to recognize the serious nature of his disease.

Anderson ended up acquiring the YRA LI executive directorship, and working with George Hinman, former commodore of the New York Yacht Club who was then president of the North American Yacht Racing Union (NAYRU), the governing body of sailing. At the time, Hinman was plotting to combine the NAYRU, YRA LI, Junior YRA, International Sailing Association, and Junior YRA LI under one roof. It was a logical solution. None of the organizations were flush. If they were consolidated, there would be enough money for a director and a secretary to keep all the affairs in order. When that came to pass in the mid-1960s, it was Harry Anderson who took charge with the titles of corresponding secretary and assistant treasurer of NAYRU. He and a secretary worked out of two small rooms connected by a bathroom on the top floor of the New York Yacht Club's Manhattan station. Story has it that the file cabinets were kept in the bathtub. He would continue as executive director of NAYRU through the presidential terms of Jim Michaels and Lynn Steadman.

During the years leading up to (and beyond)

that consolidation of yachting organizations, Anderson plunged head first into the complex, international yachting scene. It was complex because of isolationist attitudes on the part of several larger American yacht clubs unwilling to surrender their old-guard exclusivity to outside control. The New York and Eastern Yacht Clubs, for example, had blocked or delayed the formation of a national governing body for their sport until 1942, when they finally joined NAYRU. It would be another ten years before NAYRU became associated with the International Yacht Racing Union (IYRU).

It was Harry Morgan who suggested to Anderson that he become involved in the IYRU. The Morgan and Anderson families had long been close friends. Anderson's parents were also friends with the Pennoyers, with whom they had traveled and skied in Europe in the 1930s. Frances Pennoyer was Harry Morgan's sister. Both the Morgans and the Andersons had raced New York 32s, bringing them even closer together on a regular basis.

"A typical trait of the Morgans I have known is pragmatism," Anderson says. "They don't fool around or dodge issues. They take after JP, who locked up all his bankers after the crash and told them they weren't leaving the room until they had come up with a solution. Harry Morgan was a very level-headed,

practical person. When he had breakfast aboard his boat, he would take a paper napkin and wipe the egg residue off his plate to save soap and water.

"A typical example of the problems Harry Morgan faced at IYRU was trying to get the Vanderbilt rules accepted, the rules Vanderbilt started rewriting in the 1930s with the help of my father, Philip Roosevelt, and Van Merle-Smith. Vanderbilt took them to the UK. The UK ran the international body for years. He talked with Sir Ralph Gore, head of the Yacht Racing Union and commodore of the Royal Yacht Squadron. Ralph was a rugged, opinionated character. And Vanderbilt never thought he had to be polite to anyone, or be obeisant, or plead for anything. He thought common sense prevailed. So those two got nowhere. But Harry Morgan was a friend of Norway's King Olaf—Prince Olaf then. Morgan got the Norwegians to agree with Canada and the US to experiment with the new rules at some of their clubs. Other countries followed suit, and the Brits were overruled. It was a neat bit of diplomacy. Many things were like that. It was like the United Nations."

Morgan persuaded Anderson that he should attend meetings of an IYRU committee as an observer because that was where delegates from around the world got to know one another. And it would pave the way for full membership. "My first was the Centerboard Boat Committee," Anderson says, "where I sat with famous International 14 sailor Stewart Morris, and top-notch French 505 sailor Jacques Lebrun. Later International 14 sailors Dr. Stuart Walker of Annapolis and Shorty Trimmingham from Bermuda became close friends. I remember 505 Class rules permitted only one trapeze for the two-man crew. Lebrun circumvented that restriction by standing on the shoulders of his crew with the tiller extension in one hand, the trapeze wire in the other. It didn't take the class long to revise the rules, a process that international classes had to submit to the respective keel or centerboard committees for approval."

Later, George Hinman, chair of the IYRU Constitution Committee, put Anderson on a task force of the committee to completely revise the IYRU constitution. "That was a hot potato," Anderson recalls. "The committee had been delegated by the IRYU Permanent Committee to do the job, but their work had become bogged down in international politics." Anderson would get the job done, and go on to chair the IYRU's Constitution Committee.

Anderson's work on the international scene required a deft touch that combined a keen sense of diplomacy with patience, not to

mention dedication and hard work. Relationships had to be established and nurtured with care. With his worldly outlook, Harry Morgan had opened the doors and created a new, more elegant American model that had been embraced overseas. Anderson was well suited to carry on in Morgan's footsteps.

"As an example of how associations developed," Anderson says, "we became close to the representative of the Australian Yachting Federation, at the time a paper organization run out of his brokerage office. We set him up with the constitution and bylaws of the NAYRU, and later met with him when in Sydney at his office. Our association continued long after the AYF had set up office in a building contiguous to the Royal Sydney Yacht Squadron, especially during the five or more years we spent judging at the Olympic Classes winter regattas off Melbourne on Port Phillip Bay; when judging at the Soling Worlds at Pitt Water (north of Sydney) in 1974; and in connection with the America's Cup." All it took to be effective was being there—no small order.

Along with his racing and jury duties, the trick of keeping all the various administrative yachting balls up in the air would have created busy enough days for Anderson. But in addition, the revival of America's Cup competition in 1958 had triggered a raft of challenges. From

1962 to 1980, there were seven America's Cup matches—an average of one every two and a half years, a record pace. Given his participation in the Cup's revival, not to be involved would have been unthinkable for Harry Anderson.

In 1962, when the American 12 Metres *Weatherly* (US-17), *Easterner* (US-18), *Nefertiti* (US-19), and *Columbia* squared off in the trials for the right to defend the Cup, Anderson was a member of the Race Committee, and the Committee on Racing Appeals. *Weatherly* won the trials. After two races in the Cup match it quickly became evident that the Royal Sydney Yacht Squadron's *Gretel* (KA-1) was a faster boat, especially upwind. But four-time Olympian and Australia's Yachtsman of the Year (1962) Jock Sturrock, was no match for *Weatherly*'s crafty skipper, Bus Mosbacher. "Bus would carry *Gretel*, that was catching up on the weather leg, past the starboard lay line," Anderson recalls, "knowing he could reach off and match *Gretel*'s speed.

> *In the critical fourth race, Mosbacher orchestrated a wonderful move.* Weatherly *was leading two races to one.* Gretel'*s crew had made a tactical mistake in Race One, then famously won Race Two, surfing past* Weatherly *under spinnaker after* Weatherly *broke her pole, then lost a drifting match in Race Three after asking for a lay day during*

> *which it blew, another mistake. If there ever was an alarm that the Cup was in jeopardy, this was it. Race Four was critical because* Gretel *was faster, and the crew was learning the boat all the time.* Weatherly *had the lead in Race Four, but because of a wind shift the last leg turned into a close spinnaker reach.* Gretel *was gaining, sailing higher and faster under spinnaker. Bus didn't think he could hold them off until the finish. He told the crew to get the spinnaker down and put up the genoa, but to have another spinnaker ready. When* Weatherly'*s spinnaker went up,* Gretel *responded, dousing her spinnaker and putting up a genoa. Some of* Gretel'*s young crew told us about it a few days afterwards over drinks, said there had been an argument on board. The foredeck crew asked why take the sail down, they were carrying it just fine. The afterguard said the wind must be coming ahead. The afterguard won the argument, as usual. Down came* Gretel'*s spinnaker. Immediately* Weatherly *broke out the new spinnaker and bore off, catching* Gretel *unprepared.* Weatherly *won by 26 seconds, and went on to win the next race and the Cup.*

President John F. Kennedy was watching the races in 1962 from a US Navy destroyer that appeared to be drifting quite close to the starting line. "We were worried that a boat tacking to port right after the start wouldn't clear the vessel," Anderson says. "Race

Committee Chairman Briggs Dalzell radioed the ship and asked it to move 200 yards. The skipper radioed back that he didn't take orders from anyone—he had the president of the United States on board. Dalzell had to contact the Coast Guard. Once past Fort Adams, on Castle Hill, the Navy comes under the authority of the Coast Guard. It took the commandant of the Coast Guard to get the skipper to move. If we'd been able to reach the president, it wouldn't have been a problem. A sailor, Kennedy would have understood right away."

Anderson was on the Auxiliary Race Committee (and Committee for Racing Appeals) for the 1964 match between *Sovereign* (K-12) and *Constellation* (US-20), which was swept by *Constellation*. The racing was without incident that year, but after one race strong northwest winds descended upon Newport. An alert went out, and many boats were moved off piers to anchors off the Ida Lewis Yacht Club at the harbor's south end. The Race Committee boat was one of them. Race officials had dined that evening at Shamrock Cliffs, overlooking the passage into Newport. By the time Anderson had returned to his boat, the weather had piped up.

"As we were turning in," he says, "a 30-foot sloop started dragging anchor and drifting down on us.

As we warded off the sloop to our starboard, its dinghy on a long painter decided to pass along our port side, thereby hanging the whole kit and caboodle on our anchor chain. In true tradition of race committee esprit décor, I dived overboard and swam the dinghy around our bow. By the time I had climbed in the dinghy, the sloop and dinghy had swept astern of the committee boat.

The young couple on the sloop hauled me aboard in my skivvies, and we added all available line to let out scope as we were rapidly drifting toward Commodore Brown's stone pier. At the last minute the anchor held. It was after midnight, there was no launch service, and the sloop had no radio. Alas, without yachting cap or trousers, and after a few snorts of mine host's bourbon, we all turned in. When launch service resumed in the morning and I returned to the committee boat for breakfast, it was remarked that I was rather unkempt.

The following year Anderson became secretary of the Race Committee, responsible for keeping minutes of meetings and activities, and handling correspondence. He also became secretary of the New York Yacht Club, a move orchestrated by Harry Morgan, who had bigger plans for Anderson. "He called me in," Anderson says, "and said he wanted to nominate me for rear commodore in the near future. I told him I appreciated his confidence, but I was very young, I didn't have a big yacht, and I was very busy. He said it was 'now or never,' that it wouldn't come up again. That was true, so I agreed."

Anderson lent himself to several other organizations. Because of his command of the racing rules dating back to the 1950s, when he helped rewrite the team racing rules, Anderson was selected for the Appeals Committee of NAYRU in 1965. The Appeals Committee is where the buck stops when it comes to the Racing Rules of Sailing. The committee answers questions about the rules from member organizations, provides rule interpretations, and most importantly, considers and decides appeals resulting from protests. The committee also makes recommendations for rule changes that are published every four years, following the Olympics. Anderson would serve on the Appeals Committee for 25 years, becoming chairman in 1975. One of the chair's more demanding jobs is to write new rules that have been approved, and update existing rules.

"When he was appeals chairman, he'd stop by the sailing facility unannounced," says Dave Perry, a former Yale sailor who in 2012 was chair of the (now) US Sailing Appeals Committee. "I'd gotten captivated by the rules as a teenager, used them as bedside reading. So I'd have a list of questions. Harry would always

have time. We'd go sit on the grass and he'd ask what was on my list. I never felt like I was taking his time. He was patient, answered every question thoroughly. I hope I've been able to adopt the same style. Harry was my model. He was very professional.

"When I ended up on the Appeals Committee with him, the conversation got elevated. It was never a game of stump the stars. He'd always want to think about various questions, take his time."

The US Naval Academy put its feelers out for Anderson in the mid-1960s when they formed the Naval Academy Sailing Advisory Council. The seminal work by a civilian on the Academy's sailing program had been done by DeCoursey Fales, lawyer, banker, and bibliophile who had spent 20 years as USNA's principle advisor on sailing. Having grown up sailing against Fales' legendary schooner *Niña* on George Roosevelt's schooner *Mistress,* Anderson had great regard for the man whose collection of books and manuscripts exceeded 50,000 items. Given his own philosophy about how boats and the sea have a strong, educational application, joining the Academy's Sailing Advisory Council was irresistible for Anderson.

"It was DeCoursey, along with Bob Bavier and Rod Stephens, who convinced the

Academy in the late '30s that handling small craft and going to sea in them provided what is termed today character building, leadership, and experiential education," Anderson says. "Fales insisted on logging every hour of every midshipman on every vessel so that when a Congressman visited and complained about the Academy going 'yachting' it could be justified. DeCoursey's crusade went beyond the Academy grounds. I recall one evening at the New York Yacht Club bar when he was in discussion with two admirals—one could have been secretary of the navy—telling them the post of superintendent of the Academy was too important to be held by an officer on his way to retirement."

The Advisory Council was formed in the hope that the recommendations of a strong, alternative civilian entity could provide continuity of policy for the periodic changing of the guard, and would result in weeding out the deteriorating, older boats that had been donated to the academy, and attracting newer, more able vessels. The council was charged with providing "advice on solving internal problems," and providing "the basis for actions in the Navy Department that could make it possible to turn ideas into reality," according to *Sailing at the U.S. Naval Academy* by the late Admiral Robert McNitt. Given the pretzel-like density of a military bureaucracy, that was no small order.

McNitt reports that for the first meeting, the commanding officer of the naval station set a proper tone for his new job as director of the council by arriving in his own sloop. When maintenance of the existing boats was criticized, and the officer responsible for the work became defensive, council member Cornelius Shields responded sharply, pointing out the poor work he had personally observed the day before. "This appeared to be the turning point for acceptance of this civilian committee," McNitt writes. "They clearly knew what they were talking about, and were not afraid to be blunt in their assessment." Before the meeting was over, the committee was renamed the Fales Committee.

Several years later, Anderson would play a key role in establishing the Naval Academy Sailing Foundation, which facilitated the donation of yachts to the Academy. Prior to the existence of the foundation, the Naval Academy had to obtain permission from the secretary of the navy to accept the donation of a yacht, or sell one of its yachts. That load of paperwork caused a significant delay in the business that contributed heavily to the Academy's sailing program. Donors of yachts were often looking for tax breaks that could not be delayed beyond the expiration of the fiscal year in question. The idea of creating a foundation came out of a cocktail hour among Anderson and fellow members after a Fales Committee meeting. Anderson worked on the articles of incorporation for the foundation, and was elected vice president. For the first time, gifts of boats, money, or equipment—or sales of same—could be accepted within a few hours.

Beth Bonds was living at the Naval Academy grounds in those years. She and her husband, the late Captain John Bonds, who was the first director of navy sailing, lived in a large, three-story house on the parade grounds. "We provided housing and meals for visiting dignitaries," Beth Bonds says today. "It was part of the job. When I was brand new at it, the secretary called to fill me in on who was coming, and she said that a Mr. Harry Anderson would sleep in 'his customary place,' I thought, 'hmmm, I'll just see where this rolls.' He was a luminary, I knew that, an important person. And I was working hard at being a good hostess. It turned out that Mr. Anderson's customary place was any of the single rooms on the third floor. There, he would roll out his sleeping bag on the bed so as not to soil the linens. Each day he would roll it up before he left for meetings. He didn't want to be a bother. His idea was, be as innocuous as you can be. He had this wonderful way of never calling attention to himself. He had figured out how to blend into situations without being unimportant, a great skill. It's one reason we all valued him so highly."

The Naval Academy wasn't the only institution of higher learning where Anderson was helping promote sailing as a practical, educational tool. As he has written, "my avocational interests have always been directed primarily towards education and educational institutions, sometimes in connection with the formal academic regimens, but for the most part with character building aspects of education that develop the inner man and his self-respect such as the challenge offered by a sail-training experience."

Yale was tops on his list. There's a case to be made that while Anderson graduated from Yale (class of '43), he has never really left that university. After he returned from combat in World War II, it wasn't long before he resumed searching for a better location for Yale sailing. He was also helping provide boats. When he was active in the Finn class with Glen Foster in the early 1960s, both of them donated a boat to the Yale sailors. Dave Vietor, a Yale sailor who would steer one of the challenging 12 Metres during the 1987 America's Cup trials in Fremantle, says when he first met Anderson he was towing a Finn behind his Volkswagen Beetle. "The only seat in the car was for the driver," Vietor says. "The rest of the seats had been removed to make room for sailing gear."

In 1963, it was discovered that Briggs

Cunningham (Yale '28) owned a piece of waterfront in Short Beach, located in Branford, Connecticut, just a few miles east of New Haven, that looked like an ideal home base for the college sailors. The home waters for many college sailing programs are lakes and rivers. Short Beach fronts on the widest expanse of Long Island Sound, with nearly a 25-mile fetch to the Island's north shore. Harry Anderson and his family knew Cunningham well. Even though he lived in Southport, Connecticut, Cunningham had been a longtime member of Seawanhaka. He was well known for his generous support of junior sailing on Long Island Sound. "We persuaded him," Anderson says. "We went to Briggs and chatted about the Short Beach land. A couple of the undergraduates helped out. In fact the commodore of the Yale Corinthian Yacht Club paid a call on him." A fellow named Oliver May, who roomed with Cunningham at Yale, had remained active in intercollegiate sailing. Oliver May probably influenced Cunningham as well. In 1963, Cunningham and his estranged wife, Lucy, leased an old boathouse at Short Beach to the YCYC (known as "Yik Yik") for a nominal fee. If it proved to work out for the sailors, the Cunninghams were prepared to facilitate the purchase of Short Beach with the gift of stock to YCYC.

The Short Beach parcel contained the remnants of a boat yard, a small, rickety building on stilts, and some floating docks. Anderson recalls judging regattas there, bundling up and bringing food in coolers. "It was pretty drafty," he recalls.

Richard Vietor, brother of David, and in 2012 chairman of the board at Mystic Seaport, was a junior at Yale in 1963. A longtime rower, he had become disillusioned with Yale's crew situation and had switched to sailing, a sport he'd learned spending summers with his family in Edgartown, Martha's Vineyard. He soon found himself a flag officer of YCYC, charged with the responsibility of replacing the aging fleet of 420 dinghies the club owned. "The commodore suggested I talk with Harry Anderson," Richard Vietor recalls. "So I asked my father, 'who the hell is Harry Anderson?' My father, Alex, was at Yale before Harry. But both were active in sailing, and it was a small community back then. My father belonged to the New York Yacht Club, so they knew each other. And as it happened, my grandmother lived in a condo on 19 East Seventy-Second Street in Manhattan one floor above Harry's mother, so there were several connections."

At the time, Alex Vietor was curator of maps at Yale. "He had a beautiful townhouse in New Haven," Anderson recalls, "set back from the street in a landscaped setting. He took care of visiting dignitaries, and was close to Whitney

Griswold, probably had something to do with him becoming president of Yale. He also had a house in Old Lyme, and a big spread with docks in Edgartown."

Alex Vietor joined Harry in making a contribution for a new 420 fleet, and with the help of Radley Daly, provost of Yale, raised the additional funds needed. Daly was an advisor to the president of Yale at the time, associate secretary of the university, and a staunch supporter of Yale sailing.

"We started off thinking small," Richard Vietor says. "Then the realization dawned that every five years we'd have to race around to find money for a new fleet. And we needed a proper facility. Harry suggested that we start an alumni association. So Harry, Rad Daly, my father, and myself started the Yale Sailing Associates as a fund-raising entity to support Yale sailing. I was chairman, Harry was honorary chairman. I was chairman for 30 years. Harry might still be honorary chairman. We have to give Harry the lion's share of the credit for this."

There was also fun to be had. When the Vietor boys decided to take the 42-foot yawl their family had chartered for the summer on the overnight, New Bedford Whalers race, and learned they needed an adult supervisor, they called Harry Anderson. He was delighted.

"He was good at coaching," Richard Vietor says. "He was never intrusive, but we could bounce ideas off him. He took us closer to Block Island than we would have dared, and we won the race. Most of us agreed that Harry *and* the Vietors won the race. The New Bedford Yacht Club was huffy about it. They wouldn't let us take the trophy to Edgartown."

Short Beach proved to be a boon for Yale sailors, and the Cunningham's gift went through as promised. Yale Sailing Associates started raising money for a new building around 1965. At the time, Alexander Vietor was embroiled in an academic controversy about the validity of the Vinland Map, a fifteenth-century copy of a map that was supposed to provide new information about the Norse exploration of America. Vietor had written a foreword to the book released at that time by fellow Yale scholars, *The Vinland Map and the Tartar Relation*. But he made time for Yale Sailing. "Alex Vietor and I contributed, as well as our families," Anderson says. And they had good luck raising money from alumni; such good luck that a certain amount of annoyance emanated from the university development office. A professor at the university who sailed International 14s, and who was teaching architecture, set up a competition within his class to design the building. Several of the ideas put forward were included in the final design.

It was, all told, a university effort. "John Hoskins, who was a faculty advisor, did a study to determine the perfect slope for the concrete ramp to the water," Anderson says. "He figured it out based on the man pounds it took to move a wheel of a certain diameter over an obstruction of a certain thickness. So we ended up with a ramp that can be used by a person of average strength to pull a dinghy on a trailer out of the water."

The facility at Short Beach was completed in 1967. At the dedication, two permanent trophies were presented. One, a half model of the Finn dinghy to be awarded for single-handed racing, was dedicated to Harry Anderson. The other, a 420 half model for double-handed racing, was dedicated to Alexander Vietor. Kingman Brewster was there that day, resplendent in a double-breasted yachting jacket and white flannels. President of Yale at the time, Brewster was also an honorary member of YCYC. "When it was announced the competition for the trophies would be conducted during reading period," Anderson recalls, "the King responded in jest, saying if that's what the reading period is all about we'll recommend that it be discontinued."

Yale's Short Beach YCYC facility became a magnet for hot young sailors, both male and female. Among those who were attracted to

Yale in the late '60s and beyond were Steve Taylor, Steve Benjamin, J. J. Fetter, Dave Perry, Peter Isler, Stan Honey, Stuart McNay, Isabelle Kinsolving, Jonathan McKee, Jane Macky, Thomas Barrows, and Zack Leonard who, in 2012, was director of Yale Sailing. Among them and other Yale sailors since 1967, there are five Olympic medals, two America's Cup wins (and a host of participation), a Volvo win, a Jules Verne record, six Rolex Yachtsmen and Yachtswomen of the Year Awards (J. J. Fetter was so-honored a record four times), a raft of world championships in various classes, dozens of All-American skippers and crews, and four College Sailors of the Year.

Also in 1967, Harry Anderson became commodore of the Seawanhaka Corinthian Yacht Club and chair of the New York Yacht Club Race Committee. That's about the time Bill Winterer met Anderson. Winterer was running the Griswold Inn in Essex, Connecticut, a colonial landmark started in 1776 that was well known at the time for the resident orange tabby cat featured in its advertising. A financial broker, gourmet cook, shameless name dropper, sailor, and wheeler-dealer with an engaging manner and a worldly repartee, Winterer got to know Harry Anderson's step aunt, Mable James, when he was spending time in Phoenix, Arizona, in the 1950s. He was contemplating buying a casino in Carson City, and involved with the Phoenix

Art Museum. That's where he met Mabel James, whose late husband—Anderson's uncle—had a prized collection of French Impressionists and assorted American artists. The two hit it off to the extent that when Winterer had given up his house in Phoenix prior to closing a deal on a house in Carson City, and the latter deal blew up at closing, he rang Mabel James and asked if he could spend the night. "She said of course," Winterer says. "I stayed six months. It turned out to be good for her because she had to undergo a severe operation. I cooked dinner for her every night.

"In those days, you didn't just invite a girl from New York to fly out to Phoenix for the weekend. So I had Mable James ring up my girlfriend's mother who lived in Ohio and say that her friend Bill Winterer was involved in the Phoenix Art Museum with her, and we were having an opening—Claire Booth Luce, a good friend of mine, had donated her Asian collection, and a new wing was being dedicated—and Mr. Winterer wants your daughter to be his date, and she will stay with me. So I picked up my date and dropped her at Mable James' house. My date turned out to be my wife, Vicky. Later, when I picked her up, she said Bill, there is a Monet and a Manet hanging in the bathroom!"

When Helen James Anderson, Harry's mother, went to Phoenix to visit her sister-in-law, she met Bill Winterer. When Winterer moved to New York, she invited him for dinner at her apartment on Seventy-Second Street and Madison Avenue. "It was a floor-through apartment," Winterer recalls.

The elevator stopped at her door. I remember a huge foyer with a gorgeous rug. There was a music room, a library, and a servants' wing for two Irish ladies in their 70s who had come to work for Helen when they were 16. She had a Mercedes in the garage under the building with a driver on call. In her younger days she and her father, Dr. James, had huge, glorious houses in New York with coach houses attached. In her obit, the New York Times referred to her as a member of the privileged class, and she was. But she handled it well. She had real class.

Whenever I went to dinner there, always black tie, we would start with a martini in the library. She never had a Vermouth bottle. She decanted the juice from a bottle of olives and filled it with Vermouth. Dinner was beautifully served by the two women, always with finger bowls on a doily.

Helen loved opera, and had third or fourth generation family tickets to the Met. None of her three sons—Harry, David, or Jim— would take her, so I did every Monday.

One night at dinner Helen asked me what I

was doing about yacht clubs. I said I was busy getting my feet on the ground. I was a manager at Goodbody, which in those days was second only to Merrill Lynch. It was a great job for a young guy. Helen said she'd have Harry for dinner with me the following week. That's how I met Harry, through his mother, who was the most vivacious, loveliest women in the world. She reminded me of Helen Hayes. She almost looked like her. Helen took long walks for exercise every day, and played the piano very well. No wonder Harry turned out so well. He had all that good DNA. One day I rang her up and said I was looking at gas stoves for my apartment, and wondered what sort of stove she had. There was a long pause. Then she said, `Oh Bill, I've never been in the kitchen.' My God, she was wonderful.

Harry Anderson took a liking to his mother's friend, and before long Winterer was a member of both the Seawanhaka and New York Yacht Clubs.

"My first (and lasting) impression of Harry was his intelligence," Winterer says. "He is quiet, but when he says something it has import. He's probably the most interesting guy I have known, and I've been lucky to meet a lot of interesting people. He's very streetwise in a sophisticated, upper-class way. No one puts anything over on Harry Anderson."

Another America's Cup took place in 1967. Given the lengthy defender trials, members of the Race Committee logged more than 60 days of duty that summer. The Australian 12-Metre *Dame Patti* (KA-2) was challenging, and *Intrepid* (US-22) was defending for the United States. For the Race Committee, it was business as usual. *Intrepid* was the faster boat, and had a 3-0 lead going into Race Four. The series had been uneventful up to then. But the day of Race Four, the course was obscured by fog.

"The Coast Guard stopped the spectator fleet when fog set in," Anderson recalls, "but we kept moving ahead.

As we set the starting line, there were no spectator boats, and no patrol boats. Just us, and the 12 Metres that had been towed out. The weather forecast indicated there were three days ahead of us with no wind. So there was some urgency to get Race Four behind us. We were still using Navy tugs for marks, so I sent them up the course to see if the fog was breaking up. We couldn't wait for the patrol boats. We couldn't start a race after 2:00 p.m. It started to break, so we got the sequence going. Then two minutes before the start, the fog got thicker. We called the tugs, told them to keep reading the conditions to us. Commodore Dickson of the Royal Yacht Squadron in Sydney was on board as an observer. As an observer, he had no authority, but I asked him what he thought we should do. He said, "Harry, it's your decision. I'm going aft to get a drink."

With 60 seconds to the start, the tug up to weather said it was breaking up. But we couldn't see the other end of the starting line. But we knew the bearing to the other end, and we could see the upper parts of the masts of the yachts. So we'd be able to tell if they were over early. Off they went. As it happened the fog cleared and we got the fourth and final race in.

A few days later, Anderson received a letter from Dick Bertram, who had run the foredeck on *Vim* when that old 12 Metre had nearly won the 1958 defender trials, and who was head of Richard Bertram & Company in Miami, builder of powerboats designed by Ray Hunt. "The most exciting part of the series for me," Bertram wrote, "was the final Cup race when you started the boats in the fog. I'm sure the pressure on you as an individual had to be fantastic, particularly during the last couple minutes before the start. When the gun sounded for the start, all of us on *Moppie* gave a cheer for your courage. . . . it took a great deal of guts to make that decision."

At one of the many parties during that 1967 America's Cup, Anderson found himself chatting with a group of people that included

an aggressive young woman who inquired about what he did. She wasn't satisfied with Anderson's vague, conversational response, and kept pressing her question. Finally Anderson looked at her and said, "I'm much too busy to work."

Somehow, Anderson wasn't too busy to head for Long Beach, California, that same year to help his friend, Bill Dalessi, by serving on the jury for a new match-racing regatta. In 1964, Dalessi and two flag officers of the Long Beach Yacht Club had started discussing ways to promote match racing in a more open format than that afforded by the America's Cup, or the Canada Cup. The three of them sought advice from a lot of people they had known at major sailing events. Dalessi, who was on the NAYRU board with Anderson when it had become USYRU, consulted with his friend about how to structure the event.

Commodore Dalessi and his cohorts initially hoped to give the regatta presidential status. But Lyndon Johnson's people said that granting Long Beach presidential status would set a precedent, encouraging many similar requests that would be difficult to turn down. "They told me the president would have to decline," Dalessi recalls, "even though he was deeply interested in West Coast yachting." Dalessi still chuckles at that. Undeterred, he went to Congress, and through Representative

The 1980 Congressional Cup jury with winner.
Standing from left, Bill Dalessi, Bill Ficker, Pete Ives,
winner Dennis Durgan, Julian K. Roosevelt, Cy Gillette,
and Downie Muir III. Seated from left, Arthur Knapp,
Chairman Harry Anderson, and Jack H. Feller Jr.

Craig Hosmer succeeded in obtaining the blessing of Congress. Hence, the Congressional Cup was born.

"The first regatta was in 1965," Dalessi says, "and Harry came out to be on the jury not long after that. I knew all he was doing, and I always wondered how he fit it all in. But he has a one-of-a-kind mind. He remembers everything about everything and everyone, which is amazing to me."

Anderson's tenure as a Congressional Cup judge lasted more than 20 years. At the 1979 match, he became the first NYYC commodore to display his personal burgee on the West Coast. The 33rd Congressional Cup (1997) was dedicated to him. He recalls that Arthur Knapp, who raced in several Congressional Cups, was on the jury during one regatta when Ted Turner and Dennis Conner were in the protest room. "Dennis was quiet," Anderson recalls. "He wasn't very articulate back then. Ted was going on the way he does, getting him riled. After they left the jury room, Arthur followed them out. We thought he was going to the head. He returned moments later. We asked what he had done. Arthur said he'd grabbed both of them and told them any more of this nonsense and we're going to throw both of them out of the series. It wasn't a normal jury procedure, but Knappy would do that sort of thing."

Knapp always presented his book—*Race Your Boat Right*—to the tenth (last) place finisher. "Arthur loved a joke," Anderson says, "unless it was played on him. But one year he finished tenth, so we cooked up a presentation for him. Bill Ficker did the honors, and presented Arthur with a copy of his own book. He accepted it graciously."

Anderson stepped down as chair of the NYYC Race Committee in 1970, remaining on the Committee of Racing Appeals. The America's Cup match that year was between the modified *Intrepid* and *Gretel II*. Anderson went to Devereux Barker, who was then secretary of the Race Committee, and suggested he take over as chairman. Barker was 31 at the time, a columnist for *Yachting* magazine. Barker told Anderson he was flattered, but said he was concerned about his youth and inexperience. Anderson gave him a little smile, twitched his moustache, and told him it was now or never. Barker took the job.

A s a member of the Committee on Racing Appeals in 1970, Harry Anderson was in a catbird seat for one of the most vocal, protracted protests in America's Cup history. It happened in Race Two of the match between defender *Intrepid* and Australian challenger *Gretel II*. In light air at the start, *Intrepid*, with Bill Ficker at the helm, slipped between *Gretel II*, to leeward, and the Race Committee boat. Both boats were on the starboard tack. It was close, but *Intrepid* had room, she was not barging. *Gretel II* luffed *Intrepid*. After the starting gun went off, and before the boats had crossed the line, *Gretel II* continued to luff, even going beyond head to wind. There was a collision, after which both boats raised protest flags. The rule the Australians were unclear about stated that a boat may luff another boat prior to the start, but must not sail higher than a proper course to the first mark after the gun is fired. Given that the first leg was to windward, a proper course would mean full and bye on a tack—starboard tack in this case. Luffing beyond head to wind was also not allowed.

"That year was one of the first times juries accepted film as evidence of an infraction," Anderson says, "but only if the camera man was present and told them where he had shot it from. From overhead, you could tell the relationship of the boats, see when *Gretel* luffed head to wind, and see the smoke from the starting cannon—at which point they had to stop luffing. The film eventually supported the controversial decision of the Race Committee, but it was not available in time for the protest hearing.

"No one will know who was yelling 'come up!' on the Australian boat. They had three helmsmen. They had a Dutchman starting the boat, and he was hotheaded. There was no question about the collision. A piece of the Aussie boat was left on *Intrepid*'s deck. I called Dev Barker and asked if he would like to have me back. He said no, it was an open-and-shut case. But it went on for a week. Every morning Sir Frank Packer's chauffeur—Packer was *Gretel* Syndicate head—would deliver another request to reopen the hearing. Frank left no stone unturned. It was a protest heard around the world. Finally Frank sent a message that it was all over, good luck, we're not going to protest anymore."

One of the major problems with that protest was that the NYYC Race Committee was also the jury for the match, a customary practice in those days. "In disqualifying the Challenger, no matter its correctness," Dev Barker says today, "it was extremely difficult not to make it appear to be a hometown decision."

In 1970, once again the challenger was a faster boat. Once again (shades of 1962), a combination of tactics, crew work, good luck—and the rules infraction by Australia—allowed the United States to prevail, maintaining its (then) 119-year hold on sport's oldest trophy. But the renewed interest in the America's Cup, the increasing number of challengers, and as Anderson has pointed out, the global marketing of technology, were leveling the America's Cup playing field.

One of the new challengers in 1970 was Baron Marcel Bich, the ballpoint pen magnate from France who had also made a fortune in ladies' intimate apparel. Bich was a large, hefty man, a dandy who always appeared in the most colorful formal attire, white gloves included, even when steering his yachts. He carried on a 12-year crusade for the Cup, but his teams never came close to the challenger final. "He was a strange man," Anderson says.

He was like Thomas Lipton in that he had product to sell. He had a big mother ship with beautiful women on board. His father had bought titles for his sons. They flipped a coin, and Marcel got the French one, his brother got the Italian title. Bich would always say he sold more pens in Italy than France because inflation was so bad in Italy that with all those zeros the pens would run dry quicker.

Bich had been divorced. He'd had children with his first wife. She remarried. One night his ex-wife was watching TV with her daughter. Bich's picture appeared. The ex-wife says, "Oh, there's your father." That caused a stir. The daughter was 16 and wanted to meet her father. The ex-wife called Marcel, and he sent tickets for his daughter. They got along well. She became secretary of his syndicate. Apparently after he and his ex-wife were separated, they had spent another night together. She got pregnant, then remarried, but they never told anyone about their final night. It was a typical French short story. Bich told it over dinner one time.

The first meeting the America's Cup Committee had with Bich was on his dock. Chairman Harry Morgan suggested we go pay him a visit. We went over by launch, and there was a mast on the dock separating us from Bich. Harry Morgan, who was using a cane at the time, got down on his hands and knees and crawled under the mast. Bich was mortified, yelling at his crew to lift the mast.

In their red pants, navy blazers, white shirts, and New York Yacht Club ties, topped by straw boaters wrapped with a band of NYYC colors, the America's Cup Committee was a formidable group. When these esteemed gentlemen came walking down the dock during the trials to pay a visit to a syndicate, there wasn't a man among that crew without a lump in his throat. Because the committee's visits weren't usually to say, "well done." That was reserved for the last syndicate standing, after which champagne was broken out. More often they came to ask why: why the afterguard hadn't covered the opposition in the last race, or why their boat's downwind speed appeared to have diminished. Later in the trials they would arrive to express their heartfelt thanks for a syndicate's participation. This was yachting's version of the kiss on each cheek applied by a mob hit man before doing

his job. The Committee's formal thank you was a prelude to letting a syndicate know that it had been excused from further competition. The expelled team was expected to offer all its resources to the boat chosen as defender, for the good of the Cup. This nattily attired group wasn't known as "The Selection Committee" without reason. In those days a boat's superior record during the trials didn't guarantee it would be the defender. The committee kept to itself and was off-limits to the media.

The America's Cup Committee was a power,

Anderson in his well-worn America's Cup Committee straw.

and its chairman ran the show. Anderson, who was on the Cup Committee from 1974 to 1983, says that Harry Morgan, chairman in the 1970s, forbid any committee member from expressing an independent opinion. "He said the decisions of the committee were committee decisions. He didn't want to hear any individual comments. He said we had to burn our notes. That was too bad. A lot of history was turned to ash.

"Morgan started a system to sharpen the critical abilities of his committee," Anderson says. "During the trials, we'd all lay a bet on the Delta [time difference between the two boats] at the next mark. We did it for every leg. I think the bet was a nickel. Too bad we didn't have computer data on each rounding. We would have had better analysis of the boats.

"It was very sociable in those days," Anderson says. "We could wander wherever we wanted, visit syndicate headquarters and be briefed on developments. Later on they started shrouding the keels, and secrecy prevailed, even with the America's Cup Committee."

In between America's Cup challenges, Anderson was toiling away in his office on the sixth floor of the New York Yacht Club. "Those days," he wrote in a memo, "I followed the advice of Commodore Percy Chubb and the practice of Bob Bavier to lunch daily at the

Club, and improved on same with a cocktail or two at day's end when the members who worked down- and midtown dropped in for a snort or two before catching a commuter train. There were some members who also belonged to the Harvard Club next door who would stop in the morning when commuting for a snort before they caught the subway to Wall Street. Prohibition had left a permanent imprint on the lives of those who survived it."

As a scholar and an historian—and currently director of the Society for the Preservation of Long Island Antiquities—Robert MacKay, who was sailing Ravens out of Seawanhaka in those days, was impressed by what his friend Harry Anderson was doing. "I don't know how many of us were getting regular 'Harry grams,' we called them, mimeographed reports in the mail, updates and what have you about what was going on behind the scenes in yachting," MacKay says. "Harry had his lists, and that's how he kept people in touch with events. His system was the precursor of Web sites. Harry was the organization and the outreach of American yachting. He was at the center of the democratization of the sport—opening it up to more participation, more people. It was expanding. Each year it was being embraced ever more widely.

"Harry's credentials are on a par with anyone's

from his era, whether it's about relatives, money, or education. It was very Social Register in those days, and Harry is still listed in that red book. But he was taking the whole pastime in the right direction."

In the 1950s Anderson had interceded successfully with NAYRU President Harry Morgan to include the Intercollegiate Yacht Racing Association under NAYRU's auspices. A dozen years later, he was working closely with ICYRA principles Len Fowle and Eric Olsen to make sure intercollegiate racing was conforming to NAYRU guidelines. In 1970, the ICYRA recognized Anderson's sustained dedication to college sailing, from competitor to supporter, by naming him to the ICYRA Hall of Fame. At his induction, Anderson was cited for his early work on the team racing rules that proved to be the forerunner of the NAYRU and IYRU team racing rules; for his perennial judging of the McMillan Cup at the Naval Academy; for his work in establishing the Fales Committee; and for organizing and chairing the Yale Sailing Associates.

In spite of his numerous administrative duties on the sailing front, Anderson spent as much time as possible on the water. In 1967 he had bought his first sizable boat, a Hughes 38, *Witch of Atlas*, named for the subject of Percy Bysshe Shelley's longest poem, a witch who rode the streams and bays of North Africa and the Atlas Mountains. Anderson loved the poem. The witch had a boat "too feeble to be fraught," Shelley wrote, so she sold it to Apollo who had it completely refitted for his daughter,

> . . . . *Changed it to the fairest and the lightest boat which ever upon mortal stream did float.*
>
> *This boat she moored upon her fount, and lit A living spirit within all its frame, Breathing the soul of swiftness into it. Couched on the fountain, like a panther tame— One of the twin at Evan's feet that sit— Or as on Vesta's scepter a swift flame, Or on blind Homer's heart a winger thought— In joyous expectation lay the boat.*

A Sparkman & Stephens design, the boat proved to be quick. In June of 1971, Anderson won Class III with *Witch* in the New York Yacht Club's 117th annual regatta, and was awarded the Solution Trophy for overall outstanding performance. *Witch* logged a first and a second in the two races. It was the first of two Solution Trophies he would win.

A month later, Anderson had *Witch* at Seawanhaka for its Hundredth Anniversary Regatta. On the second day it was blowing dogs off chains, as sailors like to say. Bill

Dalessi, who had come east and was racing with Anderson, vividly recalls that race:

I was staying with the Stiger family across from the Seawanhaka Club. Harry and myself and a bunch of other sailors had been partying a little bit the night before at the Club. I had been playing piano, we were singing, and some crews upstairs who had been trying to sleep had given up and joined us. I woke up the next morning not feeling 100 percent. Mrs. Stiger woke me, and said she had breakfast prepared. I said "oh-my-god, I'm not sure I can handle that." I told her it sounded windy. She said it was blowing a gale. I felt miserable. I got to the boat. Harry was already on board. I said, "Harry, tell me truthfully, how do you feel?" He just shook his head back and forth. I knew he felt as bad as me. The others showed up, we were six in all.

We got a booming start among a lot of big boats including Tom Watson's Palawan, *a 70-footer. Darned if we weren't first to the weather mark. We were the only boat to set a spinnaker. The rest stayed with small headsails. We were first to the reach mark, and first to the leeward mark. About ten boat lengths from the mark, Harry finally called for a sail change. I didn't know how we could do it in time, but we did, doused the spinnaker and got a genoa up for the beat home. It turned out we could lay the finish, just barely. But no other boat got the shift. We looked back and the rest of the fleet was in a different wind, tacking back and forth. We won everything, first in class, first overall....*

What Bill Dalessi neglected to mention, perhaps because it was no big deal at the time, was that Anderson raced *Witch* with the dinghy in its cradle on deck.

When Anderson speaks about the numerous boats he has owned, one gets the feeling that *Witch* was special. "She was a beautifully balanced boat," he says. "We lost the tiller on one New York Yacht Club cruise on a run from Edgartown to Padanaram. We had to beat through Quick's Hole in the Elizabeth Islands in a fresh nor'wester into Buzzards Bay. Barely had we cleared the Hole when the tiller split in half. The bolt holding the hiking stick had never been properly sealed. Moisture had gradually rotted the core of the tiller. So finely balanced was the 38 that we steered to weather, including tacking, by using the main-sheet traveler. When we got to Padanaram, Bill Maclay went to the shipyard and found a superb, laminated Dutch tiller with a fitting that matched."

The following year, Anderson helped organize a race to Spain. There had been two previous races to Spain. The first, won by DeCoursey Fales' schooner *Niña*, was in 1928. The

Witch of Atlas, Anderson's Hughes 38.

second, in 1957, had been won by Richard S. Nye's *Carina*. The Spanish were prompted to suggest the race as a result of a visit Richard S. Nye had made to Baiona in 1969 after completing the New York-Cork (IRE) race that same year. Anderson's co-conspirator in formalizing the proceedings was Nye's son, Richard B. The plan was to hold the race in June, departing from Bermuda a week after the race from Newport had finished. First they had to engage the Spanish and select a finishing port. Anderson and Nye established their Spanish connection through "Señor B.," who had sailed with Anderson on *Witch of Atlas* a few times. "He was a jovial chap, and a bit of a wheeler and dealer," Anderson says. "The previous year he'd sailed with Commodore Clayton Ewing along the Iberian coast. Before they entered a particular harbor, he had asked to be put ashore without fanfare."

Anderson and Nye flew to Madrid, had lunch with Señor B. and members of the Spanish committee, and went on to A Coruña, a commercial harbor in northwest Spain where the 1928 race had finished. Speaking no Spanish, they had drinks with the officers of the local yacht club and port officials. Without explanation, they were soon in a convoy of cars making the long drive to Santiago on the west coast. There they were taken to a large parador, a former hospital, where they were fed dinner at midnight. "We retired to chambers the outside walls of which were four feet thick without windows," Anderson recalls. After lunch the next day they visited the yacht club at Baiona, which would become the host club for the race, and the finishing port. Anderson took delight in the sprawling Monterreal castle with its array of turrets, towers, and battlements, a fortress dating back beyond the twelfth century that guarded the harbor. It would be used as one end of the finish line. The castle offered a particularly impenetrable stone tower that would provide a perfect lair for the race committee. It was agreed to call the race, the Race of Discovery, in memory of Columbus' last vessel, *La Pinta*, which made her return landfall at Baiona.

It was a testament to the nonverbal communication skills and deft ambassadorship of Anderson and Nye that it all got done, including the signing of a Spanish sponsor (El Monte Real Club de Yates), without a common language among the organizers, and despite a certain amount of confusion. Other sponsors were the New York Yacht Club, The Cruising Club of America—which urged members to cruise over for the festivities— and the Royal Bermuda Yacht Club.

Anderson's ride for the race was *Puffin*, a Sparkman & Stephens 48-footer owned by Edward Greeff, Seawanhaka member and partner in a small New York brokerage firm.

Anderson had sailed several Bermuda races with Greeff. *Puffin*, Greeff's second boat by that name, had been built on the south coast of Denmark by Walsted's Baadevaert, a yard that prefers to build in wood and is renowned for its superb craftsmanship. Anderson recalls that even the boat's toolbox was built of mahogany and had no end grain showing on the lid. "Eddie Greeff was very fit," Anderson says, "and had so meticulous an onboard regimen that several people I knew gave up sailing with him. Forward of the anchor winch there was a triangle of plywood so neither anchor nor chain could mar the teak deck. Once, after Eddie had hit his head on the mizzen boom winch and I was pulling his scalp together with butterfly bands, he remonstrated strongly, demanding there be no scars visible after the wound healed."

The crew of eight included several younger men, including Harry Morgan's grandson and three other recent Yale graduates. The race itself was remarkable for its snail-like pace. It took 18 days, nearly a week longer than expected. Doldrums, defined by Webster as a state of listlessness or depression, is the name given to the intertropical convergence zone that exists at the equator on both the Atlantic and the Pacific sides. The area is notable for its lack of wind, and flat waters infused with seaweed. Samuel Taylor Coleridge's *The Rime of the Ancient Mariner* was set in the Doldrums: "water, water everywhere, nor any drop to drink."

So it was aboard *Puffin*. Greeff demanded weight and stowage be kept to a minimum, and he had set a very low limit on the amount of beer on board. "He had a birthday coming," Anderson recalls, "so we had a friend send three cases aboard wrapped in birthday paper. Ironically, the only place it could be stowed was in his cabin. His wife didn't mind. She was short, and used the package as a step. As it turned out, we ran out of beer off the Island of Flores, a turning mark at the north end of the Azores."

At the time of the race, the ever-shifting Doldrums extended from the Carolinas to mid-Europe. On day three, Anderson wrote in *Puffin*'s log:

> *The Atlantic has been left breathless. Water has been rationed, and we are using juices from tins of vegetables to activate de-hydrated packages of foods. The entire crew is looking forward to a few fast days of sailing so that the restrictions can be modified. Apparently the water tanks were incapable of being filled to their capacity because of air locks, but also not every last gallon can be drained from them.*

> *We are under clear skies with scattered buildup of small, towering cumuli moving barely the speed of the vessel. Splotches or cats paws of wind*

*touch the water and gently send the boat into
the next glossy flat spot. We make midnight
gybes of desperation off course to the port tack to
eke out a few more miles to the northward in the
hope of escaping the 1500 by 750 mile trap
enclosed by 30.51 isobars. Teak decks are too hot
for bare feet. We shower by bucketing salt water
over ourselves and sudsing with detergent. Fetid
heat below too hot for sleeping.*

Anderson had invited Liz Roosevelt to meet
Puffin's crew in Baiona. Roosevelt had been
a regular crew of Anderson's from Raven days
onward, but found herself being replaced by
strong young male sailors for the big boat races.
She accepted the demotion, but not without
some bristling. "By the time those people
arrived they were a psychological study," says
Roosevelt, who had been waiting in Baiona for
nearly a week with other guests for the boats
to show up. "There were all these young men
on board who had nothing to think with. They
didn't read books. Slatting around in the ocean
for days on end had just about made them nuts.
But Harry didn't mind any of that stuff. He
was happy drinking the pea water. A bad day at
sea for him is better than being anywhere else."

After the race, Anderson found himself on yet
another committee, this one convened to
discipline a crewman from a Miami boat who
had gone on an alcohol-inspired tear, ripping
a telephone off the wall of the yacht club,

urinating off the porch at cocktail hour, then
outrunning a group of angry, knife-wielding
staff members and seeking refuge on a US
Navy vessel. They arranged to get the man
out of the country before Franco's gendarmes
were called.

Before taking the train to Madrid to fly home,
a friend of Anderson's from Oyster Bay
realized he'd neglected to have his passport
stamped after finishing the race. Anderson
called Señor B., who found the customs
inspector in a café having a morning pick-
me-up. "He cordially pulled the stamp from
his pocket and officially imported our
friend," Anderson recalls. "On the train, the
conductors set us up for lunch and took our
orders ahead of the other passengers. In our
yachting uniforms, they had mistaken us for
railroad officials."

⚓

THE AMERICA'S CUP rolled on, with
a third challenge from Australia in
1974. On the Friday before the first
set of trials, Harry Anderson rang up Leith
Adams, the wife of his friend Charles C.
Adams, who was also on the America's Cup
Race Committee, to beg a ride from New York
City to Newport. Adams had left for Newport
the previous day. An energetic, full-figured

blonde who drove race cars in her younger days, Leith Adams would sculpt a handsome bust of Anderson on the occasion of his ninetieth birthday. At the time, she had met Anderson in passing, but didn't know him that well. She suggested he come to their apartment and they would depart from there. "He showed up in full yachting gear," Leith Adams recalls, "ribbons, epaulettes, you name it.

I'd never seen anything like it. I agreed to give Harry a ride, and mentioned we had to stop at Chemical Bank, where Charlie worked, to deliver these huge mum plants I had for Charlie's secretary. Harry and I got in the Mustang convertible with the mum plants and headed downtown at flank speed. Harry was a nervous wreck, with his mustache twitching away. When we got to the bank, I couldn't park, so I asked him to deliver the plants while I stayed with the car. I had to get out of the car and arrange the plants in his arms. He could barely see past them. I pointed him toward the elevators and ran back to the car.

When he came back, it was the only time I ever saw him mad. He said some man in the elevator had told him the next time he had a delivery he should take the freight elevator. He also told Harry he didn't know what florist shop he was from, but he admired the uniform. Turned out the man in the elevator was the president of Chemical Bank.

In 1974, a young Western Australian real estate and beer magnate named Alan Bond had challenged for the America's Cup through the Royal Perth Yacht Club, issuing in a summer that was notable for Bond's media bluster and not much else. His contender, *Southern Cross*, submitted to Cup-defender *Courageous* four races to nil without a fuss. It would turn out that Bond was as persistent as he was vocal, and was just getting warmed up. But the interest that year was confined to the defender trials, which were lively.

Neither *Heritage*, *Valiant*, nor *Mariner* were a match for *Courageous* or *Intrepid*, but the latter two—the new Sparkman & Stephens design and the old Sparkman & Stephens design that had been modified by Britton Chance, much to Olin Stephens' ill-concealed displeasure—were locked in combat from the start. Toward the end, with the two boats each having won four races against one another in the final trials, the Newport waterfront was set buzzing at the announcement that esteemed *Courageous* skipper Bob Bavier, who had steered *Constellation* to victory in 1964, had been replaced at the helm. The way rumors of the New York Yankees trading Alex Rodriguez after the 2012 American League playoffs dominated the baseball world is how the news of Bavier's firing reverberated in the yachting community. Sailmaker Ted Hood was brought in to steer the boat, and a hot young sailor from California named Dennis Conner was given the job of handling the starts. Bavier was openly distraught, and while pleased he had been named skipper, Hood had a frown on his face about Conner starting the boat.

Conner had survived the considerable drama taking place in the noncompetitive but confrontational *Mariner* syndicate that summer. The aluminum *Mariner*, with a radical, stepped stern designed by Britton Chance, a design element more likely to be found on a fast powerboat, was steered by Ted Turner. The boat couldn't get out of its own way. "In 1970 when *Valiant* came on the scene I was watching her before the start of one trials race," Anderson says. "Bob McCullough was steering that year. They were reaching, and suddenly for no apparent reason *Valiant* turned 90 degrees and almost T-boned another boat. *Valiant* was very unresponsive, a real dog." But the crafty, accomplished Conner, originally Ted Turner's tactician on *Mariner*, had so consistently stuffed the flamboyant Turner on the starting line when he began steering in the races between *Mariner* and *Valiant* that he was recruited by syndicate head Bob McCullough as starting helmsman on *Courageous* for the Cup match. Harry Anderson says he'd had his eye on Conner all summer.

"Bob Bavier had gotten a little rusty on match racing," Anderson says. "The others had better skills. Our America's Cup Committee didn't have much to say. Managing syndicates wasn't our job.

"Bavier had been on the other end of it during the trials in 1964 with *Constellation*," Anderson says. "Back then, skipper Eric Ridder was the syndicate's biggest contributor. It was really his syndicate. But Eric couldn't hack it. He never was that good a sailor. They finally had to fire him and replace him with Bob Bavier. That had been tricky."

Before that, in 1962, Arthur Knapp had been replaced at *Weatherly*'s helm by Bus Mosbacher, an event that had set a stunning, modern America's Cup precedent for job insecurity among legendary sailors. Later on, Knapp had confided to a reporter that his firing had sent him to a psychiatrist. "Knappy had a super ego," Anderson says. "He couldn't handle defeat."

Back in New York, Anderson played a key role in the restructuring of NAYRU. As it is written in the *Centennial History of the United States Sailing Association* (by co-authors Anderson and Robert C. MacArthur), "It was becoming evident that the Canadian Yachting Association was doing a much more effective job serving the needs of Canadian sailors than it was possible for the multi-national NAYRU to do for US sailors; an inherent conflict of interest was built into the structure that was hamstringing the growth of yachting in the US."

"Canada had gotten ahead of us," Anderson says. "They already had a system for certifying junior sailing instructors just as they had for skiing. They had a national ski patrol before we did. Paul Phelan, president of the Canadian Yachting Association and a vice president of NAYRU, pointed out at a meeting in New York after a few martinis that we had never sent an official team to the Olympics. The IOC requires the national sports governing body to select the team, and we had no such body. NAYRU was Canada *and* the USA. Lynn Steadman, who was president of NAYRU, and I went to Canada and spent several days with the CYA people and worked out a way to disengage. No one had thought about it. It was way overdue."

Official confirmation moved quickly. An ad hoc committee quickly delivered a report that recommended, "that (NAYRU) become national in nature, and authority. We suggest that our name be changed to the United States Yacht Racing Union." Steadman and Anderson met with CYA and other officials, and received "complete and enthusiastic agreement" about the plan. Paul Phelan celebrated the change, saying "our old trans-border associations are still safely in place, and both associations are now eligible for their respective national funding which we here in Canada so desperately need."

In the middle of this delicate restructuring process, Anderson had to slip over to New Haven where the Yale Sailing Association had established a fellowship in his name that would bring in world-class sailors to speak to the Yale teams, and participate in on-the-water coaching. It was YSA's way of thanking Anderson for his long and active support of Yale Sailing, including the fleet of 30 dinghies he had purchased for Yale in 1973.

The NAYRU/USYRU business wasn't finished. Anderson's administrative operation at the New York Yacht Club had outgrown that space, and for a couple years he had been working out of an office on Avenue of the Americas and Forty-Fourth Street. But it was frightfully expensive to run a nonprofit organization in New York City. Leases had escalation clauses, taxes were high, and salaries had to be in line with everything else. "Initially they wanted us to move to Newport Beach, California," Anderson says. "But Briggs Cunningham had a place out there, and they were taxing him on vertical property—the square footage of the cliff face that went down to the water from his house. The US Olympic Committee was trying to consolidate all Olympic sports at its new headquarters in Colorado Springs, which for sailing would have been remote. Annapolis, Maryland, was also considered. But Lynn Steadman and I got caught in a frightful traffic jam there one night, and that turned him off. So we ended up moving to Newport, Rhode Island."

Anderson was delighted with the decision, although moving would necessitate ending his leadership of the YRA of Long Island Sound. That group sent him off with a handsome chronometer commemorating more than a decade of service he had given them. But Newport is on every sailor's short list of best sailing locations on the East Coast, perhaps the world. From Newport it's half a day's sail to Block Island to the west, or a day to Buzzards Bay, the Elizabeth Islands, Martha's Vineyard, and Nantucket to the east. Beyond the Cape Cod Canal, the rest of the New England coast beckons, with Maine the icing on the sailors' cake. Beyond lies Nova Scotia and Labrador for the more adventurous.

The dramatic, deep, rock-bound East Passage into Newport is one of the more striking harbor entrances in the country. Outside, it's open ocean. Once you have left Nantucket to port, a course of 90 degrees true will land you on the coast of Portugal. On the inside, Fort Adams, a coastal fortification first built in 1799, guards the southern end of an expansive, well-protected harbor.

Having been a regular visitor to Newport since he was a boy, moving to Newport for

Harry Anderson was like going home. His grandmother, Mrs. Walter B. James, had died in 1944, and Rockhurst, her chateauesque cottage on Bellevue Avenue, had been sold shortly thereafter. In 1955 Rockhurst was demolished to make room for a residential subdivision. But Anderson still had family in Newport. Hugh Auchincloss III, known as Yusha, is a second cousin, a grandson of Harry's grandmother's youngest sister, Emma Jennings. Yusha was Jackie Auchincloss Kennedy's stepbrother, making him President Jack Kennedy's brother-in–law. Yusha, who grew up in Newport, says he was fond of Jackie when he was 14 and she was 12. Then her father married his mother. "I asked my stepfather what that would do to my relationship with Jackie," Yusha says today. "He said to me, well, you are usually given your family, then you choose your friends. In this case you have chosen to be friends with Jackie before she became family, so it is the best of both worlds."

An Arabic scholar who speaks Egyptian, Lebanese, and Palestinian Arabic, Yusha had graduated from the University of Beirut. He became a presidential envoy for Jack Kennedy, specializing in the Middle East. Harry and Yusha have always been good friends.

Another relative who would later show up in Newport was Robert "Zup" Campbell James, a first cousin (Yusha's second cousin). His father was Oliver Burr James Sr., a brother of Anderson's mother. Zup graduated from Yale in 1950—Korean War days—and went into the army. In a brief biographical pamphlet published after his death from cancer in 2012, *A Caviar and Champagne Diplomat,* edited by Eugene Pool and Oliver Janney, Zup James is quoted: "I was lucky to be born not with a silver spoon in my mouth, but a gold one, which with its companion little gold knife, pusher, and cup, I pawned while at Yale to buy champagne." After his army uniform was issued, James took it to Brooks Brothers for a fitting. He spent many years in Laos in the 1950s and '60s with the responsibility of training the Royal Laotian Army to fight the Pathet Lao, and as the case manager for Prince Souvanna Phouma. When Phouma was overthrown and expelled by the Laotians, James left with him. Known for his Hollywood wardrobe that often included a pince-nez, and a flamboyant style bordering on the outrageous, James later represented the CIA and the State Department in Laos.

Thanks to his participation in five America's Cups, and his frequency at the Reading Room, Anderson probably had more friends and acquaintances in Newport than anywhere else. "You could count on Harry being there Friday evenings," says Dr. Tom Cahill, a Reading Room regular. "He gets more into his day than most people. At the Reading Room he was disciplined. He'd arrive at 5:00 p.m., time for the first drink. We'd be sitting around the fireplace, and Harry would dip into his inside jacket pocket, pull out the habitual 8x10 sheet folded in half the long way that was full of notes, and say, 'Did you know that elephant trunks were used for such and such,' and we'd discuss that for 20 minutes or so, and then he'd consult his notes and say, 'When wood is not cured properly. . . .' And on it would go."

Once he took up residence, Anderson didn't waste any time getting involved in the Newport community. He became interested in the Seamen's Church Institute initially because of the "affordable" breakfast and lunch it offered in its Aloha Café on the waterfront in midtown Newport, not all that far from his NAYRU office on Goat Island. Anderson loves a bargain, and he found the quick soup-and-sandwich special offered at Aloha to his liking. One thing led to another. He joined, and before long he was on the board.

Newport's Seamen's Church Institute has religious origins that are no longer pivotal to its stated purpose of providing "A safe haven for men and women of the sea." SCI's impressive brick building on the Newport waterfront was dedicated in 1930 as a gift of the Wetmore sisters, daughters of Governor and Senator George Wetmore, whose father built Chateau-sur-Mer, a high-Victorian mansion on Bellevue Avenue. The sisters' deed of gift states that the building must be used for charitable purposes. It was placed on the National Register of Historic Places in 1983. SCI has laundry facilities, showers, a chapel, a library, the Aloha café, and lodging that is charged on a sliding scale. It is frequented by mariners from merchant sailors and fishermen to professional yacht crews. SCI's charitable work, including their Soup to Docks program that feeds 12,000 waterfront workers a year, is well known.

"Harry probably knew about SCI from New York," says David Brown, the current president. "SCI New York is the New York Yacht Club's favorite charity. Most other charitable organizations in Newport are into preserving and taking care of *things*. SCI takes care of and preserves *people*, people in need—people who go to sea. I think that is what attracted him to us."

Anderson was on SCI's board more than 30 years until he retired in the fall of 2011. "At the table," Brown says, "he was the smartest guy in the room a lot of the time. He always did his homework, and he had good ideas, well thought out. But he was never flashy. He was always a good listener who would watch how a topic evolved and jump in at the right moment. His wealth of general knowledge and broad scope of people he knows were invaluable to us. And outside of a couple foundations, he has been our largest financial contributor."

SCI dedicated its library to Harry Anderson in 2005.

Anderson was "tapped," as he puts it, to join the foundation of the Naval War College in Newport, by Harry Morgan. "He often took his boat to the War College," Anderson says, "and went to conferences there." The War College's mission is to educate and develop leaders, and conduct research, analysis, and gaming to meet strategic challenges in support of top-level navy leadership. It also aims to strengthen global marine partnerships. A portion of the New York Yacht Club's membership has always been from the US Navy, Coast Guard, and Marines. Active-duty personnel pay dues reduced by 25 percent. Today the number of military members is around 200, greatly reduced since World War II when the Brooklyn Navy Yard was at full strength. Anderson sat on the War College Foundation as an active trustee until 1985, at which point he became a trustee emeritus.

The American Sail Training Association (ASTA)— now known as Tall Ships America (TSA)—was another natural place for Anderson to hang his hat. It would be difficult to find an organization more focused on education under sail, more committed to encouraging character-building and developing leadership through sail training than TSA. Press most lifelong sailors about the origins of how they live and function in the world on a day-to-day basis, and they will credit the resourcefulness they developed as young sailors, the respect they were taught for the forces of nature, and how the most successful outcome on the sea requires an effort in harmony with those forces. As world-class racing sailor Buddy Melges is fond of saying, "You need to set up your boat for Mother Nature."

If ASTA hadn't existed, Anderson might have started it. He recalls that when he was a pre-teenager, his grandfather brought him books about ships and the sea when he came for Sunday lunch. One was titled, *Young America Afloat*, written in 1886 by Oliver Optic (pseudonym for William T. Adams). It was about a fictional 400-ton academy ship, *Young America*, an "aquatic educational institution," that dealt with "noble-hearted young men who could not tamely submit to authority, who only needed the right kind of discipline to make them earnest and faithful men and useful citizens." Anderson says the book was so successful that two more ships were added to form a squadron, and it took 12 volumes to recount the story of the trainees and the challenges they overcame.

ASTA was founded in 1973, the year after Newport yachtsman Barclay Warburton III had sailed his brigantine, *Black Pearl,* to Cowes, England, to participate in a tall ships race to Sweden. The high spirits of that international gathering of young people on a variety of school ships so impressed Warburton that he founded ASTA upon his return.

Anderson got involved with ASTA the following year, three years before his move to Newport. "He wasn't on the founding committee," says Bert Rogers, TSA executive director in 2013. "But they roped him in soon afterwards. He was on the board for 39 years, becoming chairman in 1983. Those were good years. One trait I've always admired about Harry is if he has nothing to say, he doesn't say anything. To me that's a sign of wisdom, and strength. He doesn't attract any hostility because he doesn't project any. He's a gentleman. That is pure and fundamental to his outlook. He treats people with respect when he disagrees with them. His integrity is part of who he is. He is a polite man, a gentleman."

They didn't have to use a very strong rope to corral Anderson for TSA. He summed up 40 years of his thoughts about TSA in a paper, *Philosophy and Key Values of Sail Training*, written in 2003. An excerpt: "The values from 1886 to the present have remained basically the same and are recognized via the buzzwords that you know so well—character building, challenge of the elements, experiential education, team work, building self-esteem by being stretched to accomplish, self-discipline that comes with seamanship, and so forth. . . . Barclay Warburton would have been the first to point out that perhaps the most extreme mockery of real life today is the fireplace with artificial logs and gas-fired jets—youth no longer learn the basics of how to chop wood and build a fire."

Anderson moved to Newport just in time for the 1977 America's Cup. It was another easy victory on the water, as *Courageous*—this time steered by Ted Turner with the cool-headed Gary Jobson calling tactics and, more importantly, keeping his irascible skipper focused—took four races in a row from *Australia*. But ashore there was plenty of excitement that required new interventions by the America's Cup Committee. For the first time, a syndicate from San Diego had entered the defense trials. Suddenly the staid, East Coast formality of a typical America's Cup summer was ruffled by the introduction of Southern California lifestyle, including flip-flops, Hawaiian shirts, and a large hot tub that was set up outside the dormitory at Salve Regina College where the syndicate was housed. Hot tubs, it was soon discovered, are best enjoyed completely naked, a fact

that flew in the face of existing America's Cup propriety. A cautionary phone call from the America's Cup Committee resulted in the tub being drained for the duration.

Then there was Turner, a marked departure from the string of politically correct Cup skippers who had preceded him. While Turner's willingness to say exactly what was on his mind, including whatever new material might come into his rampant consciousness while he was speaking, was manna from heaven for the quote-thirsty America's Cup press corps. But as the self-appointed keepers of decorum, the America's Cup Committee had a case of the jitters every time Turner approached the microphone, or even encountered a reporter in passing. He ran into *Sports Illustrated*'s Coles Phinizy on the street one afternoon. Phinizy asked him what he and Jobson talked about on their well-publicized morning walks. Turner replied, "What did we talk about, well, we talked about how great it was to face fearful odds for the ashes of our fathers and the temples of our gods. In fact on our way to the dock this morning Gary and I went right by the Catholic Church and listened for a moment. We talked about everything—ships and sealing wax, cabbages and kings."

Turner took Newport by storm, and was obviously relishing his notoriety, flying high.

Someone labeled him "Captain Outrageous," and it stuck like glue. But Turner crossed the line one evening at Bailey's Beach, an elite, private club on Newport's Ocean Drive that has proud roots in the town's Gilded Age. In high spirits, and quite by accident, Turner picked one of the club's more haughty dowagers to insult.

"We had to call Ted in," Anderson recalls, "and tell him to straighten up or we'd have to throw him out of the series. We had that kind of authority. We asked him to write a letter of apology to John Winslow, who was head of Bailey's Beach at the time. Ted did, Winslow accepted it, and the racing went on."

Wherever Anderson lived he would not reliably be found at home. As one sailor who often crewed with him says, "the man can't sit still to save his life." From the time he joined his first committee of the International Yacht Racing Union, he had remained active in that organization. In 1978 he became chairman of IYRU's Constitution Committee, and he oversaw a second revision of the constitution and by-laws enabling IYRU to incorporate under the UK Charities Act (similar to a 501(c)(3) in the US). "I wound up working with the IYRU counsel," Anderson says, "a partner in one of the largest corporate law firms in London, to protect the copyrights of the international classes, especially those

designated as Olympic classes. This is a process that IYRU directs and submits to the IOC for approval. The exercise cost me numerous evening receptions, as the counsel and I worked late."

He was also a member of the IYRU Permanent Committee (now Council). Between the Constitution Committee and the Permanent Committee, Anderson traveled to meetings held at various times in Rio de Janeiro, Auckland, Sydney, East Berlin (before the Wall came down), Norway, Sweden, Geneva, Alessio on the Italian Riviera, and Kingston, Ontario. Other missions for the IYRU took Anderson to Asia, South America, and the Netherlands. Once when he left a meeting in Kingston, he flew to LaGuardia Airport in New York and stopped at the Russian legation to deliver gifts of chocolate and cigarettes to a friend of fellow committee member Andre Kislov of the USSR. "I had to ring a bell at the legation for the iron grating to be opened," Anderson recalls. "When I left, the taxi was tailed until it stopped at my apartment—no doubt Secret Service or FBI."

When he was home, Anderson always made time for sailing. Over the years people have often been impudent enough to question him about why he never married. Anderson's answers have been either appropriately glib— "I came close once," he told one who inquired, "then I got the flu"—or evasive. But the truth of it is that there was no room in Harry Anderson's life for a partner, let alone a family. At the rate he was moving to keep all the various balls in the air, it was all he could do to make room for living accommodations and boats in his strenuous life.

His first house in Newport was at 209 Spring Street, a large, gambrel-roof New England colonial built between 1758 and 1777. It was completely restored in 1989 and is now listed on the National Register of Historic Places. But Leith Adams remembers that Anderson was doing it over himself in 1977. A capable handyman, Anderson put together a well-equipped shop in the basement at 209 and got to work. His ability to work with his hands came down through two generations. The favorite pastime of his grandfather, Henry B. Anderson, was making intricate, fully rigged models of sailing ships from the 1600s and 1800s. The hobby became so important to him that he moved the cars out of his garage and turned it into a workshop. "He would use discarded dentist drill bits to make fine items like blocks," Anderson says. "To obtain a weathered copper underwater look, he would paint a ship's bottom green and while it was still damp, brush gold leaf on it." His model of a whaler based on the *Charles W. Morgan* (at Mystic Seaport) is in the collection at the South Street Seaport in New York. Other of

his models reside in glass cases at the New York Yacht Club and his home.

Anderson's father was also handy. At the house in Roslyn he had built an extension on the porch, walled it in, and set up a complete workshop. So Anderson had been learning to use tools since he was old enough to pick them up. From the time he had helped raise that rustic camp in the woods at Adirondack-Florida School's northern campus, he was comfortable with tools.

"He invited a bunch of us over one day," Leith Adams recalls. "We arrived, and somehow he had removed the main beam from the living room. He said it was exciting, that we were all going to help him raise the new timber in place. There it was on the floor, it must have weighed a million tons. He had it all rigged with hoists, all figured out, and sure enough we all helped him put it up."

As for boats, in 1978 Anderson bought into the New York Yacht Club's new one-design class, a NY40 designed by Doug Peterson. It was tough giving up *Witch*, but in a year he would become commodore of the NYYC, and he wanted to support the new class. The NY40 was the first NYYC offshore race boat since the NY32s, and that provided romantic pull. And the truth was that *Witch* was slow under power. As commodore, when protocol would require the NYYC cruising fleet to follow him out of anchorages for the day's sailing, reducing those processions to below five knots would have created unrest and produced a considerable amount of ribbing from his fellow sailors. He called the new boat *Taniwha*, after his grandfather's power yacht in which he had patrolled New York Harbor during World War I. *Taniwha* is a Maui word for a demon that lives in the forests of New Zealand.

A trip Anderson made in the spring of 1979 is typical of the schedule he was keeping in the interests of IYRU and NAYRU. It started with three days of NAYRU meetings in Chicago, and continued with IYRU meetings in London, Berlin, and Paris before he flew home. He kept (and preserved) careful notes:

> Stayed in "cabin" at Royal Thames YC. . . . met with Rick Hamilton-Parks, Chairman of Royal Thames Race Committee for 1974 Cup re RTYC and NYYC relations, which are most cordial. . . . had luncheon at RTYC and sampled their wines and port—a notch or two above our own. . . . PM meeting with PR head of Royal Southern America's Cup Challenge and Slim Somerville (Imperial Poona YC) for long discussion on forthcoming September America's Cup regatta in Solent. . . . Learned what I had been told last weekend in confidence re Huey Long buying

> Independence *for his son to enter trials is known fact in UK yachting circles. . . . Thence to Commodore Elmer Ellsworth-Jones for dinner. . . . magnificent meal—fish, beef, and a most unusual pineapple potted fruit dessert served with white and red wines and followed by brandy all of which Elmer partook despite his recent rather severe bout with diabetes.*

So it went for five days with people encountered, places visited, and subjects discussed all noted, and the quality of food, drink, architecture, travel, general ambience, and social situations mentioned in some detail: "There is (in Berlin) laughter only on the lips of the young, except that the people look nowhere as grim as they did in Munich when I visited there in 1948. . . . Would it were, as King Constantine expressed at the airport, that there was a universal passport admitting one to all nations."

Jamie Hilton would be *Taniwha*'s paid captain when the boat was launched in 1979, Anderson's second year as NYYC commodore. Hilton first met Anderson in 1977, when Hilton was invited to sail on a boat in the New York Yacht Club cruise chartered by Alan Whitman, son of Betty (Mrs. Mahlon) Dickerson. "The threads of how I got into this thing are thin," Hilton says today, "but Alan Whitman and Harry Anderson had together chartered a big Trumpy as mother ship that year. Harry and

his friend Tom Josten from Seawanhaka had ordered a NY40, but had chartered another one until their boat could be delivered."

Hilton was 17 and had just finished taking a year off. He'd been working for a tree service in Stowe, Vermont. "I'm from Rumson, New Jersey," says Hilton, who in 2013 was running the Hilton Group at Smith Barney in Newport, "not a bad area, but being on a Trumpy was a far cry from anything I had experienced. Harry is unique. You might think a guy on the verge of being commodore of New York wouldn't be ready to engage with a kid who was a nobody, a guest, but they needed somebody to do the bow. I was up half the night drinking with Harry and Glen Foster, who was sailing with him, and a Newport guy named Johnny McGowan who would sail on winning America's Cup teams with Dennis Conner. We did well, sailed the boat pretty well, and at the end of the week Harry convinced Tom Josten that I should be their boat captain when *Taniwha* arrived."

In the spring of 1979, Hilton finished his year at St. Joseph's College in North Windham, Maine, mailed his kit home, and hitched a ride to Newport. "I had no idea what I was getting into," he says.

I'd been with these people for a total of one week. The next day we were taking Taniwha

from Seawanhaka to Newport. There I was, the boat captain. Harry and Tom were going out to dinner with Tom's girlfriend and Liz Roosevelt, and they wouldn't think of leaving me behind. They dressed me up, and off we went to the Clambake Club for dinner. That was so far out of the realm of anything I had experienced, but I had a great time. Everyone had a lot of drinks. That night I learned extraordinary things can happen to Harry and he just keeps rolling. At midnight we went back to the boat

LEFT: *Taniwha.* RIGHT: Jamie Hilton, *Taniwha's* captain, trims during a passage in 1981.

at Newport Offshore. It was misty. The boat was moored to the bulkhead adjoining the parking lot. In his Gucci loafers, Tom jumped down onto the boat. The deck was wet and he slipped, went down hard, hit his head. Harry calmly said we better get Tom to the hospital to get stitched up. We're there until 2:00 a.m., and none of it seemed to be a problem.

The next morning, Tom's girlfriend was sick to

her stomach. Liz Roosevelt put the woman's head in a bucket down below and off we went. It was nothing to get distraught about.

Liz Roosevelt remembers *Taniwha*. She was aboard for the initial sail from Rowayton, Connecticut, where the boat was delivered, to Oyster Bay. "Those 40s were not nice boats," Roosevelt recalls.

Taniwha, the NY40 owned by Harry Anderson and Tom Josten, during the 1979 Annapolis-Newport Race.

There wasn't much stowage space, and they rolled rhythmically downwind like you wouldn't believe. On that trip there was water in every compartment below, and not a sponge on the boat. There we were cleaning up with rags, wringing them out, on a brand new boat. It had been trucked, and rain had gotten in. I didn't get to race much after Harry became commodore of New York. He always had a lot of young. . . . men on board. One time we delivered Taniwha *to the Chesapeake for the Annapolis-Newport race. There was Harry, my cousin Fifi, and two or three strong young men there for the race. We went through New York Harbor at night. As soon as we got outside those young men got so sick, I've never seen anyone so sick. They were useless. Cousin Fifi and I sailed the boat. We had a lot of food on board. As soon as we hit Delaware Bay they came back to life and ate everything in sight.*

Anderson became Commodore of the New York Yacht Club in 1978. One of his first acts was to create the history committee, or the Collections Committee as it was officially called. It was focused on restoring the Club's valuable collection of paintings and artifacts. Anderson appointed Bob MacKay as its chairman. "There was little interest in the Club's collections when Harry became a flag officer in the early '70s," Mackay says. "It was a dirty old building. Its ceilings were greasy with cigar smoke. Harry got things focused

again. He restored the club and along with that, the value of tradition."

"Harry was always interested in history, and doing it right," says John Rousmaniere, current New York Yacht Club historian. "When I complained to him that there was no index for the 1974 club history, he told me to find an indexer and the club would take care of the rest. Within six months (an eyeblink in NYYC time), he had a complete index."

"In the '70s the Morgan-Stanley crowd was coming in wearing stick pins in their collars," MacKay says. "Harry's comment was, 'What are they doing? Just put on a button-down shirt.' He was a lot like his mentor, George Roosevelt. He had no time for pomposity."

In the 1970s, the New York Yacht Club wasn't sure it could hang on to the building on West Forty-Fourth Street. It was located in a deteriorating neighborhood with sleazy hotels. That block often reeked of garbage. There was talk of selling. Hosting so many America's Cups had taken its toll on the Club's budget.

"Harry always leaned toward the practical," MacKay says. "In communication with foreigners, working with the IYRU, he would quote the classics, setting a high tone that no one else had been able to do. When he became commodore, he was different. That was an era

of really deep-pocket people, but they all had to turn to Harry because he knew more about what was going on than anyone. He was on top of everything, and they weren't. He was a bit of an odd duck in that lineup of captains of finance and industry out there on bigger boats, but a lot of them reflected newer money without the pedigree. Harry certainly had the pedigree, and he was out there on his Hughes 38, or the NY40, giving away 30 feet to the rest of them, but they dutifully lined up

behind him. He also took home his share of the silverware, and that made a difference."

Anderson had won his class in the Marblehead-Halifax Race the first year *Taniwha* was commissioned. But he couldn't make the Bermuda Race that year, so co-owner Tom Josten skippered the boat. "On the way down," Jamie Hilton recalls, "we spent a lot of time on port tack. The diesel fill cap on the leeward side allowed water in, and we bent a

New York Yacht Club commodores gather to salute the Stephens brothers in 1996. Standing from left, Commodores Frank V. Snyder, William H. Dyer Jones, Robert W. McCullough Jr., Charles M. Leighton, Robert G. Stone Jr., Henry H. Anderson Jr., and Emil Mosbacher surround Rod (left) and Olin Stephens.

push rod on the engine. When Harry showed up, he got right into it, spent a whole week working on it mainly because Harry loves to solve problems. To Harry, life is simply an opportunity to solve problems. But he always quit in time for cocktails.

"The day we started back, we motored out of Hamilton Harbor and just beyond the entrance the engine quit. I could tell we'd bent another push rod. We didn't have ice on board because Tom was convinced that because the boat had a fridge and the engine worked we wouldn't need ice. We were only five miles out. I said, let's go back and get this fixed. Harry said, 'You know, we didn't even have an engine on the first boat I sailed to Bermuda on. Let's keep going.'"

If such records were kept, *Taniwha* would probably hold one for the longest passage from Bermuda to Newport by a 40-footer. In the Gulf Stream, the wind quit. In one 24-hour period they made 60 miles eastward with the sails down. The last few days, meals were nuts and trail mix left over from the race down. They ran out of battery power except for the radio direction finder. Off Castle Hill, marking the entrance to Newport's East Passage, the wind died again. They anchored for five hours in an outgoing tide before they were able to drift into Newport.

As Hilton remembers, during regattas and New York Yacht Club cruises the motto on board was, "'No trim is too small, no drink is too early.' Harry wanted to win, but he also wanted to have fun," Hilton says.

On one cruise we rafted up one night with a couple other boats in a remote spot in the middle of nowhere called Great Wass Island off the coast of Maine. There's no population, no lights ashore. Three guests came aboard for drinks: Harry Morgan's wife, Betty Dickerson, and her daughter, Frankie Whitman. On Taniwha it was Harry, Tom Josten, Quentin Reynolds, and myself. Harry went below and got dressed in his Breton red pants, shirt, necktie, and blazer. Then he put a dry suit on over all that. I'm not sure where the dry suit came from, but it was one of the first ones. He came up to show the ladies, drink in hand, and the next thing you knew he jumped over the side. It was wet-your-pants funny. There he was, all puffed up in this suit, lying on the water. Anything for a gag, that's Harry.

The thing is, he had the economic latitude to do anything he wanted, but the underlying theme is consistent, and that's giving back in a huge way. It doesn't matter if it's a laugh for the ladies, or his support of the various philanthropies. I don't think he ever had any big goal, or that he ever aspired to be the commodore of New York. Things like that

*claimed him because of his ability to do them.
His reason for being was a big thirst for
information and knowledge, and then giving it
back. For Harry it's always been the adventure
of sailing and the relationships that get forged
on the water, the experiences shared.*

*Harry's crew did everything together. There
was never any screaming from the helm. His
affable nature comes from the fact that he
is comfortable in his own skin. He always
included Trish. How many owners think like
that. . . . ask their paid hand if he wants to
bring his girlfriend on a trip? Once we stopped
in the Thimble Islands off Connecticut. The
main channel is narrow from the southwest,
and it's open to the east, but you can't go out
that way. It was dawn, flat water, and Harry
decided to try it. Bam! We hit, go from 6 knots
to zero in a foot. Tom Josten was flat on his face
up forward. The forestay kept him from going
overboard. Harry was calm, one hand on the
wheel, one finger on the chart. He said, "It says
here there's eight feet." He tried it again. We hit
again. I said I wasn't sure we could get out this
way. Harry says, "Hmmm. Maybe not."*

*But he could be tough. He got very mad at me
one night, the maddest I've ever seen him.
During a NYYC cruise when he was commodore,
he was ashore at a small dinner. We were in
Islesboro, Maine. The flag officers all have their
lights in the rigging at night so people can*

*identify them if necessary. It's the boat
captain's responsibility to make sure they are
turned on. And I forgot. It was pouring rain,
low visibility when they returned. I heard a
launch, people saying "There it is!" He'd been
trying to find the boat with his blue light
signal in the rain and fog. But there were no
lights. He was livid, pulled me out of my bunk.
But there was no fall out afterwards. He got
mad, chewed me out, and it was done.*

Bill Mooney, a friend of Anderson's from
Oyster Bay, remembers the *Taniwha* days.
Mooney would end up running the boat for
Tom Josten after Anderson had sold his share
to his partner. Josten had known Mooney
since he was a child. "Tom took me to my
first baseball game," Mooney says.

*Those two guys were confirmed bachelors, thick
as thieves. Tom would bring these great women
around, but the first time one of them would
have the audacity to wonder what the future
of their relationship might be, like maybe
marriage, she would be replaced. Thanks, you're
done. It was tough to keep up. In some cases it
was great news for the crew. In some cases we
missed them because they were a lot of fun.
You'd get to like having them around, then
they would be gone.*

*Harry and Tom were cut from the same piece of
cloth. They rented a house together that was*

NEWPORT

216

crawling distance from the Seawanhaka Yacht Club bar. They did what they wanted when they wanted. Their lifestyle didn't merge with the concept of family. Tom just didn't see the point. And it would have cramped Harry's lifestyle. He was used to upping and leaving without notice.

I couldn't believe these guys, so spry at 70, behaving the way they did. They were all out for the fun of it. At dinner one time they regaled me with stories. They were out of order. After a few stories Harry said he couldn't believe anyone had the nerve to complain about the youth of today. He said they are so much better behaved that we were. And I'm thinking, than you are!

Once at the New York Yacht Club I counted seven Scotches followed by a couple bottles of wine. I tried to keep up and was legless, on the floor. They seemed fine. Practice probably helped.

⚓

I N 1979, the quality of the work Anderson had been doing for the past 30 years on behalf of sailing—the leadership he had exercised—was recognized by his selection as recipient of the Nathanael G. Herreshoff Trophy. It is named after one of the great

yacht designers of all time, and is considered yachting's most prestigious award. It is given for outstanding contribution to the sport of sailing in the United States. In presenting the award, NAYRU Secretary Roger Brett said he had traced Anderson through 19 editions of the annual NAYRU yearbook, and found his name listed several times in each, either as officer or on various committees. "His greatest intangible asset," Brett said, "is that he always has the time and interest to pass his knowledge on to others. . . . With the move to Newport and the restructuring of the Union as USYRU, he was given a new title, Executive Counselor. At his own request he stepped down as a paid staff member of the Union in 1978. He is still a member of the Appeals Committee, working on cases, preparing their decisions for publication. He attends all Executive Committee meetings. His ability to distill eight hours of deliberations into five pages of minutes makes them a joy to read and refer to. . . . The Union would not be where it is today— recognized nationally and internationally as one of the best organized and operated national sports governing bodied without his strong personal interest, knowledge, and skills."

In his column in *Yachting* magazine that month, Bob Bavier wrote, "Harry Anderson typifies the best of a group of yachtsmen who do more for the sport than those who win the big races. . . . No prior recipient of the Nathanael G. Herreshoff trophy is more deserving."

That summer, his first as commodore, Anderson took the New York Yacht Club cruise to Roque Island, Maine, just 50 miles short of the Canadian border. It remains the furthest east the cruise has ever been, and it featured the commodore in an unusual role. After finishing the race to Roque Island in light air, *Brass Ring*, a Swan 44 owned by Nicholas Schaus, had run hard aground on a rocky ledge. In a report about the incident, Schaus wrote: "*Taniwha* was 50 yards away. We were encircled by deep water. Vice Commodore McCullough was in the vicinity with *Inverness*, a large yacht of 65 feet. . . . There were several dinghies circling. One took a line and it was made secure to *Inverness*. The water was boiling from her prop, but her rudder had no effect on the direction the bow was pointed as there was too much pressure from our towline at her stern. Commodore Anderson immediately saw the problem, and asked a nearby launch to take a line from *Taniwha* to *Inverness'* bow. Thus the smaller yacht was the effective rudder of the larger yacht that was doing the major pulling. It was a five star endeavor. I wish I could see a picture of what should be called the NYYC Commodore's salvage."

A large inflatable staffed with the hefty mid-

deck crew of one of the racing machines careened *Brass Ring* with its spinnaker halyard to complete the successful freeing of the Swan. The next day, alongside a dock, Schaus looked up from assaying the damage to *Brass Ring* to see a group of men approaching. They were dressed in yachting jackets, white shirts, ties, and yachting caps. "The Commodore inquired about the health and well-being of the crew," Schaus wrote. "The Vice Commodore asked if there was particular assistance that would be helpful. This visit by the flags and race committee was thoughtful, memorable, and continues to be indelible."

———————— ⚓ ————————

IN 1980 JAMIE HILTON transferred to the University of Rhode Island, where there was a sailing team, and to be closer to Newport. Trish McKenna transferred to Salve Regina. In 1980, at Block Island Race Week, Anderson, Hilton, the father of one of Hilton's friends, and four members of the URI sailing team, won the 40-foot class over 29 other boats. "The rest of the boats were crewed by friends of the owner and a couple young guys," Hilton says. "Harry loved the college kids, loved sailing with them, loved introducing them into the sport. He enjoyed them, and enjoyed learning from them.

"At regattas and on cruises, as commodore he'd be in the prime mooring spot, and have a big mother ship chartered to be with his contemporaries. *Taniwha* would be alongside. Harry would come on board and with his permission we'd be blasting Grateful Dead and Springsteen across the anchorage. Harry had written down the music he had heard us listening to and made the tapes. He had a big stereo setup with double cassettes at 209 Spring Street. We had a tape he'd labeled '*Floyd Pink*.' He couldn't ever get the idea it was *Pink Floyd*. He would listen to the lyrics and say these people are your generation's poets. He could talk about the lyrics and understand them. There was the commodore's boat, fully dressed, with the rock music cranking."

There was a Dymo Marker label in the galley on *Taniwha* that read, "Pink Floyd lives in the hearts of all young men." For sure, the young men lived in Anderson's heart. A few, with Jamie Hilton atop the list, became the sons he never had. To this day Anderson uses "the apple of my eye," a classic parental phrase of endearment, to describe Hilton. It was Hilton's transfer to University of Rhode Island that caused Anderson to become involved with the URI sailing program.

Anderson had previously interacted with URI. In the 1960s, when he was chairman of the NYYC Race Committee, Anderson had worked with the crew of an experimental plotting vessel operating out of URI's Bay Campus that was doing exercises to determine the accuracy with which America's Cup courses could be plotted. He was impressed by URI's Graduate School of Oceanography, and like so many of Anderson's seemingly casual associations, that one would sustain. Years later while having lunch at the Yale Club in New York he would run into old Yale and Columbia Law classmate George Rowe, who was counsel and executive director of two foundations supporting university-level marine biology programs. "It turned out he was not familiar with URI's GSO," Anderson says, "odd, as it is one of the top schools of its kind in the country. When I returned to Rhode Island, I reported the conversation to GSO leadership and gave them George's contacts. It was not pursued until their successors were searching the records for sources of contributions and ran across our correspondence. Contact was made with George. Since then, $2 million worth of grants for special missions have been received by GSO."

Shortly after moving to Newport, Anderson had taken advantage of an evening refresher course in celestial navigation at URI's Department of Fisheries. But as a result of Hilton helping to bring fellow members of the URI sailing team aboard *Taniwha*, Anderson became familiar with some of URI's prominent sailors, including Skip Whyte, Gregg Knapp, Cam Lewis, Henry Bossett, Henry Childers, and Ed Adams. Then he took a serious interest in improving the sailing team's lot. Given his long association with college sailing, and with Yale and the Naval Academy in particular, taking on another college project was part of a logical progression for Anderson.

The URI team had been sailing out of the East Greenwich Yacht Club. But in 1981, along with several other sports, sailing lost its varsity status. Without Department of Athletics vehicles, transportation to East Greenwich became a problem for students. And the yacht club only had one fleet of boats, which was often commandeered by recreational sailing, which had first priority.

Assistant Athletic Director Art Tuveson, who was URI's director of recreational services at the time, says an alumni group had formed to make sure the sailing team survived. "URI had a fine sailing tradition," Tuveson says. "We had won some championships in the '70s with guys like Ken Legler and Skip Whyte. Now we needed help. Harry knew Jamie Hilton of course, and I think Harry called the sailing center looking for students to sail with him in Newport. That's how it got started."

"Sailing out of East Greenwich wasn't handy to the college," Anderson says, "and it was often too rough to sail on Narragansett Bay. The team had an option to rent where they are now, at Salt Pond, a much better location. I ended up at a meeting with Art Tuveson, and Ralph Potter from the Potter-Hazelhurst advertising agency in Providence—Ralph had the sailing program under his wing at the time—and Jamie, who got me involved, and there was a big debate. The Salt Pond offered enclosed waters, and it was closer. The move got engineered, but it was a great disappointment to Ralph, since logistically at Greenwich he was able to pay close supervision to the program. Yet he recognized the advantages of Salt Pond."

Anderson's association with Yale Sailing provided an opportunity to temporarily satisfy URI's need for more boats. "Yale was replacing its fleet of dinghies at the time," Anderson says, "so I purchased them for URI. Dollars to URI to purchase the Yale fleet was also dollars to sailing at Yale, a double whammy!" It was also a double whammy for Anderson, since he was involved in purchasing Yale's new fleet of 420s. Hilton says he was living at the time in a small house in Bonnet Shores, a beach community near Narragansett, Rhode Island. "I came home one afternoon and there were more than a dozen dinghies that had been delivered to the house. There were boats all over the place."

There was more. About that time the tall ships were coming into Newport. Anderson had purchased a dozen or more sailboards to be used for competition among the crews of the ships. Afterwards, he sent half of them to URI, the other half to Yale.

"The building at Salt Pond was useless," Anderson says. "It was just a hut with no heat, and no toilet facilities. About then Ed Rumowicz got me involved in the fund-raising for a new facility and a new fleet of 420s." Rumowicz is a very active URI alumnus who has long worked with admissions. Anderson knew him from the New York Yacht Club.

Anderson and Rumowicz co-chaired the drive that raised more than $650,000 to build a sailing pavilion and acquire a fleet of new 420s. Anderson was among the top individual contributors. "We needed that campaign to do three things," Art Tuveson says: "build a facility, buy a new fleet of boats, and start an endowment. Ralph Potter kicked off the endowment by selling a boat and giving us the proceeds. And Harry single-handedly bought us the fleet. He also bought us the next fleet as well, six or seven years later. He was the driving force. The main room in the pavilion is named after him." URI bestowed an honorary degree upon Anderson in 1990. The sailing pavilion was dedicated in 1992.

"Harry has stayed involved," Tuveson says. "He became a member of the URI Foundation Boat Committee (and a trustee of the foundation), which takes in donated boats and sells them to support sailing. As such, he has been a staunch supporter of the sailing program, helping push through proposals we have submitted, and providing individual donations as well to hire coaches." Anderson has also helped send URI sailors to the Student Yachting World Cup (formerly the Course de l'Europe), a weeklong big boat regatta held annually in France. URI has attended a dozen times, winning the regatta in 1990. "Harry has always supported us with that event," Tuveson says. "And he would often give me the names of judges who might be there so I could go meet them and let them know I knew Harry. It made a difference. The man has contacts everywhere."

During the early 1980s, 209 Spring Street was the crew headquarters for whatever regatta was going on, a crash pad for sailor friends passing through. Jamie Hilton lived at 209 for several semesters while he was attending URI. A few years after Hilton had graduated, Peder Arstorp, a student from Denmark, moved into 209. Arstorp, who had worked as a boat captain in the Caribbean for a couple years before applying to college, had met Anderson in Maine. People he had met chartering invited him to visit them in Mount Desert

Island one summer. When the New York Yacht Club cruise came through, he befriended a contemporary named Nick Bell, who was Anderson's captain. Arstorp wanted to be near Newport for the sailing, so he applied to URI and was accepted. When Anderson heard he was going to URI, he told Arstorp to look him up. He did, and he began sailing with Anderson on *Taniwha*. He also sailed for URI until he felt he needed the time to concentrate on his degree work (he graduated magna cum laude in five semesters). Before long, Anderson invited Arstorp to take a room at 209 and help look after the house.

"It was awesome," Arstorp says today.

I was in college, and it was a free place to stay. It worked both ways because Harry was traveling a lot in those days and I looked after things, paid the bills, kept the house going. Friends would drop by at all hours and camp out with their crews. It got a bit ridiculous. At times there would be bodies on the antique rugs in the library. Not everyone respected the house. I would wake up to a pigsty of empty pizza boxes and beer cans all over the place.

Harry often told me how much he appreciated me being there so he didn't feel lonely in the big house in the middle of winter. I'd cook us a meal, and I was someone to talk with. And he always had advice. Once I was very upset about

how I had been treated by a wealthy Boston couple who had contacted me about running their yacht for the summer. I had traveled to Boston and spent four or five days with them on Martha's Vineyard, then moved their boat back to Boston. I went back to the Vineyard to find out if they wanted to hire me. The man was away, so I spoke with his wife. She was suddenly very formal and let me know they were looking for a college kid who had the skills and interest in taking care of the boat for free. They finally gave me $50 for travel expenses. Harry instantly replied, "That was your first mistake: never talk business with a woman." He would twitch his mustache for effect, which meant end of discussion.

But he thrives on activity. He makes all this activity for himself, sits on a raft of committees, always has something to do, places to go. He had a lot of pride in how he kept up with such a grueling schedule. He has his own agenda, and because he is used to living in his own world after being a bachelor for so long, he's uncompromising.

One summer during college days I was supposed to meet him on his new boat at some small harbor in Maine. I drove 10 hours, waited two days, and he never showed up. No one there had heard from him. There were no cell phones then, and I couldn't radio the boat. I guess he forgot about it. But it wasn't something he was

*going to feel guilty about, or cause him to say
he was really sorry.*

In addition to providing lodging for Hilton and Arstorp, Anderson was contributing to their tuitions. Those relationships were close, and long-lasting. In 1996, long after he had graduated and moved on to be an assistant vice president of sales for Ship Serve, an internet company that brokers interactions between shipping companies and their suppliers, Arstop wrote Anderson an emotional letter that Anderson still treasures.

"This is a very difficult letter for me to write," Arstorp begins. "A history of broken promises, deceitfulness, heartless accusations and impossible demands weigh heavily in favor of wrapping myself in impenetrable armor." Anderson says the remorse Arstorp expressed had to do with very high standards he had set for himself that he felt he had not met. "Yet I know the only way forward is to place my trust in those I love and to open the doors to my soul a crack at a time. When I saw you last, you touched something deep within me and I am still reeling from the incredible level of understanding and acceptance you embraced me with. It means more than anything to me." On the letter Anderson has penned: "and to me."

"We do the best we can," Arstorp continues,

"yet you have done so much for me by being open, giving, and accepting of who I am. I never knew that you were proud of me, and your incredible encouragement is an enormous support. I love that about you, and I know of no one else who is so unconditionally supportive of me in the way you are. . . . I am still afraid to say I love you, but you know that I do."

Jamie Hilton has also stayed very close with Anderson. His son, Alex, is one of Anderson's several godchildren, and Hilton manages some of Anderson's finances through his firm, Smith Barney. Anderson often spends Christmas Eve with the Hiltons. In a recent thank-you note to his adopted father-figure, Hilton writes: "Not only are you the best mentor a person could have, you also have a real flair for gift-giving. The tide charts of Narragansett Bay are a collector's item. The trophy is full of great meaning, and your generosity to the kids is greatly appreciated by Andy, Alex, Tricia and me. You are the best friend I could ever wish for. My life has been greatly so greatly enhanced by our friendship that words cannot begin to describe it."

Anderson says he lost track of the number of keys in circulation for 209 Spring Street. The repairman couldn't understand how a bachelor could destroy a washing machine. "Some of the boys," Anderson says, "learned to climb the fire escape ladder to a third-floor deck and crawl in the bathroom window." But Anderson was often in the thick of things, the point man. Once, he and Tom Josten and some of the crew returned from a black-tie function in the wee hours. Someone had presented Anderson with a weather vane for the house, and it seemed like a good idea to get it installed right away. In the darkness, they rigged a ladder to the roof peak from the third-floor deck. "With drill and lag screws in hand," Anderson recalls, "we climbed the ladder to the ridge pole and mounted the vane, fortunately getting it close to vertical column. In his patent leather shoes, Tom slid off the roof and landed on the deck without injury."

In its day, 209 Spring Street was like an annex of the Seamen's Church Institute in that it was a haven for mariners. But one could say it was a much more "happening" place. An earlier letter written by Arstorp to his mentor expressed a tone of more understandable remorse:

> Dear Harry, . . . I hope you receive this letter before returning home. Speaking of . . . I have some disturbing reports to make. Your house was the victim of an invasion of high-spirited young students from Connecticut this past weekend. Naively trusting that I would find peace and quiet at 209 Spring, I was surprised by Nick and his friends. Later, Jamie showed up

> with fresh troops to boost the decaying morale. I think your imagination will enable you to picture the scene, although only modestly. All told, everyone went out dancing and drinking. When the discotheques closed, we kept going on your first floor. Jamie saw to it that the fire drills were properly performed at 3 AM, after which the house slowly started echoing sounds of sexual pleasure-taking. A mild panic erupted when it was discovered all drawers were empty of condoms. In the morning we cleaned up and realized what a beating the living room floor had taken. We waxed it, but it is pretty scratched. I considered coating it with polyurethane, but I think it wiser to try another alternative which I will discuss upon your return. Meanwhile, everyone feels very bad about it.

Arstorp says Anderson wasn't too upset about the floor.

> I told him I'd fix it, and because he was away a lot, I could fix it without him getting in the middle of it. Because it was an antique house with old boards on the floor, you couldn't use a sander. I had to use a small pocketknife to scrape the whole floor. It took weeks. But Harry was generally unflappable. He came home one day after being in New York and the whole side of his face was banged up. He had a massive black eye, his other eye was bloodshot, I was shocked. But he was calm. He said a threesome had jumped him and stolen his wallet. I cursed,

and asked him if he wasn't furious. He said no, they just wanted my money, But they sure gave him a good whacking. He was in his 70s at the time. What a terrible thing to do to an old man on the street, but he was totally calm about it.

What did upset him was political activities. He was always screaming and yelling about the Democrats and how they were ruining the country, how it all started with FDR, how he betrayed the country, that Jimmy Carter gave the Canal back to Panama and all that. We used to fight about politics over the years. . . . not that I thought I could change his mind, but just to give a little counterpoint.

Anderson doesn't recall Arstorp's "disturbing reports" letter, or the scratched floor at 209. If he had been angry, it had passed quickly. When Arstorp was married in 1988, Anderson turned up in La Jolla, California, to be one of his ushers. When Jamie Hilton married Trish McKenna in 1988, Anderson was his best man.

TEN | Connections

T he summer of 1980, Harry Anderson's third year as commodore of the New York Yacht Club, Australia challenged for the America's Cup for the third time. If defending the America's Cup is an enormous and costly undertaking, hosting the event is an even bigger job. Everything from providing a suitable venue complete with land bases for syndicates, to organizing race committees and juries, course security and management, and setting up a media center for the world press, lands on the shoulders of the defending yacht club. The division of labor is usually well distributed among dozens of committees, but the buck stops at the commodore's desk. While keeping an eye on the big picture, Anderson continued as a member of the America's Cup Committee.

Bob McCullough took over as chairman that year. A tall, rugged man who preferred racing offshore, McCullough had been a principle in America's Cup syndicates in 1967, 1970—when he often steered *Valiant*—and 1974. He had lost all three times, so he knew this high-stakes game from the other side. Anderson says the upper deck of the committee's boat was off limits to anyone but committee members. That left wives and close friends below. "When it was time for cocktails," Anderson recalls, "Bob McCullough would stamp his foot on the deck, and the wives would send up drinks."

That was the year Dennis Conner turned the America's Cup into a professional sport. He showed up in Newport with two boats and a large crew that had logged 300 days of practice on the water over the previous year. Never again would the Cup be sailed by unpaid amateurs, Corinthians who since 1958 had managed to arrange enough time off from school or work to spend the summer in Newport, ready to give it their all for room and board and all the beer they could drink.

Liberty (left) and *Australia II* under spinnakers during the 1983 America's Cup match, which was won by *Australia II*.

Australia's team looked strong. Their boat, a revamped *Australia* (from 1977), easily knocked off Great Britain's *Lionheart* in the challenger trials. But the value of *Lionheart*'s innovative bendy mast wasn't lost on Alan Bond. When *Australia* showed up on the starting line for Race One of the Cup match against Conner's *Freedom*, Bond's boat was sporting a bendy mast of its own. The pronounced bend was at the top section, resulting in more sail area aloft. That mast was a harbinger of the "flat top" rigs that began appearing 40 years later, and at the time it caused consternation in Newport. Leave it to Alan Bond to show up with something that would require New York Yacht Club attorneys to burn midnight oil in search of a rule infraction.

"Bondy presented his mast to the NYYC committee," Anderson says. "The committee said it was illegal because it hadn't been measured. Bond said it was legal, that our measurer Harold Blumenstock had measured it on *Lionheart*. And he was right. It was foolproof. I think this is what set Bond to thinking he could win by out-designing us. He took note of the anxiety the mast issue created.

"The first race was sailed in light air," Anderson says. "It was hard to tell how the boats compared because they separated. But

Dennis Conner met with us afterwards and said *Australia* was a fast boat."

Freedom won that first race. It took two tries to get Race Two completed because of light wind. *Freedom*'s port-side tailer Tom Whidden says *Australia* was nearly five minutes ahead of *Freedom* when the time limit expired in the first try at Race Two. "So *Australia* almost won two races, because in the second attempt the next day they also beat us," says Whidden, who sailed in eight America's Cup campaigns with Dennis Conner, six of them as tactician. Elected to the America's Cup Hall of Fame (2004), in 2013 Whidden was president and CEO of North Technology Group, LLC. "They won that race on speed," Whidden says. "As I remember, it was a slight edge to us at the start and they sailed slowly away. We actually protested them for not having running lights on after dusk, but we dropped it. The rest of the races were in decent breeze and we were quite a bit faster."

Anderson remembers that protest about running lights.

> We were under pressure because of the long race the previous day when the time limit expired. We had run a race after dark in the trials, and the Coast Guard had given us holy hell. Now this race went into dusk. We were on the spot. Dennis wasn't aware of those problems. We had

*a session with Dennis because a protest would
have caused a real furor. I told him the Cup
Committee couldn't file a protest, but it was up
to him. He said he was having a crew meeting
at 6:00 a.m. and would call us. He called, said
there was no way to withdraw the protest once
it was filed. Liv Sherwood was on the jury.
Sherwood was a Canadian, a champion
International 14 sailor, a Provincial Criminal
Court judge, and a member of the Rules
Committee. He'd be chairman of the America's
Cup jury for seven Cups. Liv found a
diplomatic out, something about Dennis
having failed to note on the protest whether or
not he had attempted to inform* Australia.

Challengers had only won three of the 35
races that had been sailed in Cup matches since
1958, meaning any loss by the home team was
significant. And *Australia*'s bendy mast was
a design innovation that did make a significant
difference in light wind. The way that Cup
match played out gave Commodore Anderson
pause. "It was a close call," he says today. "We
weren't going to defend forever with a slower
boat. We had done it three times up to 1980.
Freedom was definitely slower in certain
conditions. I had made a bet with Umberta
Croce, Beppe Croce's wife. The bet was if we
lost the America's Cup, I'd get married. After
the 1980 match I called her up and canceled
the bet. I told her it was getting too risky."

Anderson says that during the trials in 1980
he got a call from Commodore Edwards, of
the Royal Perth Yacht Club that Alan Bond
was representing. "He said it was urgent,"
Anderson says.

*So he came to the house. He said he had to know
right away where the Cup would be awarded
when they won it, Newport, or New York. I said
we had never considered losing it. He said
Quantas was prepared to paint one of its planes
syndicate colors, and they planned to take the
Cup through Europe on the way home. He
needed to alert them. I told him according to
the Deed of Gift, we, not Alan Bond, were in
control of the event.*

*I remember once telling my good friend Alex
Salm, who was chairman of the House
Committee at the time, that I wanted to see
the Cup. He said I'd have to wait because it
was in a safe deposit box at Morgan Guarantee
Trust. That's where it normally was during
summers, when the Club was closed. But it
wasn't. Alex was too stingy to spend money
on that. He had just stuck it in the cellar at
the Club. He had to pretend it was under lock
and key. The room in the club where it was
customarily displayed was originally for
backgammon. It was bolted to the table not
for security, but because with its long, thin
neck, it wouldn't stand up otherwise.*

In late March of 1983, just a few months before the 12 Metres would once again start collecting in Newport for another America's Cup match, Anderson went on a "quasi-protocol" trip to the northern tier of Latin American countries. He was wearing two hats. One was that of ASTA; his mission for them being to visit various sail training vessels and promote the racing program for 1984 that included a race from Bermuda to Halifax, Nova Scotia. The other hat bore the IYRU logo, in which he covered everything from difficulties surrounding the Pan American Games (Would the Snipe Class be officially added? Should Ecuador be realigned with a West and South American group?) to an assessment of sailing's popularity in Argentina.

Anderson was back home in Newport in plenty of time for the 1983 trials, and he was dismayed about what was developing. Dennis Conner's syndicate had built two new boats, *Spirit of America,* designed by Bill Langan of the Sparkman & Stephens office (Olin Stephens was semiretired), and *Magic*, designed by Johan Valentijn. *Spirit* was meant to exploit the outer limits of 12-Metre size. *Magic* was aimed at the smaller end. *Spirit* turned out to be slow, both straight-lining and maneuvering. Through some unimaginable design miscalculation, *Magic* was too small to measure in as a 12 Metre. It was also slow. "We were screwed," says Tom Whidden, who was

Conner's tactician in 1983. "We had built two boats and didn't have anything near as fast as *Freedom*."

There was nothing for them to do but build a third boat. When it became evident that the two designers weren't the least bit interested in collaborating, the selection of Valentijn over Langan and S&S for the job was seen as a slight to Olin Stephens by older New York Yacht Club members. Valentijn's second design for 1983 was painted red and christened *Liberty*.

"Jack Sutphen always steered *Freedom*, the trial horse for Dennis," Anderson says. "And he was always Dennis Conner's sparring partner in the last on-the-water testing they would do shortly before the start." A sailmaker and talented helmsman from Long Island, the late Jack Sutphen was a perennial P-Class champion in San Diego. An unpretentious man with an easy smile and a well-considered approach to whatever he did, Sutphen was so low-key he could easily be overlooked in a room full of lesser lights. He was soft-spoken, as forthright as he was loyal to his close friend Conner. "Before one start," Anderson says, "I remember Dennis on *Liberty* saying to Jack across the water, 'I can't get by you. I've tried everything.' Jack would suggest trying another jib. Dennis would shrug and say he'd tried them all. I knew the Cup was in trouble then."

"The first day we sailed *Liberty* against *Freedom*," says Whidden, "*Liberty* was so slow I offered to go swimming because I was convinced something was attached to the bottom of the boat. And I hate swimming. The guys were all laughing at me, but I jumped in, swam down, and found the bottom clean as a whistle."

The America's Cup Committee had some discussions about alternatives. "For one," Anderson says, "we could have selected *Courageous*. *Liberty* had only gone by *Courageous* a couple times when it was blowing 20+, and that's not your average wind speed. I guess that was a possibility. But *Courageous* was underfunded, it had no new sails, and a new helmsman. Another consideration was to select Dennis and tell him to use *Freedom*. But we didn't think we had that discretion. It was up to Dennis what he sailed. *Liberty* was the new boat, and after all the fuss in that department, that's what they wanted to sail. History might have been different if the situation had been different because it's hard to beat someone like Dennis. He ranks high as a sailor, and he is a determined man."

"I think I do remember having discussions about *Liberty* and *Freedom* with the Selection Committee," Whidden says.

But there was a problem. We had worked hard on Liberty, *speeded her up, and it was never as fast as* Freedom. *But we figured we better get* Freedom *in shape in case we had to race her. We talked with Johan about how to speed the boat up in light air without hurting its fresh-breeze prowess. He said shorten the waterline, and you can increase the sail area. So he shortened the waterline, but he didn't read the rules carefully. If you shortened the waterline you would lose the grandfather part of* Freedom'*s rating which allowed a below-minimum freeboard. So when Johan shortened the waterline, he not only slowed the boat down, he raised the rating. We didn't get more sail area. In fact we had to reduce it a touch. That's why we didn't consider using* Freedom. *We used the piece of shit* Liberty *and sailed our hearts out. We made some mistakes, had a breakdown in one race, but if you go through all the races, we kicked their ass in three of them. The bad thing is we couldn't figure out how to win one of those last three races.*

Few races have been replayed more or have stimulated more discussion than Race Seven of the 1983 America's Cup, because it marked the first time in the Cup's 132-year history that the United States would be defeated; the end of the longest winning streak in all of sports. Dennis Conner had sailed the series of his life that summer, managing to establish a 3-3 tie after six races against a better boat that skipper John Bertrand and crew were learning to sail better and faster every race.

At one point, Conner and *Liberty* had a 3-1 lead, needing only one more win to conclude the series.

But in Race Two, they had dodged a bullet. *Liberty* had finished first, but had to survive a protest from *Australia II* for tacking too close. "There's probably no question that we tacked too close," Tom Whidden says today. "It was shaky. Dennis had hesitated and made it closer than it should have been. But I used footage from the blimp that was foreshortened. Harry was a big help with that. Using film for that protest was his idea. It took us a while to get the film and figure out how to use it. I distilled it into a picture book, using the frames that made us look further away than we were. It was so cool because it was film shot from behind. It showed us tacking and it made it look like we were pretty far ahead when we finished the tack. Harry was great during all that, very articulate. He had me so well prepared we couldn't lose that protest. Harry didn't stick out as much as the other guys on the committee. He was the quiet one. But he's a good sailor, and when he spoke you listened. As a young guy, I gravitated toward him." Tuning up before Race Five, *Liberty* had suffered a breakdown in 18 knots of wind. "They lost their jumpers"—the struts that tension the jumper stays, which control the bend in the portion of the mast above the forestay—"several minutes before the start,"

Anderson recalls. "They were telescoping hydraulic jumpers, but they were weak and collapsed. Bob Conner on the chase boat asked the Coast Guard to run in to his base by helicopter for replacement parts, but they refused. They couldn't take sides. *Liberty* sent its fastest chase boat in and got them. Two men went aloft and replaced them and got slammed around up there in the strong wind and choppy seas. *Liberty*'s jib was damaged in the process. They got a new jib up and were finally ready after the 10-minute warning, and still Conner got the start by more than 30 seconds. But the fix didn't hold. After a few minutes the jumpers collapsed, and *Liberty* couldn't control its sail shape. *Australia* won by almost two minutes."

In Race Six, *Australia* found a huge wind shift in an unstable nor'westerly and won by a whopping three and a half minutes.

On the day of Race Seven the wind was 8-11 knots, the sea state was calm. Both boats were conservative at the start of what was being billed as the "Race of the Century." Neither skipper wished to incur a foul, which would have required a 360-degree penalty turn, spelling almost certain defeat at the very outset. As usual in that series, *Liberty* had led across the starting line—by just eight seconds on this occasion. The two boats were quite even upwind. But thanks to smart sailing on the second beat, *Liberty*'s lead was estimated at 1:30. It was downwind where *Australia II*, with less wetted surface thanks to its minimum length and displacement, had a distinct advantage. And as Tom Whidden points out, the upside-down keel on *Australia II* was shorter at the root, where it joined the hull, and much thinner there, reducing drag.

Rounding the second-to-last mark and setting a spinnaker for the run downwind, Conner had a 57-second lead. "On the beat we had made out on the left," Whidden recalls. "Then we allowed them to get left which was probably a mistake given that we lost some time." But the lead quickly started to evaporate when the wind dropped to 6 knots or less. Whidden says that *Liberty* lost half its lead in the first 10 minutes of a 45-minute leg. He also says *Australia II's* spinnaker looked better to him. "That's hard for me to say because I was involved in designing our spinnakers, but I've looked at the pictures, and I think their sail in that wind range was better."

Harry Anderson, who had become rules advisor for *America II* that year after his work on the America's Cup Committee had concluded, was below on *Liberty*'s chase boat, looking at aerial pictures from a blimp on TV at the "unspeakable" war developing. "First," Anderson says, "*Liberty* didn't cover on that beat and lost 30 seconds."

Then, after rounding the weather mark, *Liberty* jibed away. "We had two choices," Whidden says. "Wait until they got near us and try to screw them up with a tactical move, or try to pick a couple shifts. We jibed away and they kept going. I think their side of the course did have a little more wind, but then 30 minutes later we came back together and we still had a two-boat-length lead. We jibed in front of them." *Australia II* squared away and sailed through *Liberty* to leeward, winning the race, and the America's Cup.

"If *Liberty* had held high off the wind," Anderson suggests, "the Aussies probably would have sharpened up to cover. Then *Liberty* would have had better boat speed. Dead downwind she was no match for *Australia II*. Dennis initiated a final tacking duel on the last leg, 40 or more tacks, trying to drag the Aussies into the spectator fleet, but unless you luck out the boat behind loses in that situation.

"Tactician Halsey Herreshoff is purported to have led the consensus not to stay in a covering position," Anderson says. "He thought he saw more wind, and it did appear to be so. However, in match racing, failure to cover is a no-no. You don't do that."

The congestion in Newport Harbor after that race was preposterous. Everything that floated was bobbing about, including a number of human beings. To everyone's credit, there were no lives lost, not even any sinkings. The noise level was deafening from boat engines, helicopters, and ecstatic celebrations, with "Waltzing Matilda" and other Australian standards emanating from a dozen different sources at full volume. The collective alcohol level was well into the red zone. The rooftops of every building on the waterfront were jammed with people. It was as if a war had been won. As a matter of fact, it had—a 132-year war.

"It was after 9:00 p.m. by the time we got *Liberty* back to the dock, it was so crowded," Anderson says. "I wasn't aware they had scheduled the awarding of the Cup for the following morning. The Cup had been brought up from Manhattan and taken to Marble House. Before leaving Forty-Fourth Street, a member had poured champagne in it. It had run all over the table because of the hole in the bottom. It was sent out to a Newport jeweler to be cleaned up. After finally reaching the dock, Commodore Bob Stone and I went to *Liberty* headquarters around 10:30 that evening and had a few drinks. There was no public announcement about awarding the Cup for fear of the crowd that might develop. At the prize ceremony, as a joke, Bob gave a beaten-up hubcap to Ben Lexcen, *Australia II*'s designer. After being awarded the Cup, Bond grabbed it and headed for the assembled film crews."

Anderson was relieved that his tenure as commodore had not ended with an America's Cup loss, and that he had canceled his bet with Umberta Croce in the nick of time.

THAT FALL, Anderson was part of a syndicate that bought a piece of land located on one of Cape Breton Island's Bras d'Or Lakes, an area known for its rugged, deep-green, natural beauty. Among sailors, the Bras d'Or Lakes is known as a magical destination where one dreams of dropping an anchor someday. Heavily forested with conifers, Cape Breton resembles Maine, but the protected group of long, thin, saltwater lakes running northeast-southwest are more peaceful than Maine's rocky, surf-struck coast. Cape Breton's remoteness and its sparse population are big attractions for those seeking a measure of what Anderson calls, "life in the raw." For Harry Anderson, the area is a poignant reminder of his treasured, formative years at his grandfather's Camp Junco in the Adirondacks. The land he bought with friends, a 90-acre plot called Gillis Point on the south entrance of Maskell's Harbor adjoining a 25-mile-long lake called St. Andrews Channel, had been etched in his memory since he'd seen it in 1981. Gillis is a narrow point, steeply elevated 50 feet above the water and topped by the soft grasses of a meadow. In 1981, the only buildings on it were an old barn, a boathouse, and a small lighthouse.

After the prize-giving for the Marblehead-Halifax Race that year, a race in which Anderson had won his class with *Taniwha*, a nor'wester came through clearing the fog and providing a favorable wind to sail the 125 miles to Cape Breton. Two other boats made the trip. One was *Expectation*, sailed by Devereux Barker, Anderson's friend whom he had recommended succeed him as chairman of the New York Yacht Club's Race Committee. No sooner had the boats entered the lakes through St. Peter's Canal at the south end of Cape Breton Island, than *Taniwha*'s generator quit. Breakdowns, as any cruising sailor knows, are a double-edged sword. The inconvenience and cost can be significant. On the other hand, breakdowns are part of the cruising adventure that lead to otherwise unexplored regions, challenging situations, and new relationships that can be rewarding, even life-changing. The faulty generator necessitated an urgent call to the Cape Breton Boatyard in the village of Baddeck, on a weekend. In this case, the old school tie showed its colors.

"Having raised owner Henry Fuller on the ship-to-shore phone," Anderson says, "he reminded me I had met him when he was an undergraduate at Yale. He had roomed with David Smith, who was on the sailing team."

In terms of their test strength, the ties that bind the sailing subculture—especially in Corinthian days—compare with those forged by membership in military combat units. In some ways they are even stronger, since sailors tend to have more common social backgrounds; and happier, since pleasure, not war, is what brings them together. When he was 18, having sailed with friends to Cuttyhunk Island, Massachusetts, Henry Fuller met a contemporary named David Smith at a Labor Day party. The two discovered they were both headed for Yale in a few weeks, and a friendship started. They would become roommates sophomore year. David's older brother, Mike, had also gone to Yale, had belonged to the Yale Corinthian Yacht Club, and had taught sailing at the Seawanhaka Yacht Club one summer, where he had met Harry Anderson. Fast forward a few years to 1966, and Fuller was on a 43-footer racing to Bermuda. In mid-ocean, his boat came within shouting distance of a boat named *Puffin*, owned by Ed Greeff, with Mike Smith and Harry Anderson on board. They exchanged pleasantries across the water, and more, later, at the bar of the Royal Bermuda Yacht Club. So when Harry Anderson rang up Henry Fuller 15 years later about a failed generator, Fuller knew to whom he was speaking. "I have a good memory," Fuller says. "I don't think Harry remembered me, but I remembered him."

Henry Fuller's uncle was the father of Ben Fuller, who had been curator of Mystic Seaport—another friend of Anderson. Such a raft of fortuitous connections provided immediate entrée for Anderson into a small enclave of people who were the mainstays of the rural community scattered within an hour's drive of Baddeck. Anderson met Carl Vilas, who then edited the Cruising Club of America newsletter and yearbook, another excellent connection. Anderson had been a member of the CCA since 1966. He also met Lady Barbara Russell, mother of Diana Russell. Diana had worked for Sparkman & Stephens. Anderson also knew her from the Seawanhaka and New York Yacht Clubs. Russell had focused on designing sailboards in the late 1970s. Anderson and his friend Bill Maclay, an avid windsurfer, had helped her organize the US Boardsailing Association (now called US Windsurfing). Lady Russell owned Pony's Point, the land at the north entrance of Maskell's Harbor.

"Carl Vilas wanted us to buy property he owned on the Washabuck River behind Gillis," Anderson says. "This did not materialize, but a few years later Lady Russell became alarmed that the Germans were seeking to buy Gillis Point and develop it." Every sailor who has

cruised the Bras d'Or Lakes knows Gillis Point. It's impossible to enter Maskell's Harbor, a well-known, protected anchorage, without feasting one's eyes on the high promontory with its little white lighthouse.

Dev Barker says he was sailing around the lakes a couple years later, and upon dropping the hook in Maskell's, had been invited to Lady Russell's for cocktails. "During the course of the evening," Barker says, "I told Mrs. Russell that I had been taken with Gillis Point, and said that if it ever came available she should let me know. She said it had gone on the market that very day! The next day we drove out to look at it, found the agent, told her we were interested."

Anderson and Barker initially bought the land in 1984. When they decided they wanted a third partner, Barker called his friend Larry Glenn, with whom he had shared a house in Annapolis, Maryland, when they were in the navy. Glenn was living in Japan, running Citibank's Asian operation. "Larry bought in sight unseen," Barker says. "He said he trusted our judgment in property."

In the fall of 1983, Anderson had sold his share of *Taniwha* to his co-owner, Tom Josten, and bought a 47-foot sloop named *Blue Shadow*. The boat, a take-off by a French naval architect on a Swan-type hull, had been

built of teak in a sugarcane field at Grand Baie, Mauritius, an island that lies east of Madagascar in the Indian Ocean. The original owner was a Captain Betuel, who managed a shipyard at Port Louis on the west side of the Island. Anderson recalls that the yard had a hoard of teak purchased in the days before the Burma Teak Consortium was socialized, after which teak became open season for smugglers.

The purchase happened on the spur of the moment. "Gregg Strauss, former president of the Reading Room, called me one morning and said that a Belgian named Christian Devershian was in the harbor on a yacht that he was suddenly selling instead of sailing around the world as planned," Anderson says. "Family business had gotten in the way."

In Harry Anderson's life, such events—like coming upon Henry Fuller at the Cape Breton Boat Yard—are not considered happenstance. For Anderson, they are the inevitable result of a connection, however remote, and therein lies the rhyme if not the reason. In the case of *Blue Shadow*, Devershian had looked up Strauss because Strauss was a close friend of a British friend of his named Jonathan Janson, who also happened to be a friend of Anderson. (Janson would later become a fellow vice president of IYRU). Anderson even knew how the two of them had become friendly. "Gregg knew Jonathan," Anderson says, "because Gregg's father, an investment banker in Brussels, and Jonathan's father, an investment banker in London, had both sent their sons to Gordonstoun in the north of Scotland, where the Outward Bound program was developed during World War II, for which neither Strauss or Janson had fond memories. Both HRH Prince Philip and Prince Charles had also attended." That meant that *Blue Shadow* was a part of Anderson's extended family, making it a boat worth looking at. Plus, he liked it on sight, and the boat's provenance was intriguing to such a committed researcher/historian as Anderson.

"After World War II," Anderson says, "Devershian was one of two copper commissioners in Rhodesia when there was an acute shortage of copper. He was offered

The owners of Boulaceet Farm on Gillis Point near Baddeck, Nova Scotia, gather outside the barn in 1990. From left, Devereux Barker, Lawrence Glenn, and Harry Anderson.

bribes daily of Rolls-Royces and the like. On a brief vacation he visited Mauritius, met Capt. Betuel, and purchased *Blue Shadow*. The name came from the bluish quality of the shadow cast over Port Louis when the sun was behind the mountain at the head of the harbor."

Once the book on Port Louis was opened, Anderson couldn't resist browsing further. "Port Louis was where the career of cartographer Matthew Flinders was doomed," he says. "Flinders did a 20-year survey on the Antipodes in the late 1700s. On his way back to England in 1803, he put in to Port Louis, not knowing it was under French colonial rule. The governor general was willing to let him proceed, but Flinders was too obstinate about the rights of the British. That infuriated the governor general into incarcerating him. By the time he was released, his survey work had been usurped by others, his wife was old and gray, and his career was not properly recognized nor compensated." No doubt that made the list of topics for discussion at the Reading Room.

"Devershian gave me an album with several dozen photographs of her construction," Anderson says, "and of the boat under sail. One item was a news clipping showing one of France's outstanding sailors, Eric Tabarly, at the helm during the Cape Town-Rio Race with the caption, 'Segnuer des Oceans.' Tabarly declared her one of the finest combinations of racing/cruising boats that he had sailed."

With the America's Cup challenge center stage in 1983, *Blue Shadow* didn't get much attention. But in the spring of 1984, Anderson hired Nick Bell to be his captain. Nick was 19 at the time, a student at Connecticut College. Anderson had known Nick Bell from birth. Nick's grandfather was Charles Townsend Ludington, who had helped start the Adirondack-Florida School, and who had recruited Harry Anderson for the board while Anderson was at Columbia Law School. The two families were close. The sister of Nick Bell's mother (a Ludington) had married Harry Anderson's brother, James. "My first recollection of Harry was when I was 12 years old," Nick Bell says. "He convinced my parents to buy me a Laser. Then he got Dave Perry to give me racing lessons— roll tacks, starts, tactics, the whole bit. Until then I had been sailing an old Opti with wooden spars."

One of the many key-holders at Anderson's 209 Spring Street house, Nick was a frequent guest. "Harry was great to all of us," says Nick, who today is a broker specializing in publicly traded Russian companies. "He took pleasure in leaving condoms for me. He always left me a note saying 'left the usual in the usual place.'

"Harry didn't waste any time doing his Rube Goldbergian stuff to *Blue Shadow*. Give the man a power drill, and watch out. We used to talk about how the boat had been 'Harry-ized.' But he was wonderful to sail with. There was no personality change when he stepped aboard. He was always polite, soft-spoken. He would raise his voice only to be heard."

The plan for that first summer included joining the International Sail Training races from Bermuda to Halifax, with feeder stages between various ports along the way. Sixty or more vessels had gathered in Bermuda for the start, ranging from square-riggers carrying a total of 250 cadets, to offshore race boats from half a dozen countries. "Most ships were not only on sail training missions," Anderson wrote in his annual Christmas missive to relatives and friends in 1984, "—handling craft under sail being a requirement at most of the naval academies in the world including USNA—but they are also diplomatic representatives of their respective nations." But that event was blind-sided by a calamity. On June 3, *Marques,* a three-masted barque, was lost at sea 75 miles north of Bermuda. Of the 28 people on board, 19 perished. As chairman of ASTA at the time, Harry Anderson was in the thick of it.

Built as a trader in 1917, *Marques* was rebuilt in 1947 and continued working, carrying cargoes of wine, olives, and nuts between Mediterranean ports. After further restoration in 1977, *Marques* had become the property of England's China Clipper Society, and starred as *Beagle* in a BBC television series about Charles Darwin. In 1982, *Marques* had raced around England in the Clipper Challenge. In the first leg of the 1984 series—Puerto Rico to Bermuda—*Marques* had won trophies for finishing first overall, and first in class. Less than 24 hours after the restart in Bermuda, disaster struck. The ship had been sailing in intermittent rain squalls through the night. Reports indicate sail had been reduced by two-thirds to assure a night's rest for the crew. The report Anderson wrote on the event tells the rest:

> Early in the morning of Sunday, 3rd June, the ship was sailing comfortably. The moon was out, and there were some stars in the sky. The wind was from the west at approximately 20-24 knots, with seas running about six to eight feet. The wind was coming over her port side. And the ship was heeled well over, sending up foam and spray. The crew remembers it as an exhilarating time.

> According to statements from surviving crew members, at approximately 0400 hours, at the change of watch, a sudden and unexpected local squall of indeterminable violence struck the vessel. At this time, the ship's hatch was

*open to accommodate the coming and going
of the two watch teams; this opening faced the
port side, the direction from which wind and
waves hit. The storm was upon the ship in
seconds. The masts, already leaning toward the
water as she skimmed along, began to be driven
dangerously close to the horizontal. According
to the accounts of the crew. . . . the helmsman
struggled to turn the wheel so as to swing the
ship's bow away from the wind, easing pressure
on the sails. It would have taken about 15
turns of the wheel to bring* Marques' *rudder
completely around. The helmsman managed
only one or two before the wind had its way.*

Once she was on her side, Marques' *forward
momentum—and two waves estimated by
survivors to have been 30 feet high—sent her
bow slicing forward and down into the water.
He stern came up, bringing the rudder above
water. Trainees and crew members sprung to the
lines trying desperately to cut them in the vain
hope that, shorn of the now life-threatening
weight of her sails, the ship could be righted.
But, although she made a brief attempt to do
this, it was impossible to reverse the forces that
were rapidly causing the square-rigger to drive
herself down. The surviving crew estimates that
the she ship was under water within a minute.*

*The life raft canisters released from the
pressure, surfaced, and inflated as designed.
Occupants fired flares that were seen by other*

*ships in the race. "Mayday" was broadcast,
and the survivors were soon picked up. A full
international search went on for three days
without success. Later, several other vessels in
the race reported they had suffered damage
that night from violent, local squalls and
waterspouts.*

Anderson mourned the loss, but in the
next lines he re-affirmed his solidarity with
ASTA's mission.

*It would be easy to succumb to anger and
frustration at the fates which allow such a
thing to happen, and thereby waste valuable
energy. But that is not what those who gave
their lives would have us do. Rather, we must
rededicate ourselves to those goals established
eleven years ago when our founder, Barclay H.
Warburton, had the dream of an American
group to foster education at sea for young people.*

*We must not waver from our determination to
offer youth an alternative to our plastic world,
an environment which fosters the growth of
self-knowledge, self-discipline, and self-
confidence; growth which promotes a tolerance
for—and a consideration toward—others, and
which enhances the individuals well-being
while advancing his or her emotional and
spiritual maturity. We must also continue to
offer, during sail training races, the unique
challenge of friendly competition—a situation*

which encourages each young person to use his abilities to the maximum degree possible, and which leads to growth of friendship and goodwill toward one's shipmates, and also in relating to others from all parts of this planet.

As 16-year-old Janice Ameen of Pawtucket, Rhode Island, wrote after her first sail training experience:"At sea, I have learned what teamwork is, what understanding is, how good it feels to like yourself and what you are doing. The ocean has so much to offer each one of us. You will never know what kind of person you are mentally, physically, and emotionally until you go to sea."

George Crowninshield, a retired navy officer who in 2013 was in his fourteenth year as Newport's harbormaster, was executive director of ASTA when the *Marques* went down. He said the organization suffered after the incident. "Loss of the *Marques* put a pall on things," Crowninshield says. "We had one law suit from parents over the loss of their child. ASTA was acquitted of any wrong doing, but people weren't behind it anymore. ASTA kind of died. A year afterwards I left because ASTA couldn't afford an executive director, only a girl to keep the office running. Sometimes I'd have to raise money just to pay office salaries. One time Harry and I were talking, and he took a painting off the wall of his dining room. It was a George de Forest Brush, an artist he

admired. He sent it down to Sotheby's auction house in New York, where they sold it for $250,000. He donated $125,000 to Yale Sailing, and gave $125,000 to ASTA to keep us running."

The Brush painting was called *The Indian and the Spoonbill* (1916), one of the better-known works of Brush, who lived for a period among the Indian tribes in the US and Canada. It depicts a squatting Indian soberly contemplating a dead spoonbill. Brush, who was a close friend of Anderson's grandparents, Dr. Walter and Helen James, had given them the painting in contrition when the Jameses had rejected a Brush portrait of Helen they had commissioned. Brush had painted Helen in a Queen Elizabeth I style gown (Brush later painted over Helen's face, substituting that of his daughter Nancy).

"Harry never gave up on ASTA," Crowninshield says, "never let them down. His energy and enthusiasm after the *Marques* kept a lot of us going. He's always been an ambassador for them. It's called Tall Ships America now, but they go to him for advice and council, and he still supports them financially, like he did by organizing his ninetieth birthday party as a TSA fund-raiser.

"He's remarkable, unique. My grandfather was Bowdoin B. Crowninshield, the naval architect who designed the America's Cup contender

Independence (1901), and the only seven-masted schooner ever built. I still get letters from Harry when he runs into something about my family. We had a tall ship run to Quebec one time. Harry hosted drinks and dinner for 25 of us. Afterwards we went down to the waterfront. Harry said goodnight, got on a surfboard and paddled out to his boat, disappeared into the darkness. That made me nervous. But the next morning there he was, ready to go."

Backing up the sentiment expressed in his report on the *Marques*, a month later Anderson took *Blue Shadow* into the Sail Training feeder race from Oyster Bay to Newport that was sponsored by ASTA. Racing under the Sail Training Association Rating Rule, a time-correction factor that enabled old square-riggers to compete with modern racing yachts, *Blue Shadow* beat seven other vessels to take overall and class honors.

That fall it was on to New York Yacht Club business. Dyer Jones recalls Anderson asking him to have lunch at the Newport Reading Room. Jones had first heard about Anderson from a distant great-uncle who had sailed at Seawanhaka in the 1950s in 6 Metres. At the time the two men met for lunch at the Reading Room, Jones had been running the NYYC Race Committee for two years, and while there was no direct interaction between

them, Jones had known Anderson on the America's Cup Committee. "We had sat on committees together when I was a flag officer at Ida Lewis Yacht Club," Jones says. "He was a bit of a legend in collegiate sailing, and in the yachting world in general. He got involved as an advisor on a lot of things—Admirals Cup trials, the one-ton activity in the '60s and '70s. I also sat with him when he was commodore, probably having to do with the fine arts collection at the Club. He is so well educated, so knowledgeable about so many things. He's usually way ahead of the people sitting around any table.

"I met him at the Reading Room for lunch that day," Jones says.

We sat on the porch. He said he wanted to ask me to be the next rear commodore of the New York Yacht Club. I knew he was on the nominating committee, but I was flabbergasted. I said, "Thank you, but there must be people with more experience who are more deserving." He said, "Dyer, this might be the only knock on the door. It's now or never."

I was totally surprised because I was only 36 years old! Both Commodore Frank Snyder and Arthur Santry had sons my age. It was a heck of a shock. But Harry was a great mentor. He sat down with me and provided insight, a little history here and there, and some political stuff, although Harry has never appeared to be political. But he is a great diplomat, and a diplomat is studied in politics. He schooled me in traditions. One Club tradition is when you are about to become commodore, you attend a board meeting. During the 30-minute break, the incoming and outgoing commodores adjourn to the commodore's office for a conversation. One of the speeches given is: this is not a democracy, it is a benign autocracy. The commodore reaches into his desk and hands his successor a small blue Tiffany box. He opens it. Inside is a blue velvet box. Nestled in that are two brass balls.

Blue Shadow spent the winter of 1985-86 at the Cape Breton Boat Yard in Baddeck, having the teak deck replaced. Anderson took time to fly to Florida, where the Ransom Everglades School made him a trustee for life, before traveling to Freemantle, Western Australia, for the 12-Metre World Championships that were taking place as a prelude to Australia's defense of the America's Cup in 1987. He had again been engaged as rules advisor to *America II,* which was being sailed by John Kolius. In a letter dated February 12, 1986, and addressed to Dev Barker and Larry Glenn, co-owners of Gillis Point, Anderson writes: "So far the Freemantle Doctor, the fresh sou'wester that rolls in regularly at mid-day, has kept the flies to a minimum, and the seas a jumbled dythrambic convulsion. As John Kolius says, the first two waves are predictable, but one

has no idea from which direction the third one will hit. Yesterday one Twelve opened up some plating. Jibs and spinnakers are considered disposable race by race, especially since they are using ½ oz downwind in 25 to 35 knots, so one error is fatal. Saturday, *America II* wrapped her spinnaker one gybe early on the leg and still could not get it off the head stay until half way up the next weather leg. . . . extremely close fleet racing with yachts overlapped at all marks."

So much for the racing. "Between races," Anderson writes, "there has been an opportunity to do some more layouts of the barn of which some are enclosed." Two pages follow, typed single-space. The barn, measuring 40 by 20 feet and two stories high, was on the property when it was purchased, along with the lighthouse. The three owners figured they'd have to tear it down. That possibility was mentioned in front of Liz Roosevelt, an early visitor to Gillis Point. "I heard that and said, 'Give me a pitch fork,'" Roosevelt says. She strode into the barn and started pitching the hay out. Her efforts revealed a solid structure with all the potential of being converted into a handsome dwelling.

Between races in Fremantle, Anderson had indeed been busy conceiving the renovation of the barn as his letter attests. Several pages of sketches were included.

Have lined up the plumbing on an over and under basis to save materials and labor; reversed the stairway to make space for kitchen/pantry operations; followed Larry's thought on running the gallery to east bedrooms along north wall instead of across the middle. . . . There will be vast space in central core which, of course, will be cathedral overhead to barn ridge pole . . . traps in fiberglass ceiling over each bedroom could be activated by line and pulley on overhead beam running down into each room so can get air circulation and light from the translucency. . . . Note rainwater collection system which is designed to be able to gravity feed the 1st floor cold water systems with the turn of Tap A and to the hot water tank by Tap B. . . . envisage gas generator to run electric water pump and whatever electric lighting might be installed, although believe there is available a propane gas unit for pumping water—will look further into it.

In the summer of '86, Nick Bell was back on *Blue Shadow* as mate—having studied abroad in 1985—and he had the boat standing tall as many of the usual suspects (Liz Roosevelt, Alec Salm, Bill Maclay, Steve Robinson) gathered at what was now called Boulaceet Farm on Gillis Point, for the cruise south.

The name Boulaceet had been researched by Anderson, as one might expect. He plunged resolutely into the history of the area,

exploring sources including the Beaton Institute at Cape Breton College, and the Sydney and Nova Scotia Archives at Dalhousie University in Halifax, where the research became entwined with the quest for how and when "Labrador" became "Le Bras d'Or." He discovered it dated back to John Cabot's first voyage to the area in 1497, and cited a map by Lazaro Luiz of Portuguese explorer Joao Alvares Fagundes' voyages prior to 1528 in which the area of Cape Breton and all of Nova Scotia is marked "La Terra Dos Laurador." The origin of Laurador ("landowner") Anderson found, pertained to a Portuguese pilot from the Azores named Fernandez, who was connected with that first Cabot voyage.

The research is voluminous. It ranges from extensive surveys and charts of the Maritimes done by Frederick DesBarres for the Admiralty beginning in the 1770s, to more recent history of the Alexander Graham Bell family that settled in Baddeck in 1886, seven years after Bell had invented the telephone. Bell and his family had fallen for Cape Breton on a vacation, and wasted little time becoming residents. Bell wrote, "I have travelled the globe, seen the Canadian and American Rockies, the Andes and the Alps and the highlands of Scotland, but for simple beauty Cape Breton Rivals them all."

It was from his lab in Baddeck that Bell did

the important developmental research on hydrofoil watercraft in the early 1900s. Bell's work paved the way for Christopher Hook's hydrofoil boat that Harry Anderson had helped finance in the 1950s—yet another connection. "Bell's descendants," Anderson writes, "have summer enclaves at Bein Breagh, the name of the hill on which Bell built a large home (12 chimneys). When we first visited the Lakes, two daughters were there: the oldest, Mable, summered in the house until she passed away a few years ago; a daughter Carol Meyers we knew well—we have a photo of her and Alex Salm on *Elsie* on her final trip before being hauled for restoration."

Salm, another confirmed bachelor of Anderson's age, is one of his oldest friends. *Elsie* is the 54-foot yawl that Bell had commissioned and named for his daughter as a wedding gift in 1917. With Carol Meyers, Anderson helped lead (and finance) the charge to have one of the Bras d'Or's seminal yachts restored. "The concept of the Cruising Club of America was developed aboard *Elsie* with the aid of strong spirits," Anderson writes. The reconstruction was completed and *Elsie* was relaunched in 2012.

"There was also a Bell grandson in residence when we first visited the Lakes," Anderson writes. "Melville Bell Grovesnor owned the Nevins yawl *White Mist* (1953) and sailed it on

marathon voyages during the 1960s with his family and wrote articles about those trips for *National Geographic*. Bell founded the magazine as a not-for-profit, and Melville Grovesnor's father Gilbert was the first full-time editor. Henry Fuller and I purchased *White Mist* in 1995."

From old maps and histories of the area Anderson found that Maskell's Harbor was previously known as Port Elliott (1765-67), and Boulaceet Harbor (1877), and that Gillis Point was named after an early (1805) settler. Anderson further discovered that Boulaceet was changed to Maskell's by the Coast Guard under the influence of Edward Russell, Diana's father. "Being an Anglophile," Anderson says, "Russell objected to Boulaceet as being French. Before his passing it came to light that Boulaceet is Micmac for cove, or harbor." The Micmac people are indigenous to Canada's Maritime Provinces. "Perhaps," Anderson says today, "with the assistance of Micmac Bands at Whycocomagh and Eskasoni, it can be changed back to Boulaceet Harbor."

Blue Shadow's cruise that summer, which began not long after Anderson turned 65 in June, is typical for its determined pace, and its variety of social activities, ports of call, and encounters with friends. *Blue Shadow's* crew first sailed to Halifax to pick up Peder Arstorp (connection made that time), and dine at the Royal Nova

Scotia Yacht Squadron, "where hospitality is always of the first water," according to Anderson's detailed log of the trip. At the time, Anderson was the only US member of the Squadron. The next afternoon they made Shelburne and lay at the commercial fishing pier alongside a large fishing vessel owned by a man who owned a sloop he'd been racing in a local PHRF regatta. Anderson makes note that the man told him the yacht club was being moved to a large warehouse across the street from the waterfront. No detail is insignificant.

"Next day after rounding Cape Sable the fog lifted and we made fast passage under full moon in northerlies across Gulf of Maine making landfall at Mt. Desert without charts as a result of oversight in inventorying." During that crossing of the Gulf of Maine, Liz Roosevelt accidentally jibed the boat. Nick Bell recalls the incident as an impressive example of Anderson's total coolness in a crisis. "It was blowing pretty hard, "Bell says, "it was night, we were sailing downwind, so we had a preventer on the boom that was made to a pad eye on the cap rail. When we jibed, a large piece of the cap rail was torn off. Luckily, It missed everyone. Harry hardly said anything. He was cool and collected." When reminded of the incident years later, Anderson said, simply, "It could happen to anyone." That's true of course, as any sailor who has been

steering deep downwind offshore on a windy night in a following sea will admit, at least to himself. But how many skippers would have suffered such a perilous sequence—the yacht's stern lifted by a sea, the yacht rolling hard, the rudder losing its bite, the wind clawing its way onto the wrong side of the mainsail, the boom slamming over with enough force to rip off a large and jagged hunk of the teak cap rail that was launched into the air at the whim of the whipping preventer line; the yachting version of a mace and chain out of control in the night—without a cursory rant, or more likely a prolonged, expletive-rich exclamation?

Blue Shadow joined the New York Yacht Club cruise in Maine, returning to Northeast Harbor in mid-August. After the cruise, Bill Maclay had been dropped off at Casco Passage on his sailboard to go ashore and visit a friend. "At evening," Anderson writes, "lo and behold here came Bill sailing into the harbor on the board having traversed 12 miles via Bass Strait."

On to Rockport, they joined Commodore Don Kipp and his new bride aboard *Samaru* for drinks. Anderson noted: "He is extending *Blue Dolphin* ten feet for new cabin to add to domesticity, then dined with naval architect Harry [Scheel] and wife Jean. Next morning in Harry's office in renovated 18th Century school house he showed us models of vessels with the Scheel keel and now also Scheel rudder. . . . Performance is improved as a result of using radio-controlled models used to test underwater profiles. As Scheel remarked, 'I've never had more fun or made more money.'"

They stopped at Searsport to visit the Penobscot Marine Museum and its chairman Jack Carver, and to feast their eyes on the Museum's collection of Thomas and James Butterworth's paintings. On the way east to Roque Island for a Cruising Club of America rendezvous, *Blue Shadow* anchored at Slate Island Cove on Great Wass Island, where the crew went ashore and walked the trails to the Mud Hole. At Roque, they found Sam and Ann Bell (Nick's parents) aboard *Roques Roost*. Most of the fleet heeded warnings of Hurricane Charlie and headed west to security in Somes Sound. "*Blue Shadow* being headed for Nova Scotia, and the plots on the hurricane improving, we elected to stay put," recorded Anderson. George and Sage Hall of the CCA's Essex, Connecticut, Station "radioed to find the party cancelled but came from Jonesport anyway so the two of us (Essex and Bras d'Or) celebrated for the Boston Station."

Anderson says the return passage toward Bras d'Or was tumultuous, driving into seas from the backside of the hurricane, so they put into Shelburne again. The following night they anchored in Webbs Cove, east of Halifax.

"Next day was a fresh northerly. Rounded Whitehead to beat to St. Peters under triple reefed main and reefed No. 4 genoa. After overnight at the Cape Breton Marina in Baddeck, returned to Boulaceet and spent five days with Alec working on the barn which now has the basics of propane utilities, septic tank, and well. Dev Barker, Larry Glenn and I plan to hold a barn warming next July for all members egressing the Bras d'Or en route to the [CCA] Boston Station cruise to Newfoundland."

That fall, Anderson flew to London for the Annual General Meeting (AGM) of the IYRU. He knew that his friend, IYRU President Beppe Croce, was ill, but he was surprised to learn upon his arrival that the other IYRU vice presidents had agreed Anderson should chair the IYRU General Assembly meeting in Croce's absence. That would make Anderson the only US sailor ever to chair the IYRU assembly. "He ran the meeting beautifully," says Ding Schoonmaker, who was a member of the council at that time. "He spoke so well. All the foreigners who didn't know English were so impressed by his demeanor he could have passed anything he wanted. He had them all on his side. He had a unique phrase I'll not forget. When it came to a vote, he'd say, 'All in favor,' then instead of 'opposed,' he'd say, 'those contrary-minded.'"

"Although it was not on the order of business," Anderson says of that meeting, "I deliberately presented a motion to create an International Classes Committee with a representative on the council. After some debate and apparent assent the motion was set aside as not having been on the agenda, but an ad hoc committee was formed to present the motion at next year's meeting."

It was no surprise that Anderson was selected to run the IYRU General Assembly. He had worked tirelessly and effectively for the organization, serving additionally on the International Regulations Committee that sought to reconcile conflicts in maritime regulations. One of their innovations was to foil the attempt of the European nations' attempt to characterize the sailboard as a rowboat because it made quick changes of course in narrow waterways, thereby denying its rights as a vessel under sail. He was an original member of the Judicial Review Committee, formed after the introduction of international judges. He also got involved in International Olympic Committee meetings regarding the selection of classes. He had formally introduced IOC President Juan Samaranche at the AGM in 1986. At the Asian Games in 1987, when Anderson had worked as an advisor to those who would run the 1988 sailing Olympics in Seoul, Korea, he again subbed for the ill Beppe Croce, who was always invited to IOC Executive Committee meetings prior to the games. He attended with Nigel Hacking, Secretary General of IYRU, and participated in a critical discussion of how to distribute television revenues among the various national sport governing authorities. "Nigel and I had to tread carefully," Anderson recalls, "but what saved IYRU's bacon was that no one in the sport wanted to upset the applecart by revising the system." Anderson and Hacking were also exposed to the high-level politics involved when King Constantine of Greece, and King Juan Carlos of Spain (the two were cousins) attempted to persuade Juan Samaranche to shift the site of Olympic yachting from Barcelona to islands off the southeast of Spain where the winds are arguably better, and where the Juan Carlos had a home. With the IOC already under fire for often having set the sailing locations so distant from the rest of the summer games, Samaranche side-stepped the royal pressure and kept the event in Barcelona.

Croce confided in Anderson that he wanted him as his successor as IYRU president. Anderson was flattered, but refused the suggestion. "It would have meant disengaging from many commitments in the United States," Anderson says, "a lot more travel, and spending much time at IYRU headquarters in London."

Beth Bonds went to work for ASTA in 1987. At the time her husband, John, had retired from the navy and was executive director of the USYRU. ASTA needed help, Beth Bonds had the time, so she stepped up. "Harry hired me," Bonds says.

My salary was $800 a quarter that his endowment to ASTA provided. They were hard times. Harry's phrase was that ASTA was "lying a hull," and that said it all. The Marques had to do with it, but that wasn't the only thing. Barclay Warburton was still the driving force, but he wasn't a good fund-raiser, nor did he have an organizational mind. Membership was around 200. The files were all in cardboard boxes that I took home to my basement. That's when Harry and I became great friends. I was on the phone with him every day. He knew all the answers, and he was always there with daily nuggets about what was important, how things connected, who to call about this or that.

Later on when I moved to the Armory on Thames Street, Harry would ride down the hill on his ancient bicycle. He'd always come into the office with one pant leg raised and clipped. A while ago he said the cottage he rents behind Harbour Court was too far from the Reading Room to walk. I said ride your bicycle. He said his bicycle was in Jekyll Island. I said I think you could get another bicycle. Coming from Harry, that sort of economy is always very

entertaining. As long as the old thing is serviceable, he sees no need to replace it with something new.

One winter night in Newport we had an ASTA dinner. Several board members were there, including a young man who had just joined. After dinner we were walking down the street and Harry started playing soccer with ice chunks, kicking them down the sidewalk. Our new board member couldn't believe his eyes. He had no idea what he was supposed to do with Harry.

CHAPTER
ELEVEN | Cruising

I n the fall of 1988, Harry Anderson and his good friend Tom Josten were among a crew of
23 that departed Honolulu on the *Tole Mour*, a 156-foot, three-masted tops'l schooner. They
were bound for Majuro, capitol of the Marshall Islands. Anderson had gotten wind of the
delivery trip from his friends David (a Boston attorney) and Ilona (Lonnie) Higgins (a doctor),
who had been cruising the world for five years on their 90-foot schooner, *Deliverance*. One
of their stops had been in the Marshall Islands, where they had been moved by the extensive
and complex needs facing the 35,000 people of Micronesia, spread out over 500,000 square miles of
Pacific Ocean on more than a thousand small islands. The Higginses formed the Marimed Foundation
to deliver culturally appropriate, cost-effective, and workable health care to the area. Their novel
solution was to raise several million dollars to commission a floating medical center equipped with
a dental clinic, pharmacy, lab, and x-ray facilities, and present it to the Marshallese for them to
operate and use to train their own people. The school children of Micronesia had named the vessel
Tole Mour: "giver of life and health."

Anderson had also heard about *Tole Mour* when, wearing his ASTA hat, he had visited Nichols Brothers
boat yard at Freeland on Whidbey Island, Washington, to have a look at *Spirit of New Zealand,* a sail-
training vessel that was under construction. Ewbank, Brooke & Associates (New Zealand) had
designed both *Spirit* and *Tole Mour*, which was also scheduled to be built at Nichols Brothers. As it
happened, a Yale classmate of Anderson's by the name of Dr. Charles S. Judd Jr. was a founding
trustee of Marimed, and played a key role in designing the "Queen's Healthcare Center" on *Tole
Mour*. Anderson had followed the progress of both vessels, and jumped at the chance to be part of
Tole Mour's delivery crew.

The Marshall Islands healthcare schooner *Tole Mour.*

As is the case with all of Anderson's trips, no stones of significance—or opportunity—are left unturned along the way. No schedule is ever too tight to prevent having a meal with relatives who live within a 100-mile radius of any stops he plans to make, as was the case with Thanksgiving dinner in San Francisco with a cousin, Sylvia (Coe) Tolk, and other members of the English Speaking Union, at the Tennis Club. The next day there were more cousins gathered for lunch at the St. Francis Yacht Club. The next morning, according to Anderson's log of the trip, he visited the National Maritime Museum, "whose founder and curator, Karl Kortum is responsible for stimulating more successful ancient ship preservation worldwide than any other individual." Dinner was again at St. Francis, this time including second cousin Ted Nash, "nephew of the late Ogden Nash who composed a special, unpublished poem for him on his 21st birthday while he was an undergraduate at Yale, and his wife, Ruth Coffin, daughter of the late Reverend Henry Sloan Coffin of the Union Theological Seminary at Morningside Heights (New York City) of which cousin Arthur Curtiss James was a benefactor; Jim Michael (former chair of the USYRU Appeals Committee and commodore of St. Francis, and wife Marjorie); Roger Eldridge (member of the USYRU Appeals Committee) and wife: a jolly evening of reminiscences." Perhaps moved by

the combination of relatives present, the waterfront setting on the Bay, and the salty, historic ambience of the St. Francis Yacht Club, Anderson adds this footnote to complete the big, rather remarkable picture: "Mrs. Walter B. Jennings, grandmother of Sylvia Coe Tolk and myself, who was born in San Francisco of a seafaring Connecticut family sailing cargos to the 49ers, was sister to Ted Nash's grandmother, Mrs. Hugh D. Auchincloss, whose grandson Yusha lives in Newport at Hammersmith Farm.

More relatives—his nephew David and his wife and children—met Anderson in Honolulu and took him to the grand Mauna Kea Beach Hotel on the Big Island of Hawaii, built by the Rockefellers on the Kona Coast. "Built along the lines of an Inca palace," Anderson writes, "it is furnished from the Rockefeller Asian and South American art collection, which in any normal setting would seem gargantuan and too magnificent, but not here."

Driving around with his nephew, Anderson ran into a man with a boat in the harbor who observed that Majuro, the capital, is the best and most civilized of the Marshalls, "but there is a lack of ambition and drive in the Islands and also Marshallese primitive sanitation persists. As a consequence there are flies everywhere serving as carriers of all sorts of disease." Additionally, he states, "the difficulties of operating a business is compounded by the hierarchy of the social structure. It is not possible to hire someone based solely on their ability since if advanced to a position above someone to whom they are inferior they may not exercise authority over them."

Dinner that night was at the Mauna Kea, where the wine list started with a $400 bottle of Corton Charlemagne "Hospices De Beame" Cuvee Francois de Salines 1983. Anderson did not order one.

The next day at the airport on the north end of the island, Anderson spotted the all-white, unmarked Boeing 727 belonging to his Newport neighbor, tobacco heiress Doris Duke, "in which she often transports her camels." Dinner that night was with international juror, the late Cy Gillette, who told Anderson that Michael Fay—who's rogue America's Cup challenger, KZ1, a 130-foot monohull, had been defeated by San Diego's catamaran in the match that summer after a prolonged court battle—intended to return the Cup to the former J-Class and restore it to a one-on-one challenger-defender match. Just how he would manage that was not evident.

Anderson, Josten, and other Americans on the *Tole Mour* delivery crew found themselves

reporting to the local Coast Guard office to obtain temporary ordinary seaman's papers because the crew list was below the necessary number of US citizens for a US-registered vessel. Volunteers had to be impressed to meet Coast Guard manning requirements. Then he picked up some Kona coffee as a present for Peder Arstorp, whose wedding he planned to attend in California on the way home.

The prelude ashore turned out to be considerably more lively than the passage from Honolulu to Majuro. The Pacific was in fact too peaceful at the time to empower such a large, heavy vessel. But the islands did not disappoint for either their natural beauty or their cultural surprises. The crew was advised that long pants were to be worn ashore, no children's heads were to be patted, one should descend to eye level when conversing, and one should always accept what is offered to eat or drink. The raising of the head means yes, lowering means no. Without wind, *Tole Mour* steamed into the atoll. "The new dock for which we were headed," Anderson wrote, "is a $6 million gift from Japan in return for fishing rights worth many millions annually. This is an example of Japanese 'support' for third world nations, support that provides a return for Japan, and by reason of the fish processing equipment at the pier, an export commodity for the islands."

The presentation of the vessel to the president of the Marshall Islands Republic was successful. Bands played, food was served, and many celebrants toured the Queen's Healthcare Center. *Tole Mour* sailed to another atoll for more celebration before making a beeline back to Majuro, where Anderson would barely make his connecting flight to California. Having obtained local knowledge from friends of his nephew David, who were living in Majuro, Anderson was dismayed by the degree of graft and tribal influence impeding economic progress in the islands. "Even the Japanese fishing pier was the subject of political determinism," he writes.

> *Instead of being built in the protected, northeast corner of the atoll, it was built near the old dock where it was exposed to seas from the northeast trades allegedly because a high official owned the property he sold for the site. . . . There are extremes of wealth and poverty here, and the land title customs make it morally right to peddle influence and use position to obtain government contracts. One wonders why we spend so much effort here and elsewhere when there is so much need and tragedy at home, but it is the history of the United States to "bear the white man's burden": missionaries, schools, and medicine. With a shortage of doctors and nurses at home, why are we luring prestigious professionals to the Islands and other parts of the world? The*

> *Japanese invest to enlarge their future markets, but the US continues the fatal flaws that characterized the Marshall Plan, i.e. failure to follow up on distribution and usage to ensure the effectiveness of the support.*

Anderson made it to Peder Arstorp's wedding in La Jolla, and a day later was having lunch at the San Diego Yacht Club with Malin Burnham, Tom Ehman, and their wives Roberta, and Leslie. Burnham, head of Sail America at the time, is the real estate magnate who had skippered the America's Cup hopeful, *Enterprise*, in 1977. In 1987, Burnham had masterminded Dennis Conner's America's Cup comeback win in Fremantle. He had been a major factor in the catamaran defense of the Cup at San Diego in 1988. Longtime Cup administrator Ehman was Burnham's vice present at Sail America. Together they brought Anderson up to speed on some details of the controversial, and successful, catamaran defense.

Anderson found time to help officiate at the 1988 Olympic games at Pusan, South Korea. He subbed for Beppe Croce, who was ill, as coach and advisor to the Korean Yachting Committee. He arrived the morning after the North Koreans allegedly bombed the reception center at the airport, to find security at full red alert. "The week was a bit of a sketch," Anderson recalls. "A late season typhoon came through delaying the

games for a couple days, so it was a diet of poor whiskey and garlic. We complained about the stench surrounding the waterfront— upstream was a sewage outlet that poured raw sewage out on the ebb tide. The Koreans took meticulous notes on all of our comments and proposed a cure to this problem: every hour, a fifty-gallon barrel of perfume was emptied into the river. Phew!"

Those who sail on the ocean for extended periods have perfected the mental trick of remembering the good times and forgetting those periods when the extremes of weather, or fatigue, hunger, boredom, general discomfort—and sometimes fear—made them question their sanity for having embarked on the voyage. Perhaps that's because the good times on blue water are so

satisfying: the sunrises and sunsets so primal; the dolphins cavorting under the bow so mesmerizing; the weather patterns evolving in slow motion on the immense dome of sky so compelling; the moon and stars so vibrant, so hypnotic . . . and because the only way to repeat that satisfaction is to venture forth again, and yet again. There's also the pride one feels of having been there and done that, and returned to tell about it. Passage-making under sail has got to be one of the more satisfying endeavors of the Strenuous Life.

For Harry Anderson, that's how it was with Labrador. There was very little about the conscripted trip he had made as a teenager with the Tanner Expedition in 1939 that could have been categorized as pleasurable. It was an arduous, hardscrabble trip from start to finish—from the hordes of mosquitoes encountered ashore, to the cramped accommodations and unappetizing meals (salt cod ad nauseam), to the dreaded, paralyzing leaps into 40-degree water to bathe. But as an 18 year-old who loved the outdoors, Anderson savored the adventure. He relished the associations he made, treasured the remote destinations he visited, and appreciated the historical significance of having been part of a productive, scientific exploration mounted by the legendary Doctors Tanner and Forbes. Perhaps nothing Anderson had done since that expedition lived in his memory with such

Sailing among icebergs on *Blue Shadow* during Anderson's fiftieth-anniversary cruise to Newfoundland in 1989.

poignancy. So it was that 50 years later he would set off for Labrador once again in search of closure, this time on the more comfortable *Blue Shadow*.

To add further historical significance to his trip, he included a son of Dr. Alexander Forbes, the Harvard neurophysiologist and cartographer/explorer who had been co-commander of the 1939 expedition, and two of Forbes' grandsons among his crew. Irving Forbes, from Kittery and Blue Hill, Maine, had taught music at Phillips Exeter Academy until his retirement. One of his sons, Douglas, was a student at the University of Colorado. His oldest son Alec was running a dairy farm in Maine. Anderson located the Forbeses through Bill Maclay, who had grown up with the first Mrs. Irving Forbes in Chatham, Massachusetts.

Also on board was *Blue Shadow*'s former owner, Christian Devershian; Siadhal (pronounced "Shield") Sweeney, from Newport, County Mayo, Ireland, and New York; Bill Maclay; and George Whiteley, Maclay's mentor from his days at The Hill School. Whiteley had written *Northern Seas, Hardy Sailors,* about the men and women who first settled Nova Scotia, Newfoundland, and Labrador, the "wild, bleak, beautiful islands of his ancestors," as the subtitle informs. Whiteley was an expert on the location of

John Cabot's landfall in North America. When Maclay was a student at Williams College, he had made a trip to Nova Scotia on Whiteley's motor sailer in search of the missing link in the life of the tuna fish. "George's theory was," Anderson explains, "that the tuna crossed the Atlantic in summer to the west coast of Africa where they bred and went on to the Caribbean, migrating north in the spring. Whiteley's family had the largest codfish processing plant on Bonne Esperance Island on the north tip of Quebec [near] Labrador. He joined us in the town of Nain by float plane. He never took his tweed cap off even down below the entire trip, such were the temperatures."

Anderson had met Siadhal Sweeney through Alex Salm via sailing and the Union Club. Sweeney's father was director of the Guggenheim Museum in Manhattan during its construction in 1956. "Siadhal said his father had a running gunfight with Frank Lloyd Wright," Anderson recalls, "pleading for some vertical space on which to hang artworks. He also pleaded for office space for the staff, which was added later on the first floor. He was responsible for collecting most of the museum's artwork, and he had an impressive collection of his own he kept in his home in Ireland. His vocation was as a writer of encyclopedic works for which he had a vast book collection in several languages. When he needed to write, he booked passage on a freighter headed for many ports on different oceans, so not to be disturbed. Siadahl virtually commuted between Ireland and New York, always flying via London to avoid paying both US and Irish taxes; Irish customs/immigration did not check on travelers between London and Dublin in those days."

As it was with Alice, the research often leads Anderson down winding paths that can end up connecting seemingly disparate dots. Anderson says:

> Sweeney's brother also had a home in Newport, Ireland, and between the two was the home of Walter Curley—classmate of Jim Buckley, Yale '42, who traveled with us on our European trip that summer—which is adjacent to the Keep [a fortified tower/residence usually within a castle] of Grace O'Malley. She was head of the last clan to oppose the British. One of the clan's sources of revenue was to pirate commercial vessels passing along the west coast. When O'Malley finally threw in the towel she traveled incognito to Buckingham Palace and bowed before HRH Elizabeth I in defeat. On her way home she stopped at Malahide Castle on the north edge of Dublin seeking food and shelter for the night. When denied, she abducted one of the laird's sons and took him to the west coast. The ransom that she requested, and received, was that there would

> always be bed and board for itinerants at the castle. Malahide plays an important role in literature at Yale because it is where the Boswell papers were found in a croquet bench in the garden."

The anniversary cruise to Labrador took almost two months, and included many of the same places Anderson had visited in 1939. Early in the trip, his log reads: "We were well into the Strait of Belle Isle. Fog obscures the Labrador coast and there is virtually no wind or discernible current—almost to a 'T' the conditions met in 1939 in the *George B. Cluett* as we approached Red Bay on almost the same date, the only difference being that this time there were no floes, growlers, or bergy bits. Put both radar and loran to use. . . . by noon dropped the hook behind Saddle Island. The next day, unlike 1939, the entire harbor of Red Bay became visible and there was the opportunity to go ashore and explore."

The only developments Anderson noted after 50 years were negative ones.

A big whaling station he remembered had been abandoned and was rusting away, the whale population having diminished. And the plight of the natives was still an issue. The white people were being taken care of by the Grenfell Mission, but, as Anderson says:

The Inuit Eskimos came under the Moravian Mission. The Moravian had lost much of its influence over the Inuit—it never had any influence over the Innu, (Indians), who used to migrate from Hudson Bay every summer to trade, and came under the Catholic Church. The Inuit suffered from debilitating government policies. Many Innu had stopped commuting and settled. They were consolidated in one village beset with drug and alcohol problems. Neither of our governments have done a creditable job with the native populations. There's a new village at Davis Inlet built with Federal funds to which the Innu Band was moved. In 1989, Nain, whose population is Inuit, had been transformed by a simple change of policy: family houses that were formerly government-owned were changed to private ownership, instilling the pride necessary to maintain them. This was not done for the Innu at Davis Inlet, and drugs and alcohol are such a problem we were warned to keep well offshore when passing.

The highlight of the trip for Anderson was revisiting the places he had seen in 1939, only this time with a comfortable, well-supplied offshore yacht, and with sufficient time. "Comfortable" afloat is always quantitative. In 1989, with only a bulkhead heater in *Blue Shadow*, the average temperature down below was 60 degrees. But that was a lot more comfort than the old *George B. Cluett* had

provided. "In 1939 we were working night and day," Anderson says. "This time we did a lot of hikes. Bill Maclay always had to climb the highest mountain in the area. And we looked for moose and other animals, had time to enjoy the place. As for the Forbes, it was probably the first time they really came to appreciate what their grandfather had accomplished."

Alec Forbes has vivid memories of his grandfather at holiday family gatherings when he would bring out slide shows and old 8-millimeter films of his Arctic explorations and tell stories. "Alexander was a remarkable person," Forbes says of his grandfather.

His feats of navigation are legendary, his books are wonderful, I've read all of them. They were looking for a refueling base up there for the short-range aircraft being ferried across the Atlantic to support the war effort in Europe. That was the raison d'etre for going north in the first place. Later on my father took me to Frobisher Bay, now called Iqaluit, capitol of Nunavut on Baffin Island, where the airbase was eventually built. There's a street there named after my grandfather.

As a boy, the size and scope of Labrador amazed me the way he described it. But to go up there on a small boat with Harry, to be face to face with the same conditions, that was remarkable. I couldn't make the whole trip. I had cows to milk, and a brand new baby boy in the family. But sailing self-contained was exhilarating. There was little chance to buy staples like gasoline and food, so we had to take everything with us. We were sailing in basically uncharted waters, with few aides to navigation, buying fresh salmon from fishing boats, chipping ice off little bergs for drinks, and listening to Harry and Billy Maclay telling stories of a whole other world of sailing.

My father and Harry got on even though they were very different. My father was very anti-establishment. He wouldn't have joined a club if you paid him. And Harry is quite the opposite. My father was a seat of the pants sailor, and Harry is tactician, navigator, a consummate yachtsman. But both of them liked to rough it, and meet people along the way on their own terms. And they saw eye to eye about handling a boat, unlike Christian Devershian who was very conservative, always by the book. As captain of the port watch, he was constantly insulting my father, looking down his nose at him. That made for some tension. One night when the discussion had turned to President Ronald Reagan and the upcoming election, my father, who always called a spade a spade, made a disparaging remark about Republicans. My nudging him didn't stop him from putting his foot in his mouth. He soon realized he was the only Democrat on the boat. I told him he

didn't want to get dropped off on the next rock ledge we passed.

But I'll always be grateful to Harry for letting me see Labrador the way my grandfather saw it. There aren't many people alive who have a connection to grandfather.

Douglas Forbes, who now teaches science and climate conditions at The Academy at Charlemont, Massachusetts, says the 1989 trip was one of the epic adventures of his life. "It was the most rigorous thing I had done," Forbes says.

I was a young hippie with long hair, with no time in boats since I was a kid. We were delayed by engine trouble at the start, so we sailed up the west coast of Newfoundland non-stop to save time, standing watches, getting 4 hours sleep at a time. The weather was unpleasant, raining sideways at times, cold—really cold at the helm. It was pretty intense for me at 20. People think of yachting as an aristocratic pleasure, but six people sharing a tiny space like that is not easy. It's like being in a space capsule, six people eating, drinking, and sleeping, using one little head. If you need personal space you're out of luck.

Christain Devershian didn't like me either. My father finally had to tell him he'd been handling boats since Devershian was in diapers, and my

father didn't normally mouth-off. Devershian
focused on my youth and long hair and decided
he was going to make a man out of me. He had
me pumping the bilge at every opportunity,
and I was also the dish boy. Washing greasy
dishes in cold sea water is not very satisfying.
But I have to say Devershian was a good cook.
On that trip we could always count on a good
meal and drinks. That made a big difference.

I still clearly remember the nature of the
place, sailing past mountains that plunged
into the sea, the wild landscape with
metamorphic rock and narrow passages. . . .
and no one there. If anything had happened,
who would have found us?

Forbes says he was alone on deck one sunny
afternoon steering a course dead down wind
that required the occasional jibe to maintain
bearing. He had jibed three or four times
without incident. On the next jibe the boat
rolled at an inopportune moment, and as
Forbes says, "the boom came over a little
faster than you would like." There was a bad
sound, and he looked up to see the mainsail
ripped from leech to luff. "I'm gaping at the
mains'l," Forbes recalls, "and I said 'excuse
me, all hands on deck . . . please!' I felt
horrible. We sailed under jib to an anchorage,
and got the mains'l below. Harry brought out
the sail needles and the six of us sat there and
sewed it up.

"Harry had no reaction to the accident" Forbes
continued. "He said the sail's threads were
rotten. He backed me up, said I had been
sailing smoothly. He said these things happen.
He was a fair man. He said something to me
I've never forgotten. I was flying free on my
own at the time without much direction.
I wasn't smart enough to engage Harry, ask
him any good questions, but he asked me
a bunch of key questions. My answers must
not have impressed him because the day we
parted ways he looked me in the eye and said
in a very pointed way, 'Make sure you do
something with your life.' I think he was
concerned that while I came from a good
background, I didn't have it together. That
was true, and he had spotted it. The comment
stuck with me. I think from that point on I did
become more and more focused."

Anderson spent more time cruising Labrador
before and after the 1989 trip, and along the
way there would be memorable cruises in
Scotland, the Caribbean, Newfoundland,
Sweden, and the Oxford Canal, but that 50th
anniversary cruise to Labrador was special.

Anderson and some of the usual suspects also
cruised Croatia's fabled Dalmatian Coast of
the Adriatic in chartered yachts more than
once. Not only does the Dalmatian Coast offer
some of the best cruising in the world, there's
enough history in that area to provide

unending interest for Anderson. As he put it in his comprehensive travel report, *Reflections on Dalmatian Ports and Italian Hill Towns, 1990,* "Croatia is a nation with two alphabets, three religions, four main languages, five nationalities, a Communist government and a Socialist economy run by the workers. . . . to cruise its western coast is to sail back through centuries of violent history, the maritime wars and seesawing battles between the Mediterranean nation states for control of Dalmatia that led to the erection of the medieval walled ports surviving in splendor today; through the epochs of various civilizations. . . . who imposed their cultures on the land, bequeathing layers of religious art and architecture, much of it magnificent for its simplicity of form and beauty of design. All of it that remains is gloriously revealing to the eye."

At the town of Split, in the south, Anderson and Siadhal Sweeney, who had been on the Labrador cruise the previous year, were undeterred by the barred gates and unlisted phone of the naval museum at Gripe Fortress, so eager were they to view the collection. On their third visit they found the gates ajar and came upon two young marines on a smoke break. "After the usual breaking in period associated with carrying on a discussion in languages incomprehensible to either party," Anderson writes, "it was conveyed that we could view the museum under their guidance." It was worthwhile, with full-scale weaponry; scale models of warships, seaplanes, and submarines; the history of the development of the torpedo and its ejection housings—all ranging from pre-World War I to World War II and the liberation of Yugoslavia under Marshall Tito, all with titles, script, and documentation, "needless to say all in Serbo-Croatian."

They also came upon a model of a large caique, "more of the dimensions of a Portuguese fishing caique . . . two-masted, 50 feet or more overall and moderately high-sided, the model was striking because of its similarity to the hulls of the sailing craft like our Maine schooners that ply the tourist trade along the East Coast."

Anderson's report documents two and a half weeks of visiting Dalmatian and Italian hill towns and ports, from hotel locations and tips ("in Firenze if reserving at the Mona Lisa Hotel ask for a room facing the garden in order to avoid the noise of the motor bikes on the street side") to preferred bus routes, and the nature of the food. "We contemplated the changes that have occurred over four decades epitomized by the disappearance of turbot in the Mediterranean," Anderson concludes: "no more bouillabaisse, or as the old saw goes, 'It's a piss poor port that peddles no pisces.'"

His homeport of Newport, Rhode Island, has always been Anderson's port of preference. In addition to Newport's impressive history and nautical attributes, there is no shortage of pisces. When Anderson returned from the Croatia cruise there was an especially warm welcome in store. URI awarded him an honorary doctor of laws degree. It was a way of saying thank you for the work he had done on behalf of URI sailing, including the fleets of boats he had purchased, and for spearheading the development of the new sailing pavilion. As Assistant Athletics Director Art Tuveson wrote in a letter to Anderson, "There hasn't been a single aspect in the continuing growth of URI sailing that you haven't been involved with in an extremely positive way."

Also back home, a new development fully captured Anderson's attention: the Rhode Island Marine Archeology Project (RIMAP)

was in the works. He became a cofounder as one of the first members, and served on the RIMAP Council of Advisors.

RIMAP's creator and director in 2013 is an energetic woman named Dr. D. K. Kathy Abbass, who complimented her impressive academic credentials in anthropology with post-doctoral studies in maritime history at Harvard and the University of California at Berkeley. After teaching ten years at a university in Virginia, where she learned to sail and scuba dive, she served a hands-on apprenticeship in marine surveying with Newport's well-known master of that craft, Paul Coble.

Before starting RIMAP, Abbass spent two years as director of Newport's Museum of Yachting in 1989-90, the turbulent years the restored J-Class sloops *Endeavour* and *Shamrock*

LEFT: **On Narragansett Bay, Harry Anderson steers the 12 Metre** *Columbia*, **chartered for his seventy-fifth birthday by friends.** RIGHT: **University of Rhode Island President Edward Eddy (left) with honorary degree recipients in 2009. From left, Harry Anderson, Terrence Murray, Kurt Vonnegut, Margaret M. Lanhammer, former Governor Ed DiPrete, and Albert Carlotti.**

were racing. That's where she met Harry Anderson, who later was on the Museum of Yachting board for many years. "I remember we had an educational series running at one point," Abbass says, "and Harry did a class for us on yachting etiquette. It was great fun. He did it with the commodore of the Cruising Club at the time, and it was all about flags and protocol, things most people these days don't know about."

After her stint at the Museum of Yachting, Abbass had gotten involved as the archeologist on a project at Lake George, New York, to study the remains of the *Land Tortoise,* a radeau ("raft" in French, a floating gun battery) sunk in 1758. It is the oldest warship that has been discovered in North America. Today, *Land Tortoise* is one of six ships listed as a National Historic Landmark. Her work on the Lake George project piqued Abbass' curiosity about what might be lurking beneath her home waters in Newport.

Abbass knew there were many historically important vessels to be found in Rhode Island waters. URI had identified some Royal Navy frigates in the 1970s. They had also searched for the 13 transport ships that the British had scuttled in 1778 to blockade the French fleet's siege of Newport. The RIMAP team found a few of them, but mostly found where they were not. Abbass' local historical research

identified the names of three of the transports: *Lord Sandwich, Rachael and Mary, and Grand Duke of Russia*. She discovered that *Lord Sandwich* had been a prison ship.

Abbass decided not to look for Capt. Cook's *Endeavour*, of his first circumnavigation. *Endeavour* was thought to have been lost along the Newport shore in 1793 under the name *La Liberte*. But Abbass changed her mind when two amateur Australian historians—Mike Connell and Des Liddy—published an article that suggested the *La Liberte*/ex-*Endeavour* identification was mistaken. For Australians, *Endeavour* is equal to the significance *Mayflower* holds for Americans. Cook surveyed the east coast of Australia on *Endeavour* in the late 1770s, paving the way for Great Britain to claim and colonize the continent. Connell and Liddy wrote that *La Liberte* had, in fact, been Cook's *Resolution* of his second and third voyages. This dramatic conclusion meant that all of the *Endeavour* artifacts in museums and private collections that had come from *La Liberte* had inaccurate provenance, including the sternpost lent to the Australian National Maritime Museum, and the bit sent up in the *Endeavour* space shuttle.

The Connell/Liddy article gave no clue of what had become of *Endeavour,* but it provided a key to what really happened to the famous bark. The article quoted the 1779 *Lloyd's*

Register entries indicating that *Endeavour* was carrying troops out of London, had been used as a prison ship, and that her name had been changed to *Lord Sandwich*. That information, plus the fact that *Lord Sandwich* drops out of the Register the following year, suggested that the *Lord Sandwich* lost in Newport in 1778 might be ex-*Endeavour*.

"Harry has been involved with RIMAP from the outset," Dr. Abbass says. "In the early years he would supplement our grants from NOAA, the National Parks Service, and the navy. I could go to Harry and say I needed money for stamps and he'd provide that and more. But when the *Endeavour* theory emerged, Harry immediately grasped the international implications. It's complicated, but with what we knew plus the Lloyd's information about *Endeavour* having its name changed to *Lord Sandwich*, a bark sailing out of London carrying troops to North America, and the fact we were looking for a *Lord Sandwich* that was sunk in 1778 . . . it didn't take rocket science to put the two together."

Abbass had friends with a home in Whitby, England, where all Cook's ships had been built. They donated a plane ticket to London. Abbass says:

> I went to Harry, and he gave me $500 to help with the trip. I spent most of it making copies

of documents that proved Endeavour had in fact become the Lord Sandwich transport, that she had carried troops to North America during the Revolution, and that she was the same vessel sunk with the other British transports in Newport in 1778. Harry was the first to see the documents when I returned, and understood what it meant that two of the four ships that had carried Cook around the world had ended their days in Newport—a mile and fifteen years apart.

> We decided to hold back on the publicity until we did more research, because after placing Endeavour in Newport we didn't know what happened after that. She could have been raised, rebuilt, and sailed away. That sort of thing happened. Or maybe she was in the area of the harbor that has been dredged for a steamship channel. Maybe a navy dive team blew her up in the early 1900s. Meanwhile Harry went off to Australia on boat business, attended a cocktail party, mentioned he had a friend who was about to overturn the whole Endeavour story, and all the sudden we were deluged with phone calls from Australian news services. Even The New York Times picked up the story.

Because of all the media interest, Abbass created a sister organization, the Foundation for the Preservation of Captain Cook's Ships. "Capt. Cook is one of those stellar personalities of maritime history," she says. "His three eighteenth-century voyages of discovery and exploration extended the contemporary sciences of astronomy, biology, and navigation through empirical observation. Harry immediately understood the national importance of placing Cook in Newport. He has been on the Cook board from the beginning." For promotional purposes, Anderson came up with "The Cook Hook," a catch phrase Abbass used as a title for a series of handouts she has written about Cook's global importance.

Anderson sent out a Christmas greeting that summarized the *Endeavour* situation and the work of RIMAP. At the top of the page there were two photographs. On the left was Captain Cook, captioned, "The Captain." On the right was one of Anderson, captioned, "The Commodore."

"Whenever Harry goes to London he spends a few days doing more research on *Endeavour*, and to ferret out bits of historical data about Cook," Abbass says. "He's eager to be involved, and he has provided original research for us. Other than our granting agencies, he is our major donor. He has been the quiet architect behind a lot of this. He comes to meetings, gives us advice, and it helps that he knows everyone. He has been tireless about getting the RIMAP/Cook story into his far-reaching

network, to share his passion with friends around the world. If it hadn't been for Harry, we might have folded many times over the years—not just because of his financial generosity, but also his savvy guidance."

Even after Anderson moved to Mystic, Connecticut, and absented himself from the day-to-day needs of RIMAP, he continued to keep his finger on the pulse. In the winter of 2013, when an e-mail disagreement between Abbass and one of her board members about the future makeup of the board (copied to Anderson) began taking on a strident tone, Anderson jumped in. Having assured each of them that they were too valuable to RIMAP's common goals to be offended by "wordsmithing," Anderson stressed the need to strengthen the board with people who possessed expertise in the area of fund-raising. "This lacuna has beset more than one not-for-profits on the boards of which we have served," he wrote. Then he quoted from a letter written by the secretary of the navy to Oliver Hazard Perry before the Battle of Lake Erie in 1813. The letter was in response to Perry's heated criticism of his commanding officers for their failure to supply officers and men, and suggesting his resignation from the navy as a means of assuaging the perceived slights: "Sensible as I am to your love of Country," the secretary wrote, "(your) high sense of honor and zealous devotion to the service, I cannot but believe that reflection will allay the feelings of discontent which you have expressed."

Upon receipt of Anderson's email, both Kathy Abbass and her combatant reflected, and got on with the business at hand.

How did Anderson know of the Perry letter? At the time he was reading *The Lake Erie Campaign of 1813: I Shall Fight Them This Day*, by Walter P. Rybka, as part of his ongoing research on the *Niagara*, Oliver Hazard Perry's flagship.

Research really does make Harry Anderson's world go round. Much of it is family-related. Some of it is purpose-driven, related to projects he has taken on or the needs of organizations he has decided to serve. Other research he tackles is strictly by whim, for the sheer joy of it, or, in the famous words of mountain-climber George Mallory, "because it's there." Anderson has such a thirst to ferret out the true nature of just about anything, that he can easily be diverted by a casual reference, as his brother David has suggested. While other mortals with money in their pockets and a few hours to kill on an afternoon in Manhattan might go shopping, Anderson will inevitably take that opportunity to pick up where he left off at the Union Club's venerable library, or be found checking a

nautical fact at the New York Yacht Club's cozy library of 10,000 volumes. To advance his ongoing work on his famous cousin, Arthur Curtiss James, he might make a beeline for The New-York Historical Society library. The subjects Anderson has researched number well into triple digits. In his 90s, his memory remains fluid in part because it is lubricated with constant activity. All manner of events and suggestions are constantly triggering electric, light-speed flights through myriad pathways to unearth appropriate references.

On the whimsical side, the neckties probably provide the best example. It started with a letter written by a member to New York Yacht Club Commodore A. L. Loomis III in 1995, in which the member noted that of his four club bow ties, three were butterfly "and have stripes running when worn from my left on top to my right on bottom. My one straight bow has it stripes running from my right to my left on bottom." The member's unease was that the butterflies were all showing a bar sinister, which in heraldry denotes bastardy, and he suggested that all club ties should be striped as his straight bow. Commodore Loomis forwarded the letter to Anderson for his comments.

"The serious subjects of last week's debate over the future of the America's Cup pale compared with the weighty problem raised (over the neckties)," Anderson's letter to Loomis begins. He confirmed the member's observation, and reported that since the stripes on the bow and straight ties at the Reading Room went in the same direction, recommended that the NYYC ask its current supplier for a refund, and then order ties from the Reading Room's supplier. "Although the stripes on the top and bottom parts of a four-in-hand lie in the same direction," Anderson concluded, "an insignia such as a burgee lies upside-down on the bottom part. This could be cured by ordering four times as much material and with an incremental increase in stitching."

Various other issues at the New York Yacht Club have been subject to Anderson's research. He challenged the translation of the Club's motto—"Nos Agiumr Tumidis Velis"—because while it was stated as "borne with swelling sails" by one well-versed in the Latin Language, it was "wanting in terms of scholarly research," Anderson noted, because missing was reference to the origin of the phrase and the context in which it appeared. Anderson, Commodore Percy Chubb, and other scholars he enlisted poured through concordances, found almost a match in Horace's *Epistularum liber secundus*, Epistula II (1760 edition), puzzled over a confusion with the substitution of "nos" (us/we) for "non" (not), and after many weeks of study

concluded that "We are driven by billowing sails" (present indicative passive voice) would be a more accurate translation.

One of Anderson's favorite NYYC pieces of work is what he calls "Fictitious Tabs," popular versions of history he found to be based more on romance than fact. "Why is an historical romance like the whalebone skirt on a lady?" Anderson asks: "Because it is a fictitious tab on a stern reality." Anderson's list of "Tabs" varies from questioning the validity of the oft-repeated quote from one of Queen Victoria's party at the Isle of Wight Race in 1851 ("Your Majesty, there is no second"); to the first race between American and British yachts having taken place in 1849, not 1851; to the inaccuracy of a painting hung at the Club said to depict the start of the Club's first regatta (Anderson's research included consulting the diary of Philip Hone, 1828-1851, a close-lined volume of 400 handwritten pages located at the New-York Historical Society. It turned out Hone was mistaken. The starting line was in the Hudson River off Hoboken); to the barque *Aloha* being described as a brigantine on page 36 of the Club's History; to the naval ships in the upper tier in the Model Room being erroneously referred to as the Great White Fleet. There are five pages of single-spaced "Tabs."

As for the "Commodore's Dolphins" that look to be supporting the ceiling of the NYYC

Model Room with their tails, Anderson found out from his friend Reginald Bennett, the founder of the Imperial Poona Yacht Club, that type of dolphin was carved to support the overhead on admirals' barges. Anderson found examples of similar dolphins supporting ship models at the US Naval Academy Museum, and more dolphins acting as handles on the cannons on the Academy grounds. He suggested the animals should be referred to as "'Admiral's Dolphins,' probably using single quotes to indicate that the term refers to a work of art rather than bearing verisimilitude to a denizen of the sea."

While he doesn't exactly have a degree in maritime vexillology (the study of flags), his attention over the years to flag etiquette and protocol has made Anderson well qualified on the subject.

He did some research for one of his other clubs, the Dauntless, in Essex, Connecticut, writing an addenda to a 1957 study (complete with hand-drawn sketches of construction details) of its building, the Old Ship Tavern of 1766, done by a Professor H. P. Whitcome at Yale, and further study on the Dauntless Club sign. But it was the story behind the two miniature, antique Spanish mortars flanking the entrance to the NYYC's Harbour Court station in Newport that got Anderson fully involved. No one, including Anderson,

remembers why or how the two old mortars came to his attention. It was probably an innocent remark about them made in passing, then forgotten except by Anderson, who decided to research their provenance.

He found the weapons listed erroneously in the Artifact Register of the NYYC as "10-inch high Church Mortars of Bronze from the Island of Guam, having been donated in 1900 by Naval Governor Capt. Richard P. Leary, USN." He found they had actually been repatriated from Cuba after the Spanish-American War and transferred to the NYYC through Captain Leary. Old photographs showed them initially flanking the entrance to the Club building at West Forty-Fourth Street in Manhattan. They were moved to Mystic Seaport in 1948, and on to Harbour Court when it opened in 1985. The mortars may be described as small, but they are hefty. The barrel of one is 42 inches long, and 14 inches in diameter at the muzzle. The other's barrel is 36 inches long, and 14 inches across. Their bases are almost three feet square.

"According to the 1784 edition of William Falconer's *An Universal Dictionary of the Marine*," Anderson writes, "there were 10-inch Howitzers and 10- and 13-inch mortars. . . . The covers fixed across the mouths of the two mortars at Harbour Court make it impossible to check the bore measurement."

The digging and correspondence went on for more than a year. The accumulated paperwork would fill a large three-ring binder. The material includes dates in Spanish history relevant to inscriptions on the mortars; 12 pages from *Catalogue of the Armories of Tower of London—No.1 Ordnance*; and (to mention a few) correspondence with the National Archives on Guam; the Naval Historical Center; the curator of the Tower of London Collections; the National Maritime Museum in Greenwich, UK; General Rafael Hitos Amaro, General Franco's former legal officer; and Jose Ignacio Gonzales-Aller Hierro, director of the Museo Naval, Madrid. The background of Captain Richard Leary was also thoroughly researched.

Anderson determined the mortars were cast in 1733, and learned in detail how they were "double fired," a dangerous technique requiring the lighting of two fuses. If the fuse for the propellant charge fizzled, the one for the shell could blow the mortar apart and kill the attending personnel. He learned the mortars bear the lethal names *El Manticora* (a monster of classical times), and *El Cometa* (for the sputtering, high-trajectory shells they fire). "Respecting their misnomer in the Register," Anderson concluded, "extensive research reveals no use of the term 'church mortar' in connection with ordnance."

Disturbed by a sustained academic trend begun in 1769 questioning the authorship of Shakespeare's works, Anderson's research in defense of Shakespeare began in the 1990s. It was later stimulated by some Newport Reading Room associates, contrarians who outwardly embraced the theory that an elite group of writers led by Francis Bacon had written the works attributed to a fictitious "Shakespeare." While the Reading Room gentlemen surely must have enjoyed the annoyance their position elicited from Anderson, theirs is not an argument without support. Thousands of pages and many books have been written on the subject, including Mark Twain's *Is Shakespeare Dead?*, that promote the Bacon theory.

Harry Anderson's contribution is a document addressed to his Reading Room adversaries, 50 pages of carefully organized copies of pages from the writings of Alexander Pope, Dr. Samuel Johnson, and others on Shakespeare, along with excerpts from property deeds and Shakespeare's coat of arms. Dated 2006, Anderson's cover letter reads: "Of the 21 volumes of *The Plays of William Shakespeare,* 1813, the first three are about the poet-playwright and his works. Enclosed are smatterings to illustrate how closely woven is the record of his life and the recognition by contemporaries such as Ben Johnson of his works, and therefore the improbability—aye impossibility—that anyone else could have been their author. When coupled with the later work, 1899. . . . which visited the courts, Queen's Bench, etc. for records and documents tracing Shakespeare's interest in theaters (culminating in the Rose and the Globe), legal papers, wills, etc., it puts paid to latter-day academics challenging the authorship and having the audacity to tilt with the most meticulous scholar in English literature, Dr. Samuel Johnson."

—— ⚓ ——

ANDERSON'S VISITS to Russia began in the mid 1990s. His interest in Russia had begun when he was a student at Yale. Anderson and several other students he corralled had engaged a Russian Orthodox priest to teach them the language. The trips began fifty years later thanks to Manhattan attorney Pierre Merle, who spent weekends in Newport. Merle grew up in San Francisco, where he was assistant district attorney in the late 1960s-early 1970s, and an expert by default on Chinese gangs. He got to know Harry Anderson at the Reading Room.

"I always gravitated to Harry," says Merle, a trim, congenial man in his mid-70s who could make anyone's elegantly dressed list.

"First thing I would do when I walked into the Reading Room was ask if Harry was in the house because that's where the best conversation would be. He always has an interesting angle on something, from the Peloponnesian Wars to statistics for oil and gas production in the Middle East to the current situation with American shipping to some arcane thing about how John Ledyard was arrested by Catherine the Great. He's always just back from some exotic place, and you never know what is going to come out of those papers jammed in his inside jacket pocket."

Merle also travels in exotic circles. A chance meeting at a party prompted him to begin organizing trips to Russia. It was an unusual party, given for a client's nephew, that began in Paris, after which the guests were flown to Marrakesh, Morocco, for four more days of celebrating. At the party, Merle met the Baroness Hélène de Ludinghausen, the last descendent of Russia's famed Stroganoff family, wealthy salt merchants from the sixteenth century. The baroness' great-grandmother was the brother of Count Serge Stroganoff. Of her grandmother's four daughters, only one—Princess Xenia Alexandrovna Shcherbatova-Stroganova—had a child, and that was Hélène.

"She told me she had been contacted by the

State Russian Museum seeking help and advice for restoring her family's palace in St. Petersburg," Merle says. "This was in 1992. The Russians had no money, they were disorganized, in a generally bad state. She asked me if I could help. Having had several glasses of champagne I said of course, we could set up a foundation for the preservation of the arts, and so on. Then I forgot completely about it. Two months later she called me from Paris. We set up the Stroganoff Foundation aimed at the restoration of Russia's architectural heritage. Running the trips was a way to raise money. The Baroness had been directress of couture for St. Laurent in Paris, so the first four trips were very dear for people of great

means she knew, the Who's Who of Paris and New York. As Foundation treasurer I went along. Then we opened it up. Harry signed up right away for the first trip."

Merle says for the early trips things were not so smooth. There was no commercial lighting on the streets, no store fronts, and the schedule was heavy, with museum tours all day, and cocktails, dinner, and the theater at night followed by an after theater dinner. "People were exhausted," Merle says. "It was all we could do to get up at 7:30 and make it to breakfast and start another day. But when we went down to the restaurant, Harry would often be walking in the front door of the

TOP: Anderson makes a new acquaintance over lunch at the Karma River above Perm, Russia, during a tour. INSET: Pierre Merle's Russian tour group gathers for a portrait in front of the Summer Palace in St. Petersburg. Anderson is thirteenth from left, standing, in tweed cap.

hotel, fit as a fiddle, chipper, having already been to some museum he'd found, ready to tell us a bunch of stuff we didn't know. His endurance is incredible. And he was giving the rest of us 20 years. One time he almost got locked into some artillery museum for the night. He'd gone off on his own and when they were closing for the weekend, they hadn't realized he was still in the back examining some gun."

Dr. Tom Cahill, a reading room friend, was on one of the Russian trips with Anderson. Cahill, who is 30 years younger, says he was pressed to keep up. "He was 76 at the time," Cahill says, "a dynamo. We'd been to this very noisy nightclub and had to walk home in freezing weather. Nothing bothers him. There were big mafia-type guys at the door of the club. We knew they were armed. The noise was bad, the food was awful. Harry never complained. It was just another event. He always has something planned. If it's bad tonight, it will be better tomorrow."

A woman from Newport named Virginia Smith was on that particular trip. Moscow was not on the agenda, but the idea of traveling all the way to Russia without seeing Moscow seemed ridiculous. She told Pierre Merle her intentions, and he canvassed the group to find others who might like to join her. Tom Cahill and his girlfriend (now wife) Maura Lindsay

said they would go, and Harry Anderson expressed interest. Smith knew Anderson casually from Bailey's Beach and other Newport haunts. When Smith found out the hotel would cost $600 a night, she decided she needed a roommate. "I don't know what possessed me," says Virginia Smith, an engaging woman from a military family whose hobby is battlefield strategies. Another of her hobbies is studying and writing about ghosts. "I'd probably had a stiff drink, but I called up Harry and said how'd you like to be my roommate? There was a pause, after which he said, 'Okay, sure.' I explained the hotel rates, and that $300 was much better than $600, and he said, 'You're right, let's do that.'

"The first thing I did after I hung up was call my steady beau because I knew this would get around. I told him this is what I had done and why I did it. My thought was don't try to hide it, have fun with it. I figure we saved $1000 each."

Anderson and Smith also shared a compartment on the Red Arrow, the overnight train from St. Petersburg to Moscow. Tom Cahill laughs at that. "Harry spent most of the night drinking in our compartment until we finally kicked him out," Cahill says.

Virginia Smith says Anderson was a great roommate in Moscow. She says she arranged a makeshift bundling board in the middle of the bed to keep things proper.

Pierre Merle says a month or so after each Russian trip, everyone would receive a copy of the journal about the trip Anderson had written. The journals were in the 5-10-page range, single-spaced, and had titles like "A Nifty Fifty, or Swirl With Merle," for a trip that was focused around Merle's birthday. The journals were organized on a day-to-day basis, and dealt with everything from travel difficulties to basic goals of the trips: "The entire expedition," Anderson writes in 1997, "was fine-tuned to show us as much of the culture, art, and history as possible starting with a greeting upon clearing immigration by a lady attired in an antique flamingo red dress bearing a traditional cake from which each visitor partook of a slice. On exiting the airport the Navy Band was playing under dull and dripping skies—we were not to see the sun again until airborne homewards."

On commenting on a dinner with vodka flowing through the meal and performers singing, dancing, and playing traditional instruments, Anderson notes: "Forks on the table were laid prongs down. Compare Australia where the fish and salad forks are inside of the large fork, and appetizers appear under the heading of 'Entrée', customs vary around the globe." The menu was always

reported in detail. Beef Stroganoff appeared regularly.

Visits to the Russian Museum (opened especially for the group), St. Peter and St. Paul's Cathedral, the Catherine Palace and the Chesmen Church in Tsarskoye Selo, St. Nicholas' Cathedral, the Hermitage Museum, and a score of other sites are well-documented in Anderson's report. On one trip, the group went by hydrofoil up the Neva River into the Gulf of Finland to the Grand Palace and Peterhof, Peter the Great's favorite summer place. "There, a pleasant mid-morning surprise awaited," Anderson writes—"champagne and vodka with toast-bits surmounted with caviar—all to enhance one's appreciation of the grandeur being endured. Caviar and vodka, what a pleasure! As Oscar Wilde quipped, `Pleasure is something that leaves one unsatisfied.'"

On another trip—this one in 2003 when Anderson was 83—the group traveled some distance by bus on dirt roads to a remote village (Solvychegodsk) where they were housed in a former orphanage on plywood cots. "The bathrooms lacked a shower or bath," Anderson writes, "and the toilet seats were free floating." After visiting a school and watching students weaving on shuttle looms, the group divided in three and dined at homes of families. "This included a banya (steam

bath) with customary self-flailing with birch branches to stimulate the circulation and then a multi-course dinner lasting until midnight."

In the 1997 report, Anderson wrote this insert under "Day #5: Unnerved by the gassing and robbery episode a few years ago on the midnight express, Virginia Smith of Newport, R.I., did not want a compartment by herself, hence she bunked in with me much to the amusement of the rest of the group. Likewise, being on a tight budget, she and I shared a hotel room in Moscow. *She has an amusing slant on this arrangement.*"[The italics are Anderson's].

Some of Anderson's miscellaneous entries are worthy of note: "The average American does not comprehend allegory nor the secondary meaning of proverbs." And often, news items reminded him of the home front: "Daily the

papers carried the story of the Chubias book scandal [Russian Minister of Finance Anatoly Chubias], how he and several other high-ranking public officials had accepted an advance of $90,000 each for a book on privatization from a publisher owned by one of the banks that through insiders had profited from privatization of some major companies. One could substitute the name of Newt Gingrich in the newspaper accounts and it would be a perfect fit."

Tom Cahill recalls the long flight from Moscow back to New York in 1997, through Helsinki. "We landed around 7:00 p.m. and I noticed Harry was looking at his watch. He said he was running late. He had an 8:00 o'clock dinner appointment, and was concerned he might miss it. The rest of us were shot."

⚓

NOT LONG after that, Andy Green became Anderson's latest godchild. Anderson thinks he has seven in all, but he has lost actual count. Green is now a yachting broadcaster and entrepreneur, having competed in two America's Cups and been ranked fourth in the world in match racing at one point. He was 17 in 1995 when he met Anderson as a member of the British

While not a member, Anderson (center) was pleased to support the induction of his friend Troy Johnson into the Knights of Malta, held at St. Patrick's Cathedral in New York in 1998. Standing from left, Michael Maher, Johnson, Clark Reiner, and George Hopley.

University Sailing Association (BUSA), which travels to America every four years for a series of regattas. "Harry was a longtime supporter of the BUSA event," Green says. "He would travel around with us. We'd race the Harry Anderson Trophy at Yale. We did some team racing at Yale, and used the Harry Anderson course, a modified triangle—two triangles actually—that was first introduced at Yale. It's more interesting than the usual triangle, providing a tight reach good for planing, and a run that is more tactical."

Green had been seeing Anderson at Imperial Poona Yacht Club functions for many years. Green's father, Donkey Man and Secretary Abwalla at Poona in the UK, had been bringing his son to events since Andy was five.

"I remember Harry as a distinguished member of that club," Green says. "I liked his sense of fun and joie de vivre combined with his fascination with history and the rules—aside from drinking whiskey and sailing backwards. He was interested in how to reverse all the rules."

Green says he asked Anderson to be his godfather. "I lost my godfather some time ago," Green says, "so I asked Harry and he said it would be a pleasure. As is his way, beforehand he said, 'Just so you know, this is an honorary post.' And I said, 'Yeah, an honorary title, no obligations come with it.' That's his diplomatic and wonderful way. Asking him to be my godfather simply formalized a long-standing friendship."

Members of the Revolting Colonies Outpost of the Imperial Poona Yacht Club enjoy a Tiffin (gathering) off Newport in 2000. From left are John Hele, Honourable Chaplain and Disactuary Bhoy; Harry Anderson, Pons Asinorum; and Bill Winterer, Gastronome.

TWELVE | Travels with Harry

Florida

At the age of 91, Harry Anderson was driving his nine-year-old Volkswagen Passat from his apartment in Mystic, Connecticut, to his renovated garden shed in Newport, Rhode Island, at least once a week when he wasn't in Jekyll Island, Georgia (winters), or in Cape Breton, Nova Scotia (summers). Usually there is a small stepladder and other assorted gear crammed in the back. Anderson tilts the seat at a rakish angle, drives fast and well. None of the car's many small dents and dings are the results of contact with other moving objects. The garage in the last house he owned in Newport was so small that the slightest miscalculation resulted in another scrape. And he travels light, no matter if it is the one-hour trip on Interstate 95, or flights here and there for longer stays.

When I met Harry in Florida in the fall of 2012, he had preceded me by a day to attend the trustee meeting at Ransom Everglades School. We were there two full days altogether, and his total kit consisted of two sailcloth zipper envelopes of the sort one uses to carry papers. One did contain his papers. His toilet articles, fresh socks, and underwear were in the other. He was wearing everything else he needed. Anderson's minimalist approach brought to mind stories of Steve Jobs traveling around the world in the 1990s in jeans and a T-shirt, staying at five-star hotels and packing only a spare pair of underpants in his one piece of luggage, his briefcase. For Jobs, ego was involved in making a splash. For Anderson, it is about keeping it simple. After a second, or perhaps a third day, his shirt was looking tired, but a Brooks Brothers Oxford-cloth button-down continues to pass muster even when it's been abused.

At Ransom Everglades, Anderson has celebrity status. He's one of their oldest living alumni, and he has been more involved for more years than any other alumnus in the school's fascinating history. A student at 12, he became a trustee at age 26, helped move the school to Florida, donated a ton of money along the way for various projects, helped write two histories of the school, was named a life trustee, has kept in touch with teachers and administrators over the years by sending them personal notes and clippings and books of interest, and simply loves to visit the place.

At lunch one sunny day with Head of School Ellen Moceri, who will retire in 2014 (after 12 years), she looked at Harry and then said to me, "He creates authenticity. We live in a world of pop culture. Some people forget what the culture of the school should be. It's easy to fall into being the flavor of the month. Harry reminds us of the authenticity of it, what the school should be, because he is a moral man, a leader, talented. He has made a difference in the world. He reminds us of what we are doing. He's also elegant."

Harry ordered another beer. When the waiter had left, he said, "Part of it is learning to be self-reliant. At Adirondack-Florida School we learned to take care of ourselves in the woods, paddle canoes, sail boats. How many kids today can chop wood or paddle a canoe? When we were training in Louisiana after graduating from ROTC, during maneuvers they dropped a tree across the road to stop our convoy. There was an axe in every vehicle, but I, an officer, was the one who chopped up the tree because I knew how to handle an axe. The enlisted personnel couldn't do it."

Moceri spoke about Anderson's value as a trustee, how the previous evening at a planning meeting for the commemoration of the school's new swimming pool Anderson had suggested a brochure describing the various elements that make it different.

Harry teased Moceri about sending him flowers. "She's profligate with the school's money," he said with a twinkle in his eye. "I get this basket of flowers at Thanksgiving, another at Christmas. I'm paying for them because I give money to the school. Don't send me the Christmas one because they will rot. I'm away in January and February."

"It's friend-raising, not fund-raising," Moceri said.

Anderson asked her who she'd be voting for in the 2012 Florida Republican Primary that week. She said Harry Anderson. He said he wasn't in the running yet. Moceri said she was for Obama. Anderson's mustache twitched like the tail of an annoyed cat. "As the years go by, Obama gets less and less adept at getting things done," Anderson said. He went on about Obama spending three years studying the environmental impact of the pipeline from Canada. "They don't need more time. The pipeline is a good idea, absolutely. Either way he goes Obama will lose the vote. We have two million miles of pipeline in this country. Some of it is 50 years old. If we're worried about the ecology, the old ones should be replaced tomorrow. This new one will be high tech.

"President Obama has been regionalizing high-speed trains. That's like regionalizing Amtrak, a national railway system. It's an oxymoron. He picked the Orlando-Tampa route for a 200-mph train. It's 85 miles between Orlando and Tampa. I did some figuring. You can only maintain 200 miles for 15 minutes before you have to slow down. If he introduced an Acela it would only take 15 minutes longer. But there's no national transportation policy, no national energy policy. . . . we're trying to cure problems on a hit-or-miss basis."

Moceri waited a beat. "Obama is smart," she said.

"That doesn't make him intelligent," Anderson countered.

Anderson's keen, lifelong interest in

international affairs, with an emphasis on national politics, probably began in Labrador, in 1939, when it became evident that he would have to fight in a world war. When, at age 18, one has to contemplate donning a uniform and picking up a loaded weapon that will have to be discharged at other human beings who are returning the fire, one tends to pay more attention to political events that can lead to such a grim eventuality. In a letter he wrote in 1946 to the widow of a Yale roommate killed while serving with the army in Japan, Anderson spoke of how, despite their differences, they had a common ground: "We were both thinkers of a sort," he wrote. "Although not profound or professional thinkers, we reflected much about life and people in order to resolve for ourselves the enigmatical questions of religion and philosophy, love and happiness." Politics was implicit.

Asked to comment on a social-work paper written by a niece in 2009, Anderson wrote, "When FDR was governor of New York State he introduced the rule against perpetuities. Prior thereto one could set up a trust that went down from generation to generation without incurring inheritance taxes. The new rule limited the transfer to one generation. FDR came to the Presidency he made the rule a national one. His intention was to redistribute the wealth. Unfortunately, with the collapse of the economy, there was not much wealth left. . . . Economists today compare the massive national debt to what FDR did, and analyze that the result of the 1930s and 1940s was to prolong the depression 10 more years. We may well see a repeat without a phenomenon such as WWII reviving industry and the economy. This time, the flood of 'printed' money is so great that inflation is inevitable."

Anderson is a committed, old-school Republican who has little use for President Barack Obama, saying his first-term speeches were "All bombast. He doesn't put forth a single, concrete proposition. He doesn't want to go out on a limb. He's too conservative." And when Obama criticized the black-robed justices of the Supreme Court seated front row center in his 2010 State of the Union address for their decision to allow corporations to spend as much as they wanted to influence voters in federal elections, Anderson was livid, partly for what he considered a departure from protocol on the president's part.

While some of his liberal friends consider Anderson's Republicanism on the rabid side, the omnipresent, unemotional pragmatism that has guided his life puts him mostly on the side of reason. His thoughts on gun control are an example. As a person who was properly schooled in the care and safe handling of sporting firearms at age ten, who was on Yale's

pistol team, and whose weapons' qualifications include the 155 GPF "rifle," the bazooka, and the 75 mm and 250 mm howitzers, Anderson had little patience for what he called the "spurious palaver" that was being dispensed by special interest groups during the 2013 gun control debates. "For example," Anderson says, "one governor clamors to limit the size of the clip to 10 rounds. As the late William F. Buckley would comment, the major premise is flawed, i.e. while it is not politically correct to mow down 20 youngsters, 10 is alright?"

Where guns are concerned, Anderson is for identifying and treating the mentally imbalanced; requiring background checks of buyers; limiting the type of weapons available to civilians; and correcting the spreading culture of violence. As for semiautomatic weapons, Anderson wrote this in a letter to his brother David: "Their alleged use for target practice by the mother (for example) of the demented youth at the Newtown School is ridiculous—one pull of the trigger and the target is blown out—and her leaving them available to a son who she knew was a basket case indicated a screw loose."

Anderson finds a bit of humor in the ongoing madness over guns in the United States. He recalls a friend, a member of the Yale pistol team who was also in field artillery ROTC with him, who had a huge collection of firearms after the war, mostly pistols. "He practiced with them at his camp in the Adirondacks," Anderson says. "Among his collection was a 75 mm howitzer. He painted a target on a cliff face across the pond on his property. At cocktails he would entertain his guests by letting them aim the 75 at the target and fire away. Do you suppose today that one could plead the Second Amendment to obtain a license for so doing even if one could afford the couple hundred dollars per round?"

Anderson's email signoff during the gun control debates in early 2013 was, "*If I have to shoot at something more than once, I'm not doing something right*—'Response by a Texas gun owner to the need for semi & automatics.'"

Anderson's political pragmatism was in evidence one evening in Florida. After having dinner with a fellow Ransom Everglades alumnus, the two Republicans threw up their hands over the sorry slate of candidates their party had assembled for the primary: namely Mitt Romney, Newt Gingrich, Rick Santorum, and Ron Paul. With the general election still 10 months away, the two men conceded it was already time to focus on 2016. "The right wing," Anderson said, "has destroyed the Party." His friend wholeheartedly agreed.

Anderson concluded his 2009 letter to his niece with this message:

In the end, the Great Society is still vulnerable to the whims, rapaciousness and crass stupidity of those who govern. Why did Congress on the eve of the present depression repeal the Glass-Stegall Act which separated the functions of the banks, brokers, and insurers thereby turning them into the type of speculators that triggered the economic collapse? After 18 months the administration has yet to legislate new controls except for window dressing such as limiting banker's pay to $500,000 while paying the CEO of the government controlled—and now virtually government owned—Freddie Mac a salary of $4 million? Why no movement on a plane during the last hour of flight—Al Queda have just amended their manual to require setting off the bomb at least 61 minutes before landing. The Dutch have just instituted a full body scan to which much of our public objects. Can't have your cake and eat it too.

The next evening, we spent five hours at a Coconut Grove restaurant having dinner with Ed Rumowicz and his wife, Lee. Rumowicz is the dedicated URI alumni who co-chaired the sailing pavilion drive with Anderson in the 1990s. Harry suggested we arrive at the restaurant early and have a beer. By the time the Rumowiczs arrived, Harry's beer had been followed by two scotches, with a third carried to the table, and perhaps a fourth—who could count?—before the wine began to flow.

The next morning we had a 5:00 a.m. wake-up call to catch a flight to Jekyll Island. Harry and I always bunk together on our travels. Sailors are used to tight quarters, and Harry doesn't see any logic paying for four beds when only two are required. At 5:00 a.m. my head felt glued to the pillow, but Harry popped up, jumped in the shower, got dressed, and waited patiently for me to catch up. I did have to point out that he had put on my shoes by mistake, but in all fairness, leather moccasins with boating soles look the same, especially at 5:00 a.m.

Jekyll Island

A hundred miles south of Hilton Head, near Brunswick, Georgia, lies Jekyll Island. The low, flat island with its massive live oaks draped with Spanish moss is part of a lacework of barrier islands, marshy hummocks, mudflats, and tidal creeks that covers 120 miles from Savannah in the north, to St. Mary's. Jekyll is slightly more than five miles long, and is named after Sir Joseph Jekyll, who was a member of Parliament for more than 40 years, beginning in the late 1600s, and became a supporter of the Georgia Colony.

Jekyll Island became famous in 1886 when a group of New York's most powerful financiers and industrialists started a hunting club there as a way to escape the pressures of their business lives. Members included George F. Baker, Marshall Field, J. P. Morgan, Joseph Pulitzer, William Rockefeller, and William K. Vanderbilt. The rambling, turreted clubhouse was built on Jekyll in 1888, and mansion-sized "cottages" began to pop up soon after. Jekyll Island quickly became the wealthiest, most exclusive club in the country. It was said that when the club was in full swing, one-sixth of America's wealth was "settin' on Jekyll." The captains of industry parked their private railroad cars on a siding at nearby Brunswick, Georgia, and were ferried to the island. When time allowed, they would arrive by private yacht of the 150-foot-and-up variety.

In November 1910, a "secret" meeting held at the Jekyll Island Club included Paul Warburg, a crusader for central banking in the United States; the assistant secretary of the treasury; Senator Nelson W. Aldrich (R, RI); and several high-ranking New York bankers. Security was so tight not even the employees were given the real names of the guests. That meeting laid the groundwork for the Federal Reserve Act, passed in 1913 to establish the Federal Reserve System.

The influx of Harry Anderson's relatives on Jekyll Island began around 1915. Dr. Walter James was elected president of the club in 1919, serving in that capacity for eight years. He purchased Cherokee cottage in 1925. It had 20 rooms, six baths, and a fireplace in nearly every room. Dr. James was surrounded by relatives. Club treasurer was Robert Brewster, a relative of Helen James, whose father, Benjamin Brewster, and her brother, Oliver Burr Jennings, were partners in the mercantile venture in San Francisco during the gold rush that would lead to O. B. Jennings' holdings in Standard Oil. Annie Burr Jennings (O. B.'s daughter) would become vice president of the club in 1937. "Dr. James' extended family was probably the largest and most complex on the island," says Anderson, who has done the research, "because it was also linked to the Rockefeller-Stillman-Aldrich-Jennings combination through Almira Geraldine Goodsell Rockefeller who was Mrs. James' sister-in-law." It's enough to make a genealogist quake.

Walter Jennings, Anderson's great-uncle, built a house—Villa Ospo—on the club grounds in 1927, completed the golf course begun by Dr. James (his brother-in-law), and also built an indoor tennis court. He succeeded Dr. James that year as president of the club.

Old photographs taken at the Jekyll Island Club depict halcyon days, with fashionably turned-out ladies, gentlemen, and children picnicking on the beach, playing tennis, strolling or riding horse-drawn carts on sculptured paths overhung with the impressive

oaks, buzzing around in Red Bugs—small open-air vehicles with bicycle-type wheels driven by small gas engines—or fancy dressed for dinner in the club's massive main dining room with its 100-foot-long carpet. In Tyler Bagwell's book, *The Jekyll Island Club*, Dr. Walter James is quoted as saying, "The real core of life in Jekyll Island's great days was to be found in the men's after-dinner talks. It was always of great things, of visions and developing. If they didn't have a map of the United States or the world before them, they had a map of industrial or financial empires in their minds."

Harry Anderson first visited Jekyll in 1954, while driving to Florida. The place was in disrepair, a sad sight. Changing times had made it impossible to maintain the club's lofty standards and extravagant physical plant. The cottages had been left to deteriorate. Its final season was 1942. As Bagwell writes, "The drafting during World War II of some members and employees as well as the rationing of commodities by the government prompted the decision to close." The State of Georgia bought the island in 1947, much to the relief of those remaining members who were fighting a losing battle to keep it going. In 1950, Georgia created the Jekyll Island State Park Authority. A causeway and drawbridge was built to the island in 1954. Rebuilding the island was daunting. Roads were repaired and land was leased so houses could be built (60 percent of the land must be left in its natural state). But it wasn't until the 1980s that restoration work began on the cottages in earnest, with an eye toward tourism. The renovated Jekyll Island Club Hotel opened in 1988.

As he got older and reduced his travel schedule and commitments, Anderson was inexorably drawn to the refurbished island. Since 2002, he has been spending January and February on Jekyll. For several years he rented a small, modest one-story house just outside the historic district that is centered around the Club Hotel. In 2013 he moved to a suite at the hotel. With laptop and printer humming, he can stay in touch with friends, his projects, and the world as easily from Jekyll as anywhere else. And it's a lot warmer than Connecticut. But mainly it's all those family connections that galvanize him. Anderson waxes poetic about his winters on Jekyll:

> Why the perennial return to an island
> so laid back that change is well nigh
> imperceptible? Perhaps it is like returning to
> the family summer home in the mountains or
> on the shore; familiarity breeds stability. Yet
> Jekyll provides roots into the past that enhance
> this phenomenon. The century old gnarled and
> twisted live oak trees seemingly engulfed in
> wind-borne moss, the tabby (mixture of lime,

> sand, and shells) harmonizing with the ecology
> of the island, and the architectural style of the
> members' homes running the gamut from
> wooden, colonial, Spanish, Italian, and an
> instance of Flemish, exude a gentle grandeur
> of a bygone era suspended in time. . . . Like the
> Fate, Clotho, who wove the thread of life, it is
> history woven into the fabric of Jekyll Island
> that distinguishes it from other fancy resorts.

"The Jekyll Island Club clearly was the point of greatest focus of the James and Jennings families and their immediate and collateral relatives," Anderson writes in his historical notes about the island. "Despite James and Jennings manors in close proximity in Cold Spring Harbor, Long Island, a generation earlier in Fairfield, Connecticut, and the contiguous houses on East 70th Street, the clans never gathered as closely and frequently as they did on Jekyll Island."

Anderson is no less busy in Jekyll than he is anywhere else. When he decided, one winter, to write a panegyric to the fuel-friendly Red Bug, it turned into a full-scale diatribe on energy conservation and "specious ecology cures" that included a castigation of the Clean Air Act of 1977 for exempting SUVs, thus tripling their numbers (and fuel emissions) on the road; of the auto and oil lobbies' headlock on Congress that prevents the introduction of bills to cure the SUV omission; of special interest groups fomenting opposition to new LNG terminals, thereby ignoring that LNG ships are the most bombproof ships afloat; of the ethanol subsidy as a rip-off to the taxpayer inasmuch as it is a massive subsidy to the farmer, and because it is not only corrosive to engines but not as effective in reducing emissions as promised—not to mention that the program has a deleterious effect on agricultural production; of the use of hybrid automobiles, which are expending more fuel because of their capacity for improving acceleration by cutting in both electric and petrol power simultaneously, and which are being subsidized by the federal government at the same time; and of President Jimmy Carter for dumping nuclear energy on moral grounds. "How much less intrusive on agriculture, and the imbalance of payments due to importing oil and the ecology it would be to double the tax on highway fuel and turn off the decorative lighting on the nation's bridges," he wrote. Jekyll Island does not escape Anderson's rant. He points out that legislation was in place at the time to add decorative lighting to the island's causeway bridge, and that for the sake of ambience the gas-fired log fire in the hotel's main dining room is kept going all summer, requiring more air conditioning to keep the room cool.

Much of Anderson's time on Jekyll is spent on family-related matters. He says he goes to Jekyll to "mimic" his forebears. More accurately, it is to venerate them. One of his first projects on the island was restoring the fountain at the wall built in memory of Dr. Walter James. And for many years Anderson has worked diligently to find, and underwrite high-resolution photo reproductions of portraits of Dr. and Mrs. James and Walter Jennings and have them properly framed and hung in their respective houses.

Getting to know Tyler Bagwell provided an assist to Anderson's efforts at preserving and enhancing the history of the Jekyll Island Club, his ancestors in particular. Bagwell, in 2013 an assistant professor of speech communications at the College of Coastal Georgia in Brunswick, is also a documentary filmmaker. Bagwell has known Jekyll Island from childhood. His family had a small vacation house on the island in the 1960s. He recalls riding his bicycle through the historic district as a youngster, and swimming in the old hotel pool for a dollar. He first heard about Harry Anderson through one of Anderson's cousins he interviewed in the 1990s while writing *The Jekyll Island Club*. He subsequently interviewed Anderson for an article he was writing on Annie Burr Jennings, and the two became friends. Bagwell has spent time in Newport with Anderson and both his cousins, Yusha Auchincloss and the late Zup James. Bagwell recalls walking into Harbour

Court one evening for dinner after he and Anderson had traveled from Fairfield, Connecticut, where they had been doing Annie Burr research. "Harry had on his old prep school blazer from 1938," Bagwell says. "It had holes in it, and it was frayed at the sleeves. There was a younger couple in front of us waiting to be seated. The man took one look at Harry and said he doubted if they would let him in with that type of attire. Harry mumbled that the man might be right. Then the maître d' returned, saw Harry, and said 'Commodore! Right this way.' We walked by the couple in front of us. I had to chuckle."

In the winter of 2004, Anderson provided Bagwell with the subject of his first documentary by organizing a Jennings family reunion at Jekyll. Altogether, 35 to 40 people on Anderson's distaff side showed up, including some Jameses and a Rockefeller or two. Bagwell shot interviews with most of them, which he included in a 57-minute documentary, *The Good Time Will Come—Gold, Oil & the Exclusive Jekyll Island Club—The story of Oliver Burr Jennings and his Family.* Anderson was listed as producer.

A few years later, he arranged another reunion at Jekyll for the James and Anderson side of the family. Again it was well attended. One project that came out of the reunions was Anderson's idea of a photographic album of all the homes of all the family's ancestors for distribution to all generations. That album is still a work in progress.

My second day on Jekyll, Harry suggested we hop on the open-air tram for a tour of the historic district, a 350-acre, triangular parcel of land that fronts the Intracoastal Waterway with a substantial wharf. The district was the heart of the old Jekyll Island Club. With many stops for exploring, the tram ride took two hours to tour the facilities, including the servants' dormitories, tennis courts, infirmary, and to stop so passengers could visit a dozen or so cottages that have been restored. Some are preserved as house museums, with rooms full of antiques cordoned off. Some, like the enormous Crane cottage built in 1917 by the plumbing magnate, have become annexes of the hotel. Promoted these days as a site for

Harry Anderson on one of the original electric Red Bug vehicles at Jekyll Island in 2009.

"dream weddings," Crane has its own restaurant. In keeping with the "cottage" diminutive applied tongue-in-cheek to these lavish winter getaways, many of them feel more fashionably comfortable than downright elegant. But the size of the houses, the variety of styles, and the accuracy of architectural stereotype each structure attains is striking. Harry had surely lost count of the number of times he had made this tour, but if he was at all bored by the repetition it didn't show. He asked as many questions of the guide as any of the first-timers, picking up still more details for his files.

Later on we paid a special visit to Cherokee, the house owned by Dr. James when he was president of the club. Cherokee is among the larger, grander buildings in the historic district, Crane being the largest and grandest. It is a rectangular, two-story Italian Renaissance building. The hipped roof of ceramic tile has an extended overhang that gives the house a solid look. Three sets of mullioned-glass, double front doors crowned with arches open on a raised brick terrace with a balustrade. Cherokee looks more like a small college administration building than a home. It's now part of the Jekyll Island Club Hotel system, advertised as able to accommodate meetings for 40 people, or receptions for 100.

Aware that paying guests were staying in the rooms upstairs, Harry and I confined our visit to the spacious vestibule, which takes up most of the first floor. At one end is a billiard room and library. A large fireplace is on the left wall. On the mantel is a model of *Columbia*, the huge sloop designed by Nathanael Greene Herreshoff that was the first yacht to win the America's Cup twice (1899, 1901). Her co-owner was J. P. Morgan, a member of the Jekyll Island Club. A stairway is beyond. In the middle of the room, a lounge is dominated by a large oil portrait of Walter James, seated with a golf club across his lap. His tan sports jacket is open. His necktie is red. His face is composed, friendly. His mustache looks a lot like Harry's.

As we studied the portrait, a couple joined us. Harry quickly introduced himself to them. Another couple appeared, relatives of the first. They were all from Ohio, they said, and were staying at Cherokee. Harry told them the man in the portrait was Walter James, his grandfather! The tourists were delighted, couldn't believe their luck in meeting a relative of this man who was president of the club, a Jennings. They said they could see the resemblance. One of them went upstairs to tell their teenage children, who came running. Cameras appeared and many pictures were taken of various groupings of these people from Ohio in front of the portrait with their new best friend. Harry was all smiles, totally enjoying the moment.

When he is in residence at Jekyll Island, Harry Anderson's postal communications are always on Jekyll Island letterhead bearing a photograph of the boar's head outside the main dining room. "The notation, 'Club Bore' is a spoof," Anderson says. And his email sign-off from Jekyll in 2013 is, "the ceaseless roar, from another shore, tales speechless bore, timeless and forever more." When asked for the source of this quote, Anderson chuckles. "We made that up," he said.

No sooner had Anderson arrived on Jekyll for his winter sojourn in 2013 than he got involved in Tyler Bagwell's latest project, a short documentary on the aftermath of the arrival of the slaver *Wanderer*, the last vessel to land slaves on US soil—50 years after Congress had declared such traffic illegal. In October 1858, the schooner *Wanderer* had picked up 487 captives on the African coast. Six weeks later, in the dead of the night, she landed the 409 survivors of the harsh 42-day passage on Jekyll Island.

Anderson was no stranger to this story, or its intriguing twist. It was covered in Jack Parkinson's 1975 history of the New York Yacht Club, and is well told in Dr. George S. King's *The Last Slaver* (1933). The credit for the Warren Sheppard painting of *Wanderer* in King's book reads "by permission of Walter Jennings," Anderson's great-uncle. After the Friends of Jekyll Island had erected a memorial on the beach where the captives had been landed, Anderson sent a memo to flag officers at the NYYC based on accounts from books by several authors about how a "suave and slippery Charleston, South Carolina, politician" named William Corrie—owner of *Wanderer* in 1858—had cajoled his way into the NYYC. No one knew at the time that Corrie's partner was a Savannah slave trader by the name of Charles A. Lamar. When *Wanderer* left for the Congo River to pick up her cargo of slaves, horror of horrors, she was flying the burgee of the NYYC in order to persuade various authorities that she was a private yacht.

Anderson writes:

> Well known was the decision of the Club to strike *Wanderer* from the rolls and expel Corrie after the Club learned of his nefarious activities via a letter from the secretary of the navy sent at the instigation of President Buchanan. The episode had become an embarrassment to the president. Not only was he a member of the NYYC (per its by-laws), but the episode had garnered national attention at a time when extremists in Georgia and other southern states were already militating for

secession. Buchanan was faced with judges and prosecutors in the south impeding judicial procedures that would prosecute Corrie and Lamar in Federal Admiralty Court. Buchanan's fear was that failure to indict Corrie and Lamar would add fuel to the momentum of the Lincoln-led Republicans in the forthcoming election. It was no surprise that through devious means—the kidnapping of witnesses scheduled to testify—that neither man was ever indicted.

During the two winter months Harry Anderson spends at Jekyll Island each year, he becomes part of the attraction of the historic grounds, providing the most immediate connection there is to the old, exclusive days. He keeps busy with his research, spends time with close Jekyll friends and associates, makes the occasional 200-mile drive to Charleston for lunch with old cohorts, maybe flies off to Florida for a Ransom Everglades meeting, and undertakes video projects with Tyler Bagwell.

The strenuous life continues. In 2005, Mystic Seaport selected Anderson as the recipient of its coveted W.P. Stephens Award, bestowed upon individuals who have made a lasting contribution to yachting history. The Museum planned to award it during the New York Yacht Club cruise that summer. "When we told him," Mystic Seaport Chairman of the Board Richard Vietor said, "he said he had a conflict.

He was off sailing somewhere. We had a private ceremony with a stand-in. Harry left us shaking our heads, saying, 'Imagine a guy his age still sailing around the world, too busy to be at his own award ceremony.'"

But when Anderson is on Jekyll Island, no matter where the day's events might have led him, he can reliably be found in Vincent's, the hotel pub, around 5:00 p.m., relaxing with a cocktail and enjoying conversation with whomever he happens to find there.

New York

New York City, for Harry Anderson, is about clubs and libraries. One winter day we were returning from Tuxedo Park, an hour's drive north, where we had paid a visit to Harry's old friend Alex Salm. Harry thinks they first met on *Puffin*, the boat belonging to Eddie Greef from Seawanhaka that Anderson had helped race to Spain in the 1970s. Salm's father was a count in the Austro-Hungarian Empire. His mother moved to the US and built one of the original houses in Tuxedo Park, a highly fashionable piece of real estate at the time. Salm, who is Anderson's age, went to the Kent School, then Dartmouth for the skiing. He flew B-29s for the bombing of Japan, and after running out of fuel, survived a landing on a beach that hurled him through the windscreen. His only injury was a broken nose. For many years Salm was Sumner "Huey" Long's crew liaison on a succession of ocean racers called *Ondine*. Salm has spent the last 30 years living alone in the big house in Tuxedo Park, maintaining the place and its contents fulltime. These days, that includes a startling number of succulent plants, some of them six feet tall in pots the size of washbasins, that crowd the spacious interior in cold weather.

Upon arriving at the house, we had been unable to raise Salm. We tried the enormous front door. It was open, so in we went, with Harry leading the way, repeatedly hailing his friend. No response. Finally we sat on a couch amid the imposing ranks of succulents, contemplated the dark wood paneling, the wood grid ceiling, the organized retro clutter on all sides, and waited. Salm, all six foot three of him, lean and dressed in charcoal flannels and a sweater with his hair slicked back, finally appeared, showing no sign of being surprised by the intruders. It seems he had been in his shop in the cellar, gluing handles on damaged teacups.

After lunch with Salm at a local eatery, Harry and I drove back to the city. He asked to be dropped off in Midtown. He was headed for the New York Society Library on East Seventy-Ninth Street by way of the Union Club on East Sixty-Ninth, where he would leave some

of his kit. I drove down Park Avenue and pulled over at East Sixty-Ninth Street to let him off. As he zipped up his winter coat, opened the door, and rummaged for his things in the back seat, I understood the unease George Crowninshield had felt when he watched Harry get on a surfboard after a dinner one evening and paddle into the darkness toward his boat moored in the harbor. With a slam of the door, Harry shouldered his bags and quickly disappeared into the bustling throng on Park Avenue.

We met in New York a few weeks later to attend the annual meeting of the Aaron Burr Association. We shared a room at the New York Yacht Club, outside of which happened to be a glass case containing one of the intricate ship models built by Harry's grandfather, Henry B. Anderson. A letter from Henry B. on display in the case describes the model as a compilation of three ships: *St. George*, 1701; *Prince*, 1670; and *Marlborough*, 1706. The model is brilliantly colored and gilded because Henry B. said that is what his research had revealed about the old ships.

Every spare nook and cranny of the NYYC's Manhattan Station boasts a model resplendent in a glass case, and every available wall space in the club is hung with nautical paintings and photographs. But the piece de resistance is on the second floor off the wide, steep marble

staircase that ascends from the lobby. It is called, simply, the Model Room, and the expansive (100- by 40-foot) room itself is so grand that the hundreds of full- and half-models on display there almost have to fight for attention.

The building was designed in 1898 by Whitney Warren of Warren & Wetmore in a Beaux-Arts style that reflected the "muscular glory" of Rome as influenced, with a decorative

flourish, by the French School of Beaux-Arts. Completed in 1901, the limestone exterior, with its period sailing ship's transom windows facing Forty-Fourth Street, is of distinctive nautical motif, but it is the Model Room with its stunning Tiffany window in the center of the ceiling, its ornately carved marble fireplace, and the overhanging balcony all around done in dark, hand-carved oak timbers, that provides the exuberant, Beaux-Arts statement. No matter how many times one visits the NYYC,

Old friends gather for dinner at Alex Salm's house in Tuxedo Park, New York. From left, Bill Maclay, Charlie Adams, James Gerard behind his uncle and host Alex Salm, Diana Russell, Harry Anderson, and Louis Norris.

the Model Room is always one of the first stops, such is the magnetism that room emanates.

Among the room's many showpieces are several huge, temperature- and humidity-controlled, dust-free glass cases that house fully rigged models of the yachts that have won the America's Cup. Alongside each winner is a model of the vanquished yacht. As we stood in front of that display one morning before breakfast, the years of history spread so brilliantly before him caused Harry to ruminate on the Cup, past and present. When we came to *Australia II*, the 12-Metre with the upside-down keel with wings that had pulled off the momentous defeat of *Liberty* in 1983, Anderson spoke of its designer, Ben Lexcen. "I think I was the last American to be with him," Anderson said.

He died in 1988 of a heart attack. He was a workaholic. He only had one eye. I was on the committee that was most vociferous in trying to get him into the America's Cup Hall of Fame. Alan Bond was inducted in 2003. The position of myself and some others was that without Lexcen, Bond could not have won the Cup, and logically, therefore, should also have been inducted. But others, like Bob McCullough— chair of the America's Cup Committee— considered Lexcen had exceeded the exception under the Deed of Gift for using a foreign tank

when he resorted to the aeronautical database to assay the different designs.

Others had already conceived the winged keel. Olin Stephens, for one; Peter de Savary's designer is another; a chap in Seattle threatened to sue the Club for use of a patent he claimed to own for the concept; and Ben Lexcen himself. A photo of Lexcen a few years earlier showed him knee deep in water off a beach with a model boat with a winged keel. [Lexcen was one of those inducted into the America's Cup Hall of Fame in 2006.]

When the topic turned to 2010 and the 100-foot multihulls that raced after more than two years of lawsuits, Harry's mustache switched on.

You used to be able to trust the challengers and defenders to abide by the terms of the Deed of Gift, especially those terms pertaining to match racing in stable conditions, "free of headlands." Now, syndicate heads are ignoring these key items, including usurping the Deed's authority that stipulates it is the "Yacht Club [that is] entitled to the right to sail a match." For example, both the San Diego Yacht Club and the Royal New Zealand Yacht Squadron successively turned over management of the match to the syndicate; the Swiss defender sought to appoint both the race committee and jury. Now in 2013 the Golden Gate Yacht Club is staging a race with

72-foot catamarans around a closed course on San Francisco Bay aimed at developing a television audience rather than showcasing match-racing tactics. With multi-national crews on the yachts, there's no "home team" to root for. Whatever happened to "friendly competition between foreign nations," as stated in the Deed? The late Olin Stephens once observed, "National identity of the teams?" The best efforts of New York Yacht Club flag officers to bring various parties together to resolve these extreme aberrations have been rebuffed.

Harry chuckled. "Dooley Roosevelt used to quote Mr. Dooley, the cartoon character he was named after: 'When you're dealing with yachtsmen, you're dealing with gentlemen, and when you're dealing with gentlemen, you can't be too careful.'"

Perhaps no one would have understood that advice better than Aaron Burr, who was attorney, military officer, educator, banker, and a politician who attained the second-highest office in the United States—that of vice president under President Thomas Jefferson (1801-1805). Certainly a man of Burr's elevated status was dealing with gentlemen on a daily basis. But one of them, a political rival named Alexander Hamilton, called Burr "The most unfit and dangerous man in the community" in a newspaper story, and heaped on much more provocative slander in the press at a time when words meant something. Failing to obtain an apology, Burr found it necessary to challenge Hamilton to a duel in which he shot and killed him.

Burr is surely the most controversial of the Founding Fathers, and perhaps the most fascinating. Hundreds of books (also plays, teleplays, and a movie) have been written covering Burr's military career (meritorious); his political career (he has been called the father of modern political campaigning); the duel with Hamilton (he was charged, never tried, but the event ended his political career); Burr's trial for treason in 1807 (President Jefferson found Burr's western adventures—the buying of land and the formation of a small "army"—to be sufficient to have him arrested. He was acquitted); his life and family (he was orphaned at age two); his positions against slavery and for women's rights; and his relationship with a "woman of color."

Burr first appeared in literature as a character "epitomizing worldly sophistication" in Harriet Beecher Stowe's novel, *The Minister's Wooing* (1859). A segment of the *Daniel Boone* television series (1965) was called "The Aaron Burr Story." In February 2013, a new book called *A Brief Conversation with Aaron Burr,* by Andrew J. Patrick, appeared. The subject matter, after more than 200 years, remains both evergreen and arresting.

Harry Anderson became interested in his controversial cousin, as he has said, because of "Burrabilia" that had his great-aunt Annie Burr Jennings had collected. The initial item of interest was a copy of Charles Burr Todd's history and genealogy of the Burr family that Anderson first ran across in his grandfather's library at Camp Junco in the Adirondacks when he was a teenager. "When the camp was sold I rescued the book," Anderson says. "It ended up in Annie Burr's library, and I co-opted it after her death." The original Burrs settled in Hartford in the seventeenth century, then moved to Fairfield, though Aaron Burr himself was born in Newark, New Jersey. One of Aaron Burr's collaterals married a Jennings. In fact Burrs married Jennings twice. Anderson wasn't long into his Burr research before he came down solidly on the side of his collateral ancestor. He happened upon an article in the *New Haven Register* about a fellow named Burr who was the janitor in a local theater. The article referred to the Aaron Burr Association. Anderson looked up the group, and joined.

He began collecting, buying Burr papers and memorabilia. He got involved in original Burr research in Philadelphia, where Burr's paramour, Mary Emmons grew up. He also did research on the relationship between painter John Vanderlyn—a protégé of Gilbert Stuart who painted Burr's daughter—and

Aaron Burr, the man who became Vanderlyn's mentor. Excerpts from both research projects are printed as appendices in the 2005 book, *The Conspiracy Against Aaron Burr*, a scholarly work by Oliver Perry Sturm, which Anderson coedited.

The annual meeting of the Burr Association in 2012 was held in a small, private dining room in an Irish pub in Midtown Manhattan. Sixteen people were in attendance. What this group lacks in numbers, it makes up for in commitment. The 2012 meeting was highlighted by the presence of the Hon. Brian D. Hardison, a lawyer and judge in Georgia, who in 2013 is the leading Burr collector. The meeting was arranged around Hardison's impressive road show of Burrabilia that was on display at New York's Grolier Club, the oldest (1884) society of bibliophiles in North America. Anderson had collaborated with Hardison on the 300-page catalog that describes every item in the collection, and its provenance.

The two men got to know one another as competitors. When Hardison found himself getting close to a coveted book, manuscript, pamphlet, or object relating to Burr, he would suddenly find it swept out from under him by someone named Anderson. In 2000, when Anderson's collection got too large for him to manage, he donated it to Rutgers University's existing special collection on Burr. The more than 100 items were valued at around $30,000.

We viewed Brian Hardison's Burr exhibit at the Grolier Club. The prize of the collection is Burr's pocket watch that is hand-painted with the only known likeness of Burr's wife, Theodosia, on the three-o'clock side, with a companion portrait of her mother on the nine-o'clock side.

We then adjourned to the Yale Club for drinks and dinner. Anderson has written these notes about the Yale Club:

> We became a life member after WWII: good investment since payment was only 8 times class dues. Examples of how the world has changed—perhaps for the worst: no longer are there heads of wild animals and stuffed game fish on the walls of the grill room; no longer a free daiquiri for every two purchased (during WW II, to obtain hard-to-find Scotch, bars had to purchase bottles of rum as well so this was a means on unloading the surplus of the latter); likewise steak was extremely hard to come by so whale meat frequented the menu; and of course there were no female members so bathing suits were not required in the pool.
>
> The Club had its own internal entrance to the corridor in Grand Central Station, which eventually was closed when muggings began to torment the City. When at Columbia Law School in the late 1940s, the Club was a Sunday retreat for many of us. It would be squash in the morning or sometimes tennis at the Princeton Club that had courts on the southwest corner of 39th and 40th Streets at Park Avenue South. Imagine paying taxes on such property for that kind of use today. After lunch at the Oyster Bar at Grand Central Station, the library in the Yale Club was our study hall for the rest of the day.

After getting drinks and little plates of hors d'oeuvres from the bar, the three of us adjourned to the spacious lounge with its many comfortable groupings of chairs and couches around small tables. Alas, there wasn't a seat in the place. "Do you know why there isn't any place to sit?" Harry asked. "They let women in." But we found a little spot in a corner, and were soon engaged in a lively discussion about the duel in which Aaron Burr had killed Hamilton. One might think that after nearly 210 years every last detail of that fateful day—July 11, 1804— would have been resolved. Au contraire; among historians the debate rages on about the interval between the first and second shots, whether or not Hamilton secretly set his trigger to require only a half pound of pressure instead of the usual two or three pounds, the nature of the pistols that

Hamilton purchased (they had larger-caliber barrels than customary for dueling convention, and twin sights), and whether or not Hamilton had sought an unfair advantage that proved to be his undoing. The Aaron Burr Association sponsored a re-enactment of the duel on its 200th anniversary at the very site in Weehawken, New Jersey, where the event took place. Dueling was illegal in New York in 1804. It was also illegal in New Jersey, but the consequences were less severe. Two thousand people came to watch the reenactment, and it was most successful according to a report in the Burr Association's newsletter. Those who seek to discredit Burr would probably not have agreed with the association's version of the event.

We took the elevator to the third floor for a buffet dinner. Halfway through the meal, Harry spotted a young man sitting at a nearby table by himself. Harry got up, and went over to speak with him. Brian Hardison and I exchanged amused looks, figuring it was just another person Harry knew. A few minutes later, the young man had joined us, and was talking about his work raising money for Broadway stage productions. Harry had never seen him before. But he had thought he looked interesting, and saw no reason he should be eating alone when he could be enjoying our company. And he was a Yale man, after all.

New Haven

We ate lunch at a table down at Mory's—where else? Harry said he had joined the famous eating and drinking establishment in 1940. Founded in 1849, Mory's Temple Bar is as much a part of Yale tradition as the bulldog mascot and the color blue. A private club, open these days to members of the Yale community for a one-time fee of $15 ($10 of that is a food credit), Mory's is the best-known college-associated bistro in the United States. Its current membership is more than 16,000. Mory's is famous for its tables that have been hand-carved over the years by diners with pocket knives, for its celebratory "Cups" that come in a variety of colors—one is even nonalcoholic—and for frequent performances through the years by Yale's acappella singing group, the Whiffenpoofs, who's signature, unashamedly maudlin song is about drinking at Mory's ("the dear old Temple bar we love so well"), and themselves: "Gentleman songsters off on a spree. . . ." Rudy Vallee's recording of the "Whiffenpoof Song" in 1927 swept it to national attention. Subsequently, it has been recorded by Bing Crosby, Perry Como, The Statler Brothers, and Elvis Presley—to name a few. For old Yalies, if there is one tie that binds, it is Mory's.

Mory's is in the midst of the sprawling Yale University complex. With 5,300 undergraduates, more than 6,000 graduate and professional students, and an endowment of $15 billion (second only to Harvard), Yale is New Haven's biggest taxpayer and employer. Yale also has the most arresting campus of any city university. There are block after block of architectural marvels ranging from the simple brick structures of the early days, to the many English "Collegiate Gothic" buildings crowned by the soaring Harkness Tower (1921), to the more recent work of such notables as Louis Kahn, Eero Saarinen, Philip Johnson, Caesar Pelli, and Frank Ghery. Somehow it all fits together as a grand, organic plan that is a feast for the eyes.

After lunch Harry and I walked past the massive Sterling Library then down Wall Street toward College Street and the Elizabethan Club. Harry led the way through several lush courtyards that many of the city block-size building complexes have in common. He had first walked these streets in 1939, more than 70 years ago. Did it seem any different to him? "Not really," he said.

The old, wood-frame Elizabethan Club house was practically deserted. We admired the famous contemporary painting of Queen Elizabeth, checked out the rack of clay pipes (still there), then went upstairs and relaxed in one of the small, cozy rooms with their floor-to-ceiling bookshelves. Harry talked about his

last flurry of activity with Yale Sailing. It began in 1993 when Yale Provost Rad Daley—who had been supportive in getting the team moved to Short Beach in 1967—suggested to Steve Benjamin that the time might be right to make sailing a varsity sport. Benjamin, an Olympic Silver medalist (470 Class, 1984), had just taken over as chair of Yale Sailing Associates. Title IX of the Education Amendments, which ended sex discrimination in any federally funded education program (sports included), was in its twentieth year, yet colleges were still struggling to balance programs that had been heavily male-weighted for many years. Sailing, with its co-ed make up, could help.

The first person Benjamin called was Harry Anderson. "He had a hand in founding YSA," Benjamin says, "and we've been together through thick and thin. He's the one guy I can call and rely on. He always has good advice." Together they paid a visit to Yale Athletic Director Tom Beckett, who liked the concept. But he threw them a curve. He told them all they needed was $4 million to endow Yale Sailing and renovate the boathouse.

Finding the money wasn't the only issue. Intercollegiate sailing programs had long been organized and administered by the same students who raced the boats. Taking on varsity status, and the consequent elevation

of the coach to director of sailing, would bring with it a raft of NCAA and ECAC regulations. As Anderson outlined the pros and cons of the situation in a letter to Yale President Richard Levin in the fall of 2001, "[Attaining varsity status] also includes. . . . the potential incursion on the prerogatives and responsibilities of the undergraduates thereby depriving them of the experience they gain by dint of serving as stewards in charge of running the programs, races and so forth—an experience that has led to the maturing of generations of undergraduates." Anderson was summarizing a lively, sustained exchange on the issue among the current crop of Yale sailors, alumni, and administrators. But Anderson was solidly for stepping up to varsity status.

He went on to say that NCAA and ECAC regulations could in fact be met, and that "the tugs of nostalgia for the days of yore have been subdued by a national recognition of the climate of the times." He urged Levin to respond quickly because some of the funding for the rehabilitation of the sailing center was contingent on the team attaining varsity status. He added that his pledge of $100,000 towards the project was free of contingencies.

It had taken ten years, but in February 2002, President Levin announced that Yale would have both co-ed, and women's sailing teams, bringing the number of varsity sports at Yale to 35. At the same time, sailing coach Zack Leonard was made director of sailing.

Harry Anderson with other hard-core supporters of Yale Sailing at his ninetieth birthday celebration. From left, Susan Daley, coach Zack Leonard, Anderson, and Steve Benjamin.

Ten years later, Anderson was getting involved in still another Yale Sailing project: the development of an Olympic sailing center at the Short Beach facility. The idea was prompted by the poor showing by the US Olympic Sailing Team in the last two Olympics: two medals in Beijing, 2008; no medals in the UK, 2012. Analyzing why the historically most successful Olympic sailing team had lapsed wasn't that easy. But George Atwood, in the Yale Office of Development, a sailor himself and liaison with the sailing team for the university, had some suggestions. "The pipeline for every good sailor in the US is through college sailing," Atwood says, "where they have been racing stripped-down, main-and-jib dinghies on short courses. Lots of colleges discourage Olympic campaigns because people have to take a year off. So for four years college sailors have no spinnaker boat to sail. Meanwhile, Europeans and New Zealanders are sailing spinnaker boats, learning the tweaky gear and straight-line speed. Not having straight-line speed is what killed our team in the Olympics. So the gist of the conversation is how we can get colleges to embrace the need for their sailors to have time in Olympic classes as well as the dinghies that give them such good experience with starting, tactics, and tight mark-roundings."

How to remedy the USA's Olympic slump is a complicated discussion that involves politics,

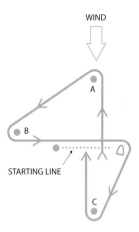

support, direction, and half a dozen factors of the sort George Atwood mentioned. One might think that at his age, Harry Anderson would be out of that loop, but that's not the case. He understands why college sailing doesn't provide the comprehensive training that is essential for Olympic competition, and that's just the beginning.

"The English are doing much better because they have in-depth programs financed by federal money," Anderson says.

Our sailors also have a problem with distance. It's easy in Europe to pop over to another country and compete against some of the best sailors. It's a big expense for USA and Canadian sailors to do that. And we don't have

First used at Yale, the Harry Anderson course concept was born in the Adirondacks, where narrow lakes often required courses of many short legs. Racing on the Anderson course, boats beat upwind after the start to the weather mark (A), reach to mark B—a good chance for planing—leave the start line to starboard, run to mark C (a deep run allows trailing boats to catch up), and finish upwind. Many college programs now use this course.

all the Olympic classes here. That's one reason we started the Finns in the 1950s.

Times have changed. When Glen Foster won his medal he was a specialist on the floor of the New York Stock Exchange. He went to the gym evenings. He had to get time off to compete. In those days it was all amateur. Lots of countries were putting their sailors in the military on special duty so they could spend all their time sailing. We hadn't caught up with that program.

At the center we envision at Yale, across from the existing facility, we'll bring in top collegiate sailors certain times of year for intense training. We'll have storage for boats, parking, sleeping facilities. The director of athletics is steamed up about it.

Zack Leonard (Yale '89) has been director of Yale Sailing since 2002, when the team achieved varsity status. Since then, Yale's 55 All-American sailors, five national championship appearances, and four Olympian sailors have made Leonard arguably the best college coach in the country. In a personal letter of thanks to Harry Anderson in 2013, Leonard wrote, "Your die-hard support of YCYC has allowed many young women and men (myself more than most) the chance to immerse themselves in the sport we love, a project worthy of our efforts. You've helped create a place where Yalies can learn about themselves as men, women, competitors, and friends. Sailing has taken me many places and opened many doors. Without my time at YCYC, that wouldn't have been possible. To be able to come back and help with the renewal of the club has been the greatest project I could ever have imagined. It's not often one gets to pay back a debt of gratitude while working at a job one loves. Thanks, Harry."

Zack Leonard says, with a flicker of incredulity, that Anderson is on the cusp of what is happening, that he doesn't miss a trick. "He's as snappy as ever," Leonard says.

He knows so much about sailing. He has seen the history of the sport evolve. His strategic thinking is amazing. His best moment was when he saw Short Beach and realized what an asset it would be.

Harry loves the details. That's why he is so strong on the rules. He's interested in all the minutiae of a subject, which is rare in this day when people want quick answers, quick indicators for making a decision instead of knowing something in depth. At a meeting the other day about the Olympic Center he brought up something we hadn't thought of. A large portion of our budget is what Yale charges us for building maintenance. Harry's first question was, if we acquire more property and build another building is our maintenance fee going to go up and cause a long-term budget problem? Being aware of that aspect will allow us to pre-negotiate before purchase and put us on a better footing. We said, "Whoa, we should have thought of that." But Harry did."

We stayed at the Elizabethan Club long enough for a cup of their famous tea, and to select from plates of delicious cookies. Several other student-members showed up, but there was little conversation. Then Harry took me to the railroad station. That involved driving down Church Street, a high-speed artery through the heart of the city with three lanes in either direction separated by a grass median. As Church approaches Union Avenue (Route 1) where the station is located, the lanes are marked for three options, left turn, right turn, and straight. A left turn was required for the station, but neither of us were sure of its location, and unfortunately the light was green, requiring a quick decision on the run. Harry got his bearings as Union Avenue loomed, and snapped a left turn from the middle lane. There was a blaring of horns, as hell-bent New Haven drivers slammed on their brakes and surely cursed. Harry made the turn without incident, accident, reaction, or comment. He dropped me without fanfare at the station, and was off to find I-95 north, to Mystic.

Cape Breton

It's a long way to Cape Breton Island, Nova Scotia, even if you live on the East Coast of the United States. From Mystic, it's 800 miles to Baddeck, a 14-hour drive. Until recently it was a drive Harry Anderson made at least twice a year. Of late, he flies and has someone pick him up in Sydney, although in June of 2013 he made the trip by car, by himself. Given the complexity of opening Boulaceet Farm for the season, and closing it up for the freezing winter months (just draining the water system involves 13 different valves opened in proper sequence), Anderson always preferred doing the job himself rather than delegating it. Alex Salm used to be a regular on those trips, Harry's preferred mate for the job.

Anderson with his good friend Bill "Coach" Maclay on board *Hector* at Pictou, Nova Scotia.

When I visited Boulaceet in the fall of 2012, I flew. A large thunderstorm cell delayed my arrival in Halifax by five hours, too late to connect to Sydney where Harry was waiting to pick me up. I got a room at the airport hotel, wondering how I would contact Harry. He rarely carries his cell phone. No sooner had I checked in than the phone rang. Seasoned traveler that he is, he'd figured it out down to where I would be spending the night. At 7:30 the next morning in Sydney, Harry was waiting at baggage claim. We jumped in his 1996 Ford Escort wagon and he drove 90 minutes west to Baddeck.

Boulaceet Farm on Gillis Point is an hour beyond Baddeck, so Harry made a beeline for Cape Breton Boatyard to finish putting *Annie B* away for the winter. By the time we got to the boat, it was raining. *Annie B* is a 40-foot lobster boat built in Nova Scotia that has been converted for cruising by a no-frills enclosure that extends the pilothouse to within ten feet of the transom, leaving a small aft deck. There's nothing Bristol about *Annie B*. She'd fit into any harbor full of hard-working boats. Inside the enclosure, she's cluttered in a very yar, well-worn way. To port there's a galley area with stove and sink with cabinet under. To starboard there's a big all-purpose counter/chart table. Aft of that is a small table that seats four. Forward, below, are three bunks, a head, and lots of miscellaneous gear. As with all of Harry's possessions, functionality is all that's required. There are lots of innovations scattered throughout the boat, like the hanging basket for fruits and vegetables that has a shock cord stretched from its bottom to a clip on the counter to prevent it from swinging.

Annie B, Anderson's converted workboat, loads up at Gillis Point, Nova Scotia, for a summer outing in 1993.

We cleaned up the aft deck, removing the steadying sail from the boom, and stowing sail and boom inside. We winterized the outboard for the dinghy and stowed it. Harry said he had to drain the water tanks. We lifted up one of the heavy floorboards between the chart table and galley. Harry grabbed a screwdriver and pliers and started below, dismissing an offer of assistance. He stepped on the engine, then down into the bilge, unscrewed the clamps and started working the plastic hoses off the metal nipples of the water tanks.

At noon, we broke for lunch. Harry had arranged to meet Henry Fuller at a local restaurant. Their friendship and mutual respect is built upon their common love of sailing, their Yale heritage, a few mutual friends, and their total lack of pretentions. They both like "life in the raw," as Harry often refers to what Cape Breton offers. As a matter of course, Fuller spends the brutal winters in Baddeck. His idea of relief from cabin fever is to go for a 40-mile hike in the mountains of Patagonia in January.

Testament to the strength of sailing, school ties, and lifestyle is how those things outweigh what the two men don't have in common. There is a considerable age gap. And while Harry fought in World War II, Fuller beat it to Canada to avoid the draft during the Vietnam War. Harry is a conservative Republican.

Fuller is a self-described renegade, a man of liberal leanings who helps raise money for the Nature Conservancy. Being with the two of them is slightly tense, because Fuller speaks almost as frankly about Harry in his presence as he would if Harry weren't there. Harry takes it all in with amusement. "I know guys like Harry," Fuller said over lunch. "I know they come from a protective covenant that they all lie under. It has to do with social networking, who you are. If you stay within it, life is fine. Get outside it, and it's a whole 'nother world."

TOP: Friends frolicking at Boulaceet Farm in 1969. From left, Lady Barbara Russell, Fifi (Mrs. Julian) Roosevelt, Charlie Adams (in drag), Sylvia Coe Tolk, Harry Anderson, Liz Roosevelt, and Diana Russell. BOTTOM: Alex Salm and Harry posturing at the pump at Boulaceet Farm.

Therein may lie the source of their biggest commonality. Fuller escaped to the wilds of the Canadian Maritime Provinces, and stayed there, like one of Joseph Conrad's perpetually voyaging sailors who realized that "whole 'nother world" ashore boded nothing but ill for him.

"Harry's always been a floater, being part of all these different organizations," Fuller said later. "And he did it well. I watched him at the Fortress at Louisbourg here in Cape Breton last summer. I'm a social critic, and watching him work the people was interesting. He smiles, says all the right things, gives 'em all a hug. But his other side is so matter of fact. Does he really mean it? That strata of society Harry came from, those people were like kings back then. They didn't have to deal with the real world. Harry has no pretentions, but he's never had to deal with people who were down and out. As I like to keep reminding him, he's only two generations removed from the robber barons."

That makes Harry chuckle: "That from someone born to the manor of a Maine squire, and a member of Skull and Bones at Yale?"

During lunch, Harry had gotten a call from one of his partners in Boulaceet Farm, Larry Glenn. Larry and his wife Anne were in residence to help winterize the place. Larry was supposed to bring the Farm's 18-foot open launch around to Baddeck for winter storage, but the engine wouldn't start. Harry said we'd come pick him up. As we drove the short distance back to *Annie B*, it was raining hard. Harry indicated foul weather gear hanging below. It was as old as the cloudy binoculars near the wheel with the plaque attached indicating that they had been given to Harry by the Japanese during the Nippon Challenge for the America's Cup in 1992. The Gore-Tex® fibers in the foulies had long since lost their magic. On deck, I was soaked through in five minutes. At the wheel, Harry got us smartly out of the little harbor.

Twenty minutes later we entered Maskell's Harbor. Harry put the nose of *Annie B* almost into the shore next to the farm's boat shed. We tied the launch alongside, got Larry on board, and ran slower back to Baddeck. We dropped the launch and Larry at one of the outer docks. Harry steered *Annie B* into the inner harbor and said he was going to back into his slip. It looked like a tall order. It was the end of the season. The place was jammed with boats rafted three deep. There was little room to maneuver. And *Annie B*'s slip is narrow and confined, like a garage. Backing and filling with care, Harry slowly spun the boat 180 degrees and backed it in on the first try with the assist of a bow thruster.

With the old Escort stuffed to the gills with oars, an anchor, assorted lines and gear, everything wet, with Larry in the front, me somehow wedged in the back, and Harry at the wheel, we headed out of Baddeck for Gillis Point. The two-lane road to Gillis is paved, but potholed, cracked and heaved by many tough winters. And it twists and turns, winding its way up and down gentle hills through the wooded landscape. Harry drove like a bat through the downpour in less than great visibility, never missing a beat, talking most of the time with Larry about what was left to do at the farm. If the Escort's heater worked, I couldn't tell. Life in the raw.

Even in the rain and gloom of that day, Boulaceet Farm is a charming place. The only clues of human residence the old red barn shows is a sliding-glass entry door, rough-finished with barn hardware, a stovepipe emerging from the roof, and a few windows. And there's a proper sign, "Boulaceet Farm," hanging next to the door. Both the barn and its companion, a new, two-story house that is 500 square feet at the most, sit side by side on the soft-tufted meadow that crowns Gillis Point. Harry apparently resisted the idea of building what's called a "manor house" companion for the barn for many years. But as he got older, the drafty, uninsulated barn finally got to him, much to the relief of the Glenns and the Barkers who had been

lobbying unsuccessfully for snugger quarters against the chilly spring and fall months. Larry and Anne were staying in the barn, so Harry and I took the cottage. Harry built a fire in the woodstove, for which I was grateful.

Anne Glenn cooked a great dinner. Diana Russell, who was in residence across the harbor, showed up, and we gathered for drinks around the woodstove that sits on a concrete pad in the middle of the open room. Above our heads, the essential wagon wheel chandelier hanging from the roof beam emitted a warm glow. Wisely, little in the way of décor has been added to the structural elegance of the old barn, which emits all the charm anyone could ever want. Renovation work has been kept functional, and rough-finished. Dinner was at the trestle table in one corner that could probably seat ten or more in a pinch. Out a small window one could look 300 feet down the meadow and see the little white lighthouse on the point.

Bright and early the next day I joined Harry and Larry at the boat shed to help secure bits and pieces and close it up for the winter. Then we got busy bolting the storm shutters onto the barn and cottage windows, a job that required one man inside, and one outside, on a ladder. When I left for the airport before lunch, they were still hard at it.

Harry Anderson at the helm of *Annie B* on a rainy
day on the Bras D'or Lakes in the fall of 2012.

Appendix 1 Pedigree Chart for Henry Hill Anderson Jr.

Parents	Grandparents	Great-Grandparents

Henry Hill Anderson

b: 09 Nov 1827 in Boston, Massachusetts
m: 26 Dec 1861
d: 17 Sep 1896 in York Harbor,
York Maine, USA

308

Henry Burrall Anderson

b: 02 Jan 1863 in New York,
New York, USA
m: 03 Dec 1891
d: 17 Mar 1938 in Sands Point,
Long Island, New York, USA

Sarah Bostwick Burrall

b: 15 Sep 1838
d:

Henry Hill Anderson

b: 19 Dec 1893 in New York,
New York, USA
m: 21 Aug 1920 in Paul Smith's,
Franklin, New York, USA
d: 16 Aug 1945 in Glen Cove,
Nassau, New York, USA

Joseph Larocque

b: 02 Apr 1831 in New York, New York, USA
m: 25 Oct 1856 in Astoria, Long Island,
New York, USA
d: 09 Jun 1908 in New York, New York, USA

Marie Whittemore Larocque

b: 17 Jul 1862
d: 30 Nov 1903 in New York,
New York USA (?)

Anna Smallwood

b: 25 Oct 1831
d: 04 Dec 1908 in New York, New York, USA

Henry Hill Anderson Jr.

b: 02 Jun 1921 in New York,
USA
m:
d:

Henry James

b: 1821
m: 1851
d: 1897

309

Dr. Walter Belknap James

b: 11 May 1858 in Baltimore,
Maryland, USA
m:
d: 06 Apr 1927 in New York,
New York, USA

Amelia Belknap Cate

b: Abt. 1834
d:

Helen Jennings James

b: 16 Aug 1898 in Newport,
Rhode Island, USA
d: 24 Nov 1977 in New York,
New York, USA

Oliver Burr Jennings

b: 03 Jun 1825
m: 13 Dec 1854
d: 12 Feb 1893

310

Helen Goodsell Jennings

b: Abt. 1860 in San Francisco,
California, USA
d: 15 Aug 1946 in New York,
New York, USA

Ester Judson Goodsell

b: 1828
d: 1908

311

Pedigree Chart for Henry Hill Anderson Jr. *continued*

Great-Grandparents	2nd Great-Grandparents	3rd Great-Grandparents	4th Great-Grandparents

James Anderson Jr
b:
m:
d: 03 May 1808

312

Rufus Anderson
b: 05 Mar 1765 in
Londonderry, New Hampshire
m:
d: 1814 in Wenham,
Massachusetts

Nancy Woodburn
b:
d:

(The Rev.) Rufus Anderson
b: 17 Aug 1796 in North
Yarmoth, Maine
m: 08 Jan 1827 in Boston,
Massachusetts
d: 30 May 1880 in Boston,
Massachusetts

Isaac Parsons
b: 04 Apr 1740 in Gloucester,
Massachusetts
m: 05 Sep 1765
d: 19 Sep 1780 in New
Gloucester, Maine

Henry Hill Anderson
b: 09 Nov 1827 in Boston,
Massachusetts
m: 26 Dec 1861
d: 17 Sep 1896 in York Harbor,
York Maine, USA

Hannah Parsons
b: 23 May 1773
d: 14 Jul 1803

Salome Merrill
b: 09 Dec 1742 in Falmouth,
Maine
d:

307

Eliza Hill
b: 1804
d: 09 Mar 1888

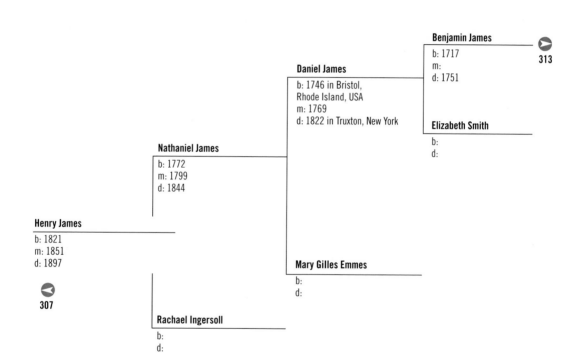

Benjamin James

b: 1717
m:
d: 1751

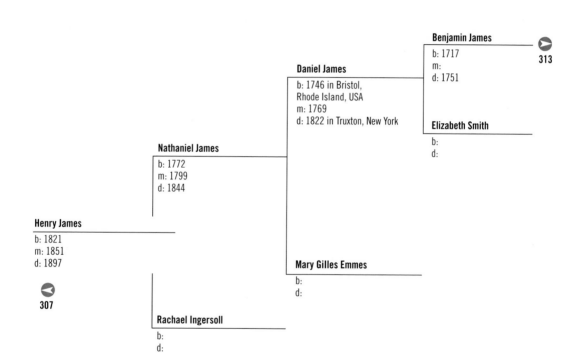

313

Daniel James

b: 1746 in Bristol,
Rhode Island, USA
m: 1769
d: 1822 in Truxton, New York

Elizabeth Smith

b:
d:

Nathaniel James

b: 1772
m: 1799
d: 1844

Henry James

b: 1821
m: 1851
d: 1897

307

Mary Gilles Emmes

b:
d:

Rachael Ingersoll

b:
d:

Pedigree Chart for Henry Hill Anderson Jr. *continued*

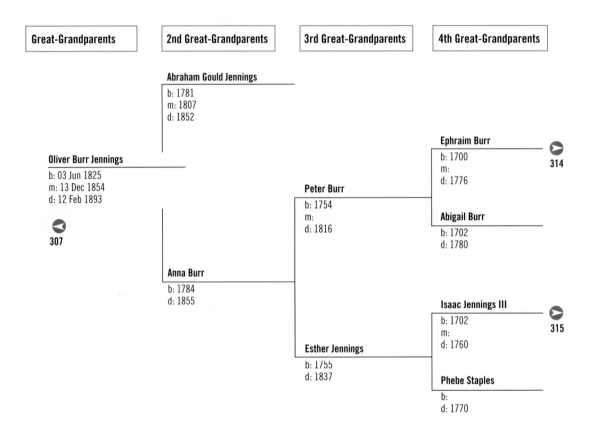

Great-Grandparents	2nd Great-Grandparents	3rd Great-Grandparents	4th Great-Grandparents

Abraham Gould Jennings
b: 1781
m: 1807
d: 1852

Oliver Burr Jennings
b: 03 Jun 1825
m: 13 Dec 1854
d: 12 Feb 1893

307

Ephraim Burr
b: 1700
m:
d: 1776

314

Peter Burr
b: 1754
m:
d: 1816

Abigail Burr
b: 1702
d: 1780

Anna Burr
b: 1784
d: 1855

Isaac Jennings III
b: 1702
m:
d: 1760

315

Esther Jennings
b: 1755
d: 1837

Phebe Staples
b:
d: 1770

Great-Grandparents	2nd Great-Grandparents

David Judson Goodsell

b: 1804
m: 1827
d: 1889

Esther Judson Goodsell

b: 1828
m: 13 Dec 1854
d: 1908

307

Ellen Bryant

b: 1808
d:

| 4th Great-Grandparents | 5th Great-Grandparents | 6th Great-Grandparents |

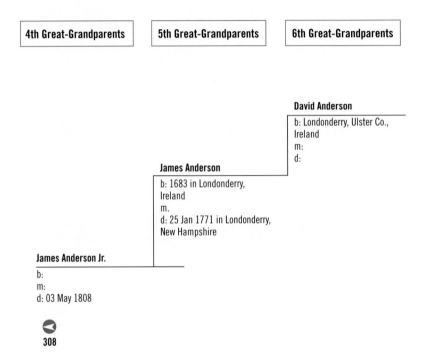

David Anderson
b: Londonderry, Ulster Co.,
Ireland
m:
d:

James Anderson
b: 1683 in Londonderry,
Ireland
m.
d: 25 Jan 1771 in Londonderry,
New Hampshire

James Anderson Jr.
b:
m:
d: 03 May 1808

308

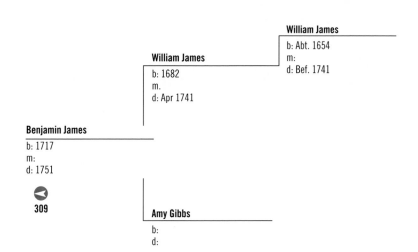

William James
b: Abt. 1654
m:
d: Bef. 1741

William James
b: 1682
m.
d: Apr 1741

Benjamin James
b: 1717
m:
d: 1751

309

Amy Gibbs
b:
d:

Pedigree Chart for Henry Hill Anderson Jr. *continued*

4th Great-Grandparents	5th Great-Grandparents	6th Great-Grandparents	7th Great-Grandparents

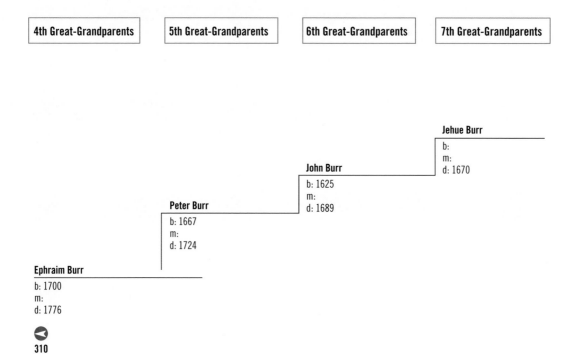

Jehue Burr
b:
m:
d: 1670

John Burr
b: 1625
m:
d: 1689

Peter Burr
b: 1667
m:
d: 1724

Ephraim Burr
b: 1700
m:
d: 1776

310

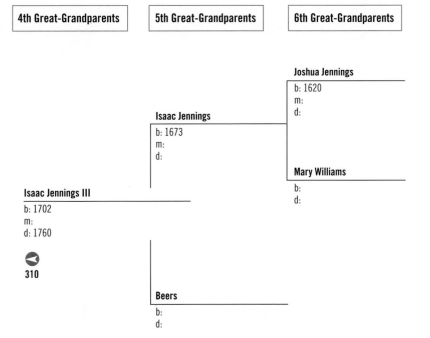

Joshua Jennings

b: 1620
m:
d:

Isaac Jennings

b: 1673
m:
d:

Mary Williams

b:
d:

Isaac Jennings III

b: 1702
m:
d: 1760

310

Beers

b:
d:

Appendix 2

Accomplishments and Memberships

BOOKS

Centennial History of the Newport Reading Room (chief editor)
Centennial History of U. S. Sailing (co-editor)
Centennial History of the Dauntless Club (assistant editor)
The Conspiracy Against Aaron Burr (co-editor)
Their Last Letters, 1930-1938: Nathanael G. Herreshoff and William P. Stephens (foreword; chief editor)
Burriana: A Catalog of Rare Books, Pamphlets, Letters, Manuscripts, Documents & Objects About of Relating to Aaron Burr (co-editor)
Arthur Curtiss James Drives the Golden Spike Connecting Commerce Coast to Coast (author, unpublished monograph)

VIDEOS

The Good Time Will Come: Gold, Oil, & the Exclusive Jekyll Island Club, The Story of Oliver Burr Jennings and his Family (producer)
The Schooner Wanderer: *The last Vessel to Land Slaves on U. S. Soil, at Jekyll Island, Georgia*

YACHTS OWNED

"1", Alden O Boat (family owned in Adirondacks)
Ouzel, Seabird, S&S 1937, co-owned with brothers at SCYC
Thistle, 1947-48, built from kit while at Columbia Law School
Ghorindinky, Finn (Acronym for Ghost Riders in the Sky)
Sleipnir, Raven (named for Norwegian winged horse, god of war)
Icarus, hydrofoil powerboat
Bertram 20, powerboat
Seiche, Shields, co-owned with Tom Josten
Witch of Atlas, 1969-1977, S&S design, Hughes 38
Taniwha, NY40 (Peterson design), co-owned with Tom Josten
Blue Shadow, 1983-1992, 47-foot Swan knockoff

Annie B, 40-foot Nova Scotia lobster boat
White Mist, 2001-2002, co-owned with Henry Fuller, 1995 S&S yawl (Nevins)
Junco, Margaree River wherry (pulling boat with sail) built by Cape Breton Boatyard (Henry Fuller, proprietor)

YACHT CLUB MEMBERSHIPS (total of 139 years as flag officer)

Upper St. Regis Junior Lake Yacht Club (vice commodore)
Seawanhaka Corinthian Junior Yacht Club (founding commodore)
Pine Knot Yacht Club (Adirondack-Florida School; rear commodore)
Yale Corinthian Yacht Club (vice commodore, later honorary commodore)
Revolting Colonies Outpost, Imperial Poona Yacht Club (commodore 50 years)
Seawanhaka Corinthian Yacht Club (rear, vice, commodore)
New York Yacht Club (vice, rear, and commodore)
Long Beach Yacht Club (honorary)
Royal Nova Scotia Yacht Squadron (honorary)
Nylandska Jaktklubben (honorary)
Royal Yacht Squadron (honorary)
Cruising Club of America
Erie Yacht Club
Bras d'Or Yacht Club
Ocean Cruising Club (past port officer, Bra d'Or Lakes)
North American Station of Royal Scandinavian Yacht Clubs & Nylandska
Yaktklubben

ORGANIZATION MEMBERSHIPS AND PHILANTHROPIES (with positions held)

Ransom Everglades School (secretary Board of Trustees, lifetime trustee, sailing advisor)
Mystic Seaport (member International Council)
Herreshoff Marine Museum and America's Cup Hall of Fame Selection Committee (past)
U. S. Sailing (past corresponding secretary, executive director, head of Appeals Committee)
U. S. International Sailing Association (past secretary and trustee)
International Yacht Racing Union (now International Sailing Federation; past vice president)
Yacht Racing Aassociation of Long Island Sound (past president)
Intercollegiate Yacht Racing Association (past judge, past chairman of Appeals Committee)
Tall Ships America (ASTA; past chairman, emeritus, member Commodore's Council)
Yale Sailing Associates (co-founder and past co-chairman; honorary commodore)
University of Rhode Island, URI Foundation (trustee)
University of Rhode Island Boat Committee of URI Foundation
New York Yacht Club, America's Cup Committee (past secretary)
International Yacht Restoration School (member, Coronet Advisory Committee)
World Ship Trust, London, UK (past vice president)

Maritime Education Initiative (past member, General Committee)
National Maritime Alliance (co-founder and first chairman)
National Maritime Historical Society (trustee, past vice president)
U.S. Naval War College Foundation (trustee)
Seamen's Church Institute, Newport, Rhode Island (past trustee, member Governing Board)
Sail Newport Foundation (co-founder and trustee)
Museum of Yachting, Newport Rhode Island (former trustee)
U. S. Naval Academy, Fales Committee (co-founder, member emeritus)
U. S. Naval Academy Sailing Foundation (co-charterer)
U. S. Naval Academy (co-chair for renovation of Inter-Collegiate Hall of Fame and Naval Academy Trophy Center at
    Robert Crown Center)
Finn Class Association (co-founder and initial secretary)
Raven Class Association (co-founder and initial president)
International 6 Metre Association (initial chairman)
International Six Metre Class (past secretary)
The Aaron Burr Association
Elizabethan Club
Dauntless Club
Newport Reading Room
Union Club
Rhode Island Marine Archeology Program (co-founder and trustee)
Foundation for the Preservation of Capt. Cook's Ships (co-founder and trustee)

AWARDS AND HONORARIA

Doctor of Laws, University of Rhode Island, 2009
Bebbe Croce Trophy, International Sailing Federation, International Yacht Racing Union
Nathanael Herreshoff Trophy, U. S. Sailing Association
Anderson Fellowship, Yale Sailing
Intercollegiate Yacht Racing Association Hall of Fame
Lifetime Service Award, Inter-Collegiate Sailing Association (formerly ICYRA)
Congressional Cup Scarlet Blazer
33rd Congressional Cup dedicated to Henry H. Anderson Jr.
Richard S. Nye Trophy, Cruising Club of America
Post Captain's Trophy, North American Station, Royal Scandinavian Yacht
Clubs & Nylandska Jaktklubben
Bronze Star, U. S. Army
Henry H. Anderson Jr. Sail Training Scholarship Fund, American Sail Training Association
Lifetime Achievement Award, American Sail Training Association
W. P. Stephens Award, Mystic Seaport
Henry H. Anderson Jr. Memorial Library at Seamen's Church Institute
Henry H. Anderson Jr. Memorial Gymnasium at Ransom Everglades School

Appendix 3

Henry H. Anderson Jr.: An Obituary
(written by Harry Anderson, December 9, 2012, in the interest of getting it right)

Born June 2, 1921 in New York City, Henry H. Anderson Jr. had early distinguished Colonial antecedents, to wit: his great-grandfather Henry Hill Anderson, counsel for the City of New York, descended from James Anderson, a co-founder of Londonderry, New Hampshire, ca. 1718; his great-grandfather Oliver Burr Jennings was a Forty-Niner whose ancestor Joshua Jennings settled in Hartford in 1645 concurrently with Jehue Burre, great-grandfather of Col. Aaron Burr of whom HHAJr is a collateral descendent [both families settled in Fairfield, Connecticut]: and William James of Scituate, Massachusetts, who moved to Newport, Rhode Island, ca. 1680.

Brought up in Oyster Bay, Long island, HHAJr was commodore of the Seawanhaka Corinthian and New York Yacht Clubs and an honorary member of yacht clubs extending from Long Beach, California, to Helsinki, Finland. He served as an officer in the Field Artillery in Patton's Third Army during World War II. He was a vice president & assistant treasurer of the Columbia Lincoln Corp., and a vice president of the Lincoln Safe Deposit Company in Manhattan before moving to Connecticut and subsequently Rhode Island. He was an associate of numerous education institutions from Newport, Rhode Island, to Coconut Grove, Florida, including Tall Ships America, University of Rhode Island, Yale University, U.S. Naval Academy, and Ransom Everglades School in Coconut Grove. He leaves a brother, Hon. David, and 45 nephews, nieces, and great nephews and nieces.

Photo Credits

Chapter Five

80: © Mystic Seaport, Rosenfeld Collection, #94491F

82: Collection of Henry H. Anderson Jr.

86: Tanner, V. *Outlines of the Geography, Life and Customs of Newfoundland-Labrador. Acta Geographic* 8, no. 1. Helsinki-Helsingfors, 1944, p. 33.

96: © Mystic Seaport, Rosenfeld Collection, #94455F

98: © Mystic Seaport, Rosenfeld Collection, #80466F

Chapter Six

104: Collection of Henry H. Anderson Jr.

106: Richard, Henry Smith Richardson, Jr., ed. *The Nineteen Forty Three Class Book Published for Yale University*. New Haven, CT, 1943, p. 29.

Chapter Seven

122: © Mystic Seaport, Rosenfeld Collection, #127147F

130: (top): Collection of Henry H. Anderson Jr.

130: (bottom): Collection of Henry H. Anderson Jr.

133: Courtesy of Beken of Cowes

134: Courtesy of Beken of Cowes

136: Courtesy of Beken of Cowes

142: © Mystic Seaport, Rosenfeld Collection, #127853F

144: © Mystic Seaport, Rosenfeld Collection, #143318F

148: © Mystic Seaport, Rosenfeld Collection, #170235.14

Chapter Eight

158: © Mystic Seaport, Rosenfeld Collection, #161392F

160: Collection of Henry H. Anderson Jr.

164: Collection of Henry H. Anderson Jr.

165: © Mystic Seaport, Rosenfeld Collection, #177195-18

166: Collection of Henry H. Anderson Jr.

186: Collection of Henry H. Anderson Jr.

Chapter Nine

188: © Mystic Seaport, Rosenfeld Collection, #188403-10

191: © Billy Black

194: © Mystic Seaport, Rosenfeld Collection, #187099

210: Collection of Henry H. Anderson Jr.

211: Collection of Henry H. Anderson Jr.

212: Collection of Henry H. Anderson Jr.

214: Collection of Henry H. Anderson Jr.

Chapter Ten

226: © Mystic Seaport, Rosenfeld Collection, #2004.20.15.9.1

237: Collection of Henry H. Anderson Jr.

Index
Page numbers in italics indicate illustrations

Roger Vaughan lives, works, and sails in Oxford on Maryland's Eastern Shore (www.rogervaughan.net).

OTHER BOOKS BY ROGER VAUGHAN

Dropping the Gloves
By Barry Melrose with Roger Vaughan

Golf, The Woman's Game

Mustique II

Listen to the Music: The Life of Hilary Koprowski

Tony Gwynn's the Art of Hitting

Nascar, The Inside Track

Mustique

America's Cup XXVII, The Official Record Stars and Stripes 1988

Herbert Von Karajan (A Biographical Portrait)

Fastnet, One Man's Voyage

Ted Turner, The Man Behind the Mouth

The Grand Gesture